Gentlemen Merchants

R G Wilson

Gentlemen Merchants

The merchant community
in Leeds
1700–1830

The Gentlemen Merchants of Leeds are now in Town and intend
making application to the House to oblige the clothiers to carry
their cloth to Leeds . . . which everybody thinks unreasonable.

Edward Elmsall to Lord Dartmouth
26 February 1775

Manchester University Press
Augustus M. Kelley, New York

© 1971 R. G. Wilson

Published by
Manchester University Press
316–324 Oxford Road
Manchester M13 9NR

ISBN 0 7190 0459 4

Published in the United States 1971 by
Augustus M. Kelley, Publishers
1140 Broadway
New York, N.Y. 10001

SBN 0 678 06785 6
LIBRARY OF CONGRESS CATALOG CARD NO. 79 149804

71-039095-2

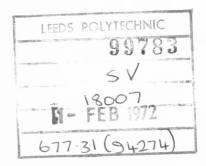
Printed in Great Britain by
Butler & Tanner Ltd
Frome and London

Contents

Maps and tables

Preface

The subject of eighteenth-century trade has always found its chroniclers, but the merchants who were engaged in it have largely been neglected. Yet economic historians have suggested that we must know a great deal more about them if we are to generalise about their economic and social role and their relationship to the processes of industrialisation. The book I have written about the merchants in the Leeds woollen industry—it has grown from a Ph.D. thesis —therefore attempts to analyse the development of a single provincial merchant community between 1700 and 1830. Such a study inevitably produces its problems.

Firstly, the evidence has its shortcomings. A good deal is known of one merchant through the fortuitous survival of his papers, while virtually nothing comes to light of his contemporaries. Those records which have been preserved are almost always incomplete, and they often represent firms which are untypical in terms of both size and organisation. Although there is a wide range of surviving evidence it is spread unevenly. Hence it is impossible to construct a detailed survey of a merchant community, either on a local or a national scale, from individual biographical studies. Completeness is an elusive goal. If there are gaps in the study and at times there is a pre-occupation with certain events, it partly reflects the fragmentary nature of the evidence.

Secondly, there is the problem of definition. What was a 'merchant'? Briefly he was a wholesale trader in the home or export markets, a *buyer*, but almost never a manufacturer, of goods and raw materials and an importer of foreign produce. But the merchants were not simply wholesale traders; they underwrote their ventures with widespread investment in land, government securities, transport facilities and industrial concerns. Frequently their commercial transactions gave them opportunities to become financial specialists. Nevertheless the merchants were neither landowners nor rentiers: they might emulate the country gentlemen's way of life, but their approach to land, industry and politics was largely conditioned by their experience in trade. Yet if the merchants shared a common viewpoint they belonged neither to a tight class nor to a profession however much they might control the country's trade and dominate the organisation of urban society.

Thirdly, a discussion about definitions brings us to a consideration of methods. Since the background, education and economic interests of merchants were multifarious it is not easy to generalise about their activities as a group. The only really satisfactory way is to estimate the total numbers involved and then for each characteristic to indicate the proportions involved. But the exiguous nature of the surviving material does not allow this. Therefore I have quoted instances of A, B and C doing X, Y, Z. Wherever possible it has been attempted to suggest what proportion of the group A, B and C was, and whether there were others who did not do X, Y and Z but deviated to insist upon U, V and W. Yet counting heads would not solve all our problems. The Leeds trade, and to a large measure, that of the West Riding, was always controlled by about 20 export firms. In 1781, when there were 73 merchant houses, two-thirds of the Leeds cloth trade was carried on by the 24 largest firms. Clearly some firms were far more important in the town and trade than others. After 1790 the problem of method and definition becomes more complex when some merchants became manufacturers. A clear distinction has been made between the two groups since there was a clear-cut social and organisational division before this date. It should be remembered, however, that they were not mutually exclusive groups. They overlapped in respect of religious affiliations, industrial interests and place of residence. But in no way does this vitiate our analysis of the eighteenth-century merchant oligarchy. Long after 1790 there were marked distinctions of background, training and outlook between members of the old merchant society and the new manufacturers.

Lastly, difficulties of organisation are implicit in an attempt to illustrate the workings of any merchant group because of its widespread interests. Ideally this book should integrate an account of the development of Leeds and a discussion of the growth of the Yorkshire wool textile industry with this analysis of the Leeds merchant community. But ideally that would take three volumes. I can only plead that I have tried to preserve an adequate balance between these three aspects of the study. Perhaps I should simply state my reasons for the shortcomings of my book in the terms one merchant gave about the problems of cloth manufacture when a customer returned his goods: ' 'tis impossible to have one piece equally good from end to end'.

But the manufacture of this book has been improved by the help I have received from a number of people. Firstly, the Pasold Research Fund has generously made a grant towards its publication. Then I must thank the many institutions which gave me access to their records. Above all I have appreciated the constant help of Mr. Michael Collinson, the Leeds City Archivist. The Earl of Harewood permitted me to consult his family's papers at Harewood. I was allowed to use the Crewe–Milnes MSS. in Sheffield City Library by courtesy of the Marchioness of Crewe; the Fitzwilliam MSS. at the same place by Earl Fitzwilliam and the Trustees of the Fitzwilliam Settled Estates; the Spencer-Stanhope MSS. at the Cartwright Hall, Bradford and Sheffield City Library by Mrs. M. E. I. Spencer-Stanhope; the Newby Hall MSS. at Leeds Central Library by Major Edward Compton and the Denison MSS. at the University of Nottingham by Lieutenant-Colonel W. M. E. Denison.

I must acknowledge my indebtedness to Mr. Roy Hay and Mr. G. C. F. Forster who read the book in draft and gave me their valuable advice. Professor R. H. Campbell, Professor Herbert Heaton, Miss Julia de L. Mann, Professor W. G. Rimmer and Professor A. J. Taylor have helped me at various stages. I have also to thank Mrs. Norma Alderson who struggled so valiantly with my writing in typing the manuscript. My wife kept our children just beyond earshot. I alone am responsible for the errors and obscurities.

Abbreviations

ACN—Papers of the Aire and Calder Navigation Company.

C.J.—*Journals of the House of Commons.*

Crump—W. B. Crump (ed.), 'The Leeds Woollen Industry: 1780–1820', *Publications of the Thoresby Society*, vol. 32 (1931).

Diary—*The Diary of Ralph Thoresby F.R.S.* (1830), 2 volumes.

Ducatus—Ralph Thoresby, *Ducatus Leodiensis* (second edition, 1816).

Ec.H.R.—*Economic History Review.*

Heaton—H. Heaton, *The Yorkshire Woollen and Worsted Industries* (1920).

H.M.C.—*Historical Manuscripts Commission.*

J. Econ. Hist.—*Journal of Economic History.*

L.I.—*Leeds Intelligencer.*

L.J.—*Journals of the House of Lords.*

L.M.—*Leeds Mercury.*

Leeds Phil. & Lit. Soc.—*Proceedings of the Leeds Philosophical and Literary Society.*

P.P.—*British Parliamentary Papers.*

Thors. Soc.—*Publications of the Thoresby Society.*

V.C.H.—*Victoria County History.*

Y.A.S.—Yorkshire Archaeological Society.

1806 Report—*P.P.* 1806, 111. Report from the Select Committee . . . [on] the State of the Woollen Manufacture in England.

1 Introduction

Accounts of our economic achievement in the eighteenth century have become largely peopled by the giants of textbook folk-lore, Richard Arkwright, Robert Owen and their like. Viewed through their eyes the pattern of change becomes distorted. For the most striking developments, at least before 1780, were linked with trade not industry. But since the merchants have always had a dull press they have remained faceless men. Writers like Postlethwayt and MacPherson seldom illuminated their treatises on trade with the examples of individual commercial successes, whereas Smiles caught the popular imagination with his studies of the inventors and captains of industry. They were heroes whose qualities every Victorian might profitably emulate. Therefore Strutt and Arkwright, Watt and Stephenson found their way into every history textbook. The merchants of London, Bristol, Liverpool and Newcastle were at best collectively dismissed in a few lines.

Such treatment is not surprising, for although the importance of the growth of trade has always been recognised as an important precondition of industrialisation, its impact on the economy and society was less dramatic. As a result it has never received adequate treatment in its own right. But worse than its relative neglect has been the tendency for historians to take the eighteenth-century trade figures as they stand and present them as an adequate index of British economic development during this period. Not only are the statistics in themselves unreliable, and not only did the proportion of manufactured goods that were exported probably never exceed 15% in the eighteenth century,[1] but also such exercises have inhibited investigation of the integration between the foreign trade sector and internal industrial development. If exports were as important as all contemporaries stated then it is essential to establish their links with the expansion of British industry. An analysis of the merchant's role is therefore central to any discussion about economic and social change in the eighteenth century.

It has always been a convenient theory in the exposition of our economic progress that those merchants who had made their fortunes in commerce in the eighteenth century—or at least their sons—became the industrial leaders after 1780. Yet the period between 1770 and 1830 was one of key technical innovation which saw the undermining of the domestic system by large-scale, factory production. Were the descendants of those men who pioneered the European, American, East and West Indian trades those who became the great entrepreneurs of the textile, iron and engineering industries which led Britain into the new age?

The history of Glasgow provided an excellent illustration of the thesis that the continuity between commerce and industry was complete, that the flow of capital and enterprise between the two sectors was uninterrupted. After the Act of Union the trade of Glasgow flourished with its merchants' appropriation of a large share of the American tobacco trade. When the Colonies broke away, the trade collapsed in 1776. Through holding large stocks and their system of resident factors the merchants were not ruined. They were believed simply to have transferred their interests from overseas trade to the nascent west of Scotland cotton industry. It was a neat explanation which accounted for the rapid growth of the industry in the 1780's: as Hamilton wrote over 30 years ago: 'when the tobacco trade was destroyed by the American War of Independence, capital accumulated in commerce overflowed into industry thus making possible the Industrial Revolution'. But the explanation does not stand closer scrutiny. Even Hamilton later admitted 'there is little evidence of tobacco merchants engaging directly in the flotation of cotton mills' although he did not substantially change his argument about the connections between Scotland's export trade and her economic growth. More recently, however, R. H. Campbell, in questioning these links, has shown that the merchants either became landowners, bankers, or switched their trading interests south to the West Indies, but only exceptionally did they direct their resources into industry.[2]

Was the position similar in England? No merchant community was obliged to make so rapid a decision about its future as that in Glasgow; nevertheless shifts in the direction of trade and the coming of industrialisation forced merchants into taking a fresh look at prospects for themselves and their families. There were several opportunities open to them. None of them were new, but events necessitated that they should examine them in a new light.

Obviously merchants remained in trade itself, although a number of factors altered its nature. The growth of the export trade beyond Europe called for extended financial facilities and increased shipping services. Therefore many merchants simply became bankers, brokers and shipowners proper. It was a logical development. Few merchants who had been involved in the import and entrepôt trades had a close knowledge of British industry. Even many export merchants, since they bought their goods through agents and factors, had only indirect connections with manufacturing. Some industries had grown up in the ports, but they were usually neither major growth industries nor did they produce for a wider market than their immediate urban community. Moreover merchants had few connections with them. And the practice for manufacturers to sell their own goods overseas without the intervention of export merchant houses, who had hitherto largely controlled this trade, was rapidly extended after 1783 when the size of all manufacturing establishments grew. These new industrialists breaking into the export trade still required certain specialised services. Therefore in London, Liverpool, Hull and Bristol, because the merchants' understanding of the mechanism of foreign trade was much more extensive than their knowledge of British industry, they were more prominent in the creation of financial, insurance and shipping functions than they were in the flotation of new industrial enterprises.

The second alternative is well known. One of the oldest features of merchant society was that those who had made the largest fortunes in trade had always invested a substantial portion of them in land, the safest form of permanent investment. The trouble is, given the state of present research, that it is impossible either to measure their total transfer of resources to land or to determine the periods and rates at which this metamorphosis was taking place. But perhaps the most important feature is not that the wealthier merchants became model improving landowners, for only the minority could afford a sizeable estate, but that the landowners' way of life became the accepted norm of achievement throughout the entire merchant community. All merchants eventually hoped to attain this ideal. Therefore they spent their surplus earnings in buying parcels of land, government stocks and transport investments so that one day their families would be provided with an independent income that was not tied to the fluctuations of trade. Moreover, they attempted in their urban communities to live their approximation of the landowners' way of life. Thus he tmanner in which they utilised their savings and the way in which they lived meant that few merchants worked on concepts of optimum firm size and profit maximisation. After 1780, however, their leisurely notions were upset by industrialisation, urban expansion and changing trade patterns. They were generally unprepared for the new era of rapid change, intense competition and big industrial units. Since they had never widely invested in industry it was not now to be expected that they should do so. Many merchants moved into landownership, other, smaller traders, especially in the declining ports, entered the professions.

If the merchants often eschewed new industrial ventures, if they as

frequently became bankers, landowners, clergymen and service officers
as they stayed in trade, then such arguments presuppose that the new
leaders of industry came from another section of society. Nearly 60
years ago Schumpeter maintained that when development took place
the inherent tendency towards equilibrium in the economic system was
broken by men who did not necessarily control the existing productive
or commercial processes which were displaced by the new.[3] Certainly
the evidence in some industries, especially textiles, suggests that the
first factory-masters were far more likely to be small producers, who
had been aided by the widespread application of a series of technical
innovations after 1770, than merchants. In 1818 one commentator on
the growth of the cotton industry wrote: 'with very few exceptions
the employers are a set of men who have sprung from the cotton shop
without education or address except so much as they have acquired by
their intercourse with the little world of merchants at the exchange at
Manchester'.[4] Since patterns of development in each industry were different, however, it is difficult to generalise. But what seems probable
is that the merchants' recruitment, training and aims were so thoroughly
established that they were unfit to innovate or make much contribution
to the new entrepreneurship between 1770 and 1830.

Before we turn to discuss the aspects of this central problem from
a detailed study of the merchants in Leeds engaged in the Yorkshire
woollen industry between 1700 and 1830, we should spend a moment
noting the unique place the industry held in the eighteenth-century
economy. For when our forefathers first believed Britannia ruled the
waves they were in no doubt that a large part of her omnipotence
was derived from the strength of the British woollen industry. From
time immemorial it had been inextricably united with the economic
progress and the political life of the nation.

Undoubtedly the industry's most notable feature was its widespread
geographical distribution. In 1700 there was no county in England that
did not boast at least a few score weavers and spinners. Admittedly
considerable concentration was already evident. As early as 1470 the
three great manufacturing areas, the West Country (Somersetshire,
Gloucestershire and Wiltshire), East Anglia and the West Riding of
Yorkshire produced two-thirds of the country's entire output.[5] It is
difficult to determine how much further concentration developed in
the next two centuries. But at the end of the seventeenth century it
was by no means complete. Exeter, Colchester, Worcester, Coventry,
Kendal and Rochdale were still important centres of industry outside
the three main areas of production.

Because the industry was so scattered, the tentacles of its organisation were second in length only to those of agriculture itself in the economy. Geoffrey King reckoned its total output was valued at £8,000,000, a computation which created an 'astonishing impression' with John James, the Victorian chronicler of the worsted industry, who commented that by King's calculation this 'was nearly equal to one-fifth of the whole annual income of the realm, and almost approaching to the value of the land' (i.e. the yearly rent of all property). Forty years later a writer in *The Gentleman's Magazine* believed the industry employed 1,500,000 persons. More cautious commentators like John Smith placed his estimate at little over half this total.[6] Even on this reckoning one in eight of England's population was employed in the wool textile industry.

The industry had perfected the domestic system of output. The details of organisation and the degree of specialisation differed slightly between all the various areas, but the great distinction was between the West Country and East Anglia on the one hand and the West Riding on the other. Basically the difference was one of capital requirements to enter the industry. In the former areas a few relatively wealthy merchants and clothiers dominated the organisation. They put out their wool for the various stages of production to be completed by an assorted army of artisans. Then most of the finished cloth was sent up to the capital for export by London merchants. In the West Riding of Yorkshire the clothier, especially in the woollen industry, was a man of small capital who, with the aid of his family, completed all the processes and then sold his weekly output to local merchants who attended the cloth halls in Leeds, Wakefield and Halifax. Unlike their counterparts in the West Country and East Anglia these merchants exported directly abroad. Therefore in the West Country organisation revolved around the traditional clothier who employed large numbers of artisan outworkers; in the West Riding it was divided between a large number of small masters and a few dozen wealthy merchants. Differences in organisation, it was argued, led to differences in enterprise. Contemporaries believed that the extraordinary expansion of the Yorkshire woollen and worsted industries in the eighteenth century was due in no small measure to its peculiar organisation.

However details differed, every commentator from Celia Fiennes to Daniel Defoe believed that increases in the population and wealth of England were only made possible by the expansion of the cloth industry. They dwelt tirelessly on the way in which the number of spinners, weavers, dyers and cloth-finishers were scattered in the country for miles around the major production centres. They always pointed out that the industry enabled workers to subsidise their meagre earnings in agriculture so that the English peasantry enjoyed the highest standard of living of any in Western Europe.

The third feature of the industry, besides its distribution and organisation, was the special place it held in the political and economic writings of the period. Probably more ink was spilled on questions about the export of raw wool and cloth than on all other economic questions put together. Every pamphleteer who made mention of the wealth of Britain felt obliged to estimate the wool clip and calculate the proportion of wool smuggled abroad. The results were often fantastic and always contradictory. William Mugliston's estimate of the number of sheep in Great Britain in 1782, not a year to warm any economic commentator's heart, was five times higher than that of John Campbell made eight years previously.[7] But it was the industry's importance which led to these wild compilations. Even the most befuddled Member of Parliament, the least well-equipped writer, understood perfectly the unique place the export of wool and cloth had held for the past 500 years. In 1640 between 80 and 90% of the exports which left London were woollen cloths. Thereafter, as English commerce took on a new, broader character, exports of cloth declined but the place they retained was still impressive. In the early years of the eighteenth century woollen cloth exports were around 70%, by value, of all English home exports; 70 years later they were still appreciably over half.[8] If its relative export position deteriorated, the cloth industry relied more and more upon its export trade. Miss Deane has estimated that the fraction of total output sold overseas grew from two-fifths to two-thirds in the course of the eighteenth century.[9] And certain areas like the Norwich stuff trade and the West Riding were committed to exporting an even higher percentage of their production.

The question which has always preoccupied historians of the woollen and worsted industry since 1750 is the reason why the West Riding sectors rapidly outstripped all the other centres of production in the course of the eighteenth century. Statistical quantification of this shift is virtually impossible: rough estimates suggest that Yorkshire's share of the total output of the woollen industry grew from less than one-fifth in 1700 to one-third in 1772 and then jumped to three-fifths by 1800.[10] Explanations have changed. In the nineteenth century it was fashionable to stress Yorkshire's superior resources of coal, iron and soft water. But as Clapham argued 60 years ago, locational factors as far as Norfolk's decline was concerned were important but not decisive. He maintained: 'it was not because Norwich lay far from the coalfields that she did not try steam-power as soon as it became available, but because power was first applied to spinning, and she was not really an important spinning centre'.[11] Clapham's explanation fits the post-1800 period; he does not explain how the West Riding's worsted industry rose from the smallest beginnings in 1700 to reach an approximately level-pegging position with the East Anglian industry by 1770. Even in the more slowly expanding woollen sector, output in the West Riding quadrupled between 1730-1800, a performance which amazed competitors in the West Country trade. The difference in labour costs was minimal and Yorkshire had little or no geographical advantage in respect of wool supplies (obtained chiefly from Lincolnshire and East Anglia) or her export markets. In both woollen and worsted production, however, Yorkshire merchants concentrated upon the cheap end of the market. For these reasons they were better placed to meet the growing competition of cotton goods at home and, first in the Mediterranean market in the 1720's and 1730's and then in America after 1760, they made a notable breakthrough in the export trade.[12] Also the West Riding was unique in comprehending both the woollen and worsted branches of the cloth industry contiguously. East Anglia concentrated entirely upon better quality worsteds, the West Country on fine broad woollen cloths, Exeter upon serges. In Yorkshire as profitability shifted it was always possible for manufacturers to switch between the manufacture of 'white' and coloured woollens and the various types of worsted cloth. Moreover the West Riding was a much more complex and forward-looking industrial area than any of the other major production centres. The stimulus of lead and coal-mining, iron and linen production, pottery-making and lime-burning, and after the 1770's cotton manufacture, made the cloth industry in the West Riding itself more responsive to change. Elsewhere the production of cloth took place in regions basically of an agricultural character. Therefore after 1770, when the pace of industrial growth quickened, cloth production in East Anglia and the West Country was divorced from the main stream of change in Lancashire and West Yorkshire. But the point which contemporaries most frequently emphasised in accounting for Yorkshire's overhaul of the two traditional centres of output was the way in which its superior organisational features gave rise to better entrepreneurship. It is with these issues so far as they affected developments in the Leeds merchant community that we shall be concerned with in the first six chapters. Chapters 7-9 consider the merchants' political and social roles and speculate on the way in which their commitments made them unsuited to the new pace of industrialism after 1800.

B

Notes to Chapter 1

[1] P. Deane and W. A. Cole, *British Economic Growth 1688–1959* (1962), p. 42; D. E. C. Eversley, 'In Pudding-time: The early stages of industrialization in England, 1730–1780', University of Birmingham Economic and Social History Discussion Paper, Series D, No. 1 (1962).

[2] H. Hamilton, *The Industrial Revolution in Scotland* (1932), p. 105, and *An Economic History of Scotland in the Eighteenth Century* (1963), p. 165; R. H. Campbell, *Scotland Since 1707* (1965), pp. 42–8, 77–83 and 'An economic history of Scotland in the eighteenth century', *Scottish Journal of Political Economy*, XI (1964), 17–24.

[3] J. A. Schumpeter, *The Theory of Economic Development* (1961 edition), pp. 65–74.

[4] 'A journeyman cotton spinner', quoted in E. P. Thompson, *The Making of the English Working Class* (1963), p. 199.

[5] E. Lipson, *The History of the Woollen and Worsted Industries* (1921), p. 222.

[6] J. James, *History of the Worsted Manufacture in England* (1857), pp. 238–9.

[7] W. Mugliston, *A Letter on the Subject of Wool* (1782), p. 9; J. Campbell, *A Political Survey of Great Britain* (1774), p. 158.

[8] W. Minchinton (ed.), *The Growth of English Overseas Trade in the Seventeenth and Eighteenth Centuries* (1969), p. 25.

[9] P. Deane, 'The output of the British woollen industry in the eighteenth century', *J. Econ. Hist.*, XVII (1957), 207–23.

[10] *ibid.*, see also below, pp. 41–4.

[11] J. H. Clapham, 'The transference of the worsted industry from Norfolk to the West Riding', *Economic Journal*, XX (1910), 195–210.

[12] See Chapter 3.

2 *The merchant group identified*

Glorioso the son of Flear is lately advanced to the Dignity of Bashaw of Pannopolis (Mayor of Leeds). He was about two years ago, the Serasquier of the largest of the Northern Provinces (High Sheriff of Yorkshire). His Father was an underclerk in the Post-Office, and his Grandfather a repairer of old Tarbants and Vests; however this Illustrious son has by his merits, Industry, and some other ways, arrived to the Favour of great men, and is supposed to be worth 400 purses.*

(I)

The emergence of a merchant community in Leeds should be seen against the backcloth of great change that was taking place in the Yorkshire woollen industry after 1400. There were two central events on which these changes hinged: the collapse of the cloth-making industry in the medieval centres of trade, York and Beverley; and its rapid expansion within the West Riding.

It is now almost 40 years since Professor Carus-Wilson shattered Professor Heaton's attempt to cite from the ullnage accounts 'statistical evidence of an accurate character' for this growth, but the fact that the transference itself took place has never been in doubt. The reasons behind the shift are best summarised by someone in York writing in 1561:

The cause of the decay of the . . . weavers and loomes for Woollen [cloth] within the sayd citie as I doe understand and learne is the lak of cloth makying in the sayd citie as was in old tyme accustomed, whiche is nowe encreased and used in the townes of Halyfax, Leedes, and Wakefield, for that not only the comodytie of the water-mylnes is ther nigh at hande, but also the poore folke as speynners, carders and other necessary work folkes . . . may ther besyde ther hand labor, have rye, fyre and other relief good cheape, which is in this citie very deare and wantyng.

Guild restrictions and high costs of production killed York's woollen industry. In the new frontier of the West Riding hills and valleys with their abundant supplies of fast-flowing soft water and cheap coal there existed no such restraints. The number of clothiers increased. Halifax became the wonder of Tudor England, whilst the population of Leeds more than doubled in the 50 years between 1576 and 1626.[1]

* The Rev. George Plaxton on Henry Iveson, merchant and Mayor of Leeds in 1710, *Thors. Soc.*, XXXVII, Part II, (1936), 95.

Parallel with this key expansion of the West Riding sector of the Yorkshire woollen industry was the emergence of local merchants in the first two of the three towns in which cloth-making tended to concentrate—Leeds, Wakefield and Halifax. The earliest references to their appearance comes in a letter to Robert Cecil from the Corporation of Hull in 1596, complaining of the government's demand that Hull should provide a ship for the expedition of that summer. The aldermen requested that the 'three great clothing townes and places belonging thereto, viz. Halifax and the Vicarage, Leeds, Wakefield and their several parishes' should contribute to the charge for: 'they are many ways relieved by this port, by the uttering their cloth to a great proportion, and so have their oils, wool, alum, etc., and like helps for their trade brought in by the shipping of this place . . . and consequently divers of them are not only clothiers, but merchants also, to the great hindrance of the merchants here and at York'. A second complaint from Hull lodged 20 years later decried 'a set of young adventurers that are lately sprung up at Leeds, and at other places amongst the clothiers who at little or no charges buy and engross as they please, to the great hurt of the inhabitants and merchants of this town'.[2] The picture was not quite as simple as the Hull merchants drew.

York's trade in cloth had flourished in the late fourteenth century, but between 1390 and 1547 the export of cloth from Hull fell away consistently, for the merchants trading through Hull completely failed to compensate for the decline in their wool exports by increasing their exports of cloth. The Hull figures for the latter provide a pattern that is completely at variance with those of London or the country as a whole, a divergence that becomes especially apparent after 1500. Not surprisingly J. M. Bartlett, in his study of York in the late Middle Ages, concluded that its trade declined in the face of West Riding competition and that the distribution of Yorkshire cloths passed to the merchants and clothiers of Wakefield and Halifax who sold their output directly to London.[3] Certainly Halifax clothiers in the sixteenth century were sending their kerseys up to St. Bartholemew's Fair and Blackwell Hall and it has always been argued that a merchant community emerged in the three towns because the small rural clothiers required markets where they could regularly buy wool and sell their cloths.[4]

The evidence for the early seventeenth century however does not entirely agree with this view that the West Riding merchants had made great inroads into the trade of York and Hull by trading directly overland with London exporters. For the trade of Hull dramatically revived in the late sixteenth century and a large part of its resuscitation was due to activity in both Leeds and York. Lionel Cranfield's correspondence reveals that the fiercest competition which London merchants met in Stade, Lübeck, Elbing and Danzig around 1600 was not from the Dutch but from merchants shipping northern kerseys and dozens directly from Hull. William Busfield, a young pushing Leeds merchant, was a principal rival, but the chief exporters of cloth from Hull to the Baltic in 1633 were York men and not those from Leeds.[5] York's role in the marketing of Yorkshire cloths should not be written off until the last decades of the seventeenth century.

One interpretation of what happened, of course, would be that York's and Hull's stagnation between 1390 and 1570 reflected a prolonged crisis in the West Riding industry. It would be tempting to arrive at this conclusion, citing the experience of York and Hull, dismissing the ullnage figures as unreliable, and pointing out the dearth of alternative supporting evidence. On the other hand it is more likely that the collapse in Hull's cloth exports was due to the decline of the industries in York and Beverley which had produced high quality cloth suitable for export. After 1400 the West Riding industry grew— probably not as quickly as Heaton suggested—and its production was sent by carrier or shipped by coastal vessels from York, or more frequently Selby (12 miles further down the Ouse), to London or sold in the home market. Once West Riding cloth became well known to home merchants they began to include it in their export samples. Its cheapness was its chief selling point; even in comparison with the 'new draperies' it was extremely competitive in price. Yorkshire broad cloths, made chiefly around Leeds, were cheaper than those made in the West Country, Kent or Worcester, and northern kerseys, less than half the cost of broad cloth, were excellent value and in enormous demand in Holland and Germany. Between 1560 and 1640 the production of kerseys and dozens (Yorkshire broad cloths) boomed in the West Riding.[6]

Table 1   Number of cloths exported from Hull (principal types)

	Kerseys	Dozens	Bays
1609	39,079	2,723	
1637	34,355	21,493	961
1682	34,399	27,656	12,221
1700	53,868	27,335	17,175

Miss François estimated that close on 100,000 kerseys were made in the parishes of Halifax, Keighley, Bingley and Bradford in 1614, and 80,000 passed through Hull in 1638. Between 1614 and 1640, although expansion after 1614 was less marked than in the last decades of the sixteenth century, textile exports from Hull increased by 160%. The export of dozens, in which the Leeds merchants always specialised, appears to have grown spectacularly between 1609 and 1637. Moreover the quality of the cloths improved. Cranfield's factors in the Baltic trade found that the cloths their northern rivals shipped from Hull were 'excellent good', far better value than the kerseys he obtained in London. One agent wrote from Stade in 1606 that the important Danzig market which served all Poland, 'will not give so much for Kersies that came from this place or from Amsterdam or London as they do for those that came from Hull though they be of the same sort of goodness'.[7]

The Yorkshire merchants had by 1600 built up an enviable reputation for selling cheap cloths of excellent value. They had broken into the preserves of London merchants for several reasons. Firstly, as multilateral trade settlements became possible through improved international monetary transactions, the simple barter of English cloth for foreign raw materials and manufactures (except in certain trading areas like the Levant and Russia) became less frequent. The export of cloth was no longer a necessary pretext for importing bar-iron or wine and therefore the functions of export and import merchants became more distinct. Cloth-merchanting itself became a more specialised function and one in which the London merchants were at a distinct disadvantage compared with their rivals in Yorkshire, Exeter and Norwich. Secondly, Hull was ideally sited for trade with Hamburg, the Baltic and the United Provinces, the chief points from which British cloth was distributed throughout Northern and Central Europe in the sixteenth and seventeenth centuries. Thirdly, the reputation in these markets which merchants shipping from Hull had built up by 1620 depended upon their superior sources of supply. Cheap cloth was a good selling line, but it had to be thoroughly sorted (it was much easier to find two dozen Spanish cloths of uniform quality than it was to supply 150 kerseys which could be bought for the same money) and not shoddy in workmanship and materials. The London merchants bought their Yorkshire cloth through factors and since they were not on the spot they had not the same influence with the clothiers as had the Yorkshire merchants. Nor in fact were the merchants operating from York and Hull well situated in this respect. Leeds and Wakefield were inaccessible to both towns by water carriage until 1700. Moreover Selby, and not York, was the point of transit for goods from the clothing area going down the Ouse to Hull, which by this route was over 60 miles away. Not surprisingly, as the Hull complaints of 1598 and 1622 out-

lined, merchants sprang up in Leeds and Wakefield when the production of Yorkshire cloths quickly accelerated after 1570. From these two
principal towns on the edge of the clothing districts (Halifax much
less favourably sited was not an export centre until the 1750's) their
merchants were able to bargain more easily with the clothiers either
in the cloth halls or in private sales. Cranfield's Danzig factor warned
him in 1608 about the kerseys he was buying in London:

I saw some of them which were very rags in comparison of the kersies the Hull
men bring. You must buy them which be exceeding good kersies or else you
shall sit still and the Hull men [i.e. Yorkshire merchants shipping through Hull]
will sell when no man will look upon yours.

By the 1680's in the Baltic trade Aström maintains: 'the London
exporters had ceased to be experts on cloth'. Their place was not taken
so much by the Blackwell Hall factors as by exporters from Leeds and
Exeter who concentrated entirely on wool manufactures.[8] Orders from
London took several weeks to complete; those from Leeds, even for
cloths that required dyeing, could be dispatched more quickly. This
was important when communications were poor and a good sale
abroad very frequently depended upon getting one's goods to market
first.

There is some confusion about the occupations from which the
merchants emerged in Leeds during the last two decades of Elizabeth's
reign to take up cloth-buying. Professor Heaton has suggested that they
advanced from clothier status.[9] Some like the Lodges and Ibbetsons
rose to eventual wealth through their long association with the town,
although it is not certain that these families were actually involved in
cloth-making. The Denisons are quoted as an outstanding example
of the merchant dynasty of clothier origins. They have a magnetic
celebrity. They eventually distinguished themselves in obtaining an
earldom and providing the Prince Regent with a middle-aged mistress.
The men, however, who made three score cloths a year could not raise
the capital nor possess the education requisite for mercantile activities
abroad. The gap, economically and socially, between clothier and merchant was wider and more difficult to bridge than has been admitted.
The Leeds men who first emulated and then out-distanced the export
merchants of London, Hull and York, by and large within the framework of the Merchant Adventurers and Eastland Companies, were
seldom one-time clothiers. Moreover the origins of the community
in Leeds are to be found in the last years of Elizabeth's reign, not in
the 1680's when Thomas Denison finally gave up making broad cloths
to begin exporting other people's.

The second Hull complaint stated explicitly that the Leeds merchants were young men who had lately 'sprung up . . . amongst the clothiers'. And Professor Rimmer has shown that those merchants who sought control of the town and its trade through the purchase of the manor of Leeds in 1628 and the charter of incorporation secured two years earlier were immigrants. He maintains that '24 of the 29 families in the 1626 Corporation were either first or second generation newcomers to the district'. Had these merchants been former clothiers we should not find this high tramontane element. The large fines levied on the minority of merchants who remained Royalist and their designation as 'gentlemen' shows that the community was composed of men of substance. We must seek their origins therefore amongst the ranks of Tudor yeomen and small landed families rather than the clothiers. Professor Hoskins has shown the Elizabethan yeomen in Leicestershire becoming increasingly wealthy, securing landed estates and grants of arms.[10] In the West Riding clothing areas the process was not dissimilar.

The late W. B. Crump worked out in some detail the position of the yeoman-clothier in the Almondbury area, an important cloth-producing centre in the sixteenth century. He noted the rise of a new Tudor gentry class from the yeoman clothiers, men who did well in the great turnover in lands following the dissolution of the monasteries. In the Aire valley the land market again was extremely fluid after the dispersal of the land belonging to Kirkstall Abbey and the sale of the Leeds estate of Sir John Nevile who was executed after the 1570 rising.[11] The clothiers around Leeds were too small to figure largely in these transactions, but there was an influx of yeomen and new gentry families around 1550. It was the sons and grandsons of these men who appeared in the last years of the sixteenth century and the early years of the next as the newcomers in Wakefield and Leeds, men of means and education who formed an easy association with the neighbouring gentry. For them the spinning-wheel and dye vat held no attractions, but they were eager to seize the prospect of good profits which an expanding market in Europe offered for Yorkshire cloth.

Examples of these families in Leeds are numerous. William Sykes, a younger son of a Cumberland yeoman settled in the clothing district in the middle years of the sixteenth century and 'improved himself considerably by the cloth trade'. His grandson Richard, principal initiator of events which led to the first Charter of Incorporation, Alderman of Leeds in 1629 and in the same year purchaser of a four-ninths share of the manor, was 'one of the most eminent merchants in these parts'. When Richard Sykes died in 1645, Thoresby (who married his great-grand-daughter) proudly related that he left 'besides vast estates to his sons, £10,000 a-piece to his daughters from whom four knights' and baronets' families are descended'.[12] Richard Milner was also of yeoman stock. He settled in Leeds before the Civil War and was elected Alderman in 1652. Three newcomers to merchanting came from North Yorkshire: Marmaduke Hickes, four times mayor, was son of a substantial farmer at Nunnington and entered the cloth trade about 1650; Richard Idle came from a similar background at nearby Bulmer; and the Kitchingmans were small landowners at Carlton Hustwaite, before a branch of the family moved to Leeds around the beginning of the seventeenth century.[13]

We know nothing of Thomas Metcalfe's origins, but he was described as early as 1630, when he was farming the ullnage collection of the West Riding, 'as a gentleman of great estate'. William Busfield, whom Cranfield came across trading in Germany in 1600, and who had married Metcalfe's sister is equally elusive, but, like his brother-in-law, he was a principal merchant in the export trade. It is known that the Dixons possessed an estate at Heaton Royds near Bradford. Of three brothers, Jeremiah succeeded to the paternal estate, William became a captain in Cromwell's army and Joshua the youngest was apprenticed into the Leeds cloth trade. Other families like the Wades, Stanhopes, Hodgsons, Lawsons, Rayners and Lowthers boasted more eminent ancestors. The Stanhopes and Foxcrofts, with whom the Wades intermarried, moved into the West Riding around 1550 on their purchase of monastic estates. Thoresby noted in his diary that the present Sir William Lowther's father 'had married Mr. Busfield's daughter of this town (where Sir William was born), was a merchant here and afterwards Parliament man for sixteen years, till his death, and one of the Council in the North.' Godfrey Lawson, mayor in 1669, was the second son of Edward Lawson Esq. of Brunton in Northumberland, a family of 'ancient descent' which perhaps explains why two of his children married into a leading North Riding landed family.[14] It is difficult to distinguish the primary occupations of these men: they balanced their accounts by a nice combination of legal fees, mercantile profits and land rents.

Not all the merchants came from the small landed class. A minority like the Denisons acquired their capital from profits made in cloth-making or allied trades in Leeds itself. Perhaps more significant is the fact that a number of merchants from Hull and York were attracted across to Leeds after 1660. Although the traders in Leeds and Wakefield had failed through York's opposition to have the Rivers Aire and Calder made navigable in the 1620's the Yorkshire cloth trade, especially after 1640, was falling increasingly into the hands of the merchants in Leeds who were better placed for marketing and finishing functions. Whether Leeds' ascendancy was gained by default it is now difficult to know. But the corporation in York allowed the Ouse above Selby to silt up and its merchants turned, depending on their wealth, either to landownership or to the inland trade, and those in Hull became increasingly involved in the import trade of the northern Baltic, an area that provided a limited market for English cloth. Yet those merchants who seemed enterprising enough to move to Leeds like Thomas Breary and George Perrot, members of leading merchant families in York, and John Skinner and George Crowle from Hull did not found notable dynasties, although Thomas Breary became mayor in 1720.[15] But the rivalry between the two ancient towns and Leeds should not be over-emphasised: there were many connections of interest and marriage.

Finally, there were a number of merchants whose antecedents are difficult to categorise easily. Richard and Robert Spencer had many connections with London merchant families. John Preston, mayor in 1691, was one of the chief merchants trading through Hull to the Baltic in 1685, which appears to have some link with the fact that his father-in-law Sir Benjamin Ayloff, a governor of the Russia Company, was the leading London trader in the Baltic trade in the 1680's.[16] The Spencers and Preston were probably drawn from London just as Breary and Perrot had been from York. Together their move is excellent testimony to the key position Leeds had achieved in the Yorkshire cloth trade towards the end of the seventeenth century.

Professor Carus-Wilson found that in fifteenth-century Bristol:

The wholesale export trade became a career no less reputable than the church or the law, with prospects no less attractive and a training no less strict, first as apprentice and then as factor. Those who professed it tended to draw apart from those lesser folk—mere shopkeepers, artisans, or small wholesale dealers.

The same was true in Leeds. Records for the reconstruction of the lives of these Stuart merchants are sparse, but their civic activities, the pedigrees that Thoresby laboriously constructed, the returns of the Hearth Tax in 1663 suggest their opulence and indicate their place in both Leeds and West Riding society. They show their interests especially socially, to be much closer to those of the neighbouring gentry than those of the clothier with whom they resided cheek by jowl in the crowded little town of the Restoration. Thoresby's diary entries, reinforced by his genealogical tables, above all emphasise this point with endless references to 'brother' Wilson and Rayner, 'uncle' Sykes and Idle, 'cousin' Fenton, Dixon, Ibbetson and Milner, which disclose the homogeneity of the town's merchant society bound by com-

mon economic interests and social activities and thoroughly cemented by
innumerable intermarriages. By 1700 the oligarchy closely resembled
those groups of 'urban gentry' which had long controlled the political
and economic life of the old urban centres of the county, York,
Scarborough, Beverley and Hull.[17] It is only the more ample records
of the eighteenth century which allow a further examination of the
composition of this community. And to this we must now turn.

(II)

Because seventeenth and eighteenth-century firms were always family
concerns, they seldom have a long or continuous history. A family
which continued more than 50 years in cloth-merchanting was exceptional. There were several reasons for this phenomenon. Some houses
were caught in the dislocations which war and uneven demand
produced. Others like the Hickes and Metcalfes produced no male
heirs, and already what was to become a familiar pattern of exodus—
the purchase of a country estate from the profits of trade—had begun.
Richard Sykes moved to Ledsham Hall around 1650; William
Busfield's son bought Ryshworth Hall, Bingley, during Charles II's
reign.[18] Moreover the type of partnership entered into by merchants
in Leeds, usually for not more than seven years, was not conducive to
producing long-lived firms.

Probably not many more than 30 recognisable merchant firms survived
the seventeenth century although it is possible a number of smaller concerns unrecognised by the corporation court-books or Thoresby's pen
continued their existence for a number of years. Of these 30 houses
less than half were in existence by the middle of the eighteenth century.
They were then amongst the largest firms in business, and all famous
names in Leeds history—Dixon, Oates, Denison, Lodge, Cookson,
Ibbetson and Blayds. Defaulting firms were replaced by newcomers.
An indication of the numerical dimension of the group gives some
idea of the extent of recruitment.

The first list of merchants was contained in the subscription list for
Holy Trinity church in 1721.[19] It includes the names of 43 merchants
who subscribed £1,100 in amounts varying from £200 to two guineas.
The partners of several houses contributed individually so in fact this
list suggests that there were about 30 merchant houses. Then there
were the Dissenters. Mill Hill and Call Lane Chapels were each run by
five or six merchant families. No Quaker or Catholic merchants were
known at this time, but in about 1715 no fewer than six foreigners
began cloth-merchanting in Leeds, two of whom appear in the church
list. From this evidence there were in 1720 just under 50 merchant

houses in Leeds, a fairly sharp increase from 1700 when perhaps there were around 30. This increase is accounted for by the influx of foreign merchants and the continued modest expansion of the Yorkshire woollen industry in these years.

Unfortunately the poor-rate assessment books do not state occupations, and the next reliable measurement of the group is not obtained until the invaluable entry made by Thomas Hill in his memorandum book in 1782.[20] It contained the names of 73 merchant houses ranging from the Denisons dealing in £50,000 worth of cloth annually to the Mirfields, just elevated from the clothiers' ranks to sell cloth valued at £1,000 a year. The group had expanded slowly over the previous 60 years. The entries in W. Bailey's directories in 1781 and 1784 suggest a lower figure than Hill's list. He included only 57 merchant houses, but these early general directories were frequently inaccurate and his second entry merely repeats that made three years earlier. The Leeds list in the *Universal British Directory* (1790) is again misleading. It was a nation-wide survey and again probably carelessly constructed when it listed 74 merchants. The 1797 *Directory*,[21] a Leeds publication, gives a list of 148 merchants although the number of firms were fewer for when the residence of the merchant was entered as well as his warehouse (where the two were separate) there was some double counting. There were in fact in 1797 about 130 firms carrying on the woollen trade in Leeds. In 1800 there were 144, in 1809, 137 and in 1814–15, 104 of whom 23 were distinguished as merchant-manufacturers. After 1815 a directory appeared almost every two years and they became increasingly complex. All of them, however, suggest a check in the number of merchant firms. Baines's 1822 *Directory* listed 97 woollen merchants of whom 30 combined the occupations of merchanting and manufacturing. In 1830 the same number was reached through a different breakdown of the figures: there were 37 woollen cloth merchants, 23 stuff merchants, 46 woollen cloth merchants and manufacturers, 10 stuff and woollen merchants and 4 woollen and blanket merchants. By 1851 there was a further decline in numbers, only 73 merchant and merchant manufacturers were recorded in that year's directory, and 30 years later the number of merchants had dwindled to 17.

Several points emerge from a consideration of this evidence. A comparison with the directory entries of Wakefield and Halifax reveal Leeds' great predominance in the merchanting and finishing side of the woollen trade. In 1830 Wakefield had 6 woollen merchants and Halifax 20, of whom 7 were merchant-manufacturers. Bradford had 14 unclassified merchants but its stuff merchants were in fact all Leeds men, save 1 from Manchester who had a warehouse in Bradford and attended market days there. Secondly, the directories indicate the great increase in the number of worsted merchants. It should be remembered however that specialisation in worsteds, as opposed to general dealing in both stuffs and woollens that had hitherto been the practice, came only with the rapid expansion of the West Riding worsted industry after 1783. Even more significant is the emergence of the merchant-manufacturers. Bailey listed only 3 in 1781, and these were engaged in the worsted branch of the industry. But in 1830 there were no fewer than 46 woollen cloth merchant-manufacturers in Leeds. On the other hand the number of true merchants, selling but not making woollen cloths, had fallen from over 120 in 1797 to 37 by 1830. Lastly, the figures permit some correlation between increased woollen cloth production and the increase in the number of merchants. Between 1700 and 1780 the number of firms doubled in comparison with the roughly fourfold growth in the West Riding broad-cloth output which was the principal item handled by the Leeds merchants. Between 1781 and 1797 the number of merchant houses increased by over 80% while output almost doubled in the great boom which followed the close of the American war. It is an interesting relationship but one neither entirely of coincidence nor rule. In years of bad trade the number of merchants did not noticeably decline: between 1776 and 1783 there was a severe contraction yet only half-a-dozen bankruptcies occurred and this included only one major firm. But in the rapid expansion after 1783, the promise of easy profits in new markets drew a large number of new-comers into the merchant ranks. Then after 1800 there was a spasmodic contraction, the result of structural changes within the industry. Many of the old-style firms began to disappear as manufacturers for the first time began to market their own output. But at least before 1780 there were other determinants of entry besides the general economic climate. Relationship and apprenticeship were the easiest routes of admission, and they cut across the pattern of economic fluctuation. Nevertheless in years of prosperity the group tended to expand and in years of depression to remain stationary.

(III)

Before we examine the categories of recruitment to the merchant group in the eighteenth century something should be said of those families who traced their antecedents back into the previous century and who formed the largest and most continuous firms after 1700. There were six of these families in 1781 the year Thomas Hill made his calculations—Blayds, Cookson, Denison, Dixon, Lee and Oates. Another seven had been equally prominent but had departed from the town at the approximate date indicated: Lodge (1776), Fenton (1760), Ibbetson (1761), Kitchingman (1725), Milner (1740), Preston (1730) and Rooke (1725). All had withdrawn to live the lives of country gentlemen with the exception of poor Sir William Rooke, William Busfield's grandson, who had died without children in 1743, very wealthy and very mad. Admittedly Thomas and William Fenton became as much involved in coal-mining as farming at Rothwell and Edmund Lodge built a cotton-spinning factory at Willow Hall near Halifax around 1780.[22] These 13 dynasties controlled the town's life down to 1780. They were the legends of Leeds: it was their houses visitors noted for their opulence, their fortunes that the newspapers speculated about. They dominated the export trade of Yorkshire cloth —even in 1781 the six families mentioned carried on a quarter of the town's trade—and calculations made for 30 years earlier would have shown them appropriating an even larger share. Their sons and sons-in-law followed in their footsteps, filling all the chief positions in the town, serving as justices also in the county and acting as the leading spokesmen of the most important sector of the country's chief industry. These families were joined by others who came through three distinct channels of recruitment.

Firstly, there was a group of foreign merchants who settled in Leeds around 1715. Secondly, there were many young men of good education and family whose fathers paid high premiums for them to train with the leading firms in the town, drawn to the trade by the wealth which merchants like William Milner and Sir Henry Ibbetson had realised in their calling. Lastly, there were those who rose from other occupations within, or associated with, the woollen industry itself—cloth-dressing, dyeing, dry-salting and retail drapery.

(i)
Numerically the foreigners formed the smallest group of newcomers. Their immigration was the result of a variety of causes—the decline of the Merchant Adventurers and Eastland Companies, the settling in England of foreign merchants with the accession of William III and George I, the Naturalisation of Foreign Protestants Act (7 Anne c. 5) and the failure of the Corporation of Leeds to form a class of freemen and organise the woollen industry on restricted lines after 1661.[23] For those men experienced in the continental cloth trade, Leeds, the centre of a thriving export trade, was a natural choice, and no fewer than six alien merchants settled in the town around 1715. Jacob Busk came from Gothenburg, John Berkenhout from Holland, Bernard Bischoff from Basle. The places of origin of Messrs. Noguier, Gautier and Clerkenbrinke are unknown.

It is not until 1717 that we first hear of Busk, Bischoff and Berkenhout, names which produced an infinite permutation of spellings in the next few years.[24] They and five other inhabitants appealed against their excessive poor-rate assessment. Their appeal was rejected, and Berkenhout's three successive pleas in the following year were all turned down. The fact that the attempts of Alderman Barstow and Dr. Kirshaw, the Rector of Ripley and the brother of a Leeds merchant, met with success showed that the justices (almost all of whom were merchants) were discriminating against the foreigners. But the matter did not drop at this point. Two years later Berkenhout, Noguier and Clerkenbrinke appealed once more 'and being offered the book to be sworn in the usual manner respectively refused to be sworne whereupon their appeals were rejected'. At the same session Busk refused the offer of an abatement in his assessment and not surprisingly his further appeal of the following April was rejected. They had ample grounds for complaint. The poor-rate was raised chiefly by a rate on property, but also by a personal assessment on the earnings of the self-employed and by a tax on the number of cloth tenters owned. The assessment on income provided an obvious area for discrimination: in the rate of August 1726 Bischoff and 'Busktt' were paying 10s. each a month, 'Klockenbrunck' £1 whilst William Milner the leading merchant in the county contributed 4s. 6d. Newcomers from elsewhere, even within Yorkshire itself, were treated little better than the foreigners. Yet it is interesting to note that in 1721 Busk and Noguier subscribed £20 and £10 respectively to Holy Trinity church and on its completion, together with Berkenhout, purchased pews there. In 1722 Busk and Berkenhout had petitioned Parliament for their legal naturalisation and by the late 1720's the resentment had died down and there were no more appeals.[25] In 1730 Busk and Noguier were amongst those serving as overseers of the poor and in the next decade all of them were to be found doing jury service and holding parish offices. In 1736 Noguier was elected to the corporation, as was Berkenhout five years later. The former never took the oaths and was fined £60, whilst the latter was found rather belatedly, through a clause in the Naturalisation Act, to be incapable of holding office.

The five men were all of substantial means, otherwise they would not have been allowed to settle at all. They all went directly into merchanting, although Jacob Busk was said to find his way there through book-keeping with a large firm.[26] Their houses proclaimed their affluence. In 1721 Busk was occupying a house in Hunslet Lane valued at £23 annually. This was no book-keeper's dwelling when a good house was assessed at £10, and a cottage from £1 to £4 per annum. John Cossin's map, illustrating in its margins the finest 15 dwelling houses in Leeds, included those of Berkenhout and Bischoff besides that of Busk.

In 1717 Jeremiah Dixon's poor assessment was reduced when he formally renounced his partnership with Noguier 'to what it was before he was assessed as in partnership aforesaid'. Dixon and Joshua Ryder, in partnership with Bischoff in 1719, realised how useful these aliens could be with their languages, foreign connections and correspondents. In 1748 Henry Ibbetson was created a baronet. Dabbling in county politics doing the rounds of London and Bath he was prevented from giving his full attention to the firm in Leeds which was the chief prop of his livelihood. In that same year he admitted a German, John Koster, on favourable terms into one of the most coveted partnerships in town. It was only broken on Koster's death 12 years later. Gamaliel Lloyd, a member of a prominent Manchester merchant family when he entered the Leeds cloth trade in the early 1760's, formed a partnership with two of Gautier's sons, and although their dyeing enterprise was a failure, Lloyd still found a partnership with a foreigner valuable. He entered into terms with Horace Cattaneo, an Italian, in 1776 to form a large and successful export house.[27]

Although little more is heard of Noguier[28] and Gautier, Berkenhout, Bischoff and Busk secured for themselves and their families eminence and prosperity in the West Riding. The three young men all made good marriages in the 1720's and that assured their acceptance on easy terms in Leeds society. Although Berkenhout's son failed to secure the lease of the Aire and Calder Navigation Tolls in 1751 and, in disgust, published a vicious satire on the Leeds gentry before turning to natural history, Jacob Busk and Bernard Bischoff founded dynasties prominent in the eighteenth century. Jacob's son Hans, who succeeded him in trade when he died in 1755, married the sole heiress of Richard Rodes of Long Houghton, and obtained the extensive Yorkshire and Derbyshire estates of the Rodes and Riches. When his two daughters married into the leading merchant family in Wakefield, the Milnes, their marriage portions were said to be £100,000 each, and he himself was reputed to have left £150,000 on his death in 1792. How much of these large sums was accrued through mercantile endeavour and how much through the Rodes's rent-roll it is impossible to know.[29] The Bischoffs have a longer history in Leeds for they were prominent in its affairs down to the middle of the nineteenth century. Being Dissenters they do not appear in the corporation, but they were notable members of the town's chapels, exemplary in their work amongst the poor in the hard years after 1795, and according to Hill the second largest firm in the town in 1781. For the Busks and Bischoffs a few short years of ostracism were followed by decades of acceptance and prosperity.

(ii)

The most usual introduction to woollen-merchanting in the eighteenth century was through a formal training arranged by the apprentice's father and a woollen merchant of his acquaintance on the payment of a substantial premium. The period of apprenticeship, varying between two and seven years, began when the trainee finished his schooling at the age of 15–18. An apprenticeship provided an invaluable, time-honoured and expensive insight into the mysteries of merchanting. In Yorkshire, as in London, the highest premiums recorded in the Apprenticeship Registers were always those paid to merchants. Hughes' assertion that around 1720 £130 was the largest premium paid to Liverpool and Yorkshire merchants is not supported by evidence from Leeds and Hull.[30] And certainly Yorkshire premiums were a good deal higher than those recorded in Wiltshire, even if they did not equal those demanded by London merchants in the Levant and East India trades. Yet in Leeds large fees were necessary to cover the apprentice's board and the final year of his training spent abroad visiting his master's correspondents. But high premiums necessarily made apprenticeship a selective method of recruitment to the merchant group. No one outside the middle sectors of society could afford the £200 or £300 which the larger firms demanded. Moreover apprenticeship was only the beginning. When training was completed a partnership had to be bought and this could not be effected for less than £1,500, and usually involved a considerably greater expenditure.

Apprenticeship fees depended largely on the standing and repute of the master. In Leeds they varied from the £40 Benjamin Horner demanded in 1715, to the £450 William Milner extracted from Thomas Snedell four years later. Lawyers and surgeons accepted far smaller premiums, although it must be remembered that the merchant usually paid for his apprentices' tours, although John Gott, when his son Benjamin was apprenticed with Wormald and Fountaine in 1780, had 'to defray the Expence of Horse Hire and also his Sons Expenses when he goes such Journies for his Improvement'. Money spent on training with a reputable firm was money well spent. But the size of the premium was not an infallible guide, as William Lupton wrote to his son: 'Coates your old companion has bound himself to Mr. Joshua Hartley, the report is that he has £200 with him—I think the poor lad is a great fool or else he wo'd not throw away money in such a manner, he might have been with the best Mercht. in Town for that sum'. Unfortunately the West Riding entries in the Apprenticeship Register

c

Table 2   Leeds merchant apprentices[a]

Master	Name of apprentice and father	No. of years	Premium (£'s)	Year apprenticeship contracted
James Ibbetson	George son of Roger Mainwaring Esq., Chester	7	300	1712
Robert Kitchingman	Thomas son of Elias Mickle-thwaite gent., Terrington	7	150	1714
Roger Marrow	Richard son of William Richardson, High Fearnley	7	150	1715
James Ibbetson	Joshua son of John Brown, Sheffield	7	305	1714
William Cookson	Robt. son of Sir Arthur Kaye, Bart. M.P., Woodsome	7	200	1715
Benjamin Horner	Thomas son of Thomas Greene dec.	7	40	1715
Benjamin Horner	Nathaniel son of David English, Leeds	7	100	1716
John Fenton	John son of John Hey, dry-salter, Leeds	7	100	1716
Thomas Breary	Thomas son of Francis Mason dec.	5	200	1718
William Cookson	John son of Sir George Cook, Bart., Adwick	7	250	1718
Richard Hey	Johnson son of Saml. Gardiner, Elkington, Derby	7	100	1719
William Milner	Thomas son of Thomas Snedell, Gawthorpe Hall, landowner	5	450	1719
John Noguier	George son of Elinor Hobson, Kirby	7	200	1722
Croft and William Preston	Walter son of John Stanhope Esq., Horsforth Hall	7	230	1721
John Brooke	Jonathan son of William Beetham, clothier, Leeds	6	40	1744
Abraham Dawson	Joseph Rose	2	100	1753
Walter Stanhope[b]	Cavendish son of John Lister Esq., Syson, Leics.	5	400	1753
Joshua Hartley[c]	—Coates	?	200	1764
John Wormald and Joseph Fountaine[d]	Benjamin son of John Gott, engineer	4	400	1780

Compiled from the Apprenticeship Registers, P.R.O. 1R1/41–53.
[a] Spencer-Stanhope MSS. 1221.
[b] Lupton MSS.
[c] Crump, 193.

are thin, especially after 1725. As the agent was always a York attorney there were inherent collection problems. Walter Stanhope's apprenticeship deed was completed in Leeds in February 1721 but it was not entered into the Register in London for another four and a half years. It is an indication of the general laxity of the returns. There is evidence that premiums did not decline after 1750: Walter Stanhope charged an apprentice £400 in 1753 for a five-year training; Wormald and Fountaine obtained the same sum from John Gott; and Thomas Lodge when he died in 1776 left £500 for his son's apprenticeship with a merchant house in Leeds.[31]

It was possible for a merchant to receive a cheaper training with a cloth-dresser, dry-salter or draper. John Douglas, mayor in 1732, was apprenticed with a linen-draper for seven years with a premium of £50 in 1711; Edward Gray, mayor in 1749 and 1768, was indentured with a cloth-worker for seven years in 1717 at a cost of only £20. Whether this type of training was recognised as an acceptable alternative to apprenticeship with a regular merchant is uncertain. It is possible that Douglas and Gray went into merchanting after they had established themselves in the trades for which they had been specifically prepared.

A high wastage rate is observable in training legalised by the more expensive indentures. Many apprentices never exported a cloth on their own account after their term was complete. Young men like John Cooke, Thomas Vavasour and Thomas Snedell inherited sufficient incomes for them to give up the idea of the cloth trade.

No single example epitomises the place of the merchant who had served a formal apprenticeship in the Leeds trade, for in spite of their preponderantly middle-class origin they showed considerable diversity. William Cookson, a merchant prominent in the first 40 years of the century, took Robert Kaye the son of Sir Arthur Kaye, M.P. for Yorkshire, as an apprentice in 1715, and three years later he accepted the son of Sir George Cook of Adwick. Sir Thomas Vavasour, a member of one of Yorkshire's oldest Catholic families, served his apprenticeship 'with one of the most respectable houses in the town' in the 1760's.[32] Other recruits like Walter Stanhope, D'arcy Molyneux, Thomas and Hatton Wolrich, John and Edward Markland, Joseph Fountaine and Henry Hall came from old, but lesser, county families of standing. Thomas and Gamaliel Lloyd belonged to a wealthy Manchester merchant family. Their father, George Lloyd, a Fellow of the Royal Society, had bought the estate of Barrowby Hall near Leeds and placed two of his four sons to serve their apprenticeships in Leeds in the early 1760's. They either made or inherited fortunes for in 1789 Gamaliel left Leeds to live in Hampstead and Thomas devoted all his time and some of his income to the Leeds Volunteers Corps which he commanded during the French wars. Eventually both brothers founded landed families in North Yorkshire.[33] Richard Sheepshanks was a well-to-do yeoman of Linton-in-Craven. Of his seven sons, four were apprenticed with Leeds merchants in the 1760's and three became clergymen, two of them holding the perpetual curacies of St. John's and Holy Trinity Church in Leeds.[34] Several merchants came from clerical families. Thomas Micklethwaite was from Terrington and Samuel Kershaw from Ripley, where his family were rectors for more than a century. Thomas Breary, mayor in 1720, was a son of the Archdeacon of the East Riding.

The Medhursts provide a well documented example of the range of a well-to-do family who came into cloth merchanting.[35] William Medhurst, the grandson of a physician, shortly after the death of his father in 1708 settled in Leeds. In 1719, the year he married the daughter of an apothecary in the town and was first elected to the corporation, he was described as a cloth-worker—a small master who finished cloth on a commission basis for the merchants (see pp. 71–73). From the evidence of the poor-rate assessment and his subscription to Holy Trinity Church he was doing well in the woollen trade, and by 1712 he had joined the merchants' ranks. No sooner had he done so than he began disposing of considerable property which he owned at Giggleswick and around 1730 began to purchase land at Kippax and Swillington (six miles from Leeds) which was to form the nucleus of the small estate the Medhursts built up around Kippax Hall during the next 50 years.[36] In 1741 he was ousted from the corporation in conformity with its rules when he ceased to live within the town. Three years later he was an unsuccessful candidate for the office of High Sheriff of Yorkshire.[37] On his death shortly afterwards his two sons, Thomas and John, who had just completed their training with their father, began to manage the firm in Leeds. From the outset they appear to have spent far more time at Kippax pursuing their rural pleasures, although they retained a house and of course their warehouses in Leeds.

Thomas Medhurst married the daughter of the Reverend Granville and Lady Catherine Wheler. Since she was also the niece of Selina, Countess of Huntingdon, it was an alliance which brought the Medhursts to the forefront of early Methodism. Both brothers, however, in spite of their religious leanings, were elected to the corporation in the 1750's. Thomas quickly became mayor in 1760 and again held the office in 1773. Besides being twice chairman of the Leeds sessions, he was also a West Riding J.P. At Kippax they farmed 200 acres themselves and were involved in mining ventures on their estate.[38]

It seems that the American War of Independence swamped the Medhursts, for they failed in the autumn of 1780, the only large Leeds firm to crash in the 1778–83 depression. The upkeep and improvement of their estate at Kippax possibly placed too great a strain on their firm for the sale of their effects is a telling postscript of their true interests. Besides their pack of harriers there was 'all the genuine and elegant household goods and furniture . . . about 800 ounces of neat and fashionable plate, a handsome post-chaise with good harness and a pair of bay horses'. The estate was resurrected only to be overtaken by a more terrible disaster in 1800. The son of Thomas Medhurst, a county J.P. and described as 'allied to some of the best families in the county and a man of very considerable fortune' (derived chiefly from his collieries), murdered his wife.[39]

There were few merchant dynasties, founded by well-to-do recruits who had served their apprenticeship in Leeds, that compared with the Dixons, Blayds, Cooksons and Denisons in importance in the economic life of the town and trade. Only a handful of them stayed in merchanting for more than one generation. They flash across the scene of Georgian Leeds taking its social life by storm. Atherton Rawsthorne came from Lancashire in the 1770's. With a brother a general and a sister married to a local baronet, he and his wife, herself a niece of Lord Chancellor Loughborough, were at the centre of the town's social round in the 1780's. Yet Thomas Hill reckoned Rawsthornes was amongst the smallest of the 73 firms in Leeds in 1781. Walter Stanhope made two good marriages and his only son, for many years an M.P., succeeded to two West Riding estates, but he himself made a poor show as a merchant in Leeds although the *Mercury* on his death labelled him as 'an eminent Merchant in this town'.[40] Nevertheless, in the space of a working life, often little more than 20 years, a hardworking and intelligent merchant just out of his apprenticeship could make a comfortable living and accumulate a small fortune. After all it was this prospect which drew recruits into the trade. Thus men like John Wormald, Edward Markland, Joseph Fountain, the Sheepshank and Lloyd brothers, all newcomers from prosperous families, who married often within the town's patrician families, did well especially in years of buoyant trade as in the late 1760's and early 1770's and again after 1783. Nevertheless only the Sheepshanks (and then not the eldest brother's family) stayed in business for more than one generation, for although John Wormald's family provided the bulk of the capital for Gott's factory their attention to business was always desultory before Gott eventually squeezed them out of the firm.

Like any good club the merchants in Leeds recruited members from their own circle. Their first preference was for their relatives and close business associates, but otherwise they welcomed recruits from well-to-do, though not necessarily wealthy, families with good social connections. The apprentices served their period of training, acquired a thorough knowledge of the cloth trade and, equally important, an insight into the mechanism of the merchant community. They married their masters' daughters and obtained places on the corporation. It was a convenient arrangement for the benefit of all concerned.

Training was one aspect of success, while another was that the apprenticed recruit could produce ready capital which made them invaluable in partnerships. Moreover they made their contribution to the life of town. Joseph Fountaine was a memorable mayor in 1777 and the first to be officially thanked for outstanding work during his term of office. Others followed his example. With a vision which comprehended more than the woollen trade itself, these wealthy newcomers were the leaven which set in process social action in late eighteenth-century Leeds.

(iii)

Well-informed contemporaries maintained that the economic and social gap between the clothier, cloth-worker and dyer on the one hand and the export merchant on the other was a wide one. When the corporation drew up its list of fines for freemen at the end of the seventeenth century the cloth-worker's payment for this privilege was fixed at 40s., the merchant's at £50. Yet although recruitment through apprenticeship, by marriage into a merchant family, and the provision of capital in buying a partnership was the easier and more usual method of entry into the merchant ranks, it was not the only one. That it was possible to move into the lower end of the trade, the indistinct area between small merchant, shopkeeper, clothier and cloth-dresser was proved time and time again especially as the eighteenth century advanced. The introduction of machinery threw open the flood gates of opportunity, but even before 1780 they had never been completely water-tight.

The greatest distinction between the Yorkshire and West Country cloth industries was that in the former the functions of merchant and clothier were quite separate. In comparison with the Wiltshire clothiers the makers of Yorkshire broad cloths were men of small capital. As John Hebblethwaite pointed out the clothiers around Leeds who made more than two cloths a week in the 1760's were exceptional. Evidence from surviving records of Leeds clothiers shows them owning their own premises, a few cottages, a close or two of land and after several generations accumulating savings of a few hundred pounds by 1780. There were, even in the broad cloth area to the south-west of Leeds, a few units of larger size which had allowed clothiers like James Armitage and Christopher Houldsworth to become as prosperous as the smaller merchants.[41] In these cases the clothier employed not only his own family but perhaps as many as a dozen journeymen. A number of these large clothiers appear to have congregated in Hunslet, the most populous out-township in Leeds parish and, as cloth-making declined in Leeds itself, an increasingly important centre of production. At least seven families—Dunderdale, Winter, Carr, Glover, Armitage, Willans and Brown—who by 1800 were prominent as merchants and significantly as early small factory-owners, had long connections with cloth manufacture in Hunslet.

The expansion of the Armitages's fortunes from their being ordinary clothiers to becoming affluent merchants by industry, intelligence and carefully planned marriages is a fascinating example of social mobility and a good illustration of the founding of a merchant house outside the usual channels of recruitment. The Armitages had been in Hunslet from at least the early seventeenth century, clothiers no different from the hundreds more who brought their weekly cloth to Leeds market from the surrounding villages. There was no hint that the family was marked out for any extraordinary advancement until the time of Joseph Armitage. When he died in 1750, the *Leeds Mercury* recorded that he was 'an eminent and ingenious clothier . . . a Man of great integrity and singularly useful by his peculiar Talents and Abilities in improving the Manufacture'. His will, leaving several properties at Hunslet to his wife and all his belongings and money with the exception of 20s. to each of his six sons suggests little either of his eminence or ingenuity. But the inventory of his goods gives some idea of his wealth with its tea-tables, bureau, 76 ounces of silver plate, its gun and sword, four pairs of looms and two cloth leads.[42] It is not known how his sons were educated but the family's resources were sufficient for the three sons who survived infancy to set themselves up as merchants. William, the eldest, was the partner of a Lisbon firm which traded as William Armitage and Bros. He died there in 1790 and left all his property equally between his two remaining brothers. Joseph, the next brother, soon followed William to the grave, and the majority of his possessions passed to James, the sole surviving brother. It was James' will, proved in 1803, which gave the real indication of the Armitages' advancement after 1750 and the profits to be made in cloth-merchanting. He made bequests alone totalling £132,000, and his property included the manors of Farnley (purchased for £49,500 in 1800) and Hunslet, besides the Field Head Estate at Birstall and land at Knowstrop. Armitage's most valuable asset, however, was his shares in the Aire and Calder Navigation which in 1806 were producing a dividend of 150% and a sum of £3,469 annually for his descendants.[43] Not surprisingly his only son Edward was able to lead the life of an extremely prosperous landowner.

Men of James Armitage's ability were rare, and few Yorkshire clothiers could have any pretensions to emulate his success. John Hebblethwaite who gave evidence before the celebrated enquiry into the woollen industry in 1806 was chosen not because of his experience or eminence in the trade—there were many candidates who could have produced better credentials—but because he was almost the sole example of a merchant who had come from the clothiers' ranks and yet was prepared to express a strong disinclination to combine merchanting with manufacturing. Before 1780 merchants with clothier origins were virtually unknown in the woollen cloth trade although, since the stuff weavers in Leeds—as numerous as the broad cloth clothiers by 1770—were men of larger capital than their counterparts in cloth manufacture, they were more evident in worsted dealings.[44]

Cloth-dressers were equally important in the composition of this group. The extent to which the dresser or cropper was able to maintain his independence from the merchant is a difficult question to decide, all that need be said here is that the master cloth-dresser was the highest paid and most skilled artisan in the woollen industry. He reached an agreement with the merchant whereby he dressed his cloth on commission at a price varying according to type and width. The four chief dressers of Sir Henry Ibbetson illustrate the place of the master cloth-dresser and indicate his potentialities. Between 1749 and 1760 William Lupton was paid £2,728 'for dressing as by note', John Wright £2,330, John Darnton £1,603 and John Scurr £1,518.[45]

Lupton was obviously a man of superior abilities for John Koster appointed him sole executor of his estate and partnership with Ibbetson. And during Sir Henry's prolonged last illness, Lupton ran the firm entirely, and he had long been in effect the manager. He sent his three sons to the grammar school. William, the eldest, was Rector of Blagdon and later perpetual curate of Headingley, whilst Francis was a partner in the Lisbon importing house of Carrett and Lupton and Arthur became a merchant in Leeds. William Lupton was a man of ambition, but the rest of the Ibbetson cloth-dressers also did well. John Wright began merchanting himself in a small way. John Scurr's son became a merchant, whilst Darnton's son became an extremely prosperous wholesale tobacconist. And these examples are drawn from the cloth-dressers of only one firm, although after 1760 there is evidence that the merchant began to take over the independent cloth-dressers' functions himself and thereafter the dresser was forced into the position of becoming merely a skilled journeyman.

The dyer occupied a relationship to the merchant similar to that of the cloth-dresser. Some merchants dyed their own white cloths, others employed independent dyers. But examples of dyers becoming cloth merchants, perhaps only through inadequate documentation, are rare. Like the master cloth-dressers they were not without means. When Edward Gilyard, self-styled 'gentleman', died in 1755, having given up the business of dyeing in 1749, he left over £2,500 and an estate in land valued at £106 per annum, of which his old dyeing premises and vats produced a yearly rental of £38. His widow, a sister of William Lupton, received three-quarters of the estate but died the following year, and the bulk of her estate passed to her brother, who acted as sole executor, and to his three sons.[46] It was a bequest which in no small measure forwarded the advancement of the Luptons to eventual fame and repute in the annals of Leeds and its trade.

More direct evidence of resources accrued in dyeing being transferred to woollen-merchanting is provided by the papers of the Rhodes family.[47] When William Rhodes 'one of the most considerable dyers in this town' died in 1772 he left 10 children and at least £5,500. His somewhat headstrong relict was not content—as so many widows are —merely to run the business on the lines established by her husband during his lifetime, and she began a number of bold innovations, installing 'a machine for Ribbing of all kinds of woollen cloths in the most fashionable stripes', and buying 16 acres of land adjoining Sheepscar Beck to erect a water-mill 'for working the stocks and other machines . . . which were then worked by horses'. Trade collapsed in the late 1770's and exacerbated the clash of strong personalities in the firm. In July 1780 the two oldest sons withdrew to form a partnership with John Hebblethwaite to commence business as merchants and cloth-workers. They very quickly gained a foothold in the European market for within 18 months Hill reckoned they were a middle-sized export house. And like the majority of Leeds houses they prospered in the decade following the American war. When Mathew Rhodes, the second son, died in 1796 his will revealed the fortunes the brothers had made in the previous 15 years. He made specific bequests alone amounting to £33,150, including £100 to the Leeds Infirmary and £50 to the town's Sunday-schools. Abraham, the only surviving son of dyer William, commenced large-scale manufacturing around 1810. Four years later he was proudly claiming, 'I have built a little Town at Woodhouse Carr for the Convenience of Business . . . which has now become one of the first in town and I have no doubt will every year increase so long as we are Blessed with Health and Strength'. The Rhodes' transition from dyer to merchant-manufacturer within the space of 30 years was a classic example of the replacement of the domestic system by factory manufacture.

Examples also exist of wholesale grocers and tobacconists, woollen- and linen-drapers becoming merchants. John and Emmanuel Elam, the sons of Gervas Elam, a prosperous Armley clothier, began life as wholesale tobacconists in the 1740's whilst their brother Samuel was a grocer. The Elams were engaged in the importing of tobacco from America and with the growth of the American market after 1740 they were obviously well placed to enter this market with their previous knowledge of its conditions.[48] The American woollen market was something of an unknown quantity in Leeds for evidence suggests an almost entirely European trade before 1750. By the mid-1770's the Elams were thoroughly entrenched in the exportation of cloth to the 13 states and they led the opposition in Leeds to the British govern- ment's colonial policy. The post-American war boom was the longest that the eighteenth century witnessed and the giver of all riches did not pass over the three Elam brothers who had largely pioneered the Leeds–American trade. When Emmanuel Elam died in 1796 he was described as a considerable American merchant 'who had retired from the trade with a fortune of £200,000'.[49] Other shopkeepers and dry- salters joined the community of merchants in a more unobtrusive manner. Richard Bramley, twice mayor, drew his capital from his father's prosperous woollen business. Henry Smithson, 'the son of the worthy and facetious Mr. John Smithson an eminent and wealthy salter' founded a firm that was amongst the largest export houses in Leeds during the latter half of the eighteenth century.[50]

The well-to-do clothier, cloth-dresser and shopkeeper who put aside their humbler callings for the more exalted role of merchanting were the lights of their several generations. Contemporaries contrasted their legendary wealth with their social origins. If they themselves were seldom acceptable in the corporation or in the well-established appren- ticed merchants' dining-rooms they were respected by all as men of integrity and acumen, examples of industry and its rewards.

The contribution of this group to the economic expansion of the Yorkshire woollen trade was significant. At first sight it seems arguable that their capital and enterprise would have been better employed in cloth-making than in merchanting which at least in the first respect was well-subscribed. Their real contribution was an entrepreneurial one. The long-established merchants were frequently conservative in their approach to new markets and business techniques. Newcomers to merchanting, like the Elams, had to take risks to break into the markets which an old merchant house would have deemed unsafe. If these ventures seldom succeeded in the traditional European market they paid large dividends in the American trade after 1760. The blazing of this trade was largely accomplished by these newcomers for the long-established merchants, who had been employed in an entirely European trade for many generations, were hesitant to switch their focus across the Atlantic where returns were slow and uncertain.

(IV)
The last two decades of the eighteenth century witnessed great changes in the woollen and worsted industries. The introduction of machinery after 1770, the infiltration of the cotton industry into the West Riding in the 1780's and new developments in the quality and variety of woollen cloths produced, revolutionised the traditional form of the industry. Some merchants in the Halifax area in the late 1780's and Benjamin Gott and two or three merchants a few years later in Leeds built factories that combined all the stages of production. As the merchants had hitherto entirely spurned making their own cloths the move made the clothiers very apprehensive. Yet it was a development that never really materialised until after 1815, and then it was the manufacturer himself who began to merchant his own cloth rather than any intensification of the process the clothiers had declared imminent in the 1790's.

If the clothier before 1780 was with rare exceptions a small man, the introduction of machinery between the 1780's and 1850's forced the industry into a new shape. Many clothiers became mere labourers, factory hands and hand-loom weavers. Others more fortunate extended their functions from a few looms or a scribbling-mill to a modest factory that combined all perhaps but the weaving or finishing of the cloth. Extensive partnerships between clothiers accelerated the latter process. Eventually and inevitably these larger manufacturers began to merchant their own production. The minutes of evidence given in 1806 and those of the large number of subsequent committees examining the woollen laws and the export of wool, abound with examples of one-time clothiers who, after 1800, were making their first tentative excursions into cloth-merchanting.[51]

The full impact of these changes as they concerned the older merchant houses are examined in a later chapter. Here it is sufficient to note that they completely upset the established pattern of recruitment. As far as actual merchanting was concerned the break-up of the apprenticeship laws was irrelevant. Training did not come to a sudden end, it was only less legalised and it had in any case, throughout the eighteenth century, varied considerably in duration. The real changes hinged on the altered structure of the industry. After 1800 an increasing proportion of the Yorkshire woollen trade was handled by the large manufacturers who were beginning to market their own cloths. It was seen, however, that those merchants who consistently refused to manufacture were finding it increasingly difficult to keep their heads above water. William Cookson and Jeremiah Naylor, who in 1806 were so outspoken in their intentions never to have the trouble of making a piece of cloth in their lives, later both faced serious financial crises.[52] The number of merchants engaged solely in buying and selling woollen cloths declined, as we have seen, sharply after 1800. Recruitment of apprentices from the neighbouring smaller gentry and the wealthy middle class in the West Riding, the chief source of merchant trainees before 1780, dwindled as the prospects of making a large fortune in woollen merchanting receded. Not only was it far more difficult to acquire a knowledge of manufacturing than it had been of merchanting, but also factory production required a bigger outlay of both time and money. Another deterrent was that cloth-making, as opposed to cloth-selling, carried a social stigma that hung over from the old strict division between the two functions. The old merchant dynasties were proud that they had no connections with cloth-making. Sir Henry Ibbetson and William Milner would have been horrified to learn that any of their sons had become manufacturers or their daughters had married one. Therefore the vast majority of factory-owners, since their channels of recruitment were quite different, had a lower social status than the eighteenth century export merchant.

In Leeds the old Dissenting merchant families tended to retain their businesses, and a few newcomers were recruited from amongst the 'better sort'. William Morritt's brother was High Sheriff of Yorkshire, patron of Sir Walter Scott and owner of the well-known Rokeby Park estate; Robert Holt Leigh, elected to the corporation in 1803, was the son of a Lancashire baronet; whilst Robert Coulman came from a landed family near Selby and married the daughter of an East Riding landowner.[53] Yet after 1800 these men seldom stayed long in Leeds, and they were lost in the crowd of those who came to merchanting through manufacturing channels. The classic period of merchanting was at an end.

Notes to Chapter 2

[1] E. M. Carus-Wilson, 'The Aulnage Accounts: a criticism' in *Ec.H.R.*, II (1929), reprinted in *Medieval Merchant Venturers* (1967 edition), pp. 279–91; Heaton, pp. 54–5, 60, 72–75, 79–80, 220; P. J. Bowden, *The Wool Trade in Tudor and Stuart England* (1962), pp. 44, 54–5.

[2] *H.M.C.* Salisbury MSS., VI, 58–9; G. Hadley, *History of the Town of Kingston-upon-Hull* (1788), p. 115.

[3] J. M. Bartlett, 'The expansion and decline of York in the later Middle Ages', *Ec.H.R.*, XII (1959), 17–33; E. M. Carus-Wilson and O. Coleman, *England's Export Trade 1275–1547* (1963), pp. 138–9, 146–7.

[4] Heaton, pp. 146–9; W. G. Rimmer, 'The evolution of Leeds to 1700', *Thors. Soc.*, Vol. L, Part 2 (1967), 91–129.

[5] *H.M.C.* Sackville (Knole) MSS., II (1966), *passim*; S-E. Aström, *From Cloth to Iron: The Anglo-Baltic Trade in the Late Seventeenth Century* (1963), pp. 230–1.

[6] *H.M.C.* Sackville MSS., II, 146. The table is taken from R. Davis, 'The trade and shipping of Hull 1500–1700', *East Yorkshire Local History Series: No. 17* (1964).

[7] *H.M.C.* Sackville MSS., II, 184, 205; M. E. François, 'The social and economic development of Halifax, 1558–1640', *Proceedings of the Leeds Philosophical and Literary Society*, Vol. XI, Part VIII (1966), 261–3.

[8] *H.M.C.* Sackville MSS., II, 205; S-E. Aström, *op. cit.*, pp. 171–2.

[9] Heaton, pp. 99, 169–70. The Denison papers (DB/36) give an outline of the family's slow progression from cloth-making in the 1580's to Thomas Denison's first commercial ventures in 1680.

[10] W. G. Rimmer, *op. cit.*, 121–4; W. G. Hoskins, *Essays in Leicestershire History* (1950), pp. 154–9.

[11] W. B. Crump and G. Ghorbal, *History of the Huddersfield Woollen Industry* (1935), pp. 29–30, 44–6, 108–9; M. E. François, *op. cit.*, 280.

[12] *Ducatus*, pp. 3, 36; R. V. Taylor, *The Biographia Leodiensis* (1865), p. 338; Stowe MSS., 748, f. 31.

[13] *Ducatus*, pp. 7, 43, 49, 136, 214–5, 256–7.

[14] *Ibid.*, pp. 5–6, 24, 34–5, 72, 154–6, 168–9, 249; W. Cudworth, *Round about Bradford* (1876), pp. 261, 281; A. M. W. Stirling, *Annals of a Yorkshire House* (1911), pp. 62–90; N. Scatcherd, *The History of Morley* (1830), pp. 312–3; *Diary*, I, p. 418.

[15] B.M. Add. MSS., 21, 427, ff. 225–6; S-E. Aström, *op. cit.*, pp. 66–71; *Ducatus*, pp. 12, 72, 98, infra,

[16] Ducatus, p. 125; S-E. Aström, *op. cit.*, pp. 161–2, 234.

[17] E. M. Carus-Wilson, *Merchant Venturers*, p. xxix; J. Wardell, *The Municipal History of the Borough of Leeds* (1846), Appendix XIV; R. Carroll, 'Yorkshire Parliamentary boroughs in the seventeenth century', *Northern History*, III (1968), 70–104. A word must be said about the sources of this first section. Infinite shadings between 'merchant', 'chapman', 'factor', 'cloth-worker' and 'clothier' cannot always be elucidated by the stray reference in sparse records. W. B. Crump and G. Ghorbal (*op. cit.*, pp. 29–30) were in a dilemma when they found several important families in the 1470's ullnage accounts designated 'clothiers'. They thought they were more probably merchants, but there is no evidence to support their assumption. Moreover these paragraphs rely heavily on the mass of genealogical material collected by the Leeds antiquary Ralph Thoresby. It should be said in its favour, however, that Thoresby was himself a merchant as were his grandfather, father and uncles before him. He knew the Leeds merchant community thoroughly and began collecting his writings as early as 1680.

[18] R. V. Taylor, *op. cit.*, p. 338; W. Cudworth, *op. cit.*, pp. 195–8.

[19] DB/204/3.

[20] See Appendix A.

[21] See the bibliography for the Leeds directories after 1797.

[22] A few papers relating to Sir William Rooke have strayed into the Spencer-Stanhope MSS. (Bradford). See also J. Batty, *A History of Rothwell* (1877), p. 191.

[23] Of the 61 freemen enrolled between 1670 and 1734 only one, William Medhurst, was a merchant. Yet the corporation minutes drew up a list of fines ranging from £2 for a cloth-worker to as much as £50 for a merchant coming into the town. And when foreign merchants began to settle in Leeds after 1700 they were ordered to pay fines of between £100–£500 'for any freedom to be taken by such ffreeign merchant, who shall be naturalized before such ffreedom

is taken'. See S. and B. Webb, *The Manor and the Borough*, Part II (1908), pp. 415–16; J. Wardell, *op. cit.*, Appendix XXIV and Leeds Corporation Minutes (L/C2 ff. 155, 165).

[24] This section is largely based upon the Leeds Quarter Sessions Order Books, LC/QS3 (1714–25) and the Poor-Rate Assessment Books for the Township of Leeds.

[25] *C.J.*, XX, 129.

[26] J. Hunter, 'Familae Minorum Gentium', *Publications of the Harleian Society*, XXXII–XL (1894–6), 10–11.

[27] Lupton MSS. Second deed of partnership, 1 July 1755; *L.M.*, 16 Oct. 1764, 14 May 1776.

[28] In fact Noguier prospered in Leeds. When he died in 1753 he left his daughter a marriage dowry of £3,000, his wife £1,000 and an annuity of £50 together with his furniture, jewels and plate (*C.J.*, XXVI, 964).

[29] R. V. Taylor, *op. cit.*, pp. 187–91; ACN 4/115; 'Pendavid Bitterzwigg: John Berkenhout', *Thors. Soc.*, 41 (1950), 1–17; J. Wilkinson, *Worthies, Families and Celebrities of Barnsley and District* (1883), pp. 160–4; *L.I.*, 3 March 1778, 5 June 1781, 18 Feb. 1792.

[30] E. Hughes, *North Country Life in the Eighteenth Century* (1952), pp. 106–7.

[31] Lupton MSS., W. to A. Lupton, 2 June 1764, 3 June 1764; Spencer-Stanhope MSS., 1221; Crump, 193; Will of Thomas Lodge proved at York, Nov. 1776. See also *L.M.*, 17 Oct. 1786.

[32] R. V. Taylor, *op. cit.*, pp. 305–6.

[33] *ibid.*, pp. 307–11. See also Burke's *Landed Gentry* (1952 edition), 'Lloyd of Stockton Hall', and 'Lloyd of Cowesby Hall'.

[34] R. V. Taylor, *op. cit.*, pp. 239–42, 457–9, 514–15.

[35] Medhurst MSS. in Leeds City Archives, L.D. 205. See also Burke's *Landed Gentry* (1952 edition), 'Wheler of Otterden Place'.

[36] Wakefield Deeds Registry, P 729/932–4, Q 375/422–3, Q 432/579–80, EE 681/995, FF 134/188. In 1830 the Kippax estates produced £1,962 per annum.

[37] *L.M.*, 13 Nov. 1744.

[38] *L.M.*, 21 Dec. 1779; *L.I.*, 6 Aug. 1782. Details of the Medhursts' activities appear in the manuscript diary of the Rev. Henry Crooke (Leeds City Archives, Clark MSS.).

[39] *L.M.*, 5 Dec. 1780; *L.I.*, 4 Aug. 1800.

[40] Oates MSS. (Leeds); for a longer account of the Stanhope family see R. G. Wilson, 'Three brothers: A study of the fortunes of a landed family in the mid-eighteenth century', *The Journal of the Bradford Textile Society* (1964–5), 111–21.

[41] DB 58/25, Will of Christopher Houldsworth. See also wills of the Beetham family amongst the Armitage papers M.D. 279, B2/21.

[42] *ibid.*, B2/16, 20.

[43] *ibid.*, B2/23, B6/36, B9/9 and ACN 2/5.

[44] Heaton, pp. 296–7.

[45] Lupton MSS., account books of Ibbetson and Koster.

[46] *ibid.*, material relating to Edward and Elizabeth Gilyard.

[47] DB/39.

[48] Apprenticeship registers, IRI, 50/224, 51/27, 180.

[49] *L.I.*, 16 Dec. 1793, 29 Feb. 1796.

[50] *L.M.*, 16 Jan. 1750.

[51] See especially *P.P.* 1821 (437) vi, Laws Relating to the Stamping of Woollen Cloth, and 1828 (515) viii, The State of the British Woollen Trade.

3 Trade and manufacture 1700-83

Who is so well entitled to a comfortable maintenance as the
labouring clothier, from the fruits of whose toils the merchants
etc. amass their immense fortunes?*

R. Brown (1799)

That the West Riding of Yorkshire emerged as the most dynamic,
important and progressive of the three regions devoted to woollen
textile production is a commonplace fact of eighteenth-century history.
As early as 1750 the idea that the Yorkshire industry was doing great
harm to the East Anglian and the West Country trade in cheaper
cloths was prevalent in these two areas and by the 1770's it was known
that Yorkshire's worsted industry, only introduced in the last decades
of the seventeenth century, was as large as that centred upon Norwich.[1]
It has been estimated that Yorkshire's share of the total English output
of woollen cloths grew from less than 20% in 1700 to around 60% in
1800.[2] It was this expansion which led observers like Dean Tucker and
Arthur Young to make disparaging comparisons between the backwardness of the West Country industry and the enterprise of Yorkshire.

In spite of the increasing share of the cloth export trade appropriated
by the West Riding and the impression that the West Country
clothiers gave of the constant threat of the Yorkshire industry there
were notable set-backs throughout the period that were linked principally to the state of the export market. At first sight it appears
that no other eighteenth-century industry is so adequately covered
statistically as the West Riding woollen trade with the customs accounts
and a production series in the figures of broad and narrow cloth
produced after 1726. Unfortunately both sources provide innumerable
problems.

The customs accounts are perhaps the more unreliable or at least
bewildering. The Inspector-General after 1696 compiled his figures
from quarterly returns collected from each port. But these detailed
returns have been lost and the final ledger entries only differentiate

---

* R. Brown, *A General view of the Agriculture of the West Riding of Yorkshire*
(1799)

between London and the outports collectively. When the latter are
compared with extracts from individual Port Books the figures do not
agree. It is informative to compare the total figures of two of the
leading types of cloth exported, kerseys and northern dozens, extracted
by Mrs. Schumpeter—and since the Devonshire kerseys and dozen
trades were virtually extinct by 1700 these cloths were almost entirely
produced in Yorkshire—with the quantities of these goods exported
from Hull.[3]

Table 3   The export of kerseys and northern dozens, 1702–83.
Figures indicate number of pieces:
a, total English exports; b, Hull exports alone.

	Kerseys		Northern dozens (single and double)	
	a	b	a	b
1702	71,517	108,267	27,222	45,833
1717	72,064	68,474	35,059	28,990
1728	39,144	40,297	33,295	40,022
1737	31,771	33,083	45,789	76,157
1758	31,722	33,378	40,090	69,728
1768	23,383	33,399	47,989	122,710
1783	6,758	13,340	54,587	163,710

The discrepancy is marked but the result is perhaps not surprising.
Over 30 years ago W. G. Hoskins, discussing the Devonshire serge
trade, wrote:

The Port Books for Exeter are not, therefore, the reliable sources they might
have been for statistics of the serge trade. Smuggling, false entries of quantities
and values, and the complete exclusion from the custom's record of some
commodities add to the difficulties of computation.[4]

Since the quarterly accounts have been destroyed it is impossible to
place much reliance on either the national figures or those for individual ports.

The Stamping Acts of 1725, 1738 and 1765–6 which attempted to
enforce standards of manufacture by an inspectorate in the West
Riding broad and narrow cloth (but not worsted) industries produced
figures of these types of cloth milled in the county's fulling mills
(see Table III). They are an important production series which have
been used by economic historians for wider purposes than a delineation
of the Yorkshire woollen industry.[5] They should be treated with
caution. It has always been maintained that they were much less
reliable after 1790 when the beginnings of factory production and the

introduction of a whole range of new woollen fabrics outside the scope of the Acts resulted in many cloths never reaching the fulling mills where the cloths were measured and stamped by the cloth-searcher. Although before the 1780's they comprehended almost all woollen cloths they seem little more satisfactory since the mechanism of stamping did not change and the laxity of the searchers was reputedly perennial. Increasingly after 1800 evidence was given before a succession of parliamentary committees of evasion of the laws, but it should be remembered that the deponents were out to remove all statutes relating to the woollen industry. Moreover the figures stand up to closer scrutiny. It has recently been established that after 1790 other trade indices moved in unison with them.[6] And in the discussion surrounding the Acts in the mid-1760's, at a point when legislation seemed particularly ineffectual, complaints emphasised that the cloths were sealed and counted but not carefully measured to the regulation widths and therefore they were often unduly stretched by the merchants afterwards to the discredit of Yorkshire exports. This was a consequence of the poorly paid searchers being unable to stand up to the merchants' pressures to have cloths of the size they wanted, whether within the regulations or not, rather than the formers' laxity.[7] In the history of the Acts between 1725 and 1821 there were three major types of evasion that the laws were unable to keep pace with. Firstly, cloths were ordered directly from the clothiers which never passed through the cloth halls. As the clothiers' advocate wrote in 1765 'believe me ye stamps of all cloths by ye inspectors does not go well down with those yt have hence benefitted by private bargains'. But it is significant for a defence of the veracity of the broad cloth figures that Sir Henty Ibbetson's direct orders in the 1750's were for kerseys and worsteds, but never broad cloths which he bought entirely in the cloth halls.[7] Secondly, the factory system, although it was only producing a small proportion of broad cloths before 1815, further increased the tendency to by-pass the cloth halls where the clothiers could keep an eye on affairs in their interest. It should be remembered on the other hand that many of the early factories were public fulling-mills and the cloth-searcher visited them frequently. By no means all factory-produced cloths went unstamped before the repeal of the Acts. Thirdly, the new 'fancy' cloths produced were right outside the scope of the Acts, and this was perhaps the most serious limitation of the figures for this was the fastest growing sector of the woollen branch of the trade after the 1780's.

Thus, although the West Riding cloth figures produce difficulties, particularly in the 1760's, they should not be discarded as useless simply

D

Table 4 Broad and narrow cloth milled in the West Riding of Yorkshire 1726–1820[a]

Year[b]	Broad cloth (thousand pieces)	Narrow cloth (thousand pieces)	Year[b]	Broad cloth (thousand pieces)	Narrow cloth (thousand pieces)
1727	29·0		1774	87·2	88·3
1728	25·2		1775	95·9	96·8
1729	29·6		1776	99·7	99·6
1730	31·6		1777	107·8	95·8
1731	35·6		1778	132·5	101·6
1732	35·5		1779	110·9	93·1
1733	34·6		1780	94·6	87·3
1734	31·1		1781	102·0	98·7
1735	31·7		1782	112·5	96·7
1736	38·9		1783	131·1	108·6
1737	42·3		1784	138·0	115·5
1738	42·4		1785	157·3	116·0
1739	43·1	58·8	1786	158·8	123·0
1740	41·4	58·6	1787	155·7	128·1
1741	46·4	61·2	1788	139·4	132·1
1742	45·0	62·8	1789	154·1	145·5
1743	45·2	63·5	1790	172·6	140·4
1744	54·6	63·1	1791	187·6	154·4
1745	50·5	63·4	1792	214·9	190·5
1746	56·6	68·8	1793	190·3	150·7
1747	62·5	68·4	1794	191·0	130·4
1748	60·8	68·1	1795	251·0	155·1
1749	60·7	68·9	1796	246·8	151·6
1750	60·4	78·1	1797	229·3	156·7
1751	61·0	74·0	1798	224·2	148·6
1752	60·7	72·4	1799	272·8	180·2
1753	55·4	71·6	1800	285·9	169·3
1754	56·1	72·4	1801	264·1	137·2
1755	57·1	76·3	1802	265·7	137·1
1756	33·6	79·3	1803	266·8	139·6
1757	55·8	77·1	1804	298·2	150·0
1758	60·4	66·4	1805	300·2	165·8
1759	51·9	65·5	1806	290·3	175·3
1760	49·4	69·6	1807	262·0	161·8
1761	48·9	75·5	1808	279·9	144·6
1762	48·6	72·9	1809	311·2	151·9
1763	48·0	72·1	1810	273·7	158·3
1764	54·9	79·5	1811	269·9	141·8
1765	54·7	77·4	1812	316·4	136·9
1766	72·6	78·9	1813	369·9	142·9
1767	102·4	78·8	1814	338·9	147·5
1768	90·0	74·5	1815	330·3	162·4
1769	92·5	87·8	1816	325·4	120·9
1770	93·1	85·4	1817	351·1	132·6
1771	92·8	89·9	1818	324·5	140·3
1772	112·4	95·5	1819	363·3	119·7
1773	120·2	89·9	1820	286·7	129·3

a B. R. Mitchell and P. Deane, *op. cit.*, 189.
b Figures of broad-cloth pieces are for years ending 25 March up to and including 1752, and for years ending 5 April thereafter. The narrow-cloth pieces statistics are for years ending 20 January up to and including 1752, and for years ending 31 January thereafter.

because they do not fit in with theories of Yorkshire's constant expansion at the expense of all other cloth-producing regions or that growth between 1800 and 1820, at least in the old woollen cloth lines, was not spectacular. However much the searchers neglected their work, the millman still recorded the number of cloths that passed through the fulling-mills, and the figures were dutifully produced at the Easter Quarter Sessions each year. As some contemporaries admitted this counting was by 1800 the most useful function performed by the Cloth Acts. For broad and narrow woollen cloths at least they provide an adequate minimum production series.

If the statistical sources seem questionable it is frequently possible to reinforce them with other types of evidence. Taken altogether this suggests that the Yorkshire woollen trade experienced a very modest growth in the first 30 years of the eighteenth century, a performance that was disappointing in view of the activity between 1697 and 1709. There were two decades of good trade after 1730 with no prolonged set-backs. 1750 saw the beginning of a more difficult period. Continuous stagnation throughout the 1750's was followed by an upward trend, especially marked between 1768 and 1771, that was broken by major recessions in 1772–5 and 1778–83. But before we look at the breakdown of the reasons for these movements we should first say something of the proportion of Yorkshire cloth that was exported.

Some historians have suggested that the Yorkshire industry had hardly begun to invade the export markets by 1700. The customs figures support these views. Over two-thirds of the cloth exported in 1699–1701 went from London. Only in the German and Dutch markets had the outports the edge on London. In these years £1,354,000 worth of cloth, or 44% of total cloth exports, was shipped on average yearly to Germany, Holland, Flanders and France. London's average share was £553,000 and in 1700 Exeter shipped £327,000 worth of serges to Germany and Holland alone. For 1700 this leaves the other outports with just less than a £500,000 share of this market. Hull, much the most important of these ports, probably shipped rather more than Exeter, or shared around a quarter of the north-west European trade. To other areas Hull shipped, as did the other outports, small quantities, even to the Baltic for this was in fact never a large market for cloth.[9] The customs figures suggest that between 12 and 15% of Britain's total woollen exports passed through Hull from the West Riding in 1700. Such a figure appears misleading for Yorkshire cloths were not entirely exported by Leeds and Wakefield merchants and factors shipping through Hull. London merchants who monopolised the south European market and the Levant and East India trades bought supplies of Yorkshire cloths either through a resident factor, directly from the larger clothiers in the kersey and worsted branches, or from Leeds and Wakefield merchants who charged a small commission of around $1\frac{1}{2}\%$. By 1700 these cloths were largely finished in Leeds before being sent up to London. Defoe—and, by implication, the custom figures—suggested that this trade was a large one. Again the evidence in detail is controversial. The values of kerseys and northern dozens (Leeds broad cloths were traditionally entered as dozens in the customs accounts) exported, and these were by far the most numerous types of West Riding cloth which found their way overseas, suggest that they accounted for $12\cdot6\%$ of total woollen exports in 1699–1701. This neatly corroborates the figure of Hull cloth exports above. There were no worsted cloths exported from Yorkshire worth speaking of in 1700 and Jackson maintains that the coastal trade in cloth between Hull and London was relatively insignificant.[10] Therefore unless very large amounts of cloth went overland to London by pack-horse the Yorkshire trade accounted for less than 20% of exports. Unfortunately we have no indication of West Riding output retained for the home market at this date, but there is little reason to believe it was much different from the national ratio. Miss Deane has reckoned that about 40% of the national output was exported in 1695.

In 1770 Yorkshire's position had changed radically. Thomas Wolrich, a Leeds merchant, who produced a set of figures for the output of the West Riding woollen and worsted industries from Easter 1771 to Easter 1772, indicated that $72\cdot3\%$ of a total production valued at £3,273,000 found its way overseas (see Table 5). James, writing 80 years later, maintained these figures were 'the only ones during this century on which implicit confidence can be placed', and it is significant that these figures are very closely corroborated by Thomas Hill's estimates which show that of both woollen and worsted cloths handled by the Leeds merchants $73\cdot0\%$ were exported.[11] These percentages are considerably higher than Miss Deane's estimate of national woollen output where the amount exported grew from 40% in 1695 to $66\frac{2}{3}\%$ in 1800. This difference is accounted for in part by the fact the Yorkshire broad cloths were almost all exported (Thomas Wolrich reckoned 90%), and is also testimony to the success of the Yorkshire merchants after 1730 in the south European and later the American markets. The proportion of cloths handled by the Leeds merchants showed the extent of this breakthrough. Hill computed the value of cloth passing through the Leeds firms during 1781 at £1,011,000, of which £273,000 represented sales in the home market. The closure of both the European and American markets during this year halved the

Table 5 General estimate of the export and home consumption of Yorkshire woollen manufactures for the year ending Easter 1772[a]

Type of cloth	Exports £ s. d.	Home consumption £ s. d.	Ratio	Total £ s. d.
Broad cloth	772,405 9 7½	85,822 16 7½	9:1	858,288 6 3
Narrow cloth	101,044 9 10½	404,177 19 6	1:4	505,222 9 4½
Bays and Rochdale goods	224,000 0 0	56,000 0 0	4:1	280,000 0 0
Kersies and half thicks	100,125 0 0	11,125 0 0	9:1	111,250 0 0
Blankets	46,666 13 4	23,333 6 8	2:1	70,000 0 0
Hose, colne serges, etc.	4,500 0 0	40,500 0 0	1:9	45,000 0 0
Long wool manufactures (i.e. worsteds)	1,123,200 0 0	280,800 0 0	4:1	1,404,000 0 0
	2,371,941 12 10	901,759 2 9½		3,273,700 15 7½

[a] From the estimate of Thomas Wolrich in J. Bischoff, A Comprehensive History of the Woollen and Worsted Manufacture (1842) I, p. 189.

export trade of the Leeds merchants and the depression in fact led to
Hill's enquiry. In a good year during the early 1770's exports from
Leeds were more probably in the region of £1,500,000 which suggests that its merchants were handling around 60% of Yorkshire's
export trade. As by this time Yorkshire accounted, according to
Wolrich's estimates, for almost half the national total of all woollens
exported, it is easy to see the importance of the Leeds merchants in
conducting a large proportion of the cloth trade. In 1700 Yorkshire
had contributed less than 20% of woollen exports; now in the 1770's
30% passed through the hands of the Leeds firms alone and Yorkshire
produced almost a half of the country's most important export com-
modity.

This increasing significance of the West Riding in the woollen
export trade naturally led to its subsequent reliance on the state of
overseas markets. It is this dependence and the shift in markets after
1700 which largely accounts for the periods of fluctuation outlined
above.

(I)
The impression is that the opening decade of the eighteenth century
was one generally of good trade, although West Riding petitions in
1702 and 1708 maintained that 'the Trade in the Woollen Manufactures
is greatly decayed'. Since both complaints blamed the export of wool,
a constant and overstated reason, perhaps too much should not be read
into them. Trade declined after 1710 and from then until around 1730
the trend was only slightly upwards with occasional good years like
1717 and 1725 broken by very real depression between 1718 and 1722
associated with the 'universal wear of East India goods, printed cal-
licoes and linen', the export of wool and the South Sea Bubble.[12]
These reasons accounted for depression in the home markets, but exporters advanced other arguments for the stagnation which dwelt on
the state of the German and Dutch markets.

The West Riding export trade in the late seventeenth century was,
as we have seen, almost entirely centred upon Holland and Germany.
Around 1700, one ship a week, on average, left Hull for Amsterdam
and almost every fortnight one for Germany, and it was a very rare
ship that sailed down the Humber without at least a few packs of cloth
on board. From Amsterdam, Rotterdam, Hamburg and Danzig,
Yorkshire cloths were distributed throughout northern and central
Europe. In the Dutch towns large numbers of Leeds merchants congregated. Thoresby was well entertained by them during his brief training
there in 1678 and William Milner's two elder brothers resided at

Rotterdam for many years after 1685. As was customary for merchant apprentices Milner and his cousin James Ibbetson spent five years training in Holland in the 1690's to familiarise themselves thoroughly with the European trade.[13] The traffic was a two-way one with a number of Dutch and German merchants and factors settling in the West Riding clothing towns to buy cloths for their fellow countrymen. But their numbers were never as large as those who settled in Exeter nor indeed of the Leeds men who settled in the German and Dutch North Sea ports.

Although the fastest expanding market for English cloth in the seventeenth century was in south Europe, the north-west European trade was a growing one for Yorkshire cloth at least. As early as 1600 Yorkshire kerseys and dozens were in great demand and throughout the century Yorkshire merchants cut into the preserves of London merchants who specialised in the traditional expensive West Country broad cloths. Although the German market expanded rapidly after the abolition of the Merchant Adventurers privileges in 1688 and William Milner claimed in the 1730's to have had returns of around £80,000 yearly from the Hamburg market for over 40 years, the German and Dutch trades had reached their zenith by 1710. Thereafter a rapid decline followed particularly in the German market. Haynes noted it in 1715, the *Leeds Mercury* in 1726. There were two principal reasons. Dutch and German finishing, commission and distribution merchants who had formerly sold English cloth throughout Europe were being by-passed by English merchants selling directly to customers. More important, even the cheap Yorkshire cloth met with increasing competition from cloths produced in Germany, Austria and France.[14] This rivalry, particularly evident in Germany, Holland, Poland and the Levant, accounted for our seemingly excessive concern with wool exports down to 1800. It was widely held that only high Continental prices for inferior wools stopped French and German manufacturers sweeping the entire European market.

Total woollen exports to Holland, Germany, Flanders and France fell from an average of £1,354,000 in 1699–1701 to £847,000 in 1772–4.[15] In Yorkshire the downward trend of exports to these countries was equally obvious. Increasing sales of worsteds did not offset the collapse of the woollen cloth trade that affected even Yorkshire kerseys and dozens. From Hull the number of ships sailing annually for Holland fell from 56 in 1699 to 28 in 1768. No more is heard after 1710 of the flourishing colony of Yorkshiremen in Amsterdam and Rotterdam. The decline in activity in these markets together with the problems of imported cottons in the home trade accounts for the stagnation in the Yorkshire woollen industry between 1710 and 1730.

(II)

The West Riding cloth industry recovered from the doldrums of George I's reign in 1730–1, and although there was a modest depression in 1732–5, production mounted steadily to reach new levels in 1739. A sharp recession exacerbated by very high food prices followed in 1740–1. The depression was short and the rest of the 1740's were good years. This ten-year period of expansion between 1742 and 1752, with a trough in 1744–5 and a peak in 1746–7, gives some substance to Miss Deane's notion of Britain's two-phased industrial 'take-off' in the 1740's and the 1780's.[16] Moreover, Yorkshire's advance took place at a time when trade in the West Country was stagnant. Experience in Wiltshire, Exeter and Norwich was believed to be general. John Smith in 1747 clung grimly to his two-volume argument that the complaints of decay were greatly exaggerated, but few accepted his opinions. The price of wool, always the most sensitive indicator of activity in the industry, and at an extremely low level in the 1730's and early 1740's, seemed to confirm the general view of complete stagnation. Smith attributed the depression to a contraction in the home market where purchasing power was reduced by low agricultural prices.[17] In fact low wool prices—it was maintained they were 50–60% below the European level—enabled the small Yorkshire clothiers who employed little labour outside the family to improve the quality of their product and at the same time effect some price reduction whereas the large West Country clothiers were unable to force down labour costs and prices to keep in line with Yorkshire's progress.[18] The improvement of quality achieved without price increases was extremely important and West Riding broad cloths were able to compete with the middle range of Wiltshire cloths, and with these and the cheap Yorkshire stuffs the merchants of Leeds and Wakefield were able to invade the home and overseas markets hitherto dominated by London, Norwich and Exeter.

If Yorkshire cloths gave the West Riding merchants the edge in our markets by the 1730's the improvement of the West Riding river navigations (see Chapter 7) allowed them to escape the domination of London merchants in the south European trade. Access to Hull, before the Aire and Calder Navigation opened up the rivers to Leeds and Wakefield in 1701, was difficult and many goods went overland to London. Although the Navigation's progress was menaced by the declining trade with Holland and Germany before the 1730's trade settled much more firmly on a Leeds–Wakefield–Hull axis. When the improved quality of Yorkshire cloth enabled the Leeds merchants to get a foothold in the Mediterranean trade the navigation meant that it was not channelled through London.

There are few indications that the south European market, rather smaller than the north-west European one for cloth in 1699–1701, was really significant to the Leeds merchants before the late 1720's. Jackson maintains that it was not important before the 1750's although this statement is difficult to reconcile with his figures. Statistics for the national woollen exports disclose that the south European trade was almost double that with Holland, Flanders and Germany in the early 1720's. West Riding cloth swelled the flood waters of the new channel. Whereas only 5 ships had departed from Hull for Portugal, Spain and Italy in 1717, and 10 in 1728, no fewer than 51 set sail in 1738.[19] By 1750 there was a similar congregation of Leeds merchants and factors in Oporto and Lisbon to that which had existed 80 years earlier in Amsterdam and Rotterdam. Thus although the home trade was depressed (and even here there is evidence that the competition of Yorkshire cloth was making inroads into the order-books of Norwich and Exeter merchants and West Country clothiers),[20] the proportion of exports, as every petition that came out of the West Riding stated, to total production was so high, and the south European market so generally buoyant between the late 1720's and 1750, that the West Riding industry could enjoy a virtually unbroken generation of prosperity and progress.

(III)

The depression which set in after 1750 was protracted. Although national recovery had begun by 1756 and between 1758 and 1761 total exports rose to a new level, the figures of broad woollen cloth indicate that Yorkshire cloth production was stagnant after 1750. The number of broads milled in the 1750's was fewer than in the 1740's and the export levels of the three chief cloth exports from Hull, kerseys, bays and dozens were, in 1758, all below the level of 1738. The Leeds newspapers with weekly reports of unemployment and high food prices indicate that the depression reached its nadir in 1757.[21]

As we have seen, the broad cloth figures present difficulties in the 1760's, but the national woollen export figures, except in 1764, reveal no great activity in the 1760's, especially in the American trade after 1765. There were bitter complaints from the West Country of Yorkshire competition in the middle 1760's, and certainly after 1768 production moved sharply upwards. Between March 1769 and 1773 broad cloth yardage increased by 31·4%. The boom was real but short-lived. 1772 saw the beginning of a depression which Ashton ascribed to various causes, but notably to the collapse of the American trade. The worsted trade was hardest hit as its chief export market was now across the Atlantic. Stuff-weavers' wage rates fell by some 28% between 1771 and 1774 and there were numerous riots in Leeds. An unusual number of bankruptcies in the town amongst its merchants— five in the six months following August 1772—showed the seriousness of the recession,[22] and it in fact led Wolrich to make his investigations of the West Riding woollen and worsted industries.

It is a feature of the milled cloth figures that they respond slowly to the export market for the clothier tended to manufacture through a depression. The domestic system was always lauded for its high level of employment and only in the most acute trade slumps were large numbers of clothiers thrown completely out of work when they could no longer obtain credit with the wool stapler. Therefore the figures do not necessarily indicate the depth of trade recessions as they affected the export merchants in Leeds, Wakefield and Halifax. But in 1773 the crisis was complete. The newspapers became full of the talk of large-scale emigration of the Yorkshire agricultural and woollen labourers and carried letters from America describing events there and the collapse of Anglo-American trade. Cloth piled high in the cloth halls. The clothiers admitted to Thomas Hill that there were 18,742 cloths in the Coloured Cloth Halls at Leeds alone, and Hill wrote in his notebook: 'N.B. It was supposed that the no. was greater as many of ye makers would not tell what Qty they had for fear as they said the Merchants would take advantage of it'. At a meeting of the merchants trading with North America which met at the King's Arms in Leeds in the New Year of 1775, Samuel Elam made a statement which received widespread coverage in the London newspapers.

The unhappy difference betwixt Great Britain and America throws the merchants of this country into great distress; there are now a great many cloth dressers in this Town out of Employ and a much greater number of cloth workers such as carders, spinners and weavers in the country adjacent. The poor rate at Dewsbury is already got up to 8s. in the £ and at Batley, Heckmondwike and other towns thereabouts, the poor rate is nearly as much, and it is my firm belief, that if the trade to America is shut up until this time twelve months, all the rents of the lands and houses in the above townships will not be sufficient to support the poor alone.[23]

Since Elam supported conciliation he was accused of exaggeration, but in the following week he substantiated his argument by attaching the signatures of 353 unemployed master clothiers which included 63 from Armley, 63 from Hunslet and 66 from Holbeck, all townships within the borough of Leeds.

A brief recovery took place in 1777 only to be followed by four of the gloomiest years the Yorkshire woollen trade had ever known. All the figures which contemporaries relied upon—the number of cloths milled, bankruptcies, export returns and the poor-rates—pointed to acute distress. Half a dozen merchant firms closed their doors in Leeds in 1779–80, and total dues on the Aire and Calder Navigation fell from £52,241 in 1777 to £41,667 in 1778 and remained below this figure for the next four years.[24] The trouble was not simply that the American markets were closed tight after 1775, but that the French entry into the war in March 1778 badly hit the Mediterranean trade. The hesitancy of the British government to protect merchant shipping resulted in insurance rates rising to 18–20%. In July 1778 at least £250,000 worth of West Riding cloth was waiting at Hull for a convoy to Portugal, Leghorn and Genoa. William Denison, senior partner in the largest merchant house in Leeds, whose dealings were exclusively in the Italian market, maintained his firm was at a standstill after the summer of 1778. He reckoned that he had been 'deprived of about £20,000 . . . by our blundering people at the helm' and that he 'had better lend his money at one per cent Interest than trade with it up the Straits [of Gibraltar]'.[25] His frustration was shared by cloth exporters throughout the West Riding. Not until the summer of 1782 did the upward movement of trade begin in anticipation of the end of war. A 'most luxuriant harvest' in the following year aided the rapid return to normality and a decade of almost unbroken progress in the West Riding.

Again fluctuations in activity between 1750 and 1783 are explained largely by the performance of woollen exports. The Portuguese and Spanish markets reached saturation point in the 1750's, although the Italian trade held more buoyant. Recurrent wars between Spain and England, French competition and the attempts of both the Spanish and Portuguese governments to foster their own woollen industries were the chief reasons for the diminution of English cloth exports.[26] The south European market, which had accounted for very nearly half of all the woollens exported in the early 1750's declined after 1760 with only a slight recovery in the middle and late 1770's owing to renewed efforts after the collapse of the American trade. Like the stagnation in the German and Dutch markets, this decline was sufficient to account for the long periods of relative inactivity in the Yorkshire woollen industry between 1750 and after 1783 when the American trade became stabilised.

There is little evidence that the American market was a very dynamic element in the woollen trade before the 1750's. The customs accounts suggest that in 1752–4 exports there formed just less than 10% of our total foreign trade in woollens which was in fact a rather smaller percentage than the American trade had taken in 1722–4. By 1772, however, America was the largest single purchaser of English woollens and between 1772–4 the 13 states and the West Indies bought about 30% of our total woollen exports.[27]

The extent of the participation of Yorkshire merchants in the American trade is very difficult to determine before 1783. The West Riding cloths were shipped from three ports—Hull, Liverpool and London. Hull, whose fortunes were built on the Yorkshire woollen trade, was never very important in the American trade although attempts were made to make it the outlet for Yorkshire goods destined for America, before the completion of the Rochdale canal at the turn of the century further concentrated the flow through Liverpool.[28] It was in the late 1750's, with stagnation of the south European markets, that the American trade was opened up with Yorkshire. Its pioneers were new men to cloth-merchanting like the Elam brothers, who had earlier been importing large quantities of tobacco from the American colonies. They slipped almost imperceptibly into merchanting the cheaper woollen and worsted cloths.[29] Other merchants, often dealing in worsteds, who had not found a footing in the intensely competitive European markets followed their lead. The activities of the corporation throughout the War of American Independence suggest that the large firms were still almost wholly concerned with the European trade. Houses having often a century's tradition of trading with Europe did not turn easily to the more speculative American market. Nevertheless by 1770 America had rapidly become an important area for the West Riding manufacture. Only 1 ship sailed from Hull for America in 1737; 20 years later there were 6 and in 1772, 10. Those merchants who laid the foundations of the American trade in the generation before the Colonies broke away made possible a very rapid expansion of this trade after 1783. In 1799 the United States took 40% of all British woollen exports.[30] It was this large-scale swing from the declining European markets, where increased and sometimes prohibitive duties sheltered native industries and deterred trade after 1760, that largely accounted for the fast growth of the Yorkshire woollen and worsted industries in the late 1760's and early 1770's and again after 1783.

Although the fluctuations in the West Riding industry outlined above broadly coincide with Ashton's delineation of the country's export trends, they disagree widely with Deane's figures for the output of the British woollen industry in the eighteenth century.[31] She maintains that 'from the end of the seventeenth century up to about 1741, the average rate of growth was apparently about 8 per cent per decade'. Between 1741 and 1772 it seems to have risen to 13–14% and then to have dropped back to as little as 6% in the last quarter of the century. The relative decline of the West Country and East Anglian industry and expansion in the West Riding—Deane suggests that Yorkshire's share of national output doubled between 1772 and 1799— and the different acceleration rates of the worsted and woollen sectors make estimates of the rate of growth of the total industry very misleading, especially since the figures of the consumed wool clip which she uses, and admits, are little more than inspired guesses. The long gaps of time between the estimates lead her into creating periods of growth which are both arbitrary and artificial. Moreover they are contradicted by Mrs. Schumpeter's export figures. The increase between 1700 and 1741 of the main sorts of woollen and worsted piece goods exported gives an average of just over 8% per decade which exactly fits Deane's estimates, but between 1741 and 1775 instead of moving up to 13 or 14% per decade they remain exactly the same. Of course home consumption might have increased along the lines recently suggested by Eversley in this period to account for her figures.[32] Even so one does not then expect them to fall suddenly away after 1780 especially in view of the rapid expansion of the West Riding industry that the first stages of mechanisation allowed after 1783.

Although it is dangerous to place much reliance on the statistical evidence, estimates show that between 1700 and the early 1770's Yorkshire's share of the woollen export trade increased from less than 20% to just under half the national total. Wolrich's figures suggest that this progress had not been paralleled in the home market, but it should be remembered that woollen cloths of every description met acute competition from linens and cottons after 1740 and contemporaries maintained that Yorkshire cloth, especially worsteds, were making real inroads into the inland trade after the 1720's. But the fastest periods of growth in the West Riding came in three periods which coincided with the capture of a succession of the key export markets. By 1700 Yorkshire merchants had achieved at least parity with London merchants in the Dutch and German markets and were effectively meeting the competition of them and Exeter merchants selling high-grade cloths and serges; in the 1730's and 1740's they invaded the south European market with Yorkshire woollens and worsteds and after 1750 they were in the forefront of the rapid expansion of the American trade. The strength of the West Riding industry's position was due to the fact that its cloth became increasingly competitive as prices were stabilised and improvements in quality were achieved by the use of better wools and careful finishing in a period when wool and, to a lesser extent, labour prices fell. Secondly, Yorkshire merchants traded in both woollens and worsteds. Therefore they could easily switch their orders with the clothiers as demand shifted from one to the other. It was the existence of the two industries together in the area between Halifax, Bradford, Leeds and Wakefield that gave the area its great strength in the eighteenth century. Other cloth-producing areas, such as Wiltshire and Gloucestershire, Devonshire and East Anglia relied on one or the other but not both. Moreover their exports were handled by London merchants to a greater extent than those of Yorkshire. And the London merchants were involved in a varied trade, often in imports rather than exports, whereas those in Leeds and Wakefield concentrated entirely on the export of cloth; they knew their business as woollen exporters backwards and they had a deep knowledge of the actual production of cloth unlike their counterparts in London who relied on factors for their cloth purchases. Through the Aire and Calder Navigation, by their initiative and close contacts with the producers they were able to outdistance their rivals in every free market in the eighteenth century.

(IV)
In the second half of this chapter it is necessary to examine the relationship between the merchant and clothier in Yorkshire during the eighteenth century for it is significant that contemporaries accounted for the West Riding industry's growth *vis-à-vis* those in the West Country and East Anglia not in terms of export performance or factor endowments, which as Clapham argued, discussing the transference of the Norfolk worsted industry to the West Riding, were 'important but not necessarily decisive', but by the different regional structures of the industry.[33] It is well known that the manufacture of cloth in the West Country was dominated by large-scale clothiers who 'put out' their wool to journeymen and their families to complete the various stages of production, whereas in Yorkshire the clothier was almost always a man of small capital who owned his materials and tools and carried his cloth weekly to sell in the nearest cloth hall. Here the cloth was bought by merchants primarily from Leeds and Wakefield who paid the clothier his cash, carried the cloth back to their warehouses and there finished or 'dressed' the cloth before selling it to the inland or export trades. Participants in the Yorkshire trade drew important conclusions from these differences.

Since in the West Country trade it was rare for journeymen weavers to become clothiers, the cloth industry there was represented in Yorkshire as being 'founded on a Monopoly erected and supported by great capitals'. In the West Riding on the other hand young men of good character out of their apprenticeships, could, with the credit facilities given by wool staplers and the use of the public fulling-mills at easy rates:

with a very trifling Capital, aided by the unremitting Labour of themselves and Families united under one Roof, decently and independently [maintain] themselves and [keep] the Home Trade and Foreign Markets constantly and equally supplied.[34]

In other words the Yorkshire clothiers believed their success was due to their superior entrepreneurial opportunities, for they were, unlike

Map 1   The West Riding clothing districts in 1775. From a contemporary map in the Dartmouth MSS. (Leeds City Archives)

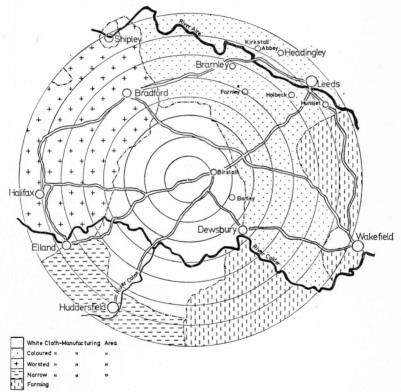

their West Country counterparts, recruited from the widest range of the community and openings were allowed to all men of enterprise and initiative. This freedom of opportunity was much more significant than the duality of their interests, cloth-making and farming, which Defoe stressed and that every history book has repeated since. As

Brown pointed out, although the clothiers lived in the country for a variety of reasons including 'less temptation to vice' and kept a couple of horses and cows they had 'little if any pretensions to the character of farmers'.[35]

Even when we examine the second prop of the system, the merchants, the entrepreneurial explanation is a convincing one. A writer maintained in 1800:

> that the real, natural, regular demand for their [i.e. the clothiers] goods, either for home or foreign consumption can be, and is always supplied by those who possess the necessary capitals, education, and every requisite for conducting the important business of a Merchant as it ought to be.[36]

Even if these qualifications implied a restriction of entry to their number and placed the emphasis on capital requirements for commerce rather than industry, there were a handful of the most prosperous and forward looking clothiers and cloth-dressers who joined their ranks before 1783. And after this date mechanisation of industry, especially in the worsted branch, led to increases in the size of their establishments so that they were themselves eventually able to break into the markets traditionally monopolised by the non-manufacturing merchant.

(V)

The manufacture of cloth and yarn was widespread throughout Yorkshire during the eighteenth century, but this diffusion was insignificant when compared with its concentration in the area lying between the five market centres—Halifax, Bradford, Leeds, Wakefield and Huddersfield. Woollen cloths were produced in three largely distinct regions. The first two produced broad woollen cloths which were marketed almost entirely in Leeds. The mixed cloths, in which the wool had been dyed before it was spun, were manufactured partly in the parish of Leeds, but chiefly in the villages to the west of Leeds in the Aire valley. The area also included villages to the south of Leeds which were situated near the watershed of the Aire and Calder —Batley, Dewsbury, Morley and Ossett. Aikin noted: 'not a single manufacturer is to be found more than one mile east or two north of Leeds . . . nor are there many in the town of Leeds, and these only in the outskirts'. The manufacture of white, or undyed cloths, was concentrated in a

> tract of country forming an oblique belt across the hills that separate the Vale of Calder from the Vale of Aire, beginning a mile West of Wakefield, leaving Huddersfield and Bradford a little to the left, terminating at Shipley in the Aire and not coming within less than six miles of Leeds on the right.

Although the Calder valley was the centre of the white cloth area, Leeds, not Wakefield (its focal point), was the principal market for these cloths since the Wakefield merchants said that they 'might as well buy white cloths at Leeds as their colored'.[37] The third area, Huddersfield, Halifax and the neighbouring villages of the upper Colne and Calder valleys were famed for their narrow cloths, particularly kerseys. But changes were taking place in both centres. The Huddersfield area turned to making fancy cloths after 1780, especially kerseymeres which began to compete with the West Country superfines. Huddersfield itself became an increasingly important centre for broad cloths, especially for those made in the large parishes of Saddleworth and Rochdale, just across the Lancashire border, which were, Aikin claimed, the finest manufactured in the North. Halifax turned to producing worsteds around 1700, and as early as the 1720's Defoe reckoned that 100,000 pieces of shalloons alone were made yearly in the parish.[38] It, together with Bradford later, became the centre of the rapidly expanding worsted industry. A line drawn between the two formed the base of the worsted area which stretched for 15 miles to the west and north-west. Wakefield and Leeds themselves were also important in the production and marketing of worsteds.

The number of clothiers is difficult to estimate. In the 1806 enquiry witnesses gave extremely contradictory evidence about an increase or decrease in the previous 30 years. Everyone, however, maintained that machinery had increased productivity. John Hebblethwaite was most succinct: 'fifty years ago he was thought a great clothier that made two pieces [i.e. one cloth] in a week, and now if he make six or eight or ten he is not the largest by far'. Aikin estimated there were 3,240 master broad clothiers in 1795. Since he was a careful commentator it is likely that he obtained his figures from the Leeds Cloth Hall trustees. David Farrer's assertion that in 1765 there were 4,000–5,000 clothiers who brought 4,000–5,000 cloths into the market weekly fits in neatly with Hebblethwaite's evidence but he was not explicit about either the type of clothier he referred to or whether the market included others besides Leeds.[39] The number of manufacturers in the kersey, fancy and worsted sections of the industry was supposedly smaller since they were bigger producers, but there are no estimates extant. Putting the question of numbers aside two trends were evident after 1770. Many broad-cloth makers and kersey manufacturers turned to the fancy, worsted and even cotton trades, and machinery increased the output of all manufacturers whether they made stuffs, kerseymere, white or coloured cloths.

Long before the introduction of machinery, however, inroads were

E

being made into the traditional picture of the West Riding system whereby the small clothier sold his cloth publicly at the cloth halls to a merchant who offered the best price. As early as 1700 the merchant was buying by direct order from the clothier, by-passing the halls and markets. William Milner purchased a batch of 200 kerseys from W. Sutcliffe in 1706; Sam Hill, the great Soyland clothier, received orders from Tottie and Markham, Thomas Lee, the Cooksons and Fentons besides others, in the three weeks of 1737 which his fragmentary letter-book covers.[40]

Even more compelling evidence of this practice comes from the account-books of Ibbetson and Koster. Here were entered their transactions with the large clothiers of the Halifax district. Between 1749–60 they ordered no less than £23,838 worth of goods from Samuel and Thomas Lee, kersey-makers of Willow Hall, Halifax. Other orders were on a smaller scale, but from their quarterly account-book it transpires that between 30 September 1757 and 10 December 1761 they purchased £19,054 worth of woollen and worsted cloths in the cloth halls and £10,997 worth by direct order.[41] It seems probable that the other large export merchants in Leeds bought a similar proportion of their goods directly without having any resort to the cloth halls.

Professor Heaton suggested that two results stemmed from the merchants' increasing tendency to order directly from the clothier: that the latter became dependent on the merchant and worked directly to the latter's order and price and that the merchant became so involved in production that he himself became a manufacturer.[42] If this phenomenon was evident to a certain extent in the worsted industry and kersey trade of the Halifax area, it was certainly not noticeable in the Leeds broad-cloth district, and even in the worsted and narrow-cloth industries the more usual transition was from manufacturing to merchanting.

In answer to Heaton's first assertion there is little evidence of price-fixing by the merchants. Dealings in the cloth halls were subject to innumerable by-laws which appear to have been thoroughly enforced by their trustees, clothiers elected from the general body of manufacturers in the clothing villages.[43] But the price of wool was the best guarantee of the clothiers' position. Although labour was the chief cost factor in cloth manufacture, wool prices—forming around 30% of total costs—were much more variable. The merchants' letter-books were full of references to increases in wool prices driving up their cloth charges. It was this elasticity of wool prices in itself which prevented the merchant stating his price. During the spring markets when the chief export requirements were purchased the clothier commanded the price he wanted. Demand sent cloth prices rising. It was only in a depression and, to a lesser extent, during the annual slack period between September and January that the merchants could call the tune. They knew the margins they could operate within and these probably remained steady at least down to the 1780's. Again, however, they were fixed by a combination of elements, the relative scarcity of cloth, the clothiers' agreements and intense competition amongst the merchants themselves rather than as a result of deliberate calculations by the body of exporters in Leeds.

Even in the direct-order system which was an obvious infringement of the cloth markets, there was little to point to the fact that through it the merchant had any more direct control of price than in the open market. Certainly the merchant stated the colour and quality of the cloth he wanted, but large manufacturers like Sam Hill always offered several varieties of the types of cloth they produced. Hill's kerseys varied in price from 30s. to 60s. each. And if the relationship between Ibbetson and Lees and Edwards was typical of that subsisting between merchant and large manufacturer there is little to suggest that the latter's position was inferior. Ibbetson lamented:

. . . we have of late had some disagreeable complaints from our Friends advising us that they had carsays of your Marks 1s. per piece lower than we charg'd, now we always understood that we had them from you 1s. lower than other people on acct. of our quick payments but in lately seeing a Bill of parcels of yrs. to another House we find you therein made no difference. Now you must naturally suppose that by other people being able to undersell us in these sorts of goods they will consequently judge that our cloths are also of an inferior quality and may be a means of friends deserting us.

William Denison bullied the clothiers with whom he dealt about delays and inferior workmanship, and occasionally threatened withdrawal of his custom, but he made no attempt to dictate his own price terms.[44] A large reputable clothier—and the firms involved in direct ordering were, by Yorkshire standards, all big units—did not solely rely on the orders of one merchant, however large. Moreover since the Yorkshire merchants' competitive weakness abroad was in quality rather than price they attempted to secure an improved manufacture, which the direct-order system guaranteed, rather than rigorous price controls.

In a consideration of Heaton's second argument, that the merchants became so involved with the manufacturers that they tended to become cloth-producers themselves, it is necessary to distinguish between the clothiers in the broad-cloth industry and those making kerseys and worsteds. It is significant that all the large clothiers with whom

Ibbetson placed his orders dwelt near Halifax and Rochdale. Here they made cheap kerseys, used for army clothing and garments for the poor throughout Europe, and worsted shalloons and bays, lighter cloths which replaced the kersey manufacture in the eighteenth century. In their output, if not organisation, they resembled the great West Country clothiers rather than the white and mixed clothiers who made the more expensive broad cloths in the Leeds area. Sam Hill's annual returns between 1744 and 1750 were in the region of £30,000, or slightly larger than the turnover of Sir Henry Ibbetson in the following decade.[45] The Lees of Willow Hall and the Edwards of Pye Nest, famed Halifax manufacturers, were producers on a similar scale. Certainly the industrial units in the kersey and worsted industry were much larger than those in the broad woollen cloth manufacture. Joseph Armitage of Hunslet was one of the largest broad clothiers of his day, and yet when he died in 1750 his capital equipment was valued for probate at only £84 13s., which included his two horses, a cow and calf and books worth £5. All that singled him out from the ordinary broad woollen clothier was the fact that he owned four looms and two dyeing vats.[46] Even in 1806 when the average master broad clothier was employing eight or ten journeymen they were much smaller employers than their counterparts in the fancy cloth and worsted trades.

In the Halifax area these large manufacturers attempted to merchant the cloth they made. A letter concerning turnpike improvements in 1740 explained the situation with great clarity.

> This town (Leeds) has long been possessed of the Bays and White Kersey Trades, which woollen goods are made mostly in Rochdale parish in Lancashire and in Halifax parish, and have been usually vended here—of late some of the makers in both parish have sent their goods abroad without the Intervention of our Merchants.

Sam Hill's letter-book shows the activities of one of these manufacturers three years earlier. Besides the orders he received from various London and Leeds merchants, letters to his shipping agent in Hull and packer in Leeds show that he was breaking into the export market on his own account.[47]

The chief obstacle preventing the easy and complete transition of the clothiers of the Halifax area into export merchants was the fact that their cloths had to be sent by road to Leeds. Here the horse packs were remade into larger bales for transit by the Aire and Calder Navigation to Hull. This meant that the Leeds merchants who did the repacking and finishing had a tight hold of the Halifax manufacture. The campaign between 1740 and 1758 to make the River Calder navigable as far west as Halifax should be seen in the light of this arrangement. The eventual procuration of the Calder–Hebble Act in 1758 was secured by the financial support and persistent efforts of the large merchant-manufacturers in the Halifax district. After this date their dyehouses and dressing shops began to appear in Halifax and cloths were then finished there, rather than in Leeds as they had been previously.[48]

If in Halifax the merchant community was created by the larger clothiers' assumption of mercantile activities in the middle years of the eighteenth century, there was no similar movement in and around Leeds. Manufacturing and merchanting were never combined in the Leeds area. It was only after many generations of saving, that a clothier of property and capital like Joseph Armitage was able to launch his sons into cloth-merchanting. Moreover these few merchants with their clothier origins did not retain the manufacturing side of the business. There was no tendency for the merchant to take on the production of cloth before the 1790's. In Leeds itself a few large worsted manufacturers also acted as merchants, but here, as in Halifax, the tendency was for the manufacturer to break into merchanting and not vice versa.

It might be thought that the same reasons for the merchants' taking over the finishing processes—quality control and profit—were operative in the merchants' consideration of manufacturing the cloth themselves. Why not take the clothiers' profits also? It is significant that Cookson and Naylor, the doyens of the merchant communities in Leeds and Wakefield who appeared before the 1806 Committee, replied to this question in terms of trouble not profit. They had no tradition of manufacturing and they had no desire to copy the Halifax merchant-manufacturers who now combined the two functions. The supervision of the finishing processes was important, especially in broad cloth where all depended on the final dressing, but it was something which could easily be deputed to a competent master cloth-dresser. It was a very different matter from overlooking the entire manufacture. To the eighteenth-century merchants this close daily supervision was unthinkable and alien to their whole concept of their place in industry and in society. 'Merchants', wrote a correspondent in the *Intelligencer* in 1793, 'are superior links of that chain which connects the various ranks of Society in the firm bonds of mutual necessities'. Even if this observation was a little coloured by events across the Channel, it was true that both the clothier and the merchant were well aware of their clearly defined place in the organisation of the woollen industry. A Stanningley white clothier the following year attributed the West Riding's extraordinary progress to 'merchants and manufacturers having hitherto been different persons'.[49] The distinction was based upon the merchants' knowledge that the largest profits were made in their branch of the trade and their belief, expressed by John Hebblethwaite in 1806, that they could buy cloth cheaper and more conveniently than they could manufacture it themselves.

This strict definition of the separate roles of the merchant and manufacturer in the Leeds area caused the great outcry against those merchants who commenced large-scale factory production after 1790. In Halifax and Huddersfield there was hardly a protest for here the two operations had long been combined. The lead in the earliest step towards complete factory production was taken by the large merchant-manufacturers in the Halifax and Huddersfield area, men like John Edwards and Law Atkinson rather than the better known Benjamin Gott in Leeds. One has only to compare the evidence of Atkinson and Edwards before the committee examining the woollen manufacture in 1806 with that of Cookson and Naylor to realise the gap in their thinking and position. The former spoke of their factories, their progress and their desire to have all the laws abolished within the industry. Cookson and Naylor confirmed, to the committee's satisfaction, that they abhorred the idea of manufacturing their own cloth. The latters' opinions were typical of those held by the Leeds and Wakefield merchant communities. Their attitude to the rapid introduction of machinery and the consequent growth of factories was conditioned by the fact that they saw the role of the merchant and manufacturer to be quite separate. It was an arrangement that through experience they much preferred. The result was that the lead in the woollen industry and the changes which took place were centred on the manufacturers of Halifax, Huddersfield and Bradford rather than those of Leeds and Wakefield who possessed the larger capitals.

Notes to Chapter 3
[1] *V.C.H.* Wiltshire, iv, p. 161; J. James, *op. cit.*, pp. 258–88.
[2] P. Deane, *op. cit.*, 203–23.
[3] G. N. Clark, *Guide to English Commercial Statistics* (1938), pp. 52–6; E. B. Schumpeter, *English Overseas Trade Statistics 1697–1808* (1960), pp. 40, 46–7; G. Jackson, *The Economic Development of Hull in the Eighteenth Century*, unpublished Hull University Ph.D. thesis (1960), pp. 208, 212.
[4] W. G. Hoskins, *Industry, Trade and People in Exeter 1688–1800* (1935), p. 62.
[5] A. D. Gayer, W. W. Rostow and A. J. Schwartz, *The Growth and Fluctuation of the British Economy* (1953), I, pp. 10–170; P. Deane and W. A. Cole, *op. cit.*, p. 52; T. S. Ashton, *Economic Fluctuations in England, 1700–1800* (1959), p. 30.
[6] R. G. Wilson, 'Transport dues as indices of economic growth, 1775–1820', *Ec.H.R.*, XIX (1966), 110–23.
[7] Spencer-Stanhope MSS./464–489.
[8] *ibid.*, J. Senior to J. Stanhope 21 March 1766.

⁹ R. Davis, 'English foreign trade, 1660–1700', *Ec.H.R.*, VII (1954), 150–67; W. G. Hoskins, *op. cit.*, pp. 18–19, 155.

¹⁰ E. B. Schumpeter, *op. cit.*, pp. 46–47; G. Jackson, *op. cit.*, p. 143.

¹¹ J. Bischoff, *A Comprehensive History of the Woollen and Worsted Manufactures* (1842), I, pp. 186–90; J. James, *op. cit.*, pp. 279–86; See Appendix A, p. 239 below. Wolrich, a Leeds cloth and worsted merchant in Leeds, collected these figures to present before a Parliamentary Committee investigating the decline of the stuff trade in Yorkshire during 1771–3. As Wolrich was a prominent member of Joseph Priestley's Mill Hill congregation at this period he possibly was inspired by the latter's scientific method, and certainly he knew the trade thoroughly.

¹² *C.J.*, xiii, 185–6, xvi, 50; xix, 191, 458, 530.

¹³ G. Jackson, *op. cit.*, pp. 111, 196; *Diary*, I, pp. 16–28; *Ducatus*, p. 214.

¹⁴ J. Haynes, *Provision for the Poor, or a View of the Decay'd State of the Woollen Manufacture* (second edition, 1715), p. 16; *L.M.* 13 Oct. 1726; M. Postlethwayt, *The Universal Dictionary of Trade and Commerce* (third edition, 1766), see under 'cloth'.

¹⁵ R. Davis, 'English foreign trade, 1700–1774', *Ec.H.R.*, XV (1962), 285–303.

¹⁶ See especially P. Deane and H. J. Habakkuk, 'The take-off in Britain' in W. W. Rostow (ed.), *The Economics of Take-Off into Sustained Growth* (1963), pp. 44–62.

¹⁷ J. Smith, *Chronicon Rusticum Commerciale; or, Memoirs of Wool, Etc.* (1747), ii, pp. 468, 519–56.

¹⁸ J. de L. Mann, 'Clothiers and weavers in eighteenth century Wiltshire' in L. S. Pressnell (ed.), *Studies in the Industrial Revolution* (1960), pp. 66–96; *V.C.H.* Wiltshire IV, pp. 161–4.

¹⁹ G. Jackson, *op. cit.*, Table 18; R. Davies, 'English foreign trade, 1700–1774', 302–3.

²⁰ *Gentleman's Magazine* (1743), 139ff.

²¹ P. Deane and W. A. Cole, *op. cit.*, p. 59; T. S. Ashton, *op. cit.*, p. 149; *LI.* 1 Feb., 6 Dec. 1757.

²² T. S. Ashton, *op. cit.*, pp. 156–60; Leeds General Quarter Sessions Books, LC/QS9 (1766–75); J. James, *op. cit.*, p. 281; (W.) Bailey, *List of Bankrupts, Dividends and Certificates 1771–1793* (1794).

²³ *L.M.* 1 March, 19 April, 27 Sept. 1774, 24 Jan. 1775; *Thors. Soc.*, XXIV (1919), 37.

²⁴ R. G. Wilson, 'Transport dues', 110–123.

²⁵ Denison MSS. H/46.

²⁶ M. Postlethwayt, *op. cit.*, see under 'Portugal' and 'Spain'; H. S. E. Fisher, 'Anglo–Portuguese trade, 1700–1774', *Ec.H.R.*, XVI (1963), 219–33.

²⁷ R. Davis, 'English foreign trade, 1700–1774', listed above *Ec. H. R.*, XV (1962).

²⁸ J. Priestley, *Historical Account of the Navigable Rivers, Canals and Railways of Great Britain* (1830), pp. 578–83.

²⁹ *supra*, pp. 41–2. There were no fewer than 14 wholesale tobacco manufacturers in Leeds in 1782 (*L.I.* 22 Jan. 1782).

³⁰ H. Heaton, 'Yorkshire cloth traders in the United States: 1770–1840', *Thors. Soc.*, XXVII (1941), 225–87; see also his 'Benjamin Gott and the Anglo-American cloth trade', *Journal of Economic and Business History*, II (1929), 146–62.

³¹ P. Deane, *op. cit.*, pp. 203–23.

³² E. L. Jones and G. E. Mingay (eds) *Land, Labour and Population in the Industrial Revolution* (1967), pp. 206–59.

³³ J. H. Clapham, loc. cit.

³⁴ *C.J.*, XLIX, 431.

³⁵ R. Brown, *A General View of the Agriculture of the West Riding of Yorkshire* (1799), p. 229.

³⁶ *L.M.* 15 March 1800.

[37] J. Aikin, *A Description of the Country for Thirty or Forty Miles around Manchester* (1795), pp. 558, 574; H. Clarkson, *Memories of Merry Wakefield* (second edition, 1889), p. 44.

[38] J. Aikin, *op. cit.*, p. 558; W. B. Crump and G. Ghorbal, *op. cit.*, p. 74; D. Defoe, *A Tour thro' the Whole Island of Great Britain* (1927 edition), p. 605.

[39] 1806 Report, 160; J. Aikin, *op. cit.*, pp. 573–4; Spencer-Stanhope MSS., 1170.

[40] F. Atkinson (ed.), *Some Aspects of the Eighteenth Century Woollen and Worsted Trade in Halifax* (1956), *passim*.

[41] Lupton MSS. Figures extracted from the two account-books of Ibbetson and Koster.

[42] Heaton, p. 300.

[43] White Cloth Hall MSS. (Brotherton Library, Leeds).

[44] F. Atkinson, *op. cit.*, p. 2; Lupton MSS. Letter-book of Ibbetson and Koster, 26 March 1761; Denison MSS. De/H, 46.

[45] F. Atkinson, *op. cit.*, p. 1.

[46] *Supra*, pp. 29–30.

[47] ACN 4/120 R. Wilson to G. Fox, M.P., 15 Dec. 1740; F. Atkinson, *op. cit.*, pp. 1–16.

[48] J. H. Crabtree, *A Concise History of the Parish and Vicarage of Halifax* (1836), pp. 304–5.

[49] *L.I.*, 21 Oct. 1793; *C.J.*, XLIX, 431.

4   *The merchants at work*

> At Leeds the clothing trade, that staple manufacture of the King-
> dom, that employs such innumerable hands and which is a more
> genuine source of wealth than the mines of Peru, is seen in all its
> glory.*

When William Milner jotted down in 1736 an account of the successes
in his long and full life he paid chief tribute to a 'wonderfully good
and Gracious God Almighty' and his 'very vertuous discreet and good
wyfe'. Few merchants would probably have paid Milner's uxorious
tribute, but almost all of them would have replied to questions about
their prosperity in terms of God and hard work. At the height of the
American war in 1780 a cheerful correspondent in the *Intelligencer*
wrote: 'I will venture to assert that the merchants of Leeds come nearer
to the Dutch in their practical knowledge of trade than any others in
the Kingdom. Cool, cautious, frugal and industrious they will always
survive.'[1] It is now difficult to test these claims by any eighteenth-
century standards, but certainly financial success was almost always the
reward of diligent attention to business. Although prices and profits
naturally loomed large in the merchants' ledgers, discussions with their
partners, arguments with the clothiers and instructions to their cloth-
dressers filled a large part of their daily round. It is these aspects of their
work, as well as their rewards in trade that we must consider in this
chapter.

(I)
The ideal merchant apprenticeship in the eighteenth century provided
instruction in trade, accounts and languages. Young men in the Leeds
trade had a good deal to learn in the five years that they spent, on
average, training to be merchants. Besides a working knowledge of
German, Dutch and Portuguese, they had to acquire a familiarity with
continental mercantile practices and a thorough knowledge of the
Yorkshire industry, especially in cloth-finishing techniques. In the late
seventeenth century it had been simpler to send apprentices to Rotter-

---

* W. Bray, *Sketch of a Tour into Derbyshire and Yorkshire* (1783)

dam or Amsterdam for four or five years' experience, but after the
decline of woollen exports through Holland and the improvement of
finishing processes in the West Riding, training was usually largely
completed in Leeds, although all apprentices contemplating the export
trade spent a year abroad. A long letter that William Denison wrote to
his young nephew in 1779 gives a good impression of the purpose of
this part of their training. The advice was not dissimilar to that which
every gentleman gave before his son embarked on the Grand Tour;
and where they culled wisdom derived from the experience of their
own lives, Denison distilled some of the knowledge he had acquired in
40 years of foreign trade. He began in fine style: 'If you think yourself
properly qualified in language, address and politeness to make the
tour of Italy, the sooner you do it the better, provided you can meet
with a proper companion amongst the Exeter or Norwich travellers.'
Trade in 1779 was bad, but the nephew was sent patterns and instructed
to make comments on the general trade with Italy and lists of dealers
and bankers in almost every sizeable town, 'so that in ten or twenty
years hence everything may occur to your memory the same as if you
was present'. The uncle again stressed that 'nothing can be done but
by politeness and civility', but concluded with a comment which
must have given some relief to the youth: 'it requires more knowledge and experience than it can be presumed to possess people at
your age'.[2]

Postlethwayt believed that the instruction given by busy merchants
was often inadequate and that apprentices from well-to-do homes, who
often had had an indifferent basic education, 'looked upon it in the
light of hackney drudgery'. He suggested that a mercantile college
should be founded to give instruction to students over 15 who would
study accounts, mathematics, commerce and languages.[3] It is quite
possible that his strictures would have been applicable in Leeds,
although Denison's nephew and Benjamin Gott appear to have been
well instructed, and it was of course necessary in the West Riding trade
to acquire an understanding of the cloth halls and the finishing processes that no mercantile college could have properly provided.

A likely youth who had just completed his apprenticeship, or anyone
else who entertained ambitions of becoming a woollen merchant,
usually looked around for a partner to join him in the venture. In 1782
at least 46 of the 73 firms in Leeds were formed through partnerships
and of the 61 that signed a resolution in favour of gig-mills in 1791 no
fewer than 47 had two or more partners.[4] Many of those that were
apparently one-man concerns were in fact family enterprises, like the
Denisons, Blayds, Bischoffs and Oates, who had no need to look

beyond their immediate relations for partners, but whose partnership deeds were drawn up as carefully as those firms which combined more diverse elements.

There were three reasons for the formation of these partnerships. Firstly, they spread risk, although this element was insignificant in comparison with its importance in the formation of partnerships in the Far Eastern and slave trades and shipping ventures in general. Secondly, two or more partners came together so that by their joint efforts they could raise the required minimum capital. Such a partnership was that made by Mathew and Timothy Rhodes and John Hebblethwaite in July 1780. They signed a deed agreeing to raise £3,600 within the next nine months. Mathew was to contribute £1,550, Timothy Rhodes £1,200 and Hebblethwaite £850. The two Rhodes, who had been brought up as dyers, agreed to lend Hebblethwaite £350 without interest as he alone knew 'the business of a merchant'. Lastly, partnerships were formed for convenience. The West Riding trade required that the merchant perform three distinct operations: he had to attend cloth markets throughout the county, supervise the cloth-finishing in Leeds and occasionally visit his correspondents to renew acquaintances, solicit orders and collect bad debts. It was not easy for one man to combine all these functions especially if he had to go abroad or enjoy any social life, nor in the eighteenth century was the delegation of responsibility to managers believed to be wise. Therefore not only were firms with two or three partners who contributed equal capital shares numerous, but there were many examples of partnerships which were formed for the convenience of one partner, who was prepared to admit another of inferior capital and social standing, provided he carry out the more arduous duties. In 1819 William Lupton joined forces with his nephew David Rider in a seven-year partnership. Rider at no time contributed more than £1,000 to the firm's capital, although Lupton's share was reckoned at £38,065 on the day the deeds were signed. It emerges from the letter-books that Rider was little more than a well-paid traveller for the firm. Lupton could terminate the partnership at a month's notice and it was stated: '. . . the said David Rider shall diligently apply himself to the best of his skill and power in managing the said joint trade, and that Mr. Lupton shall be at liberty to give such attention and assistance only as may be agreeable to him'.[5] These eager junior partners, who shouldered the daily running of the business, were invaluable to the older, established merchants who were thereby enabled to devote ample time to town administration and social recreations.

A study of the motivation behind the formation of partnerships entails a consideration of the amount of capital required to float a woollen-merchanting house. Requirements changed after 1783, and information before 1780 is scarce. The firm of Ibbetson and Koster was a medium-sized Leeds firm trading abroad in the 1750's, at least judged by the standard of Hill's list 20 years later. In their second deed of partnership made in 1755 they agreed to raise £9,500 which had risen to almost £12,300 by 1760. William Milner, who was the largest merchant of his day, claimed in 1737 he had for 'many years returned £70–80,000 and upwards a year in way of business'. If the ratio between his capital and turnover was in the same proportion as that of Ibbetson and Koster the former must have been at least in the region of £25,000. Towards the other end of the scale Walter Stanhope and Nathaniel Heald, a cloth-worker, were to raise £3,000 in 1737, although in the event the partnership collapsed because Heald was unable to find the £1,000 he had promised.[6] Those cloth-dressers who entered merchanting possessed only a few hundred pounds, their premises and finishing equipment. Their trade, usually in the home market, was small, but neither Stanhope nor these small inland merchants were typical of the Leeds trade which was always largely an export one. Since the annual turnover in the European market was at best two and a half times the capital outlay, and two or three partners had to share profits, individual merchants before 1780 had to be able to raise at least £1,500 to enter the trade and ensure a fair livelihood. Although some merchants like Milner were eventually trading on large capitals of £20,000 and more, initial requirements in the Leeds trade, compared with the Levant and Far Eastern trades, was small.[7] Of course returns in the European market were quicker, but profits were smaller. Nevertheless the relatively small initial sums necessary to break into woollen-merchanting in the West Riding, especially in the home market, created openings for a much wider section of the community than the restricted recruitment to the old trading companies and to that circle of London merchants who monopolised the Asian trade had allowed. Partly for this reason, the Yorkshire industry gained its reputation as the land of opportunity in the eighteenth century.

After the 1780's there were a number of changes which affected the size of outlay in the Leeds trade. Inflation, the shift from the European to American markets, the effects of large-scale manufacture after the introduction of machinery were all factors necessitating an increased capital contribution. This was particularly the case if the merchant contemplated manufacturing. Wormald and Gott's total proprietorship was £20,229 in January 1792, the year they built the famous Bean Ing factory; by 1808 it had increased to £272,937. An advertiser in the

Leeds Mercury sought a partner in 1819 for a 'Large Manufacturing and Mercantile concern in the Woollen cloth line in Leeds' who could advance £30,000 within a year. Even for the majority of merchants, who never contemplated manufacturing, the amounts of capital required had increased. When Robert Denison, who had been a partner with his brother William in the largest export house in the town, died in 1785, he left £20,000 to his nephews, 'for or towards carrying on the said business of merchants at Leeds'. But if this was to form their sole outlay he was thinking in terms of requirements in his youth 40 years earlier. In the same year that Denison died the partnership of Wormald, Fountaine and the young Benjamin Gott (his father found £3,660) raised a capital of £40,320. Mathew Rhodes who in 1780 had struggled to collect £1,550 together, brought £18,000 into a partnership he founded with Martin Hird in 1793.[8] Regular advertisements for partners begin to appear in the newspapers around 1800, occasionally specifying the amount they wished the partner to advance. In most cases the firms were concerned with the smaller home trade, but even in this the prospective partners were requested to advance sums varying from at least £2,000 to £8,000.[9] Houses trading with Europe and the Americas required their partners to contribute even larger sums. Mathew Rhodes' £18,000 was not untypical.

It does not follow that these increases made entry to business either more difficult or more selective. In real terms the increase in capital requirements between 1740 and 1800 was less than the amounts indicated above would suggest. Moreover, machine scribbling and spinning and the buoyancy of trade after 1783 advanced the fortunes of many, besides the merchants, both in and beyond the woollen industry. Far more men were able to raise £5,000 within the town in 1800 than could advance £1,500 in 1740.[10]

How were these sums raised? The long-established dynasties like the Ibbetsons, Denisons and Cooksons had few difficulties, they could call upon the reserves of ploughed-back profits which had been invested in property and government stocks by successive generations. The merchant recently out of his apprenticeship and those men who entered the occupation from another trade were in a different situation. The well-to-do parent who afforded a large premium for his son's training usually provided the capital for his first trading ventures. Many were like John Gott who saved hard to launch Benjamin into his masters' firm. Often female relatives were requested to lend money to their nephews, for the provision of funds was a family affair. The cloth-dresser and clothier met with the greatest problems. They owned their premises, some equipment and a deal of skill and enterprise; but, at least before 1780, they found it difficult to raise the money for their own or their son's first excursion into cloth-selling. More money was required than the gradual transition from one occupation to the other provided. Delays in remittances could eat into their careful savings with remarkable rapidity. A closer study of William Lupton's efforts suggests that the affairs of the entire Lupton family—brothers, sisters, uncles and cousins included—were directed with the single aim that William should be enabled to launch his two sons into woollen merchanting. He was allowed to borrow substantial sums and became sole executor of, and chief beneficiary in, his sisters' wills.[11] John Hebblethwaite and William Rhodes' sons began merchanting after much the same struggle. Personal drive and the ability to inspire confidence were all important. This enabled the struggling merchants to secure loans from their families and occasionally their friends. Banks were unimportant even after 1780 in the provision of initial capital. A man had to be well on the way to apparent success before a bank would consider making him a loan. Clothiers and cloth-workers at least had to rely on a purely personal network.

There is no indication that, unlike merchants concerned in shipping, the woollen merchants were partners in more than one firm. Most houses consisted of two or three partners. The notices of partnership dissolutions that appeared in the newspapers very occasionally revealed that a firm had more than this number. The Quaker firm of Pease, Heaton and Pease, formerly Bensons, formed in 1804, had six partners, but this was quite exceptional. These notices were usually only advertisements that a firm had dissolved after the term stipulated in the partnership deeds, a period which varied from 5 to 11 years—7 was the most popular span. Occasionally firms were terminated before the date of expiry when one of the partners had become a financial embarrassment. David Dunderdale and John Plowes, who was mayor in 1790, were partners both in a woollen merchanting house and Castleford pottery. The partnership was dissolved on Plowes' bankruptcy in 1803. Dunderdale immediately advertised for a new partner who could advance not less than £15,000–£20,000.[12]

The tight wording and detail of the partnership deeds, which was intended to prevent disputes, in fact often led to friction within a firm. The notice which appeared in the *Mercury* in 1796 of the dissolution of partnership between Richard and John Micklethwaite did not suggest anything more than that their term of agreement had come to an end. Yet a great family feud was created over John's conduct of business. Letters were written without salutations, Chancery proceedings threatened and finally arbitrators were called in to settle the whole affair. Thomas Micklethwaite, a third brother with money in the firm wrote to John: 'its a shocking life to lead always at enmity . . . I really cannot imagine why you wish not to have done with this unpleasant Business. What pleasure can you have in it'.[13] The partnership was not finally wound up until 1800. Others went the same way, but those concluded in this fashion were in the minority for harmonious partnerships left few testimonies to their successful association. Jeremiah Dixon and Thomas Lee ran a leading firm together for almost 40 years, and the Clapham and Hall families were partners for over 50 years until political differences severed their connection after 1815.[14] Some men held together in one firm for many years, others split their commissions and moved every seven years or so from one house to another.

(II)

Having entered into a partnership the new recruit to the cloth trade sought suitable premises from which to carry on his business. The size of the establishment depended largely on whether the merchant finished his own cloth. He was much more likely to do this after 1750 than were his seventeenth- and early eighteenth-century predecessors. The result was that the premises a merchant occupied were far more commodious in 1800 than they had been a hundred years previously. In 1700 the chief requirement had been a good warehouse and counting-house adjoining the dwelling. Mr. Bell's establishment in Hunslet Lane, advertised in 1757, was typical of these smaller premises: 'a good dwelling house of twelve rooms with a Packing shop, stable, an orchard, a close of land adjoining and other conveniences fit for a Merchant'. Richard Lee's premises in Woodhouse Lane sold in 1809 suggest the changes that had taken place in 50 years. They included a 'capital Freehold Mansion House . . . with stabling for eight horses, coach house, saddle house, Brew House and Laundry, and other attached and detached offices and Gardens, together with the Plantations, Pleasure Grounds, and Paddock adjoining containing upwards of five acres'. Near the house, but detached from it, were Lee's large warehouse, counting-house, cropping chambers, row shops, drawing chambers, wool warehouse, etc.[15] From their inception, the Leeds newspapers contained scores of these advertisements which ran the entire gamut from Bell's premises to the large establishment of Richard Lee. The merchants' houses and their appendages lined Hunslet Lane, Meadow Lane, Boar Lane, eventually Woodhouse Lane and were scattered throughout the northern half of the township. Only after 1780 with the building of the squares and terraces in the west end of the town was there any tendency to separate the dwelling-house from the warehouses and dressing shops. Even then the break was not complete as Park Lane became lined with the appendages of the finishing trade (see p. 202 below).

The long-established firms, like the Blayds, Dixons and Denisons, tended to occupy the same premises throughout the eighteenth century. Only when they were unable to extend their workshops or when they wished to build a grander town house did they contemplate moving. Newcomers and the men who formed partnerships in the smaller houses shifted from one set of premises to another as they acquired sufficient means to afford a larger house and more extensive warehousing and finishing facilities.

The cost of a good dwelling-house with ample facilities for cloth-dressing and a close or two of land is not easy to determine. The poor-rate assessments are informative but not necessarily helpful. Merchant owner-occupiers were assessed for the town dues on an annual rateable value which varied from £10 on the smallest premises to the £50 levied on the fine town house which John Carr built for Jeremiah Dixon in 1750. Yet the ratio between this valuation and the actual market value makes little sense. Henry Atkinson wrote to his sister-in-law, the widowed Mrs. Walter Stanhope in 1765: 'Bro. Stanhope informed me he had sold yr. House and premises to my neighbour Wormald over ye way for £2,000, a very good price'. The house was rated at £20 annual value in the 1754 assessment. Jeremiah Dixon sold his fine house to his partner Thomas Lee in 1763 for £4,500, 'much less than the Building had cost'.[16] Market prices appear to have been around 90–100 times their assessed annual value in the 1760's. Whether these assessments bore any relation to an economic rent is unknown although many smaller merchants rented their premises before 1780. A merchant had to be prepared to pay from £1,000 to £5,000 to obtain a decent house with good facilities for his business before the boom, which began in 1783 and, more especially, inflation after 1795, sent property prices soaring. By any eighteenth-century standards the merchant's outlay on suitable premises was a substantial one.

(III)

A glance at the merchants' premises brings us to a consideration of the numbers of men they employed, and a study of their role in the finishing processes of the woollen industry. These stages—raising, cropping or shearing, burling, fine-drawing and finally pressing the cloth—known together as cloth-dressing had been carried out at Leeds since at least 1600. The tendency to discourage the export of 'white' or unfinished cloths to Holland and the decline of the great chartered companies which had been principally engaged in this trade, stimulated the growth of dressing and dyeing in England. Kerseys, and the majority of Yorkshire broad cloths, the chief exports from the West Riding, were still sold by the clothiers after fulling in a 'white' state, but they were increasingly dyed and dressed in Leeds, and to a lesser extent Wakefield, rather than in the Dutch towns and London.

The Apprenticeship Registers and the subscription to Holy Trinity Church in 1721 show the large numbers and prominence of the cloth-workers in both towns. Yet it is easier to cite the importance of the Leeds and Wakefield dressers in the Yorkshire woollen industry, than discover their exact relationship with the merchants. Around 1700 the merchant having bought his cloth then arranged for it to be dyed, if necessary, and finished with a master dresser who employed a number of journeymen and apprentices to carry out the various final processes. The master dresser was paid by the yard an amount that varied with the quality of the cloth. Sir Henry Ibbetson who bought a fine livery cloth in 1760 for 9 guineas, paid 18s. for having it dressed and 12s. for dyeing. The rate for cheaper coarser cloths was nearer 1s. in the pound than this livery cloth dressed at 2s. per guinea. The merchant tended to have his cloth finished by the same dresser each time. Between 1749 and 1760 Ibbetson paid £8,179 to the four master dressers whom he most frequently engaged. In 1758 he paid £1,525 for cloth dressing to no fewer than nine master dressers.[17]

The arrangement between the merchant and cloth-dresser, however, was not as loose as it might appear. Already by 1700 inroads were made into the system. Dressing was a vital stage in production especially in the manufacture of broad cloths where, since they were always sold in plain colours, all depended upon the dyeing and finishing. Faults could be disguised and the cloth given its necessary stretch, or, as the clothiers believed, dressing allowed the merchants to obtain an extra yard in 20 at their expense. For these reasons and because finishing was an important item in the merchants' costs (Ibbetson paid £16,513 to his dressers, 1751–60)[18] it was in their interest to have the cloth-dressers under their closer supervision. William Milner as usual appears to have taken the lead. From a note to Thoresby in 1708 it would appear that he was employing his own dressers.

Three of my dressers are now abroad upon the Jury, and I understand that Anthony Harrison is likewise summoned to be of the maine-riding Jury, which will take him much off my business and I can very ill spare him, therefore doe begg the favour of you to excuse him whereby you'll very much oblige.[19]

Milner's lead was obviously followed. In 1725 'several hundred' cloth

F

dressers 'in and around the town of Leeds' petitioned the Commons that:

the Trade of a cloth dresser hath been a Trade time out of mind; and the Petitioners have all along exercised the said trade themselves; but of late years, several Merchants, Clothiers and others have assumed to themselves the said Trade and Business of a cloth dresser.

Moreover the merchant seems to have owned the dressing utensils. In 1737 the immigrant merchant John Berkenhout had stolen from him: 'two presses, two setts of plates with papers, seventeen pairs of sheers, five shear boards, thirty pairs of Lead Weights, handles, Racks and foot Boards of the value of £50'.

Even the relationship between Ibbetson and his cloth-dressers was closer than at first appears. 'Mr. Ibbetson's dressers' subscribed £36 15s. to the Archbishop of York's fund for the defence of Yorkshire in 1745, and John Darnton stated himself in 1754 to be 'dresser to Sir Henry Ibbetson, Bart.'[20] The master dyers' position appears to have been threatened in the same way. Ibbetson bought regular consignments of dyestuffs for 'our dyers'.

By 1750 there were numerous indications besides the evidence concerning Milner and Ibbetson to suggest that the merchant was taking over the finishing stages of production. He now owned his own dressing shops which were managed by master cloth-dressers, who, as the method of payment negotiated between them and the merchant indicates, still retained a quasi-independent status, but which, in effect, amounted to their under-employment during the annual slack periods in the cloth trade. Many similar advertisements to that inserted by Rayner and Wolrich seeking a journeyman dyer and hot-presser appeared in the newspapers.[21] Now almost all premises advertised as being suitable for merchants made reference to dressing shops, dyehouses and tenters. The 1798 directory contained the names of only 22 independent master dressers, a notable decline since 1721, especially in relation to the greatly increased output of the Yorkshire woollen and worsted industries. By 1800 it was only the smallest merchants and those who could not at periods of peak activity complete their commissions themselves who put out their cloth for finishing with the few remaining independent master dressers. It was their reduced status in the eighteenth century as well as the introduction of the gig-mill in the 1790's which drove the cloth-workers into forming their well known 'Institution' or union after 1795.

The number of cloth-dressers a merchant employed is difficult to determine. In 1806 it was reckoned that there were 500 master dressers and 5,000–6,000 journeymen croppers employed in the West Riding. Of these a large proportion found work in Leeds, where John Tate, a Halifax cloth-dresser, maintained there were eight times more employed than at Halifax. Wakefield and Huddersfield were the only other finishing centres of importance. Either Tate's ratio was erroneous or the total estimate was too high for there are numerous references around 1806 to about 1,500 croppers occupied in Leeds which, given the number of merchants and the few independent masters left in 1806, suggests that the average merchant employed around 10 dressers. John Naylor, the great Wakefield merchant, had 28 croppers under his immediate supervision in that year, although he also employed others who were not.[22] A dressing shop advertised in 1775 in Leeds was described as 'very proper for a Merchant or cloth dresser in great business, it will hold 20 or 30 men at work'. Benjamin Gott, who in 1813 employed 257 men in the finishing departments at Bean Ing out of a total of 761 work people, was certainly not a typical merchant, but this figure underlines the importance of the finishing processes and the large numbers employed in these branches.[23]

Besides the cloth-dressers, the dyers and fine-drawers, who concealed faults in manufacture and damage done to the cloth in finishing, the merchant employed clerks, packers and travellers as well as instructing any apprentices he might take. Although the merchants were reluctant to depute responsibility to managers, clerks and book-keepers who kept the firm's letter-books and accounts often crept into positions of authority within the firms. Their offices, or counting-houses as they were always known, were the hub of the business. A first-rate clerk was well paid. When William Denison was looking for a book-keeper in 1780, he offered to pay a good salary to applicants who could write Italian, German and French. But the London clerk who came up to Leeds for interview told him he had 'a good Fortune in Funds' and had understood his prospective employer lived in Hampstead. In a letter redolent of the Yorkshireman's age-old suspicion of the southerner, William replied to the London merchant who had recommended him: 'I told him in answer if there were any mistakes, the ready way to remedy them was to return immediately as he came . . . as I keep nobody to look at I think I am well rid of this fruitful Genius'.[24] Some clerks did well like William Reed who had been William Milner's book-keeper for years before he established a cloth export house in the 1740's. Packers, who pressed and baled the finished cloth and acted as general warehousemen and occasionally as buyers in the halls were never numerous, and the largest export houses employed no more than four men and a couple of boys in this department.

Travellers were employed only by the large home merchants, for those in the export trade, or more usually their apprentices in the final year of their training, visited their correspondents much less frequently.

The merchant's role in the cloth finishing processes is indicative of his position in the woollen trade throughout the entire period under review, and herein lies the significance of this discussion of the merchants' relationships *vis-à-vis* the cloth workers. The same questions were posed by the decision of the merchant to finish the cloth himself in his own premises, as those raised when he sought, after 1800 to take up the entire manufacturing processes. Should the merchant take for himself the profit of the cloth-dresser to cut his costs? What were the advantages of close personal supervision of this important stage in production? Those who made a negative reply raised a point often heard again after 1780. The woollen trade had always known cyclical recessions. Indeed the trade itself was of a seasonal nature. Was it then wise to employ a large number of cloth-workers who could not easily be turned away during slack periods? Was it not better to employ an independent cloth-dresser only when there was work for him? The majority of merchants, however, came to the conclusion that higher profits and closer supervision were worth additional capital expenditure. But the two systems always existed side by side to a certain extent. This duality of methods, paralleled as we have seen in the manufacture of cloth, was typical of the older woollen industry in contrast with the worsted and cotton industries. It meant that innovations and improvements were often slow to be assimilated.

(IV)

Once the merchant had formed a partnership and entered his warehouse and finishing shops, he thumbed through the order-book which was compiled from correspondents which the partners had each brought into the firm. Purchases to execute commissions were made in the weekly cloth markets held throughout the textile area. Merchants rode to the cloth halls at Bradford, Wakefield and Halifax with their patterns to buy worsteds and, at the latter market, kerseys. After 1766 they frequently went across to Huddersfield in search of fancy cloths and Saddleworth broad cloth. Of course the majority of broad cloth purchases were made regularly in the two cloth halls at Leeds which were the largest in the county. Defoe has left a famous description of the merchants buying cloth in the coloured cloth market at Leeds, held in Briggate until the Mixed Cloth Hall was built in 1755.

As soon as the bell has done ringing, the merchants and factors, and buyers of all sorts, come down, and coming along all the spaces between the rows of boards, they walk up the rows, and down as their occasions direct. Some of them have their foreign letters of orders, with patterns seal'd in them, in their hands; and with these they match colours, holding them to the cloths as they think they agree to; when they see any cloths to their colours, or that suit their occasions, they reach over to the clothier and whisper, and in the fewest words imaginable the price is stated; one asks, the other bids; and 'tis agree, or not agree in a moment. . . . If a Merchant has bidden a clothier a price, and he will not take it he may go after him to his house, and tell him he has considered of it, and is willing to let him have it; but they are not to make any new agreement for it, so as to remove the market from the street to the merchant's house.[25]

This was the description of the perfect market. In practice it probably never existed for neither manufacturing nor selling practices were uniform, nor did all merchants or clothiers conform to what visitors believed to be common practice. And during recessions the bargaining was loud and protracted when the clothier had his back against the wall. Moreover the direct-order system, as we have seen in the previous chapter, was already eating into the marketing mechanism Defoe described in the 1720's. Nevertheless probably the majority of cloths before 1800, especially in the Leeds area, was bought in the cloth halls. After 1800 their position declined rapidly. One clothier in 1821 estimated that even around Leeds not more than one in five broad cloths ever passed the doors of the Leeds cloth halls.[26]

When the clothier carried his cloth to the merchant's warehouse it was thoroughly inspected for faults over a strong light, measured (since no one paid attention to the measurements on the lead seal) and the bargain concluded. This stage was essential for long before the range of cloths was extended after 1770 broad cloths and kerseys, especially those dyed in the wool, varied enormously in quality. As D'arcy Molyneux wrote: "'tis almost impossible to have one piece equally good from end to end and much more to have a number of equal quality'. The direct-order system guaranteed little more uniformity of standards than open buying in the halls since improvement rested with the mechanisation of spinning and weaving. Methods of payment for cloth varied. Some merchants like Henry Ibbetson, who had an interest in the return of the land-tax, secured good terms with the clothiers by paying them cash on the spot, others paid a percentage on delivery and paid the rest over varying periods of time, whilst a minority settled their accounts only after the cloth had been finished.[27] Yet even with direct orders the domestic system entirely relied on a quick settlement with cash and small bills of the clothiers' accounts.

(V)

A view of sales procedures in the mid-eighteenth century, before mass marketing technique which accompanied the upsurge of industrialism broke into the earlier more leisurely commercial world, is provided by three folio volumes of letters and accounts of the partnership of Ibbetson and Koster between 1748 and 1761.[28] At first sight the firm's trade appears similar to that of the score of the largest export houses in Leeds, but there is evidence that it was being deliberately run down throughout the 1750's. Sir Henry Ibbetson, the senior partner, was a very wealthy man. His father had made a fortune in the woollen trade between 1695 and 1739. If Ralph Thoresby, the Leeds antiquary and one-time merchant, is to be believed—and he was the mildest of men in opinions about both events and people—cunning and deceit formed a large part of James Ibbetson's stock in trade. A satire on the Leeds gentry, which appeared in 1751 representing Henry Ibbetson as an ox, suggests he was a very different man from his father, but does not necessarily disclose the reasons for his inactivity in the cloth trade during the 1750's. Although he was the second son he succeeded to the major share of his father's property which after 1739 provided him with an income of well over £1,000 a year from land alone. This, together with an excellent marriage to the daughter of Ralph Carr of Cocken, a prominent businessman and landowner in county Durham, and the knowledge that his son would one day inherit his elder brother's delightful Wharfedale estate (bought by James Ibbetson from Lord Fairfax in 1717), provided him with a livelihood and prospects that allowed his interest in affairs to range beyond those of the woollen industry itself. Close attention to business in the 1740's gave way to involvement in politics. In 1745 he was prominent in securing York for the government and although some of his zeal in raising 100 men at his own expense for the defence of the county was to be explained by his return of the county's land-tax, his services were sufficiently meritorious for him to be given a baronetcy in 1748. He served office as High Sheriff of Yorkshire and contemplated standing for election at York in 1747. Authority in the county gave him ascendency in the town. In the entire history of the corporation he was the only mayor to be elected to office in the same year that he was first elected to the council. During the 1750's political dabbling gave way to increasing participation in ventures outside the cloth trade. He appears to have become involved with another merchant Peter Birt in coal-mining and in 1758 they took a 14-year lease of the Aire and Calder Navigation Tolls. The rewards of the latter were apparently excellent for Ibbetson readily agreed to the proprietors' request that they give up merchanting in order to forestall traders' protests that their goods would receive preferential treatment on the rivers. The management of the cloth firm in Leeds was left entirely to John Koster but his direction of its concerns, since he was very much the junior partner never providing more than five-nineteenths of the firm's capital, was geared to Ibbetson's opinions. The merchant house, whose antecedents went back to the Civil War, was being sacrificed to Ibbetson's other economic interests. Yet whatever the peculiarities of the firm's management its few surviving papers provide a fair impression of the goods, direction of trade and salesmanship of a middle-sized export house in the Yorkshire cloth trade.

The cloths sent abroad showed no great basic variety, although many changes were rung in quality, colour and finish on the three major types of cloth Ibbetson dealt in, broad cloths, worsteds and kerseys.[29] The firm's buyer ordered no fewer than 10 different sorts of bays alone from one Rochdale maker in 1761. Ibbetson dispatched his cloth in three main directions—London; Germany, Brussels and Basle; and Portugal, Spain and Italy. The majority of his shipments were made from Hull, although cloths for London, where many were reshipped to south Europe, were sent by carrier's waggon as frequently as they were shipped down the coast from Hull. Agents in Hull and London handled insurance and shipping arrangements and their charges were passed directly to the customer.

The firm's trade was carried on by three distinct methods. Firstly— and this was by far the most important category—cloths were shipped to the direct order of merchants residing abroad. In Germany, Flanders and Italy these merchants were all natives, whereas in Portugal they were Englishmen at the Lisbon factory who handled the woollen trade of Portugal and to a large extent that of Spain and its colonies also. Secondly, Ibbetson supplied cloths for London export merchants who traded in northern cloths. As returns were speedier, charges for these commissions were proportionately lower; but the relationship between Ibbetson and the London merchants was otherwise the same as that which existed between him and his foreign correspondents. In no sense was he their factor buying in the Leeds markets to their direct order on a percentage commission basis. Lastly, and least importantly, he was shipping goods to Portugal to agents who disposed of the cloth on his behalf. In these enterprises he seems to have been involved with his London agents and brokers, de Neuville and Schuman and, after 1749, Battier and Zornlin, on a risk- and profit-sharing basis. Such consignments were usually only made in times of good trading conditions: when the markets became glutted and slack they dwindled away.

Ibbetson wrote in October 1760 to Carrett and Lupton in Lisbon: 'We are out of love with having goods lye for our own acct. in your part of the world having already been too great sufferers by that kind of traffic'. Two stoppages he went on to explain had laid them 'under many difficulties'. Later Battier and Zornlin were cautioned from Leeds that the Portuguese market had reached a critical position and returns from the consignment trade were so slow and abatements made so large, that they were better out of such activities. Consignments were unimportant to Ibbetson and were frowned upon by the most reputable export merchants, but after 1790 they became a very significant part of the American trade.

The terms of credit laid down between the merchant and his customers always appear to have been the most controversial issue between the two parties. It was obviously in the interest of the customer to demand the longest terms possible and on the other hand the merchant naturally wanted to stipulate the shortest period to secure his returns. The merchant could exert less pressure and during trade recessions credit was extended beyond the six-month maximum which was deemed safe by the majority of merchants trading in south Europe. It was these extensions of credit which led many unwary merchants down the path to ruin. As Ibbetson well realised a correspondent who requested longer and longer periods to meet his payments was almost always financially unsound.

Ibbetson's golden rule was to allow credit for six months after the customer's receipt of the invoice. Accounts were to be settled preferably by bill of short date. If for any reason the debt was outstanding after the six months allowed, interest was charged at 6% on all accounts. A letter to Thomas Jacomb, a London bill-broker with whom two merchants in Lisbon, Benjamin and Thomas Whiting, kept their accounts, brought out the inexpediency of long credit terms. Jacomb had claimed, on the Whitings' behalf, that he had been unable to remit Ibbetson because of the Portuguese 'fleets not regularly sailing' for South America. Ibbetson replied:

We have been oblige(d) to refuse severall good commissions for want of capitall where with all to execute them, as a great part of ours is detained in the hands of people who acted quite contrary to their agreement with us.

Charging overdue accounts with interest was all very well but as he admitted: '. . . between us Sir, the money would be ten times as useful to us in our present situation than having it lye in your hand at six per cent'. Other export merchants offered more lenient terms, but they did not have the reputation or tradition of the old firm of

Ibbetsons. William Lupton writing on behalf of Ibbetson to George and Thomas Allen in Lisbon reveals arrangements very different from those insisted upon by his master. Thanking them for their kind wishes he continued:

. . . as also giving us the preference of your Business on such terms as other offer you, which is to have a credit from receipt of the invoice of six, nine and twelve months, after the expiration of six months to allow interest and at that Time to remit one-third, another at nine and the remainder at twelve months, wherein you promise punctually, and in the case of failure to allow interest. Should these be the generall Terms on which we trade, our capitall would speedily be set fast, and our Hands ty'd for want of return, and should we agree to send goods on these terms, 'tis a greater indulgence by many months than we give to any other House we are concerned with.

The Allens, however, who had been brought into Ibbetson's books by his cousin D'arcy Molyneux, who swore for their honour and punctuality, were accepted with some reluctance. After checking on their credit in London and extracting a promise of remittance in London bills at three months date, Ibbetson agreed 'to carry on this business of long credit with some tolerable degree of care'. But they were requested to order their worsteds elsewhere, 'it being out of our power to execute these orders [without] a loss with the long credit we give you'.

Not all merchants could afford to be so fastidious as Sir Henry Ibbetson. To capture trade newcomers extended credit facilities and allowed abatements on their invoices. These features became especially prevalent in the American market. The six-month rule which guided merchants like Ibbetson was extended until credit was given over periods extending up to two years. In no small measure it accounted for the uneven returns and general instability of the American market. But long before the opening-up of the American market it was all too easy, as many merchants knew to their sorrow, to become involved with an unsafe firm. Even a small house like Levi Sousine of Leghorn when it stopped payment in 1782 involved four firms in Leeds to the extent of £15,500. William Denison in 1779 had difficulties in extracting £6,200 from a Geneva import house, 'about a sum sufficient to have ruined a family of moderate good circumstances in trade'. When his brother died in 1785 debts of £61,259 were due to the estate from 143 foreign firms in amounts ranging from 6d. to £3,652. Three and a half years later the executors still had almost £10,000 outstanding from 31 firms including £1,917 from the ubiquitous firm of George and Thomas Allen.[30] Even with caution things could get out of hand. Robert Denison's debts in 1785 were not far short of his annual turnover. It was all too easy to allow the firm's capital to get locked up in bad debts. That bankruptcies amongst the larger Leeds merchants in the eighteenth century were almost unheard of was the result of their care in establishing the reputation of their clients and unwillingness to jeopardise regular returns by lengthening their credit terms. But so long as the West Riding trade was controlled by men who operated on these principles, as they did until the 1780's, expansion of exports was modest in comparison with trends after 1783.

Ibbetson's papers illustrate the contemporary bill remittance and exchange activities of an export house. As in other extant collections of eighteenth-century mercantile letters, a high proportion of them are concerned with the complicated process of drawing and discounting bills. Ibbetson instructed his London agents Battier and Zornlin to draw on the houses in Paris, Hamburg and Brussels, with whom his customers kept their accounts, when he calculated that the exchange rates, within the credit period he allowed, were favourable. The customer was then informed that a bill had been drawn upon him and his account adjusted by that amount. The Portuguese market was almost entirely in the hands of English merchants who, as Portuguese bills were not encouraged, drew on London firms. The bills were immediately forwarded to the Bank of England and discounted at easy rates through Ibbetson's return of the land-tax (see pp. 150–153 below).

Only when the alternative was no payment at all did merchants accept consignments of foreign produce in lieu of good bills. It was not deemed wise amongst the Yorkshire merchants to become general import merchants although all imported the odd pipe of wine or parcel of dyestuffs for their own requirements. Nevertheless newspaper advertisements reveal that at times they were obliged to accept anything from turnip seeds to deer skins. Wine, dyestuffs and olive oil were more regular and acceptable goods taken to settle accounts. In isolated cases merchants went into the wine trade. Elam and Buck sold every description of wine from their Burley Bar wine-vaults, and George Oates was selling Portuguese and Spanish wines by the gallon and pipe from his Briggate warehouses in the 1770's.[31] But the vast majority of merchants preferred an early settlement of accounts that allowed them to go again into the cloth markets more quickly. They did not want their returns invested in goods which would take a further six months to convert into cash. Thus the Yorkshire woollen merchants in general avoided involvement in importing, shipping and insurance ventures.

Merchanting practice changed with the rapid expansion of the American market after 1783. By its very distance this market posed new problems. Newcomers to the trade were prepared to take risks which would have seemed inconceivable to Sir Henry Ibbetson. When this tendency increased further after 1800 many merchants who consigned goods for auction to the United States and South America might well have dwelt on Ibbetson's guiding rules. Through his letters we see the best side of the eighteenth-century commercial world. Relationships with customers were most cordial, disputes detested. Mirrors, barrels of oysters and silver cutlery—although Ibbetson instructed: 'We would not choose them to be of the best sort'—were exchanged with old correspondents. Constant advice was given on market trends. To one firm Molyneux wrote: 'We should have sent the bales of Tammies along with them but they are so excessive dear, that we durst not do it, they were never known higher'. Another customer complained of the cloth dispatched to them, and although Ibbetson maintained they bought their cloth cheaper than anyone in the market and employed an excellent cloth-dresser, he agreed that they should be given the profits on the cloth. Abatements were always made on faulty cloth. Attention to detail was meticulous. There was no attempt to squeeze a quick, easy profit. Calculations of returns were based not simply on securing an adequate percentage on capital employed but also on retaining the goodwill of customers. Whatever charges were made against the dubious practices of the Yorkshire clothiers, no such charge can be levelled at the Leeds merchants on the basis of Ibbetson's accounts. The business was run on such thoroughly established principles that Ibbetson could depute the management to his junior partners and on occasions his chief cloth-dresser, and absent himself for weeks on end in Bath and the country. It was small wonder that the life of a well-established merchant was considered inferior only to that of the country gentleman.

(VI)

Finally, before we discuss the profits made in the eighteenth century woollen trade, something should be said of the home merchant and cloth factor. In his description of the Leeds coloured cloth market Defoe divided the buyers into three categories, the home merchant, the factor and the export merchant. His account of the inland merchants in the days before improvements in transportation is a good one.

There are . . . a set of travelling merchants in Leeds, who go all over England with droves of pack horses, and to all the fairs and market towns over the whole island, I think I may say none excepted. Here they supply, not the common people by retail, which would denominate them pedlars indeed, but they supply the shops by wholesale or whole pieces, and not only so, but give large credit too, so that they are really travelling merchants, and as such they sell a very great quantity of goods, 'tis ordinary for one of these men to carry a thousand pounds value of cloth with them at a time, and having sold it at the fairs or towns where they go, they send their horses back for as much more, and is very often in a summer for they chuse to travel in the summer, and perhaps towards the winter time, tho' as little in winter as they can, because of the badness of the roads.[32]

In fact the inland traders were always less numerous than the export merchants in Leeds. The town was famed as the principal centre for the manufacture and marketing of Yorkshire broad cloth which was almost entirely exported, whilst the home merchants dealt chiefly in kerseys and worsted stuffs. Thomas Hill reckoned in 1782 that there were 39 houses engaged solely in the export trade, 18 in the inland markets and 16 who combined both. Of a total of £1,011,000 worth of cloth which passed through the Leeds merchants' hands in 1781 the home trade accounted for only £273,000 in value. These home firms were much smaller than the export houses save for two or three large firms dealing entirely in worsteds like Clapham and Hall, William Thompson and Rayner, Dawson and Co.[33] With these three exceptions the inland traders employed a much smaller capital than the export houses, although there is ample evidence from the Lupton papers that their returns were neither larger nor more regular.

The home merchant himself, his partner or a traveller for the firm were obliged to visit customers, the small local dealers and shopkeepers, at least twice a year with patterns to solicit orders and collect accounts due. If Defoe's account is reliable, practices had changed very much by the late eighteenth century when goods, as in the export trade, were dispatched by land- and water-carriage on the receipt of orders. No inland merchant travelled with pack-horses by this time.

The importance of the factor in the Yorkshire woollen trade is difficult to estimate although his functions, through Professor Heaton's discovery of Joseph Holroyd's papers, are well known.[34] Holroyd, of Sowerby near Halifax, was executing commissions from London, Amsterdam and Rotterdam merchants to the extent of around £30,000 annually in the first decade of the eighteenth century. On these commissions he received a small percentage, $1-1\frac{1}{2}$%, for the goods he shipped. Defoe mentioned factors buying in the markets at Leeds on behalf of London shop-keepers and merchants who supplied London itself, the plantations, the Baltic and Russian trades, although he said nothing of men like Holroyd buying directly for merchants in Holland.[35] After the 1720's there is little evidence of factors buying goods on commission for foreign merchants. The very survival of Holroyd's letters has perhaps served to give undue prominence to the factor's position. It was obviously against the interests of the Yorkshire merchants exporting abroad to allow these men to buy large quantities on low commission. The stagnation of the German and Dutch markets after 1710 curtailed the factor's activities and they never found the same footing in the south European trade. London merchants increasingly purchased their northern cloths either directly from the manufacturer or from the West Riding merchants. The latter scoured the Yorkshire markets for suitable cloths for their London brethren in return for a small profit and quick settlement of accounts. Certainly by the 1780's, when the first directories were published, the cloth factor had disappeared. His functions, even in the Halifax area where he had been most active, had been assumed by cloth merchants resident in Wakefield, Leeds and Halifax.

(VII)
By far the most valuable evidence of actual profits to be made in the woollen trade comes again from the accounts of Sir Henry Ibbetson and John Koster, whose returns cover the years 1749–60. In these 12 years profits of £12,091 were paid into the partners' accounts. For the first three years the debit side of Ibbetson's own account is missing, but in the following nine years profits as a percentage of capital invested were 8·2%. Over the entire period profits averaged 4·8% on total turnover (see Table 6). The decade as far as it concerned the Leeds trade was not a good one. Sales slumped and returns were so slow in 1753 that the accounts went unbalanced. Trade appears to have recovered in 1756 and 1759–60 to some extent however. Furthermore it must be remembered that Ibbetson was deliberately running the firm down. Before he admitted Koster to the partnership in 1748 his capital was in the region of £20,000 since he drew at least £10,000 out of the firm in the four years before 1752. His second deed of partnership with Koster in 1755 showed that his personal interest in the firm was fast diminishing.

Returns for the decade fluctuate too wildly to suggest that merchants aimed at a profit margin similar to that secured by Ibbetson in the 1750's. No two years in the export trade were ever alike. Ibbetson's profit in 1755 was only £414, in 1756 it had risen to £1,471. There is no apparent reason for this dramatic up-turn. The famous Lisbon earthquake of November 1755 seems to have done Ibbetson nothing but good. As slow returns and bad debts were endemic in the export trade, even the most cautious merchants' profit calculations were frequently upset. Therefore they probably aimed rather above the profits returned by Ibbetson. A gross profit of 12–15% on their capital, secured by a safe 5% on their sales, would satisfy even the

Table 6   Profit and loss of Ibbetson and Koster, 1749–60a

Year ending 31 Dec.	Capital		Total profits added to partners' accounts	Profit as % of capital	Annual remittances
	Ibbetson	Koster			
1749	⎫	1945	1197	15·1 ⎫	26,164
1750	⎬b	2016	1263	15·3 ⎬c	24,257
1751	⎭	1986	942	11·8 ⎭	25,741
1752	7937	2031	900	9·0	21,924
1753	7062	1750	d		17,868
1754	8332	1701	1534	17·0	23,064
1755	7003	2471	414	4·4	23,559
1756	8129	2919	1471	14·6	25,616
1757	9089	2757	767	6·5	20,945
1758	8268	2952	1101	9·7	20,031
1759 ⎱ June 1760 ⎰	8971	3318	2502	10·0	41,170

a Figures to the nearest £. The year's profit was calculated by adding the profit and loss of four distinct accounts: the 'accompt of merchandize'; 'charges of merchandize' (i.e. profits on charges made to customers for postage, packing etc.); 'accompt of provision'; 'Insurance accompt'. The second and fourth categories were much less important than the other two. The 'provision accompt' appears to have been a 2% charge on all invoices dispatched (see 'provision' in *Oxford English Dictionary*). The actual profits on the cloth were entered in the 'accompt of merchandize'. This method allowed a calculation to be made of the profit and loss of each transaction.

b Debit side of his account missing.

c Calculated on Koster's capital alone. Profits were shared in the ratio 3 : 1, 1749–55; 2 : 1, 1756–60.

d No profit declared.

e Figures combined in all accounts.

merchant who had borrowed money to enter the industry. In a rare revelation Thomas Wolrich reckoned in 1772 that a merchant estimated a profit of between 6*d.* and 7*d.* on cloth sold at 5–6*s.* a yard. But since his statement was a public one it was probably an underestimate for the reckonings of the majority of merchants.

Conditions of both manufacture and trade changed so rapidly after 1780 that a collation of the profit of the merchant-manufacturer and the pre-1780 merchant can be misleading. Intense competition in the unsettled years after 1800 cut profit margins considerably. What became the practice of securing a small profit on a large capital was in contrast with the traditional merchants' *modus operandi* of returning a reasonably large profit on a relatively small capital.

In fact the lament of small profit margins and intense competition amongst the West Riding merchants themselves and with their Norwich and West Country counterparts was one constantly heard. And by twentieth-century standards profits were generally small although they fluctuated wildly from year to year. In the Yorkshire woollen trade they appear to have been rather higher on average than the 4–5% on capital that merchants trading to the Levant received. But then the Leeds merchants never realised the killings that could be made by the Levant and East India merchants when import prices rose sharply in London.[36] Altogether profits in the woollen trade were not excessive, and although the Leeds merchants aimed at something above Adam Smith's 'good, moderate, reasonable profit' this only offset the years of poor returns.

In 1781 Hill reckoned that there were 19 firms that had sales of £20,000 and upwards during the year. During more normal trading conditions turnover was at least 50% higher and they would anticipate profits in the region of £1,500 and above, although it should be remembered that these amounts were usually divided amongst two or three partners. Other firms at the top of this group returned more spectacular dividends. With a capital of £40,000 in 1785 Wormald, Fountain and Gott could expect to share profits of around £4,000 a year. In the first 40 years of the century William Milner secured a similar sum on his annual turnover of £80,000. When William Denison died in 1782 the *Mercury* reckoned 'he had acquired by diligent and unwearied attention to business the immense fortune of £700,000'.[37] Men like Denison and Milner were very wealthy even by the standards of the largest London merchants.

Of course the larger merchants did not rely solely on profits from the woollen trade for their income. They began business with adequate resources and they inherited and acquired considerable property. As William Denison admitted to the Duke of Newcastle when he wrote about the land-tax:

My security I believe will be acknowledged superior to that of any other house here. Although it is indecent for a Merchant to brag of his circumstances I must beg leave to tell you as my Confidential friend that my annual Income is upwards of £— in land and the Funds besides a Capital in Trade.[38]

Land provided the merchants' most important additional source of income. In 1742, 23 merchants owned property in the township alone valued—on the very low assessment of the poor-rate officers—at over £80 per annum. The capital value of these 23 estates was upwards of £7,000 each. Merchants also owned property in the out-township of

Leeds parish and the county ranging from Denison's several thousand acres in four counties downwards. Thomas Kitchingman's rentals were around £700 in the 1720's. Even a small merchant like Joshua Hartley, when he went bankrupt in 1773, could fall back upon a small 332-acre estate that he owned in the West Riding.[39]

Purchases of government securities were the next most popular form of investment. Walter Stanhope and Sir Henry Ibbetson both had holdings in the funds in the 1750's, and in this way they were typical of many merchants. The tendency to increase purchases in these securities became marked towards the end of the century. Mathew Rhodes purchased £12,500 worth of 3% consols in 1796–8; his brother Abraham invested £33,600 in the same fund in 1805. Even Nathan Rider, a Mabgate clothier, left £2,000 in 3% consols when he died in 1813.[40] Before the great issues of foreign loans and railway stock, government securities were far the most convenient and secure short-term form of investment. Money placed out in canals and turn-pikes provided another popular form of income, whilst a minority of merchants advanced capital for banking and industrial ventures. But however varied the merchant's source of income might appear, it was usually derived from profits in the woollen trade well-invested by himself and often his forefathers also.

The incomes of the small home and export merchants were much smaller than those of the leading export merchants who derived theirs from a range of investments, besides profits in trade. In 1781 there were 32 firms with an annual turnover of less than £10,000 that provided the partners in these houses with an income, on average, of probably no more than £300 or £400. Merchant incomes, like those of the landed gentry, showed great variations, even in a provincial community like Leeds. They differed from the £100 acquired by the smallest home merchant to the total income of William Denison which was not far short of £10,000 yearly.

How do these figures compare with national estimates of merchant incomes during the eighteenth century? Gregory King in 1688 reckoned that there were 8,000 merchants 'by land' whose income averaged £200, and 2,000 'by sea' whose earnings were £400 each. Joseph Massie in 1759 estimated that there were 13,000 merchant families in England.[41] He split the group into three categories: 1,000 earned £600 per annum; 2,000, £400 and 10,000, £200. In Leeds a similar picture emerges. The number of merchants grew by about the same ratio and there is little evidence that capital requirements and profits grew appreciably before 1780. The majority—perhaps two-thirds—of the Leeds merchants fit into Massie's income brackets if their profits

from trade alone are considered. Income from property and investments would push some of those at the top of this bracket beyond
Massie's highest average figure. The other third's total earnings were
appreciably higher than £600 yearly. These men were for the most
part to be found in the corporation, although there was also a sprinkling of leading Dissenters in this group. In comparison with every
other occupation merchanting provided a handsome livelihood. By
comparison Massie reckoned that the average earnings of 'superior'
clergy, and of the 12,000 gentlemen professing the law, were only
£100. It was these large incomes that gave the principal merchants
their status in both town and country. If the nobleman could jog
along on £10,000 a year, the provincial merchant could manage very
comfortably before 1780 with £1,000 a year. That celebrated diarist
Parson Woodforde kept five servants and a princely table in the last
quarter of the century on less than £400 a year.[42]

Profits made in woollen-merchanting were then very variable. The
returns of some merchants were so remunerative that they and their
descendants were enabled to join the ranks of the wealthier country
gentry. Every merchant in town envied the careers of Sir Henry
Ibbetson and William Denison. Yet the fate of merchants like Thomas
Medhurst showed that excessive expenditure of time and money on
rural pursuits and inattention to the details of business and unsound
commercial practices could be disastrous. In fact the majority of
merchants steered a middle-of-the-way course. Through hard work
they secured an ample income that compared very favourably with
those of the small landed gentry and the wealthy clergymen.

Notes to Chapter 4
    [1] J. Mawman, *An Excursion to the Highlands of Scotland and the English Lakes*
(1805) pp. 33–4; *L.I.* 15 Aug. 1780.
    [2] Denison MSS. De/H46, W. Denison to J. Wilkinson, jun., 13 Feb., 6 March
1779.
    [3] M. Postlethwayt, *op. cit.*, see under 'merchants'.
    [4] Appendix A, Crump, 319.
    [5] DB/39 Armitage-Rhodes MSS.; Lupton MSS.
    [6] J. Mawman, *op. cit.*, p. 36; Lupton MSS. and Spencer-Stanhope MSS. 1162.
    [7] R. Davis, *Aleppo and Devonshire Square* (1967), p. 69.
    [8] Gott MSS.; Crump, 194–5; H. Heaton, 'Benjamin Gott and the industrial
revolution in Yorkshire', *Ec.H.R.*, III (1931), 45–66; *L.M.* 2 Jan. 1819; Denison
MSS. De/H47; DB/39 Armitage-Rhodes MSS.
    [9] e.g., *L.M.* 20 Aug. 1798; 29 Sept. 1804; 14 June 1806; 23 March 1811;
19 Oct. 1816; 11 March 1820; *L.I.* 25 June 1804; 9 Nov. 1811.
    [10] For an example of a family (Rhodes) who made a rapid advance after 1783
see R. G. Wilson, 'Fortunes of a Leeds merchant house', *Business History*, X (1967).
    [11] Lupton MSS. See especially the material relating to Edward Gilyard.
    [12] *L.M.* 28 Jan. 1804.

[13] *L.M.* 2 Jan. 1796; Micklethwaite MSS. (John Ryland's Library), English MSS. 1138/21–37. Compare R. G. Wilson, 'Fortunes of a Leeds merchant house'.

[14] S. Brooke, 'Notes on the Hall family of Stumperlow and Leeds', *Thors. Soc.*, part 4 (1953), 309–51.

[15] *L.I.* 12 April 1757; *L.M.* 9 Dec. 1809.

[16] LO/RB, poor-rate assessment, 2 May 1754; Spencer-Stanhope MSS. 2719; *Ducatus*, 5n.

[17] Lupton MSS. Account-books of Ibbetson and Koster, extracted from 'Merchandize Accompts'.

[18] *ibid.* This figure includes dyeing also, although this item appears to have been only about 10% of the total figure.

[19] Thoresby MSS. Correspondence, 12 April 1708.

[20] *L.I.* 31 Dec. 1754; 'A List of Voluntary subscribers . . . for the Defence of the County of York begun at Bishopthorpe 23 September 1745'. Besides Ibbetson's dressers Jeremiah Dixon's contributed 40 gns, Francis Milner's £20 and Mr. Denison's 10 gns Ibbetson and Dixon made large personal subscriptions. There was doubtless a connection between these and their desire to retain the deputy-receiverships of the land-tax for East Yorkshire which they then held.

[21] *L.M.* 9 April 1751.

[22] 1806 Report, 250, 374–5; *P.P.* 1802–3 (95) vii, 227; *L.M.* 29 Jan., 5 Feb. 1803; J. Bigland, *A Topographical and Historical Description of the County of York* (1812), p. 789.

[23] Crump, 37, 307.

[24] Denison MSS. De/H46, W. Denison to J. Simpson, 13 Dec. 1780.

[25] D. Defoe, *op. cit.*, II, pp. 205–6.

[26] *P.P.*, 1821 (437) vi, 51.

[27] *ibid.*, 63–70; Lupton MSS. Letter-book of Ibbetson and Koster, 1 April 1761.

[28] This section is based upon two volumes of accounts (1748–61), a letter-book (June 1760–June 1761), and a few stray papers which have survived in the Lupton MSS. William Lupton was Koster's executor, and the former's son filled the letter-book with copies of his own firm's letters, when there was a shortage of paper during the Napoleonic Wars. The account books were probably abbreviated and specially made up for Lupton since they include nothing of Ibbetson's own other extensive business interests. The year the letters cover was a momentous one for the firm: Koster died in the spring of 1760; Ibbetson was in poor health and died in June 1761. The management of the firm was deputed first to Lupton, their head cloth dresser, and after December 1760 to Ibbetson's cousin D'arcy Molyneux.

[29] The chief types of cloth the firm handled were kerseys, Leeds broad cloths (cloths, plains and coatings) and a whole range of worsteds (everlastings, amens, barragons, flannels, bays, tammies, serges and shalloons).

[30] 'Extracts from an Old Leeds Merchant's Memorandum Book: 1770–1786', *op. cit.*, 38; De/H46, W. Denison to J. Baumgartner, 20 March 1779; De/H47.

[31] *L.I.* 28 Oct. 1777; *L.M.* 21 Aug. 1781.

[32] D. Defoe, *op. cit.*, II, pp. 206–7. See also R. B. Westerfield, *The Middleman in English Business Particularly Between 1660–1760* (1916), pp. 313–8.

[33] See Appendix A, and J. James, *op. cit.*, pp. 311–13.

[34] Heaton, pp. 386–8, and especially his introduction to *The Letter Books of Joseph Holroyd and Sam Hill* (1914).

[35] D. Defoe, *op. cit.*, 206–7.

[36] R. Davis, *Aleppo and Devonshire Square*, pp. 222–50.

[37] *L.M.* 30 April 1782.

[38] Denison MSS. De/H46, 27 Feb. 1781. I have been unable to trace the letter itself, disclosing Denison's income, amongst the Newcastle papers in the British Museum and Nottingham University. The amount is not disclosed in Denison's letter copy-book.

[39] LO/RB, poor rate assessment for May 1742; DB 129/2; *L.M.* 14 Sept. 1773.

[40] DB/39 Armitage-Rhodes MSS; Lupton MSS.

[41] P. Mathias, 'The social structure in the eighteenth century: a calculation by Joseph Massie', *Ec.H.R.*, X (1957), 30–45.

[42] J. Beresford (ed.), *The Diary of a Country Parson* (1926), II, Introduction p. x.

5   *Expansion 1783–1806*

> Perseverance, industry and skill have seldom or ever failed to acquire not only competence but affluence. Thus a very preponderating portion of the rich manufacturers and traders of the district, consists of men who, much to their own honour, have risen by their own exertions and diligence from the most humble circumstances to ease and opulence.*

Now that marked changes in industrial output and technological invention are discovered to have occurred far back in the Middle Ages the term 'Industrial Revolution' has long lost much of the cogency it was once invested with. As far as the woollen industry itself was concerned it was never very applicable. Even in Yorkshire, the industry's most forward-looking sector, change came slowly and tended to follow innovations that had first taken place across the Pennines in Lancashire. And for a variety of reasons, part technical, part entrepreneurial and part change in fashion, the woollen manufacture in Yorkshire was some 20 years behind the worsted industry's assimilation of the great mechanical inventions. The gig-mill was first introduced in the 1750's and the fly-shuttle shortly afterwards and yet the power-loom did not entirely replace the hand-loom weaver until the 1870's. The shift from a purely domestic manufacture to complete factory production took almost 100 years.

It was the relative speed in the application of the technological inventions that delineated the two periods of greatest change. Between 1780 and 1800 the fly-shuttle, the scribbling, slubbing- and carding-machines and the spinning-jenny were all more or less absorbed within the framework of the domestic system. Efforts to combine the entire processes of large-scale manufacture with merchanting met with strong opposition. The progress towards a complete factory system was halted by uncertain conditions after 1800, the long post-war depression and the great financial crisis of 1825–6, but above all by the surprising adaptability of the domestic system to all the inventions with the exception of the power-loom. Improved prospects, however, after 1830 led to the rapid installation of the self-acting mule and power-loom—both technically perfected in the 1820's—and after the 1840's combing machinery in the worsted industry. In this chapter we must

* E. Parsons, *The . . . History of Leeds* (1834), ii, p. 208.

look at the implications for the merchant and clothier of the application of the first round of inventions between 1783 and 1806.

(I)

John Kay's fly-shuttle was known in Yorkshire by 1737, but it was not extensively used until the 1760's at the earliest. At first there was strong opposition from the clothiers. But neither their riots nor attempts to prove that it was 'detrimental to the Fabric and Manufacture of cloth' obscured the fact that it was too invaluable to cause a prolonged furore. Physically weaving became an easier task for the earlier method was hurtful to the clothiers' chests.[1] As far as the spinning-jenny was concerned there appears to have been little time lag between its invention and widespread use. Both it and the fly-shuttle were well known by the early 1780's.[2] Although the fly-shuttle halved the labour required in weaving broad cloth and enabled an increased output and the jenny quickly speeded up the hitherto slow spinning processes, the two inventions made not the slightest change in the organisation of the woollen industry. Since neither improved loom nor jenny was expensive and both were easily made the clothier was able to afford them and absorb them within his existing premises. A rapidly expanding home and export market after 1783 meant that neither invention caused operatives to become redundant.

It was Arkwright's adaptation of earlier inventions in the initial processes of manufacture—willeying, scribbling, carding and slubbing —which when introduced from the Lancashire cotton industry into Yorkshire in the late 1770's and early 1780's altered the structure of the West Riding woollen industry. At first scribbling-machinery was hand-operated, although a revolving 'gin' worked by a horse was soon adopted to drive them. The next stage—very quickly reached—saw the removal of the scribbler, carder and slubbing-billy into a mill driven by water power. Fulling-mills, always driven by water power, installed scribbling-machinery and most after 1785 combined both functions. To these mills the clothiers resorted with their wool to have the preparatory processes completed. They returned home with the slubbings, spun them on the jenny, wove their cloth and once more went to the mill to have it fulled.

At first sight it seems difficult to see that the extension of the fulling-mills' function to include the preparatory processes could alter the structure of the woollen industry. After all, the fulling-mill was a centuries-old institution, and that the clothier now took his wool there to be scribbled and slubbed at a few pence per pound simply seemed to add to its usefulness in the domestic system. As one observer noted in 1783 they had created no unemployment and: 'a clothier may as he did formerly, spend a fortnight or more in doing that which he may now get done in one day; and 'tis my poor opinion that a great part of our coarse wool could not have been made into cloth but for these machines'. The fulling–scribbling-mills spread rapidly especially in the Calder and Colne valleys. In 1786 it was reckoned there were 170 in an area extending 17 miles south-west of Leeds and that about the same number were to be found in the other West Riding clothing districts.[3] The increase in the number of cloth-searchers who measured the fulled cloth at the mills confirms that many new fulling–scribbling-mills came into operation after 1783; 48 full and part-time broad-cloth searchers found work in 1783, 85 in 1794; the establishment of narrow-cloth searchers grew from 68 to 105 during the same period.[4] With the installation of steam power in the largest scribbling-mills after 1792 their functions grew. Equally as important as the application of steam, however, was when the owners or lessees of the mills began to install a few jennies and occasionally cloth-looms. Neither were steam driven, but this assembly of machinery capable of executing all the stages of manufacture was the first step taken towards a complete factory system. The typical evolution of the woollen and worsted mill in the West Riding was not that which followed Gott's pattern—the scale of his enterprise was entirely exceptional before 1815—but that which grew from the fulling–scribbling-mill, installing a steam-engine to drive the fulling-stocks, billies, willeys, carding and scribbling-machines and then extending its premises to include a few jennies and looms to become the 'Complete Manufactory' of the war years. Of course not all the early West Riding mills developed in this fashion. Some always relied on outside hand-loom weavers, others included extensive dyeing facilities, and in the worsted industry the pivot of change was the establishment which installed jennies, for worsted yarn was hand combed (a process not mechanised successfully until the 1840's) not scribbled and carded. Many early mills seemed remarkably adaptable in producing either wool, worsted or cotton yarn as comparative profitability shifted and ownerships changed. The example of the technological achievements in the cotton industry was important. It was not simply that events in Lancashire were closely watched in the West Riding, but that the cotton industry itself swept westwards across the Pennines. The *Mercury* reported in 1802:

the rapid increase of Cotton Manufactories in the North of England has lately been almost incredible . . . so considerable has its progress been in Yorkshire, that the labouring poor in the western part of this Riding are at present principally employed in it. In the neighbourhood of Halifax, Huddersfield,

Bradford and even Dewsbury, several large Manufactories have lately been erected.[5]

Rapid technological advances in the cotton industry were closely followed, at least in the mechanisation of the preparatory processes, in the Yorkshire wool textile industries.

The question of the ownership of the early scribbling and spinning-mills is crucial to a discussion of the respective roles of the merchant and the clothier in the changes that took place in both the woollen and worsted industries before 1806. Who provided the capital for the introduction of the fly-shuttle, jenny, the scribbling-, carding- and slubbing-mills in the 25 years following 1783? Was it the Leeds and Wakefield merchants as is usually assumed? Mantoux was in little doubt. He saw that when the merchant became the employer of cloth-dressers and dyers, 'this was the first stage in the gradual transformation of commercial capital to industrial capital'. Dr. Hartwell gives weight to Mantoux's opinion when he writes: 'Not only did the merchants become manufacturers, but they did so on a large scale, and in the woollen industry, tended to concentrate the whole process of making cloth, from the raw material to the finished piece under one roof.' Professor Heaton maintained the process was double-edged:

These larger clothiers began to have their cloths finished and then set out to try to sell them, thus side-stepping the merchants. They sought to establish contacts, wholesale or retail with the buyers of finished cloth at home or abroad, or both. Some merchants, on the other hand, not content with buying in the halls or with ordering pieces privately, began to organise the production of cloth.[6]

But his emphasis has not always been consistent; in 1915 he maintained:

the new possibilities could be taken advantage of only by those men who had sufficient money to lay out in mill building, machines and steam-engines. The merchants had these supplies of available capital, but the small clothiers had not;

but 20 years later he argued: 'The textile industry was *the* land of opportunity for the energetic and ambitious man with little capital.'[7] The idea that change rested with the clothier who increased his capital by the application of the new inventions was most persuasively argued by an extremely knowledgeable local historian, W. B. Crump. He believed that the scribbling-mill was the pivot on which the entire changes in the structure of the woollen industry revolved:

The clothier owner was at once in the position to reap the benefit of the use of power-driven machinery and put out more wool to be spun and woven to his order. He might even put a few jennies and hand-looms into premises adjacent to his scribbling mill if he saw any reason for exercising closer super-vision. Other clothiers followed his example and sought a stream site where they could erect a small mill, mainly though not exclusively for the treatment of their own wool.[8]

Does the evidence support Crump rather than Mantoux? The answer is in general, yes. Heaton argued in his article 'Financing the Industrial Revolution' that several factors smoothed the path for the clothier. Firstly, capital expenditure in building and equipment was not neces-sarily heavy: mill space could be rented; a 40-spindle jenny cost £6 in 1792 and a big scribbling- or carding-engine £50. Secondly, a mill-owner could provide services for other clothiers so that he did not necessarily have high raw material costs. Lastly, the small mill was not at a great disadvantage in competing with a large rival especially before 1830. Specialisation allowed the small firm to operate efficiently. There are several additional points which further substantiate the line taken by Crump and Heaton in this essay. The scribbling-mill required a small circulating as well as a small fixed capital. Professor Pollard, citing Gott as an example, has suggested that 'the problem of finding capital was largely a problem of finding circulating capital'.[9] But Gott, whose ratio of fixed to circulating capital was 4:9 in 1801, considered himself to be primarily a merchant. The scribbling-miller, even if he manufactured some cloth himself, required circulating capital for rents, wages and interest payments only. His raw materials could be obtained from the wool-stapler and dry-salter on credit, and, if he did not allow those clothiers for whom he scribbled and fulled undue credit, he was guaranteed regular payments himself. He was able to sell his own manufactured cloth to the merchants on virtual cash terms. It was the stapler in the sale of wool and the merchants in the sale of the finished cloth who provided credit terms in the industry and who therefore required the largest amounts of circulating capital. Furthermore the early scribbling- and spinning-mills were very profitable ventures. A clothier could rapidly build up by the plough-back of profits a con-siderable capital which enabled him to extend his enterprise in both manufacturing and eventually in selling his cloth without the interven-tion of the merchants. When Walter Spencer-Stanhope proposed erecting a scribbling-mill on his Horsforth estate in 1784, a Leeds machine-maker estimated that an expenditure of £550 on building and machinery would return a 'neat' annual profit of £522. Of course these figures which took no account of the seasonal depression in the woollen trade were optimistic, but the profits declared by John Rogerson in his diary—he ran a scribbling-mill at Bramley—confirms that returns from these mills were good. His profits were £1,337 in 1812, a notoriously bad year, and when trade improved in the following year they had risen to £1,787. In December 1809 he reckoned, three years after the mill had opened, 'It costs (the Close, Dam, Houses and everything) £5,700 and rather better.' In another passage he reckoned that a mill with three fulling-stocks, three billies and three scribblers—a modest mill—would cost £24 14s. a week and leave £12 9s. 6d. profit 'recovering Nothing for Repairs'.[10]

But there are more general reasons for accepting Crump's thesis that change stemmed from the larger clothiers' mechanisation of the preparatory and spinning processes, than that the profits to be made in scribbling and spinning were good. The same progress was experienced in every area in both the woollen and worsted industry. Indeed it can be argued that structural changes in the wool textile industries during the 1780's occurred more rapidly around Halifax, Bradford and Huddersfield than they did in the commercial centres of Leeds and especially Wakefield. Already by 1786 there were 300 scribbling-mills in the West Riding, particularly concentrated in the Colne and Calder valleys. They spread rapidly down to 1815. Yet there were not more than 250 merchant firms in Halifax, Wakefield and Leeds, and the majority before 1815 never contemplated running a mill of any kind. Thus the scribbling- and spinning-mills were usually built by clothiers, often in partnerships amongst themselves or with others engaged in the ancillary trades of dyeing, cloth-dressing and dry-salting. Some of the early scribbling-mills to be met along the banks of the Calder and its tributary streams were owned by the large manufacturing merchants whom we have already met around Halifax. The transition of the large clothiers around Huddersfield, who were exploiting the trade in kerseymeres, into merchant-manufacturers was largely facilitated by their ownership of scribbling-mills in the area. Some landowners and a few merchants in Leeds and Wakefield had always owned fulling-mills and after 1783 good prospects had induced them to introduce scribbling machinery. Yet their owners did not tend to become cloth manufacturers. Thomas Lloyd, a leading merchant in Leeds, was typical of these owners. He bought Armley mills in 1788 and in the following year extended the fulling-stocks and corn grinding gear so that it became the largest fulling-mill in the country, 'allowed by all who have seen them to be built and finished upon an excellent construction, and supposed to be one of the most capital corn mills of its size in the Kingdom'.[11] But the management was deputed to servants. Lloyd, who ran the Volunteers Corps after 1794, lived the life of the complete country gentleman at Horsforth Hall and never dreamt of manufacturing a cloth in his life.

The result of the facts that large profits were to be made in the early mills and that technological developments on an entirely unprecedented scale were taking place in every sizeable village between Rochdale and Leeds, Keighley and Wakefield, in the 25 years after the end of the American war, was a rapid expansion of West Riding industry during these years. No figures exist to chart the courses of either the worsted, linen or cotton industries, but all moved faster than the traditional woollen industry itself. Nevertheless even in the latter growth was dramatic. Although developments were not quite so impressive as those Rostow traced in the expansion of cotton and iron industries in his analysis of that famous seminal period in British economic history, 1783–1802, they are sufficiently volatile to have considerably buttressed his thesis had he cared to look beyond the two industries which somewhat perilously prop his analysis. The statistics for the West Riding woollen industry are unambiguous. Production of broad cloths in the West Riding trebled between 1781 and 1800. The increase in the value of the lease of the Leeds–Bradford–Halifax turnpike, the main trunk-road of the wool textile area, from £852 to £3,500 between 1785 and 1800 and the jump in receipts on the Aire and Calder Navigation from £40,033 in 1782 to £150,268 in 1802 provides a good positive correlation with the broad-cloth figures.[12] Growth was due primarily to two factors. The stagnation of the traditional European export market was more than offset by the rapid expansion of the home and American markets between 1783 and 1806. It was a growth virtually without check during these years. Yet the implications of the mechanisation of the first stages of the wool textile industries were even more significant. The structure of the woollen industry especially had fundamentally changed little in the 200 years after 1570. The largest profits had always been reaped by the merchant, whereas the clothier had had little incentive, or indeed the means, to extend his manufacture. Suddenly the technical innovations gave every master clothier his chance. All could afford the jenny and broad-loom and many the scribbling- and carding-machines. The increased level of investment in the 1780's led to changes in productivity which amazed contemporaries and allowed the bolder innovators to return a fat entrepreneurial profit during this period of excellent trading conditions. Therefore the lead in events was taken not so much by the wealthiest merchants, the Denisons, Blayds, Cooksons and Milnes in Wakefield who had made the biggest fortunes over the past 100 years—their aims in life were very different—but with the small struggling merchant, the merchant-manufacturers of the Halifax area, and above all by the larger clothiers of Huddersfield, Bradford and the villages which stretched away south from Hunslet and Holbeck. It was their vision, their capacity for hard work, their ability to save which lifted the Yorkshire textile industry out of the rut of domestic manufacture on to the rails of nineteenth-century factory production.

(II)

Yet the view given above of the transformation of the Yorkshire woollen industry through the evolution of the scribbling- and spinning-mill to the first nascent factory completing all the stages of manufacture was not that always emphasised by contemporaries. A few perceptive observers noted the increase in the size of all the clothiers' establishments after the introduction of the fly-shuttle and especially the jenny in the 1780's. But the various parliamentary enquiries between 1794 and 1806 into the state of the Yorkshire woollen industry emphasised the clothiers' fears of the merchant turning manufacturer and threatening thereby to annihilate the domestic system. It is now proposed to examine more closely how real these threats were.

On the surface, especially between 1792 and 1797, the suspicion that the merchant would turn manufacturer seemed well grounded. It was the establishment of the Bean Ing factory by the young merchant Benjamin Gott—he was under 30—in 1792 which gave cause for great alarm throughout the West Riding. Although Gott's venture would have caused little stir in Lancashire, in the context of the woollen and worsted industry it was entirely exceptional. Crump wrote:

the boldness of Gott's conception of a factory in 1792 is perhaps without a parallel . . . other great mills, either in the woollen or the worsted industry, grew from very humble beginnings, or arose at a later period. But Bean Ing sprang out of nothing; it was an ideal, a dream of the new age of industrialism, materialised forthwith in bricks and iron, in steam and machinery.[13]

As the Commons committee investigating the woollen industry in 1806 discovered, however, there were other merchants who had become manufacturers. Pim Nevins, a Quaker merchant in Hunslet, claimed to have commenced manufacturing in 1779. Fisher and Nixon of Holbeck and John and Edward Brooke of Hunslet Lane built mills around the same time as Gott.[14] Fisher and the Brookes were small merchants, but like Gott they seem to have simultaneously installed jennies and looms as well as scribbling- and fulling-machinery so that, since they had long been finishing cloth, they now included every stage of manufacture under the roofs of their own mills. And, in the same month that Gott was installing his 40 h.p. Boulton and Watt engine, another well-known merchant partnership, Markland, Cookson

—he was a cousin of William Cookson—and Fawcett, ordered a large engine from the same firm for their Leeds mill which was variously described as a cotton, worsted twist and carpet factory.

In the broad-cloth area, where it was unknown for the merchant to manufacture, there was immediate consternation. Wormald and Gott, one of the largest and best known merchant houses in the West Riding, whose two founder partners had been mayors of Leeds, had begun manufacturing. That others, albeit smaller firms, like Fisher and Nixon's and the Brookes, should follow Gott's lead led the clothiers to believe that the Leeds merchants would all fast become factory-owners and swallow them up. The great factories already flourishing in Lancashire were very much in their minds. It was in vain that a correspondent in the *Intelligencer* wrote: 'To prove the reality of this danger [i.e. merchants becoming manufacturers] few arguments will be necessary, if it be supposed probable, or even possible that such a custom may soon be either universal or very general.' He pointed out that the profits of the manufacturer were very small, that the merchant had enough work and responsibility already and in any case he doubted if all the merchants had the capital necessary for such a large-scale undertaking as that embarked upon by Benjamin Gott.[15] And it is informative of the intentions of the generality of merchants in Leeds not to become clothmakers ·that when the scribbling-mills sprang up in the Colne and Calder valleys they decided to take steps to stop the functions of manufacturer and merchant becoming combined. Aikin related the story:

the success of these factories [*sic*] has been such to excite the jealousies of the Leeds merchants, who are accustomed to buy the same articles from the lower manufacturers at their cloth halls; and so aware were they of the danger of competition, that in 1794 a deputation was sent from thence to petition for an act to prevent any merchants from becoming a manufacturer; but on consideration the idea was dropped.[16]

They thought better of their proposed action for two reasons. Firstly, the clothiers were planning to discourage merchants becoming factory-owners by tightening up the apprenticeship laws which would have led to an acute labour shortage. But 1793 was no year for the merchants to be dictated to by the clothiers about their position in the industry. Therefore at a meeting of merchants in December resolutions were passed 'that the Practice of merchants becoming Manufacturers is not likely to encrease so as to diminish the number of Master Clothiers' and 'that the free exercise of Men's abilities is a Privelege which this County has long enjoyed, and to which it owes much of its

present Prosperity'.[17] The clothiers were now so alarmed at the merchants' advocacy of *laissez-faire* that they had recourse to Parliament. But
plans to devise a scheme for the Leeds cloth halls trustees to prevent
merchants becoming manufacturers were dropped in April 1794.[18]
Secondly, the merchants were not prepared to oppose changes in the
structure of the domestic industry because they themselves ran into
trouble with the cloth-workers. For the first time in the history of
the Yorkshire industry, in contrast with the endemic disputes between
the West Country clothiers and weavers, relationships seriously
deteriorated.

It was the introduction of the gig-mill and shearing-frame that
aroused the wrath of the cloth-workers. The gig-mill was a very simple
mechanism consisting of a revolving cylinder with rows of teasles set
in parallel holders on its surface. The cloth was passed over the teasles
by a couple of rollers on to which the cloth was wound and unwound.
Without modification the clumsy hand shears with which the cloth-
workers 'cropped' the raised cloth were now mounted on to a carriage
that allowed one man to operate two pairs of shears. The gig-mills and
shearing-frames threatened many croppers with immediate redundancy.
As early as 1806 many cloth-workers felt 'that the cropper's trade
will not, by and by, be worth following' and although there was no
agreement about the extent of unemployment caused by the shearing-
frame one man could do as much work as three or more had before its
introduction.[19]

The gig-mill's use was actually prohibited by an act of Edward VI,
but it had been quietly, if unlawfully, introduced from the West
Country into Yorkshire in the 1750's. D'arcy Molyneux saw one
working in Leeds in 1761, although he formed the opinion—like many
merchants on first sight—that they were only suitable for certain types
of cloth. In Halifax the gig-mills soon came into general use for dressing
coatings produced in the area, and after 1780 they gradually increased
in the Huddersfield area, until in 1802 there were half-a-dozen, some
of which were power driven.[20] In Leeds itself, by far the most important
finishing centre in the county, they made no progress although it was
well proved that they were superior in the dressing of fine cloths and
reduced finishing costs. The croppers were united in preventing their
introduction. Meetings of the Leeds merchants and letters in the press
lamented that the trade of Leeds must dwindle if the merchants were
not allowed to keep abreast of inventions in use in other parts of the
county, and pointed out that the scribbling-mill, fly-shuttle and jenny
had reduced manual labour by a third and yet contributed to increase
both wages and trade.[21] William Cookson was questioned closely in

1806 about the use of finishing machinery in Leeds. A member of the Committee enquired whether his hesitancy to install gig-mills and shearing frames into his dressing shops was 'from apprehension or from choice'. After relating how he had sent 1,000 cloths to Halifax and Huddersfield to be experimently dressed by gigs he continued:

> I certainly would send the finer cloths to be dressed by machinery, than if I lived anywhere else than where I do; I do not wish to breed disturbance, or breed disquiet as a magistrate, but I am convinced that the gentlemen, who do use machinery, are superior to me in dressing.[22]

Yet the cloth-workers were unmoved by either warnings or the quiet arguments of moderate men like William Cookson. When Johnsons of Holbeck installed a gig-mill in their finishing shops they were pulled down and totally destroyed one dark November night in 1799.[23] The croppers through their well organised union—'the Institution'— were determined to enforce the apprenticeship laws against the merchants. They threatened strike action if the merchant employed a journeyman who was neither a member of the croppers' union nor who had served a legal apprenticeship. But behind the croppers' façade of resisting the introduction of shearing frames by strictly enforcing the apprenticeship laws was concealed the threat of redundancy, their own diminished status and a profound distrust of changes that had taken place since the 1780's. Their skill, unity and absolute control of the finishing processes gave them a voice in affairs that was quite disproportionate to their numbers.[24]

In the summer of 1802 Benjamin Gott decided to call the croppers' bluff. When he engaged two croppers above the legal minimum age for apprenticeship (14), his whole finishing department walked out. At a meeting of merchants to discuss the 'most effectual means of preventing illegal Combinations amongst their workmen', arising out of the strike in Gott's dressing shops, it was maintained that it was perfectly legal to take apprentices above the age of 14 years. The 88 firms who signed the resolutions agreed to resist all combinations and:

> . . . that if the workmen shall turn out or refuse to work with any master, in consequence of these Resolutions, we . . . hereby agree to make the names of such Workmen public, by a Circular Letter to each subscriber, and that we will severely assist any Merchant, whose Workmen shall so turn out or refuse to work by employing in our respective shops, if required, two or more workmen in the service of such merchants.

But the resistance of the croppers was not to be broken by 300 handbills and notices in the two Leeds newspapers printing these resolutions. In January an agreement was patched up between the merchants and croppers, when the former agreed that no apprentices should be taken above 15 years of age. It was not until 1816, however, that gig-mills were introduced into Leeds.[25] Previous attempts to do so were met by strikes and savage reprisals, especially during 1811–12. This successful resistance of the croppers to mechanised dressing in Leeds—their success around Huddersfield and Halifax was less complete hence the most serious outbreaks of Luddism in these areas in 1812—made many merchants hesitant to begin manufacturing. The finishing operations were troublesome enough, they argued, without concerning themselves with the entire manufacture.

But whatever the merchants' innermost thoughts about the changing industry and their lamentations that life and trade had both been easier before mechanisation they recognised the great steps forward made in the Yorkshire manufacture since the close of the American war. Although it was the intention of the majority never to make a yard of cloth in their lives they were not prepared to halt progress because the small clothiers and cloth-workers were apprehensive that their old way of life was threatened. Therefore all the merchants condoned the break-up of the domestic system of manufacture, and some, especially those who had entered the trade and done well after 1783, were prepared to take the lead in events to reap the profits of factory manufacture.

(III)
The opposition of the smaller clothiers and cloth-dressers to innovations in the industry appeared to be becoming so successful that the only way out of the impasse, for those bent on enlarging and modernising their manufactories, was recourse to Parliament for the repeal of the multitude of Acts that made such obstruction possible. A glance at the extraordinary expansion of the cotton industry reminded the large manufacturers and merchants of the disadvantages occasioned by the woollen laws. In the summer of 1796 the merchant-manufacturers of the Huddersfield district had met to discuss the necessity for application to Parliament for amending or replacing the Stamping Acts.[26] The enforcement of these acts, causing bottle-necks in production at the fulling-mills and insisting on standard cloth widths, were an old area of contention. Now the larger manufacturers wished to remove those laws, which protected the artisans' rights within the domestic system, and whose rigid application would have threatened the growth of the factory system.

The next move came from an unexpected quarter. During the ummer of 1802 there were serious riots in the West Country against the

s

introduction of both the fly-shuttle and the gig-mill, and in December 'several persons concerned in the Woollen Trade and Manufactories within the counties of Somerset, Wiltshire and Gloucester' petitioned that the existing statutes in force for the woollen industry 'should be altered, amended or wholly repealed'. The eventual Bill sought to suspend proceedings emanating from the woollen laws for a short probationary period. Although it passed quickly through the Commons, the House of Lords agreed that further consideration of amendments should be adjourned for three months. In the spring of the following year the controversy was extended to Yorkshire, when the West Riding cloth-dressers appealed against the renewed efforts of the West Country clothiers to secure their Bill, and the merchants and manufacturers of Halifax and Huddersfield petitioned to have the Bill 'extended to the County of York, if not the manufacture at large'. Soon a second round of petitions from Yorkshire sought that a Bill be produced to secure the repeal of the entire collection of laws relating to the woollen industry. There were, in fact, therefore, two Bills in Parliament at the same time: one sought to suspend all proceedings under the woollen laws until 1 July 1804 and the other to repeal all the Acts concerning the woollen manufacture. The first was passed in July. The second met with defeat.[27]

Early in 1804 the Yorkshire clothiers petitioned Parliament that the great increase in production and the introduction of machinery necessitated a new Act to regulate the industry. In their evidence they expressed their desire to see the apprenticeship laws tightened up and the number of looms gathered in one building restricted. After the second reading of their Bill, which would have imposed severe restrictions on the size of manufacturing units, was deferred several times it was eventually dropped. In the following year a second attempt by the small clothiers and cloth-dressers of the West Riding and West Country to reinforce the Tudor Acts, especially the one—in fact never enforced —which limited the number of looms installed under one roof, failed.[28]

Yet as in 1803 a Bill to suspend proceedings under the woollen laws for 12 months was quickly hurried through Parliament in 1804. This procedure was revived annually until 1809 when the most controversial of the Acts concerning the woollen industry were repealed. It seemed that this expensive, see-saw struggle between the large manufacturers on the one hand and the cloth-workers and small clothiers on the other was interminable. Out of this festering of perpetual disquiet that surrounded the argument about mechanisation and the impending collapse of the old system to which the small master and journeyman was entirely attached, grew the sore of Luddism. Only in 1806, when the Gloucestershire weavers complained that the large manufacturers promised each year to procure a Bill for the general revision of the laws and then merely rush through a temporary Suspension Bill, did the Commons set up a Select Committee in March 'to consider the state of the Woollen Manufacture of England'.[29] At last Parliament appeared to be making some attempt to sort out the mound of accumulated law and settle the claims of both interests.

The Committee was distinguished by the progressive economic views of its members. Several members had a long and close knowledge of at least the Yorkshire woollen industry: Sir James Graham had married a Leeds merchant heiress; Henry Lascelles had many friends in the town corporation; Wilberforce, who actually wrote the report, was well known to the merchant community and a close friend of William Cookson; Walter Spencer-Stanhope was the son of a Leeds merchant. Recognising the considerable merits of domestic manufacture the committee nevertheless came down firmly in favour of the system of factory production. The woollen industry could only prosper in a free atmosphere:

the rapid and prodigious increase of late years in the Manufacture and Commerce of this Country is universally known, as well as the effects of that increase on our Revenue and National Strength; and in considering the immediate causes of that Augmentation, it will appear that under the favour of Providence, it is principally to be ascribed to the general spirit of enterprise and industry among a free and enlightened People, left to the unrestrained exercise of their talents in the employment of a vast capital; pushing to the utmost the principle of the division of labour, calling on all the resources of scientific research and mechanical ingenuity.[30]

The report divided the 70 laws relating to the woollen manufacture into three categories: those which regulated the conduct of masters and labourers and prevented frauds and embezzlement; those which prevented the exportation of machinery and materials; and those which controlled the making and selling of cloth and prohibiting the use of certain machines like the gig-mill and the law of Philip and Mary's reign that limited the number of looms to be worked in one house. The committee recommended that the first and second classes should be enforced, and the third—save that cloth should be exported only in a finished state—repealed.[31]

It was a bold and not entirely consistent attempt to sort out the vast mass of law that had accumulated over five centuries in the statute book. Parliament had hedged issues for four years. Now the Committee, listening largely to merchants and big manufacturers, and thoroughly alarmed by disclosures about the croppers' trade union, produced

H

a report that was anathema to the small clothiers and cloth workers. Many of their spokesmen made confused witnesses under the pressure of interrogation of confirmed *laissez-faire* members like Henry Lascelles (see p. 169). The committee maintained that the domestic system, already partly undermined, could not be buttressed by the restrictive laws the clothiers would have them enforce. And the old system, they believed, would not in any case collapse quickly. The recommendations proved to be too strong for a further committee to accept in 1807, and it was not until the following summer when a third committee was appointed, that the report was adopted. Then all its recommendations, including the more controversial clauses of the apprenticeship act, were conceded.[32] In June 1809 the Woollen Manufacturers Bill embodying the changes finally passed into law.

The minutes of evidence published in the 1806 report, and to a lesser extent those recorded in reports made during the previous four years of Parliamentary agitation,[33] provide an invaluable review of the great changes taking place within the woollen industry in the preceding generation and isolate the position of the three major groups affected by the transition from domestic to factory production— the croppers, the clothiers and the merchants. Since the croppers' union of not far short of 5,000 men was almost 100% effective and links were quickly proved with a similar movement in the West Country, the committee was entirely hostile to the croppers' case. It exposed their threats to burn down mills where the gig and shearing-frame were used; it deplored their attempts to lever up wages; it emphasised the political danger of their union. No chance was lost to underline the inconveniences the merchants were subjected to by the croppers' hostility.[34]

In a discussion of the steps towards a factory system the evidence of the clothiers and merchants is more informative. The croppers' unity in opposing change was not shared by the clothiers for the reports revealed two types of manufacturer. There were those small clothiers in the broad-cloth area, often driven out of Leeds by recent high land prices and increasing rents. They had absorbed the spring-shuttle and spinning-jenny into their premises, and they had accepted the value of the scribbling-mill in completing the preparatory processes of manufacture. But beyond this they would not go for they were utterly opposed to the large factories. Robert Cookson, a Holbeck clothier, stated the small clothier's position clearly:

the use of which machinery [scribbling-mills] in the preparatory processes of the raw material, is conceived by the Master Clothiers . . . to be useful in carrying on the trade; but the collecting of looms in large manufactories, where the raw material goes through the preparatory processes, which is becoming very prevalent, will, if not restrained, tend to destroy the domestic system.

Only if the laws were enforced, Cookson reckoned, would it be possible 'to prevent large Manufacturers . . . from swallowing up and totally annihilating the domestic trade'.[35] John Ellis, an Armley clothier, thought there were about 3,500 master clothiers in a similar position to him and Robert Cookson each employing on average eight to ten journeymen. On the other hand there was a small proportion of large clothiers in the worsted and fancy cloth trades, who wanted all restrictions removed. James Walker of Wortley was typical of those men who abounded around Bradford, Halifax and Huddersfield. An ordinary clothier in 1780, he had prospered during the following decade. In 1793 he installed a 20 h.p. Boulton and Watt engine in the slubbing- and scribbling-mills that were the base of his success. By 1806 he was 'half a factory man' employing, according to one of his employees, 100 workers in his own premises and 30 out. Already Walker was finishing his own cloths and selling them independently of the merchants when possible, and he was pleased to state that these direct orders were increasing yearly.[36] It was with men like Walker, already embryonic factory merchant-manufacturers, that the future of the woollen, and, especially the worsted industry lay. They pioneered power-spinning and weaving after 1826 and built the great factories of the early Victorian age.

Lastly the minutes of evidence revealed that the merchants were split into a similar grouping as that found amongst the manufacturers. The long-established merchants of Leeds and Wakefield represented by William Cookson and Jeremiah Naylor showed no inclination towards manufacturing. Gott and John and Edward Brook were examples that few wished to follow. Without any misrepresentation the committee could therefore state:

in fact, there are many merchants, of very large capitals and of the highest credit, who for several generations have gone on purchasing in the Halls, and some of this very description of Persons state . . . that they not only had no thoughts of setting up Factories themselves but that they believed many of those who had established them, were not greatly attached to that system, but only persisted in it because their Buildings and Machinery must otherwise be a dead weight upon their hands.

But the report also disclosed a large number of merchant-manufacturers in the Halifax and Huddersfield area, who combined all the stages of manufacture in their factories. John Edwards of Pye-Nest near Halifax had made 150–200 pieces weekly since 1760, which was over 30 years

before Gott began to make his own cloths. Law Atkinson of Bradley
Mills, Huddersfield, had become a merchant-manufacturer in the 1770's.
And the report made a distinction between the number of mills in the
Halifax and Huddersfield area established for many years and the four
or five factories recently built near Leeds. The tendency in Halifax in
the 1750's had been for the manufacturer to begin selling his cloth
without the intervention of the merchant. This trend continued to
prevail and in Halifax and Huddersfield the question of the merchant
commencing manufacturing did not arise. It was significant that the
agitation after 1800 for the repeal of the woollen laws came from this
area. When John Edwards said, 'I think they ought all to be done
away entirely, all restrictions upon Trade; I do not see the utility of
them: every manufacturer will make his goods fit for the market', he
was speaking on behalf of these large merchant-manufacturers.[37]
The Leeds and Wakefield merchants were very quiet throughout
the whole unrest: but then their dealings with the clothiers had been
going on for over 200 years. Edwards and his like knew no such tradition.

The most significant changes towards a complete factory system
were therefore taking place around Huddersfield, Bradford and Halifax.
Those clothiers who owned scribbling-mills became large-scale manufacturers and eventual merchants.[38] Even the fly-shuttle and jenny
altered the size of the clothiers' establishments. One witness reckoned
the large manufactories had been 'gradually increasing ever since the
spring-shuttle came up' and another maintained that in the same period
since 1760 the average clothier had increased his output by at least five
times.[39] The years between 1783 and 1795, before the great inflation
set in, were looked on as a halcyon period by those clothiers giving
evidence in 1806. Capital investment in the new machinery and mills
came almost entirely from profits accumulated in manufacturing during
these years. The contribution of those merchants who had made their
fortunes in commerce through the preceding century has been greatly
over-estimated. Certainly the investment of the Leeds and Wakefield
merchants in these early important developments was insignificant
when compared with the money pumped into the mills by the large
manufacturers of every clothing area in the county. When, as we shall
see in Chapter 7, merchants contemplated investment outside land and
government stocks it tended to be in transport securities and banking
ventures and, only exceptionally, on any scale directly in industry. The
aim of a wealthy merchant in life was to lead the life of a solid country
gentleman, not to spend 15 hours a day running the largest factory in
town. The merchant's daily round, especially when duties were effec-

tively delegated to a young junior partner, had always allowed him
to achieve some approximation to the landowner's ideal life: controlling a factory was as great a threat to his ease, as life on its shop-floor
was a sentence to the average journeyman in 1800. Furthermore it is
easy to overstate the significance of Benjamin Gott as a merchant
turned manufacturer. Gott was a man of bold initiative. He had few
imitators from amongst the merchant community and none at all on
his scale of production. Those merchants who contemplated manufacture after 1793 had usually come from another trade and only made
their money in the post-war boom. The long-established merchants
who had steadily amassed great fortunes during the eighteenth century
in the woollen trade spurned the idea that they should manufacture.
Not surprisingly, therefore, the committee in 1806 could conclude
that the fears of a total factory system engendered by three or four
factories around Leeds and the movement of many clothiers out of the
town and 'two or three populous Hamlets adjoining Leeds' were
largely exaggerated. The report continued that out of 300,000 broad
cloths and 166,000 narrows manufactured in the West Riding in 1805,
only 8,000 were produced in the factories near Leeds, and the committee inferred that there was no alarm 'lest the Halls should be deserted
and the generality of Merchants should set up Factories'.[40]

The committee's evidence is confirmed from two further sources.
The resolutions of a meeting held in August 1805 to consider action
against 400 journeymen clothiers in the Leeds area, who had turned
out because of their employers' objections to the croppers' union, was
signed by 54 'Principal Woollen Manufacturers of Leeds and the
neighbourhood'.[41] Of these 54 firms traced in the *Directory* for 1809,
only 9 were merchant-manufacturers. A mere 3, Gott's, Fisher and
Nixon's and J. and E. Brooke's, had any connection with cloth-merchanting in 1781. The majority were one-time clothiers like James
Walker of Wortley—who was included in the list—and who had
prospered after 1783. Furthermore the ledgers of the Jowetts, leading
wool-staplers in the town, who had dealings with every woollen
manufacturer in and around Leeds at one time or another after 1775,
emphasise two points we have been discussing.[42] Firstly, they show
that before 1815 Leeds township itself was not an important centre of
manufacture and that few merchants were involved in that side of the
trade. Secondly, those manufacturers on a large scale in Leeds and its
vicinity were frequently once clothiers: David Dunderdale, who had
a woollen factory at Woodhouse Carr, and the Willans, the largest
manufacturers in Hunslet, were both one-time clothiers. The Nusseys
and David Farrer were dyers and Jeremiah and Robert Glover former

tobacconists. Through the pages of their accounts can be traced the growth of these men from small beginnings in the 1770's until after 1795 when they had become semi-factory-owners.

(IV)

The few factories that were established in 1806 were still very much a novelty in the wool textile industries. Even including scribbling, spinning- and finishing-mills, which did not often employ more than a score or two of men, calculations about the increased size of manufacturing establishments are not very impressive. As Professor Rimmer has shown, in Leeds, except for a handful of large factories, business units did not noticeably increase in size until after 1840.[43] Admittedly the woollen industry always lagged behind the mechanisation of the cotton and worsted industries. Nevertheless the changes that took place down to 1806 should not be dismissed in an attempt to debunk the notion of an 'Industrial Revolution'. Contemporaries believed that innovations in the generation after 1783 meant the destruction of the old organisation of the woollen and worsted industries which had depended upon the separation of the merchants' and clothiers' functions. Now the growth of the cloth-makers' output, the tendency to by-pass the cloth halls, the introduction of looms into the scribbling- and spinning-mills, all threatened the independence of the small clothier, menacing a freedom which was believed to be at the very centre of the success of the Yorkshire wool textile industries. But the threat was not simply an economic one. The new machinery was the basis of new social relationships. As many observers noted industrialism brought an increase in the division between master and man. Previously the merchants' connections with the clothiers had not been close. Because they never produced cloth they did not threaten the independent existence of the master clothier. There was a wide division of wealth. But the clothiers were left in their work to their own devices and as small masters they enjoyed considerable status in their own village community. Now the merchants stood aside to watch a new breed of masters, men without their traditional obligations and authority, who built their mills across the county. Wealthy mill-owners gratuitously doled out the recipe of their success. Writers like Edward Parsons in his *History of Leeds* captured their meaning and diction perfectly.

Perseverance, industry and skill have seldom or ever failed to acquire not only competence but affluence. Thus a very preponderating portion of the rich manufacturers and traders of the district, consists of men who, much to their honour, have risen by their own exertions and diligence from the most humble circumstances to ease and opulence.[44]

Mechanisation introduced a human lottery. Some men 'were raised by their own efforts' but the majority of workers in the textile industries saw the evolution of the factories undermining their old position in the industry. The process was by no means complete by 1806, but divisions in the industry were clearly defined and the merchant's old easy leadership of the industry was threatened.

Notes to Chapter 5

[1] *L.M.*, 29 May 1770; *P.P.* 1802–3 (95) vii, 285–6; 1806 Report, 166.

[2] *P.P.* 1802–3 (95) vii, 285.

[3] *L.M.*, 11 Nov. 1783; 13 June 1786. See also Crump, 17–24, and 'The diary of John Rogerson', printed in Crump, 59–166, which provides an excellent insight into the workings of a Bramley scribbling-mill for the years 1808–14.

[4] West Riding Quarter Sessions Order Books, 1783, 1794 (Wakefield County Record Office).

[5] *L.M.*, 2 Oct. 1802.

[6] P. Mantoux, *The Industrial Revolution in the Eighteenth Century* (1961 edition), p. 62; R. M. Hartwell, *The Yorkshire Woollen and Worsted Industries, 1800–1850*, unpublished Oxford University D.Phil. thesis (1955), p. 304; H. Heaton, 'The Yorkshire cloth traders in the United States, 1770–1840', p. 229.

[7] H. Heaton, 'The Leeds White Cloth Hall', *Thors. Soc.*, vol. 22 (1915), 131–71; 'Financing the Industrial Revolution', *Bulletin of the Business History Society*, XI (1937), 1–10.

[8] W. B. Crump and G. Ghorbal, *op. cit.*, p. 90.

[9] S. Pollard, 'Fixed capital in the Industrial Revolution in Britain', *J. Econ. Hist.*, XXIV (1964), 299–314.

[10] Spencer-Stanhope MSS.; Crump, 103, 108, 147, 160.

[11] *L.I.*, 5 Feb., 1788; 16 Nov. 1789; *L.M.*, 12 Jan. 1790.

[12] R. G. Wilson, 'Transport dues as Indices of Economic Growth', *Ec.H.R.* XIX (1966) 110–123.

[13] Crump, 255.

[14] 1806 Report, 71–3; *P.P.* 1816 (272) vi, 149–50. Nevins' premises were offered for sale several times—*L.M.*, 3 March 1804, gives a full description of an early factory in the woollen industry.

[15] *L.I.*, 21 Oct. 1793.

[16] J. Aikin, *op. cit.*, pp. 564–5. The story is repeated in J. H. Crabtree, *op. cit.*, p. 305.

[17] *L.I.*, 30 Dec. 1793.

[18] *C.J.*, XLIX, 275–6, 431–2, 496.

[19] 1806 Report, 284.

[20] Lupton MSS. Letter-book of Ibbetson and Koster, 11 March 1761; *P.P.* 1802–1803 (95) vii, 246.

[21] Crump, 317–19.

[22] 1806 Report, 366–372.

[23] *L.I.*, 6 Dec. 1799.

[24] For a full survey of the croppers' problems in these years see the 1806 Report; A. Aspinall, *The Early English Trade Unions* (1949), pp. 40–69; and especially E. P. Thompson, *op. cit.* (1968 edition), pp. 570–80, 595–9.

[25] *L.M.*, 2 Oct. 1802; *L.I.*, 4 Oct. 1802; Crump, 180; W. Hirst, *A History of the Woollen Trade during the Last Sixty Years* (1844), pp. 12–19.

[26] *L.M.*, 25 June, 9 July 1796.

[27] *C.J.*, LVIII, 75, 351, 375, 379, 386, 391–3, 884–9; *L.J.*, XLIV, 335–6, 354, 366.

[28] *C.J.*, LIX, 81, 226, 245, 295, 302; LX, 224, 235, 306–7, 339, 347.

[29] *C.J.*, LIX, 341, 346, 363; LXI, 45, 70, 136, 512.

[30] 1806 Report, 7.

[31] *ibid.*, 7–9; *C.J.*, LXIII, 344–7.

[32] *C.J.*, LXII, 24, 110, 228, 764; LXIII, 132, 344–7; *L.M.*, 28 May, 18 June, 2 July 1808.

[33] *P.P.* 1802–3 (71) v; 1802–3 (95) vii; 1803–4 (66) v.

[34] 1806 Report, 14–17 and the evidence especially of James Tate.

[35] *C.J.*, LIX, 226.

[36] 1806 Report, evidence of John Ellis, James Walker and William Child.

[37] *ibid.*, 9, 11, 220–1, 398–9, 401. See also *C.J.*, LVIII, 392; *P.P.* 1802–3 (95) vii, 371–80.

[38] Many members of this group gave evidence before various committees: the Walkers and Batesons of Wortley, Law Atkinson of Bradley Mill, the Brookes of Honley and Armitage Bridge and all the Halifax merchant-manufacturers. Besides the Reports and Minutes of Evidence of 1803 and 1806, see also *P.P.* 1821 (437) vi, Laws relating to the Stamping of Woollen Cloth; 1828 (515) viii, State of the British Wool Trade; 1833 (690) vi, Manufactures, Commerce and Shipping.

[39] 1806 Report, 126, 160.

[40] *ibid.*, 12.

[41] *L.M.*, 24 Aug.; *L.I.*, 2 Sept. 1805.

[42] Business Records of John Jowett and Son in the Brotherton Library (Leeds), Ledger Nos. 1–4 (1775–1824).

[43] W. G. Rimmer, 'The industrial profile of Leeds, 1740–1840', *Thors. Soc.*, vol. 50, part 2 (1967), 134–57.

[44] E. Parsons, *The Civil, Ecclesiastical, Literary, Commercial and Mercantile History of Leeds* (1834), II, p. 208. P. Gaskell in *The Manufacturing Population of England* (1833), pp. 53–4, gave an exactly parallel account of the rise of the cotton masters in Lancashire.

6   The causes of defection 1806–30

Brown, James (1758–1813), merchant in Leeds. Two sons: (1) *James* (1786–1845), D.L., J.P., merchant manufacturer, married daughter of another Leeds merchant, Mathew Rhodes. His son *James* (1814–1877), D.L., J.P., bought two Yorkshire estates, Copgrove and Rossington when he succeeded to his father's ample fortune. M.P. for Malton (1857–1875) and High Sheriff of Yorkshire. (2) *William* (1788–1855), J.P. Banker in Leeds and London. His only son left Leeds on marrying daughter of Sir Joseph Radcliffe Bart. of Rudding Park.*

The agitation that culminated in the 1806 Report marks the end of the first step taken towards a complete factory system. Not until the generation after the passing of the Great Reform Act was the final move made in this direction. For the intervening years were ones of difficult trade that slowed down developments in the textile industries. It is against this background of general uncertainty that the merchants' continued hesitancy to manufacture and desire to leave the trade entirely must be viewed.

The 20 years following 1782 had witnessed an unprecedented expansion in the Yorkshire woollen industry.[1] Although the decade after the outbreak of war with France was plagued by high prices and industrial unrest there was no slackening in foreign trade on which Leeds had always depended. The chief feature had been the growth of the American market: in 1772 the American colonies had imported 20% of England's woollen and worsted exports; by 1800 it absorbed double that proportion.[2] Even our exports of woollens to Portugal and Germany had revived. The handsome profits that no one denied were to be made in these years, were invested by the clothiers in scribbling-machines, jennies and a general expansion of their premises. Those realised by the merchants were channelled into their usual outgoings—land, government funds and good living.

The strong upward trend in activity after 1783 was broken when the bubble of prosperity burst in 1801. Thirty generally lean years followed. The four years after 1801, although they witnessed some recovery and a steady advance in the price of wool, saw trade becoming increasingly difficult. After the resumption of war in 1803 the German and Dutch markets were virtually closed and the slight recovery which took place after the 1802-3 depression relied heavily on contracts

* Burke's *Landed Gentry* (1875)

for army clothing and the U.S. market. Then in 1806 the Berlin Decrees and the Orders in Council resulted in Britain's exports being entirely recast. It was, however, impossible to switch at once to a completely transatlantic trade and a very severe recession occurred. In Leeds three small merchant houses collapsed in the autumn of 1807, providing a prelude to the failure of more important firms in the following years. In May 1808 Thomas Storey, 'one of the many who have severely suffered by the Continental disturbances', died in Amsterdam harassed by debt. Five months later report ran like fire amongst the clothiers that R. R. Bramley and William Cookson, two of the largest merchants in the town and both former mayors, had failed.[3] Both the entries in Rogerson's diary and the letters of William Lupton, the grandson of Sir Henry Ibbetson's chief cloth-dresser, lament the complete stagnation in the woollen industry in 1808. Lupton wrote to his brother-in-law John Luccock, who had been sent to South America to revive the firm's fortunes: 'We cannot expect any settled good trade untill the American business is settled or the Continent more opened. Some people already are adventuring to Spain, but it can only yet be a barter trade.'[4]

Nevertheless in spite of Lupton's disillusionment trade recovered more quickly than anyone believed possible. The price of wool was rising rapidly in the spring of 1809—always a good augury, for these price shifts provided the merchant with his most reliable indicator of market conditions. A brief respite during 1809-10 in the virtual prohibition of trade with the United States between 1808 and 1814 and the rapid opening up of the South American market by a number of Leeds men for the consignment of Yorkshire cloth provided the conditions for a short, sharp boom in 1809. Even the Mediterranean trade was briefly resumed. Returns, however, were disappointing from all markets. Abraham Rhodes complained to his partner in Rio de Janeiro: 'I am as poor as Job, I get nothing from America nor from you. I am obliged to lock up the shop for want of the needful.' Rhodes' experience was common, and the severe depression of 1810-12 the result.[5] The price of South Down wool fell from 36d. per pound in 1809 to 17d. in 1811. 'We are kept tolerably quiet only by the immense military force in the neighbourhood,' recalled William Lupton, during the disturbances throughout the clothing districts in 1811-12, when the croppers resorted to machine-breaking and mill-burning. The Orders in Council were repealed in June 1812. On the receipt of the news in Leeds 'more business was done in Woollens . . . than on any day for eight years past'. But recovery thereafter was slow. Trade with the United States was completely closed 1812-14 and the advance depended on the 'immense demand of our Armies and those of our allies'. In August 1814 Lupton reported: 'a very great demand for the Continent has caused coarse wool to advance to the highest prices that have been known. Bockings have risen 30s. per Piece and our markets are much cleared of low goods of every description.'[6]

Yet peace did not bring prosperity. By the early summer of 1815 Lupton reckoned the market to be at a critical stage; wool was 'actually at this moment higher than ever was known'. Trade with Portugal, however, was the worst Abraham Rhodes remembered, although he admitted: 'Our American trade is so large that if we had £30,000 more capital we could employ it.' All depended on the returns from the United States. They could not have been more disastrous. 'The state of trade is worse than ever I saw it,' observed William Lupton in May 1816, 'and bankruptcies more numerous.' Not until August 1817 could he report to John Luccock:

Trade here seems to be improving a little—wool of all kinds is rather upon the advance—the stocks are small—a considerable demand for low woollens for Germany—the harvest is promising, and we look for good home trade as soon as the prices of corn are sufficiently reduced to allow our manufacturers to spare anything from the more pressing demands of their families.[7]

As in 1815 a permanent advance depended almost entirely on the American trade. Wool prices continued to rise during the summer of 1818, but yet again news of failures in the U.S.A., already reaching England, proved to be the harbinger of depression at home. Throughout 1819 Lupton was lamenting the consequences that had attended those too far committed in the American market. By early 1820 he thought: 'the glut on your side must soon be over, for the ruinous prices have nearly finished all the consigning houses in this part'. In June he confessed to his own considerable losses and he resolved to steer clear of the vastly overstocked U.S. market.[8]

If the returns from America were frequently disappointing after 1815, the European market at least as far as woollen cloths were concerned never recovered. Portugal remained the best area, but there was no expansion even there, and after 1820 exports of woollen cloth to Germany and Holland became virtually negligible. 'There is not any state in Europe which has not duties imposed for the purpose of protecting their own manufacturers,' complained a witness to the committee enquiring into 'The State of the British Wool Trade (1828)', 'I think the governments of the Continent do everything in their power to exclude our manufactures.'[9] Moreover the 6d. tax on imported wool, introduced in 1819 to aid the country's stricken agriculturists, hit the Leeds trade particularly hard. Worsteds were still entirely made of British long wool. But the quality of British short staple wool had deteriorated so much since 1780 as to be largely unfit for the manufacture of all but the coarsest woollen cloth. In 1820 it was reckoned that the Yorkshire woollen industry relied on imports for two-thirds of its wool supply. For the woollen trade the tax had deplorable effects: exports of cloth made from short clothing wool fell by about 36% between 1819 and 1821.[10] A slow recovery took place in 1823, which by 1825 had developed into a boom. 'You can have no idea without seeing it of the avidity with which goods are purchased at every day increasing prices', wrote Lupton to a correspondent in London. By June 1825 he admitted they had more orders than they could cope with. The impetus of the advance had come from the South and Central American market, where total exports from Britain had increased by 120% between 1821 and 1825. But in the summer of 1825 the market in South American government shares—the largest single area of new investment in the early 1820's—collapsed. The woollen trade remained in a critical state during the autumn. Again as in 1816 and 1819 all depended on the remittances from the Americas. By late November the melancholy news of disastrous failures in America was spreading through the Lancashire ports to Leeds. Lupton in early December spoke of credit being annihilated, and though he discountenanced rumours that the Leeds banks were in difficulty he had 'never known money to be so scarce'.[11] Joshua Oates, a member of one of the oldest and largest merchant firms in Leeds, was in bad straits as he confessed to his brother: 'I have actually suspended what? payment? No! not exactly, but I have suspended purchases of every description except bread, meat and potatoes, and I have *driven* clothiers away with a "can't you call again next month?" ' He owed Beckett's Bank so much money that without putting a bill into their hands he dared not ask for a renewal of credit with their London agents, Glyn Mills and Co. But as he stated he was by no means alone in his difficulties:

there is literally next to nothing doing by our foreign merchants and such numbers of them are in back water that I should hardly know where to begin with introductions—it is said by the Dyers and clothiers that with the exception of six or eight houses in Leeds no payments have been made since last November.[12]

William Lupton fared even worse than Joshua Oates. His only profit declared between 1820 and 1827 was £959 in 1822. He claimed the firm was so busy in 1824-5 that the accounts were 'not re-examined nor was the stock proceeded in'; but he was deluding himself for the firm's affairs were in a chronic state. Net losses of £8,555 and £19,690 were declared on 31 December 1826 and 30 June 1827 respectively. On the latter day it was revealed that he owed Beckett's Bank £13,084 and his father-in-law, £15,259. Lupton died the following year worn out by his troubles.[13]

Gott attributed the depression of 1825-6 to the collapse of the South American market, the increase of the United States tariff on imported woollens from the 25% imposed in 1816 to 33⅓% in 1825, and the low price of cotton which had upset the American economy.[14] For the woollen merchants the results were more important than its causes. The woollen trade never recovered again in the 1820's and not until 1832 did a prolonged advance take place.

These difficult years took their toll on the eighteenth-century merchant community. By 1830 few of the merchant houses that Thomas Hill listed in 1782 survived. Of the 135 firms in Leeds engaged in the sale and manufacture of woollens, worsteds and blankets only 21 houses had partners who could provide a direct link with those in 1782. 37 houses were concerned solely in woollen merchanting and 46 were described as woollen merchant-manufacturers, and yet only seven of these firms had been in existence half a century earlier as cloth merchants. Of the 19 largest which Hill reckoned had a turnover of £20,000 and upwards in 1781, five survived of which no fewer than four were headed by Dissenters.[15]

Of course most firms had a low survival rate in this period, but this wholesale defection was caused by something more than recurrent recessions, bankruptcies, retirements and failure to produce a male heir that had always decimated the merchants' ranks. Bankruptcies were certainly more evident in the slumps caused by the frequent dislocations of the European and American markets after 1800, yet they provide little clue to this general withdrawal, for the affairs of the large merchants seldom deteriorated to the extent of being dragged through the Bankruptcy Courts, although as we have seen Joshua Oates believed the entire merchant community to be in at least temporary difficulties in 1825-6, and the same observation appears to have been true to a lesser extent in 1808, 1811-12, 1816 and 1819. There were four main factors, which will be discussed in detail but which do not pretend to be an account of the development of the Yorkshire woollen and worsted industries in this period, that rendered the position of the non-manufacturing merchant untenable and speeded up his departure from business. Firstly, the transition from a primary European to an American trade after 1793 moved against the established export merchant whose experience was confined largely to the former area. Secondly, the manufacturers made deliberate attempts to outpace the merchants in all markets by price-cutting and extended credit facilities. Thirdly, the woollen cloth itself declined. Broad cloths that had been the staple item of the Leeds export trade became unfashionable. They were replaced by a wide range of 'fancy' cloths and light worsteds. Finally, the economic opinions and social attitudes of the traditional woollen merchants themselves was not conducive to the rapid changes taking place within the West Riding.

(I)

There are two main trends in the woollen export trade after 1800 which vitally affected the Leeds cloth merchants. The European markets never recovered after the Napoleonic Wars. The new sectors of growth in the overall export of woollens were in South America and the Far East for the United States' market—which had been the great area of expansion after 1760—showed signs of stagnation after 1815. In Leeds the bigger firms had always been largely engaged in the export trade. Although Bischoff maintained in 1828 that the home market, 'in point of extent is the best for woollen manufactures' he produced no supporting evidence for his statement. It is unlikely that the percentage of woollens sold at home, estimated by Miss Deane to be $33\frac{1}{3}\%$ in 1800 and by Wolrich to be $27 \cdot 7\%$ of Yorkshire's output in 1772, rose sharply for the competition from cottons and cheap worsteds became increasingly acute during the 30-year depression of prices and incomes after 1814.[16]

Through the long years of the French wars the merchants had believed that once peace was declared the European cloth trade would settle down at its pre-war level. Their hope was misplaced. In 1820 Benjamin Gott admitted that the Mediterranean trade had 'considerably diminished'. Exports of woollen cloths to the Netherlands and Germany collapsed, after a brief post-war boom, in 1817 (see Table 5). Henry Hughes shipped some woollens to Germany in 1827 for the great fairs at Frankfurt and Leipzig. In the following year he related his experiences before a Parliamentary Committee:

> I believe they were in their market for the space of from 10 to 13 months, and the principal part of them I received back again within the last three months, because, although repeated trials had been made to sell them, no market could be found, without great loss.

Yorkshire exporters blamed flourishing home woollen industries in France and Germany for their dwindling returns. They maintained

Table 7 British woollen and worsted exports, 1816–28[a]. (C 'cloths of all sorts', W 'stuffs, woollens and worsted'[b])

	Germany	United Netherlands	Portugal	Italy	E. Indies & China	United States	Brazil	Total[c]
[d]1816								
C	20	21	50	9	28	375	20	638
W	25	30	36	17	195	186	7	593
1817								
C	9	13	40	8	19	195	24	467
W	38	37	27	15	188	202	8	585
1818								
C	12	11	50	16	22	178	33	478
W	96	30	31	29	147	229	8	683
1819								
C	10	10	25	29	25	213	46	447
W	126	36	29	37	181	356	13	938
1820								
C	6	9	42	28	27	122	30	340
W	123	35	17	33	175	181	27	717
1821								
C	5	6	42	23	43	75	28	288
W	206	36	22	31	212	147	19	829
1822								
C	4	3	39	18	60	145	15	375
W	207	35	26	56	205	303	24	1021
1823								
C	2	4	37	27	47	200	29	420
W	276	56	24	123	169	262	26	1078
1824								
C	2	2	32	15	48	127	32	356
W	322	58	23	125	220	215	19	1150
1825								
C	2	2	61	19	51	111	36	407
W	360	65	40	88	166	25	29	1242
1826								
C	1	1	47	17	45	136	55	385
W	332	46	29	57	185	264	37	1139
1827								
C	2	1	45	15	50	113	24	328
W	395	75	28	55	242	180	15	1123
1828								
C	2	2	30	16	53	144	37	371
W	454	85	26	86	137	263	41	1259

[a] Figures to nearest thousand. Compiled from *P.P.* 1828 (515) vii, The State of the British Wool Trade, and J. Bischoff, *A Comprehensive History of the Woollen and Worsted Manufacture* (1842) II, Appendix, Table VII.
[b] These were far the most important categories listed: kerseymeres, baizes, napped coatings, duffils and flannels all declined absolutely in the export figures after 1816.
[c] Total exports to *all* countries—not just those listed.
[d] Year ending 5 Jan.

that German merchants were successfully invading the Italian and Levant markets. Certainly during the imposition of the 6*d.* tax on imported wool (1819-24) German woollens were cheaper, although their finish was inferior to the Yorkshire cloths. In the early 1820's James Bischoff found it profitable to buy cheap Prussian cloths for re-export to South America and Gibraltar.[17] This trade was terminated after 1824 with the reduction of the wool tax to 1*d.*, but it indicated the competition on the Continent that the British cloth export merchants had to face after 1815.

The woollen export trade with the U.S.A. was still very important. In 1800 it absorbed 40% of all British woollen and worsted exports. From this high point it declined relatively for the next 50 years until by 1850 the figure had fallen to 30%.[18] As far as the Leeds merchants were concerned the decline was more marked than these figures would suggest for woollens were replaced to a large extent by cheaper worsted cloths. In 1816, 375,000 'cloths of all sorts', a description that included the Leeds broad cloths, were exported to the U.S.A. Twelve years later they had dwindled to 144,000. Worsteds on the other hand increased from 186,000 to 263,000 pieces in the same period. This movement is partly accounted for by the U.S.A. tariffs which favoured worsteds at the expense of woollen cloths. Various tariffs imposed after 1789 mounted rapidly after 1812. By 1828 there was a 45% *ad valorem* duty on woollen cloths, although that on worsteds and the cheapest woollens remained at 25%. Although the tariffs were reduced somewhat after 1832, they clearly moved against the woollen cloth merchants and favoured the exporting manufacturers, particularly those concerned in making cheap worsteds. Moreover exports to America met with increasing competition from its own woollen industry. Gott reckoned in 1828 that the U.S.A. produced six-sevenths of its superfine cloth consumption.[19]

This stagnation in the American market was offset to some extent by the opening up of the South American trade after 1808 and with the Far East after 1815. Although the demand for worsteds in the Far East was far greater than for woollens cloths, exportation of both, hitherto controlled by London merchants, increased when the monopoly of the East India Company came to an end.[20] Like Portugal and Spain—of which the South American trade was an offshoot—demand in Brazil and Argentina was largely for the broad woollen cloths in which the Leeds merchants and manufacturers specialised. Yet as in the opening up of the North American trade in the 1750's and 1760's the established merchant was very hesitant to risk his capital in the Brazilian and Far Eastern markets. He could curtail his orders with the clothiers and attempt to switch to the home market when the European markets were virtually closed after 1806. But manufacturers could not shut down their mills and during depressions they were forced into merchanting themselves. In 1807 therefore when the closure of the Portuguese market coincided with the beginning of restraints and stoppages in the trade with America a number of Leeds merchants and manufacturers sent out representatives to Brazil in the wake of the fleeing Portuguese court. In fact there was little alternative. As Joseph Rogerson wrote of the Brazilian trade in his diary: 'it makes people venture very hard now as there is no port scarce open but it for cloth'.

Henry Glover was in the van of the little West Riding contingent that sailed for Rio in 1807. The firm of Rhodes and Glover, of which he was junior partner, had only recently made a name for itself in Leeds. Abraham Rhodes, a dyer's son, was an enterprising man who in 1811 established a woollen factory. The house had formerly traded to Portugal and the United States: now it was forced into sending spot consignments to the Mediterranean, the Caribbean and South America. But from the outset the Brazilian trade—long indirectly controlled by British factors in Lisbon—was disappointing. There was a cycle of dearth and glut linked with the irregular arrival of ships from Britain. Yet the demand for woollen goods did not exceed £200,000 a year. Therefore from the beginning the Leeds firms had to rely on commission sales for other manufacturers sending out a varied range of goods. The experience of young men like Henry Glover was, however, largely limited to a specialised knowledge of the woollen cloth trade. Suddenly they were asked to manage a varied and complex consignment business where connections were unproved and financial arrangements primitive. Glover persuaded his partner in Leeds to buy three ships to get round the problem of shipping delays, but his remittance of what appeared in the books in Leeds to be substantial profits from his trade in sugar, cotton, deer skins and jerk beef was so fitful that it almost brought the firm into ruin.

Ventures like these embarked upon by Henry Glover abrogated every tenet of the old mercantile faith. Yet only the boldest adventurers survived. And the North and South American trades relied on personal contacts and initiative to an extent unknown in the old rule of thumb European trade. These new markets were built up by English traders on the spot, men like Henry Glover, who spent long hard years representing their firms, selling woollens and dealing in everything from pins to beaver hats to make a precarious living. Professor Heaton discovered a whole colony of Yorkshire traders, almost always representatives of manufacturers, who broke into the American trade after

1783. They began to outpace these more progressive merchants who had been moving into the market since the 1760's. The diary of one such traveller has survived.[21] John Kighley was a junior partner successively in two old established merchant houses, the Oates and Bischoffs. He was a diffident and sensitive man who had, to his distaste, to make his way in trade. At first he thought the pace of life not dissimilar to that in Leeds. Business was leisurely: the afternoons and evenings were taken up with Leeds' acquaintances in walking, riding and eating. Even the crossings could be agreeable, for cabin passages at £40–£50 each usually ensured at least a good table and interesting company. But the novelty wore off. Kighley made 10 crossings in 13 years. In America the tales about Leeds grew longer. A glimpse of 'that Arch fiend that disorganizor of Civilised Man' Tom Paine walking down Broadway ('a shabby dirty old fellow in a bottle green Bearskin coat, buttoned round with a Belt of the same, pantaloons and dirty stockings, a face covered with carbuncles and the whole appearance of the person bespoke an old debauchee'), Jefferson, 'taking a ride without any attendents whatever', even dining with Jerome Buonaparte did not long stop Kighley's laments for civilised company and entertainments. On one trip he spent eight or nine months 'on the move betwixt New York and Alexandria—something like a marching regiment, sometimes travelling by land, at other times by water—nipped with the winter frost or boiled by the Summer sun, choaked with dust or drenched with Rain'. One old Leeds merchant found the threat of yellow fever and the June heat so unbearable that he took the first boat back east for Liverpool telling Kighley: 'they may talk o't West Indies as they will but by God it's nought to be compared to this. I'll try t'oud spot a bit longer.' When Kighley arrived back in Leeds in 1805 he had had enough: 'I . . . am comparatively speaking a free man, but without a shilling, after near 12 years servitude, during which times I have been fours times abroad, and have been exposed to "plague pestilance and famine" to battle, shipwreck and loss of Liberty in France.'

The sons of the Dixons, Denisons, Milnes and their like were not prepared to pass their time in similar excursions. They preferred hunting and assemblies, Bath and Scarborough and sought a commission in the army or a good benefice. A few months' trip to Portugal and Italy was pleasant indeed but a few years' sojourn in Buenos Aires selling shawls and swords was quite unthinkable. Yet almost all merchants at some time after 1783 were forced into the United States market. But the old guide lines of Sir Henry Ibbetson's generation were useless in a trade of vast distances and long credits. Mercantile theory eschewed the practice of deputing affairs to managers and agents, and some old-fashioned merchants like William Cookson had their fingers very badly burned by the chicanery of their American agents. On the spot assessments of the business climate was essential: replies by letter took on average, three months. In South America, where the development of trade after 1807 was largely pioneered by Leeds men, there was not one representative of an old merchant house to be found. Kighley's diary shows that the lead in woollen cloth sales in the United States was taken by speculating manufacturers whose sons and brothers spent long years abroad. The eighteenth-century dynasties who governed the town and controlled its trade with Europe would not commit themselves to the degree of involvement that these new markets made essential.

(II)
Professor Heaton observed that the most important step towards a complete factory system was taken when some merchants began manufacturing and the clothiers commenced selling their own cloths without the intervention of the merchant. The pressure, however, was upon the manufacturer and not the merchant as some subsequent writers have suggested.[22] For the greatest profits had always been made by the merchants. The attractions of cost reduction and quality control did not force them into making their own cloth. As late as 1830 with wise buying both inside and outside the cloth halls and by controlling the finishing processes they could still compete with the large exporting manufacturer. In 1806 John Hebblethwaite was convinced that he could buy cloth as cheaply as he could make it, and in 1828 James Varley, a Stanningley merchant-manufacturer, with a weekly wage bill of £300–£400, declared that he was able to buy cloths and coatings 'less than I can make them for'.[23]

In fact the relationship between merchanting and manufacturing profits shifted. Between 1800 and 1815 trade passed through a period of rising prices and good although often wildly fluctuating profit margins. The clothiers maintained in 1806, somewhat paradoxically, that their own profits were small but that the merchants were being pushed into manufacturing. Certainly the argument of economies of scale was not compelling for they were not, especially at this early stage, very notable since wool textile technology tended naturally towards small units of production. James Ellis reckoned the factory producer was able to undersell the merchants by 5% or about 9d. a yard in the superfine trade that the few factories in 1806 were entirely concerned with. Most merchants did not find this margin a sufficient incentive although the evidence of Gott and Abraham Rhodes—the latter claimed to make £60,000 in the four years after he began manufacturing in 1811— suggests the profitability of the early factories. Admittedly it is impossible to establish in both cases the percentage of profits accrued in selling cloth bought in the cloth halls and that produced in their own factories. It should be remembered that Gott sold three times more cloth than he made himself.[24] But whatever news leaked into Leeds of the success of Gott, Rhodes and the Brookes, the majority of merchants remained unmoved. Mercantile practice always dismissed the notion of merchants turning manufacturers. Before 1790 a modest capital in merchanting secured a good livelihood. There was no rush either to maximise profits consistently or expand the firm continually. Few firms by 1790 exceeded the size of that founded by William Milner a century earlier. Surplus earnings were invested in land, government securities, occasionally another industrial venture in order to underwrite commitments in the cloth trade. Many economic historians depict all eighteenth-century entrepreneurs as ants tirelessly maximising profits to lift the graph of economic growth. Such a picture has no resemblance to the activities of the Leeds merchants. Business decisions were taken on the strength of discussions where social considerations outweighed the hard economic facts. Men like Hebblethwaite and Cookson maintained there was no advantage in setting up a factory. When Hebblethwaite was asked if he would 'engage in a factory which unites the profits of a Manufacturer and Merchant', he replied emphatically: 'if there is no alternative I would give up business wholly before I would be a Factory Manufacturer'. On being pressed to state his reasons, he continued: 'In the first place because I should not like to have the trouble of it, and it is not beneficial, I have trouble enough with the cloth after it is made, I do not wish to have trouble with it.'[25] Other merchants came to a similar conclusion by extending the range of their arguments. Trade between 1800 and 1815 was unsettled. Capital expenditure to launch a factory was increasing. Why lock money up in mills to return an uncertain profit? Certainly there were a great number of mills to lease, but this does not mean that building them was a good investment so much that bankruptcies were so numerous that it was impossible to sell them. Labour problems were not made easier by the political situation. Running a factory 15 hours a day, 6 days a week, might be all very well for ex-clothiers but it was not a gentleman's occupation. And it was not deemed prudent to depute responsibilities to a manager.

During the second period between 1815 and 1830 competition, within the woollen industry itself and from cottons and worsteds, cheap raw materials and improved machinery, forced prices down. Profit margins fell. Although the committee enquiring into the 'state of Manufactures, Commerce and Shipping' in 1833 attempted to drag out of witnesses the profitability of their factories all they would disclose was that profits were better 15–20 years earlier. John Marshall, the great Leeds linen manufacturer, thought that mills realised an average profit compared with other concerns. Dr. Glover's study of Hague and Cook, the Dewsbury blanket manufacturers, showed a sharp deterioration in profits between 1811–21 and the early 1830's; 'a margin of two-and-a-half per cent added to total cost per unit of output seems to have been considered adequate by the partners after they had revised their price lists'.[26] Declining profit margins and the merchants' hesitancy to extend themselves in the difficult post-war markets and their consequent restriction of cloth purchases forced the manufacturers into handling their own sales.

Let us examine the steps by which the manufacturer also became a merchant. Before 1800 the clothier had always manufactured through a depression. The cloth piles mounted in his shop, but when spring came and the market improved he usually managed to sell his accumulated stocks to the merchants. When the clothier expanded his premises this fortuitous system became impossible. Machinery could not stand idle nor hands be turned off at the onset of every seasonal slump. John Hopton, a clothier trustee of the White Cloth Hall at Leeds, when questioned by the Committee enquiring into the Stamping Laws in 1821: 'Do you in point of fact merchandise yourself', replied: 'Sometimes when I have a stock in hand.' James Varley appearing before the same committee provided a similar answer. He was more explicit in 1828 when he described the route by which he had become a merchant-manufacturer: 'I was not what we call a merchant then [1820], I did a bit bye the bye; that is to say I was a cloth manufacturer; and I only exported goods then when I could not find a market at home for them, to give my poor men employment, and give them cheese and bread.' When pressed by the committee to state the reason for his having a 'surplus quantity of goods in hand' he answered, 'We generally have during the Winter months; we consider it a flat time then, and we manufacture goods, or used to do, on speculation, and when I had a market for them in Leeds I sold them, and when not, I used to send them to Rio Janeiro and New York, to keep my machinery going during the Winter months.'[27] Many large clothiers began merchanting in similar circumstances to those described by James Varley. As William Hague, a Manchester merchant, said in 1833: 'they are driven to make shipments; formerly manufacturers would never ship if they could sell their goods at a profit; but when a stagnation takes place . . . they then prefer to try the markets themselves, and to take the profit of the merchant and manufacturers'. One factor, with a modern ring, moved in favour of these manufacturers taking these steps. Many customers believed 'they can supply them better, being the manufacturers, than a middle man coming in between them; they conceive there is only one profit'.[28]

The rapid exploitation of the New World markets after 1793 gave the manufacturers their opportunity. Here was an area where the traditional merchants were hesitant to move. As a result the large manufacturers, especially during the numerous depressions after 1800 when the merchants stopped buying their cloths, were forced to export in order to survive. N. S. Buck, delineating the three main periods in the development of the Anglo-American trade in the first half of the nineteenth century, noted the breakthrough of the manufacturer.

In the first period [1800–15] we find the British merchant the outstanding figure; he received orders from America for goods, and he himself also assumed the risks of Commerce by sending out goods on consignment to his agents and correspondents in America. In the second period [1815–30] . . . the British Manufacturer attracts our attention, for he seems to have been forced into marketing his own goods because of the inability or the unwillingness of the merchant to purchase his entire output. And in the third period [1830–50] the American merchant became a much more important factor in the foreign commerce than he had been previously.[29]

Moreover the structure of the Yorkshire textile industries helped the manufacturer. When he took the decision to market his own cloth he was able to have it finished by commission dressers and dyers to bypass the merchants. Finishing costs were slashed when the gig-mill and shearing-frames spread rapidly after 1816 and, at periods when the merchants' regular trade was slack, the finishing firms had surplus capacity available for the manufacturers' cloths. Then if his departure into marketing was successful the manufacturer could easily set up his own finishing department. By these stages it was much simpler for the manufacturer to integrate the final stages of production than it was for the merchant to commence manufacturing where capital outlay was much greater. And if the manufacturer's departure into marketing meant that he required greater financial resources or additional credit facilities—a point not always appreciated and a misunderstanding which led to innumerable bankruptcies—he was forced into this action by a failure to market his output through the intermediary services of the merchants in Leeds. Any sale was better than no sale at all once the size of manufacturing establishments increased.

The manufacturers' encroachment on the merchants' trade after 1790 changed the pattern of the export of woollen cloths in a number of ways. And it was the methods by which the manufacturers achieved their ends, rather than their competition in itself, which sickened the merchants who had been long in business. The *modus operandi* of trading only by direct order with respectable houses who made quick returns, that had guided Sir Henry Ibbetson, was now largely forgotten. Not only did the very distance and the pioneering elements in the American trade lead to an extension of credit terms after 1783 which permeated every trading area, but also the manufacturers deliberately undercut the merchants in prices and payment facilities. Increasing competition forced the merchants to lengthen the period of payment from 6 months to a year, 18 months and occasionally 2 years. After 1800 these arrangements, when reliance on the American sector of the export market was total, frequently ended in disaster. Exporters were often powerless even to enforce interest charges on overdue accounts and were obliged to take bills at 12, 18 and occasionally 21 months. Recourse to what Kighley described as the 'glorious uncertainty of the law' was taken only in the last resort when no terms of settlement could be agreed upon. Credit restrictions made during recessions were all too often precautions taken after the event. With bad debts mounting in his ledgers, William Lupton wrote to a customer in 1806: 'We have therefore come to the determination of having our money in 12 months or to give up the trade for the extra credit runs away with all our profits.' As an incentive he offered a $7\frac{1}{2}\%$ discount if bills were settled within three months, but as he admitted to his Scottish traveller, 'with the opposition in our line it is not possible to be over strict'.[30] The lesson proved hard to learn: merchants and manufacturers restricted speculations in the year following a payments crisis, only time and time again to launch out to the full extent of their capital without adequate precautions. Frequently William Lupton and Abraham Rhodes declared their disgust with the consignment trade and their desire to recall their partners, yet they realised during the Napoleonic Wars and indeed after 1815 when the European markets never recovered, that there was little alternative.

Equally serious with the manufacturers' pressure in extending credit terms was their wholesale dumping of cloth on the export market. As we have seen, when the large manufacturer was unable to dispose of his cloth to the merchants he had no choice but to sell it under the hammer in the West Riding or London, or more frequently consign it abroad for auction. The auction system discredited the merchants' regular trade after 1800. David Crowther, partner with his brothers

in a mill near Leeds, writing from New York in 1819 disclosed practices
that made the old-established merchant community shudder.

Our friends the Thompsons [they had a mill at Rawden] are getting sick of
doing so little business. Jeremiah can scarcely conceal his Chagrin. Their losses
on bad debts are immense . . . They have sold off their goods generally as they
arrive at auction at ruinously low prices, but are now going on the plan of
spreading them over the United States . . . In fact every town of any consideration where there is an auctioneer is supplied with their goods.

Not only was the system prevalent in America, but also even in Lisbon.
James Waterhouse, a large Halifax merchant, lamented in 1821:

Trade of every description is much overdone, and there are many adventurers
who go to great lengths, and who after a certain time, are obliged to bring the
goods to the hammer . . . furnishing the article at the cheapest price is the
great point of consideration with half the world at present.[31]

Not only did cloth consignments and auctions undermine the old
order system, but also they prevailed. In 1869 it was estimated that at
least 60% of the textiles exported to America were consignments from
needy manufacturers or speculators, many of them sold by auction.[32]

   Intense competition, the collapse of the old European market and
the successful attempts of the manufacturer to break into the merchants'
trade by price cutting and extended credit facilities resulted in changes
that the traditional merchant was unable to face. William Lee, a fourth
generation member of an old Leeds family, gave some important
evidence before the Committee examining the Stamping Laws in 1821.
Lee, now treasurer of the Stamping Fund and a West Riding J.P. and
living at Grove Hall near Pontefract, had given up cloth-merchanting
in Leeds around 1793. He viewed changes in the woollen cloth trade
with disapproval:

   Lee: 'That is a regular trade, where a merchant gets an order from
        an old established house; it is in his interest to stand as high
        as he can with that house, but the trade is very much changed.
   Q.: Is the observation you have been making applicable to
        merchants who are sending out goods on speculation, with-
        out any regular order?
   Lee: It is applicable to people who send out goods on speculation,
        who do not care what the goods are so long as they get a
        profit on it, which is very injurious to the regular established
        merchant.'[33]

   The old merchant community in Leeds and Wakefield supported
Lee's view in lamenting that trade was 'very much changed'. Many

between 1780 and 1830 quietly relinquished their interests in cloth-merchanting. Others carried on only half-accepting the changes forced upon them by the manufacturers. They refused to manufacture and hesitated to commit themselves in the American markets. Yet the pressure of the manufacturers made it impossible for the non-manufacturing merchant to stand still. Mechanisation of the industry allowed manufacturers to force the pace of trade after 1793, and many entrants to the merchants' ranks crept in without the traditional training. Thomas Butler noted in his diary in 1798 when his father, an ironmaster, contemplated entering the Leeds trade: 'those persons who begin concerns they are not thoroughly acquainted with seldom succeed . . . Yet very Rapid Fortunes have been made in the Leeds Trade, even by mere novices.' Eighteenth-century trading practices became out of date in the rapidly changing situation after 1800. Merchants like William Cookson, Richard Bramley and Jeremiah Naylor, who clung to the old beliefs were overtaken by financial disaster. Naylor, 'bold Jerey' to his friends and perhaps the leading merchant in Yorkshire in 1800, who had boasted in 1821: 'I conducted my business in my own way and I had no consideration of what other people did; I conducted my business with a great deal of pleasure to myself', was bankrupt in 1825. He was unable to pay a total dividend of more than 5s. in the £ to his debtors.[34] Even merchants who made more attempts to move with the times like Samuel Elam, William Lupton, the Stansfelds and Oates frequently found themselves in difficulties. Only those few merchants like Benjamin Gott, Abraham Rhodes and John and Edward Brookes who diversified into making superfine cloths and blankets survived the upheavals of the first 30 years of the nineteenth century. They had come to terms with the changes that the large manufacturers had forced upon the woollen industry during these years.

(III)
Before 1780 the Leeds and Wakefield merchants had dealt in both woollen and worsted cloths. Specialisation was rare. Bailey's 1784 directory noted only five Leeds firms dealing solely in worsted stuffs. The two decades following 1783 saw a rapid growth in the varieties of both woollen and worsted cloths. A whole new range of 'fancy' cloths, some like swansdowns and toilinets with a cotton warp and woollen weft, were introduced after the American war. After 1800 merchants tended to deal only in woollen or worsteds, seldom both. William Lupton, although he sold the 'fancy' cloths produced in the Huddersfield area, still largely dealt in the old broad cloths. When a Glasgow wholesale draper ordered some flannel Lupton advised him to obtain it

in Rochdale. Lupton shipped some worsteds to South America, but they were direct consignments by stuff merchants like Samuel Blagborough. As he explained to Thomas Luccock, 'we have always avoided as much as possible deviating from our own line'.[35] The reasons for this separation are obscure: whether they derived from the differing degree of finish required for the two major types of cloth, or the increasing varieties produced within both trades or that the worsted manufacturers, organised in larger units than in the woollen sector of the industry, increasingly traded directly without the intervention of merchants in Leeds, is difficult to say. But the significance of the tighter classification between woollens and worsteds became evident after 1815 when the export of the traditional broad and narrow cloths, in which the dressing and dyeing was all important, dwindled sharply.

James Bischoff, in a somewhat gloomy conclusion to his *History of the Woollen and Worsted Manufactures* produced a simple set of figures to establish the extent to which the woollen cloth export trade had declined in the generation after 1815.

	1816	1826	1840
Cloths exported (pieces)	636,368	384,508	215,746
Worsteds exported (pieces)	593,308	1,138,588	1,718,617

He blamed the loss of the trade with the Continent, the tax on imported wool introduced in 1819 (from which the woollen trade never recovered), and the increasing unsuitability of English wool for woollen cloth manufacture.[36] Yet perhaps the most important reason for the decline of the woollen export trade was the change in demand from the old heavy broad cloths to the lighter 'fancy' cloths of the Huddersfield area on the one hand and the cheaper worsted stuffs of the Bradford region on the other. The Leeds merchants whose fortunes had depended for two centuries on the export of the famous Leeds broad cloths to Europe found themselves outpriced and outmanœuvred by the manufacturers of Huddersfield and Bradford in the New World markets.

The worsted industry grew very rapidly in Bradford after 1800. Unhampered by commercial traditions and old-established firms which acted as a brake upon industrial progress Bradford's trade expanded at a faster rate in the nineteenth century. The adoption of the mule, and, more importantly, the power-loom, the key factor in the second stage of industrialisation, came almost 20 years earlier in the worsted industry. A growing demand, cheap wool prices (the worsted, unlike the woollen, industry was able to utilise low price coarse British wools), and an easier solution of technological problems in power weaving stimulated rapid change in the worsted industry in the two difficult decades after 1815. Corresponding developments in the woollen industry came only in the 1840's and 1850's. Something of the contrast between Leeds and Bradford was brought out at the Great Exhibition of 1851. Even a progressive firm like Benjamin Gott's showed how tradition-bound the Leeds woollen trade had become. When other firms were exhibiting an infinite variety of woollen cloths, worsteds and mohair and cotton mixtures, Gotts merely displayed the old broad cloths in a wide range of shades. On the other hand Forsters of Black Dyke Mills increased the number of their different types of worsted cloth from 14 to 70 in the 20 years after 1840.[37] An even more instructive illustration of the different rates of progress in the woollen and worsted industries in the West Riding is the comparison of factory sizes shown below.

	No. of firms		Employment		Average per factory	
	Woollens	*Worsteds*	*Woollens*	*Worsteds*	*Woollens*	*Worsted*
1838	606	348	27,548	26,603	45	76
1850	880	492	40,611	70,905	46	170

These figures reflect the extraordinary survival of the jenny and handloom in the woollen industry. The average worsted factory employed four times more labour in 1850. Furthermore the degree of concentration in the worsted industry was far greater than in the woollen industry. In 1851, 86% of worsted spindles and 94% of power-looms in the worsted industry were collected in the West Riding. On the other hand only 40% of all woollen workers were employed in the same region.[38]

The change in demand from woollens to worsteds and the growth of Bradford and other West Riding centres like Batley and Dewsbury resulted in the eclipse of the Leeds merchant export houses. Their paramountcy in the Yorkshire cloth trade was threatened by an army of thrusting manufacturers in every production centre of any size in both the woollen and worsted areas. As late as the 1820's Leeds firms had handled most of the output of Bradford, Huddersfield and the smaller towns. Now after 1830, and aided by the railways, manufacturers in these towns and some immigrant merchants, like the Halifax clothiers a century earlier, set up finishing establishments and their own export sales connections. In 1841 John James, the Bradford historian, noted with pride that the trade in worsteds was almost entirely handled by Bradford men who had broken the control of the Leeds merchants during the previous decade.[39]

Developments in Huddersfield, Dewsbury and Batley were very

similar. The latter towns had concentrated on the use of shoddy or rags—introduced when the price of wool was high at the end of the Napoleonic Wars—to produce cheap blankets and coarse woollens. By 1830 they were dominating the blanket trade without recourse to the Leeds merchants who had formerly handled the trade. In the next generation the two towns achieved a similar commanding position in the heavy woollen industry which had formerly been concentrated in Leeds.[40]

It was inevitable that after the 1820's, when Bradford, Huddersfield, Dewsbury and Batley began to handle their own sales and exports, that the number of Leeds merchants should sharply decline. In 1851 there were still 40 woollen cloth merchants in Leeds, although 30 years later the number had fallen to 17. Bradford had become the centre of the worsted industry, and Huddersfield of the woollen trade.[41] In 1797 there had been no fewer than 130 merchant firms in the town handling the major share of the Yorkshire wool textile industry.

(IV)

The merchants' defection from the woollen trade had important consequences. The belief that capital accrued in commerce before 1780 was gradually and imperceptibly channelled into industrial concerns in the nineteenth century has little basis of truth in the West Riding wool textile industries. The real input of capital for increasing mechanisation after 1783 came from the manufacturers themselves. With the introduction of the jenny and scribbling-mill and by their organisation of joint-stock concerns clothiers were able to increase the size of their concerns. The pace of change was not rapid and until the 1830's the independent clothier was able to survive. Then the mule and powerloom divided the way. The majority of clothiers' families became factory-workers, although a substantial number of men engaged in cloth-making and other ancillary branches of the textile industry succeeded in establishing mills of their own. Cudworth, the local Bradford historian, found the Aire valley and the town and vicinity of Bradford crowded with the large factories of mill-owners who had risen from very small beginnings, such as the Fosters of Denholme, typical Victorian mill-owners. He writes:

If an instance were required of the ultimate reward of indomitable perseverance no better could be provided than that furnished by the experience of the Fosters of Denholme. We believe the brothers made no secret of the fact that the sum total they could get together with which to commence business was £200. We should imagine that the present plant and stock could not be purchased for £200,000.[42]

It must be remembered that the scale of enterprise in the woollen industry was always small. As late as 1850 the average West Riding woollen factory employed only 46 persons. Moreover the factories before this date seldom completed all the production processes. In 1833 out of 129 woollen factories in the county only 12 took the raw wool through every stage of manufacture. The majority were devoted either to scribbling, spinning or finishing, or combinations of these three functions. Both woollen and worsted industries utilised small supplies of motive power: in 1838 the average mill in both industries relied on engines or water-wheels producing 17 h.p.[43] Much the most significant changes in the scale of factory production came with the power-loom and mule-spinning, changes only evident in the worsted industry after 1830 and the woollen industry after 1850. Because the complete factory system was reached only gradually, the small manufacturer was given his chance. In 1833 John Brooke, a large Huddersfield mill-owner, recommended the woollen industry to the small man of enterprise: 'if I were an apprentice to a woollen manufacturer, and when I became of age I had a small capital, I should embark in the business with every prospect of success'. His words were not the unctuous wanderings of an old man who had done well. Between 1834 and 1838 inclusive the number of woollen factories, if the returns are reliable, increased from 129 to 542. The growth in the numbers of worsted mills was almost as spectacular, expanding from 204 in 1836 to 388 within three years. In Bradford alone there were four times more mills in 1836 than there had been five years earlier.[44]

Of course, Brooke did not stress the enormous risk in these early factories. H. Burgess, writing in 1836, and speaking of industry generally, reckoned that 9 out of 10 of the large manufacturing concerns had changed hands since 1819 through insolvency. Robert Baker, a West Riding sub-inspector of factories, estimated that of 318 firms in his district in 1836 only 127 survived 10 years later.[45] Merchants who had carefully nurtured their resources were not prepared to squander them in this lottery. Moreover, numerically it was simply impossible for the merchants collected in Leeds, Wakefield and Halifax to have provided any great portion of capital to the vast total number of mills that had been established, successfully or otherwise, before 1840. And even in Leeds, where some merchant newcomers to the woollen trade after 1783 had invested the fat profits of the following two decades in mills there is little evidence of their survival in the trade or their impact on the town's industry. Leeds' position as the premier seat of woollen manufacture in the county declined, and of the 68 woollen factories that existed in 1858 these were no different in scale than the other 800 woollen factories scattered across the county. Their average labour force was only 54, a figure which closely approximated the county average.[46]

As the merchant took the decision not to begin manufacturing his capital found other outlets. Although resources had never been entirely tied up in the cloth trade they were now increasingly diverted to land, government stocks and transport securities. Instead of seeking out a good apprenticeship for his sons, the merchant examined the possibilities of the professions when he was unable to set them up with an independent income derived from land or other investments. Large sums, accrued in commerce during the eighteenth century, were diverted in this way. When the Denisons and the Milnes in Wakefield withdrew from trade to their estates during the first crucial stages of rapid industrialisation their resources were far larger than Gott's or any other of the early factory owners. In fact the loss of capital channelled away from the textile trade and industry was really unimportant. Or at least it was unimportant when linked with their outlook. The Denisons and Milnes and those who emulated their example lacked the entrepreneurial qualities necessary to lead the industry from a domestic to a factory-based system of production. The Milnes' heir in the 1820's won the St. Leger with his horses no fewer than five times in eight years. It is not a distinction one normally associates with the scion of a leading Unitarian merchant family. Sir Wymess Reid, the family biographer, drew a stern account of Rodes Milnes stationing himself in an inn window at the conclusion of York races, inviting every passer-by to join him in a bottle of wine.[47] With such vignettes the textbook image of the tireless endeavour of the Dissenters in their business pursuits loses some of its precision, and the suspicion grows that the continuity between eighteenth-century trade and nineteenth-century industry has been much overstressed by historians.

Even men of real worth like John Hebblethwaite and William Cookson, who declared that they could not possibly conceive becoming merchant-manufacturers because they believed such a step was 'incompatible for the comfort of either', were of an entirely conservative outlook. It was far better that merchants of these opinions should move out of the industry at the end of their working lives rather than attempt to burden it with their old-fashioned views. Lipson maintained that one of the chief reasons for the backwardness of the West Country woollen industry after 1815 was that the structure of the industry never changed and the large clothiers there were conservative. They were able to retard the use of machinery which destroyed their vested interests and they lacked enterprise and energy. A Hand-Loom Commissioner noted in 1839:

While the men of Leeds and Huddersfield were constantly in their mills and taking their meals at the same hours as their workpeople, the clothiers of Gloucestershire, some of them, were indulging in the habits and mixing with the 'gentle blood' of the land.

In Yorkshire the manufacturers replaced the merchants in the leadership of the industry between 1783 and 1815. It was an important move that meant Yorkshire could take every advantage of its resources of skill, good labour and fuel to overhaul finally its two rivals, the West Country and Norwich trades.[48]

If the Yorkshire merchants frequently made excellent improving landowners, they tended after 1790 merely to put a brake on the progress towards a complete factory system in Leeds, Wakefield and Halifax. When Wakefield was eclipsed by Huddersfield and Bradford after 1800 one Victorian commentator attributed a large share of the blame to its merchants.

It is a well known fact that at the time when manufacturers began to excite considerable interest in the West Riding, the aristocracy of Wakefield, who had already made their fortunes, refused to permit mills or factories to be established here, they were well content to ride in their carriages and fours, and attend the markets in other towns, but would not have manufactures brought to Wakefield. Indeed they went so far as to have inserted in the indentures of apprenticeship, that those thus bound should not exercise their trade etc. within seven miles of Wakefield, and soon this aristocracy left Wakefield altogether.[49]

In Leeds itself it was impossible for the merchants to ossify developments to this extent for as Professor Rimmer has shown the town's economy by 1820 was broadening to include the engineering, shoemaking and linen trades. Moreover the number of firms grew from around 1,076 in 1797 to over 7,000 in 1842. Although the overwhelming proportion of new ventures were domestic units and craft shops, not factories, they altered the industrial profile of Leeds and swamped the merchants who had dominated its economic life before 1815. The proportion of firms associated with textile production fell from 58% in 1728–59 to 14% in 1834. In woollen manufacturing the number of firms remained constant between 1797 and 1834 and the majority of new textile firms made linens, worsteds and cottons.[50] The relative decline in woollen manufacturing in Leeds, diversification into other textile trades and the town's diminishing importance as a finishing centre after 1830 was due to the Leeds merchants' failure to maintain their hold on the county's cloth export trade and their refusal to contemplate large-scale change. As the manufacturer established successful sales connections of their own, the merchants became less competitive after 1815 in a world of falling prices and profits. Therefore the advance of the Yorkshire wool textile industries in the nineteenth century was directed by manufacturers who were prepared to take a far bolder initiative to meet new requirements brought about by industrialisation and intense competition at home and abroad.

Notes to Chapter 6

[1] Recessions were marked in 1788, 1793–4 and 1797–8 in the Yorkshire woollen industry. Orders were plentiful, but returns poor. The third depression is well documented in *The Diary of Thomas Butler of Kirkstall Forge, 1796–1799* (1906).

[2] H. Heaton, 'Yorkshire cloth traders', 227.

[3] *L.I.*, 16 Nov. 1807; *L.M.*, 28 May 1808; Crump, 88.

[4] Lupton MSS., 5 Sept. 1808.

[5] *ibid.*, 26 Feb. 1809.

[6] *ibid.*, 15 May, 8 Sept. 1812, 6 Dec. 1813, 29 Aug. 1814.

[7] *ibid.*, 28 March, 14, 28 June 1815, 16 May, 18 June, 8 July, 24 Oct. 1816, 4 Aug., 12 Sept., 6 Oct. 1817.

[8] *ibid.*, 22 June 1818, 31 Jan., 21 June 1819, 20 Jan., 23 May, 30 June 1820.

[9] *P.P.* 1828 (515) viii, 51.

[10] *P.P.* 1820 (56) xii, 75; J. Bischoff, *op. cit.*, II, p. 16.

[11] A. D. Gayer, W. W. Rostow and A. J. Schwartz, *op. cit.*, I, p. 182.

[12] Oates MSS., J. H. to E. Oates, 1, 9 Feb., 13 May 1826.

[13] Lupton MSS. Annual stock-taking accounts, 1815–28.

[14] *P.P.* 1828 (515) viii, 284–92.

[15] W. Parson and W. White, *Directory of . . . Leeds and the Clothing District of Yorkshire* (1830).

[16] J. Bischoff, *op. cit.*, II, p. 171.

[17] *P.P.* 1820 (56) xii, 78; *P.P.* 1828 (515) viii, 40; J. Bischoff, *op. cit.*, II, pp. 167–8.

[18] H. Heaton, 'Yorkshire cloth traders', 227.

[19] *ibid.*, 266; F. J. Glover, 'Dewsbury Mills,' unpublished University of Leeds Ph.D. thesis (1959), pp. 116–129; *P.P.* 1828 (515) viii, 284–292.

[20] The following two paragraphs are based upon letters of William Lupton to John Luccock and Abraham Rhodes to Henry Glover in the Lupton MSS. Both Luccock and Glover represented their firms in Brazil between 1808 and 1816. See also H. Heaton, 'A merchant adventurer in Brazil 1808–1818', *J. Econ. Hist.*, VI (1946), 1–23; R. G. Wilson, 'Fortunes of a Leeds merchant house'.

[21] H. Heaton, 'Yorkshire cloth traders'. I am grateful to Professor Heaton for allowing me to see Kighley's diary which he bought in a London saleroom during World War II. It covers the period 10 Sept. 1804–14 May 1807.

[22] Heaton, 300–1; also his 'Yorkshire cloth traders', 119; R. M. Hartwell, *op. cit.*, pp. 297–304; F. J. Glover, *op. cit.*, pp. 99–101.

[23] 1806 Report, 159; *P.P.* 1828 (515) viii, 154.

[24] 1806 Report, 30; Gott MSS.; R. G. Wilson, 'Fortunes of a Leeds merchant house'.

[25] 1806 Report, 156. See also the evidence of William Cookson and Jeremiah Naylor before the same committee.

[26] *P.P.* 1833 (690) vi, 152, 158–9; F. J. Glover, *op. cit.*, pp. 370–2.

[27] *P.P.* 1821 (437) vi, 51, 73–4; *P.P.* 1828 (515) viii, 143, 158.

[28] *ibid.*, 252 and *P.P.* 1833 (690) vi, evidence of William Hague especially Q. 4957.

[29] N. S. Buck, *The Development of the Organisation of Anglo-American Trade, 1800–1850* (1925), p. 150.

[30] Lupton MSS., 14 March, 18 Dec. 1806.

[31] H. Heaton, 'Yorkshire Cloth Traders', 267; *P.P.* 1821 (437) vi, 11–12.

[32] N. S. Buck, *op. cit.*, p. 151.

[33] *P.P.* 1821 (437) vi, 101–2, 105.

[34] *The Diary of Thomas Butler*, *op. cit.*, p. 226; R. V. Taylor, *op. cit.*, p. 481, and Cookson's will proved at York, April 1811; J. W. Walker, *Wakefield, Its History and People* (1934), p. 399; H. Clarkson, *op. cit.*, p. 52.

[35] Crump, 52–56, gives a description of the various types of woollen cloth produced around 1800. W. Lupton to Borland and Abbott, Boston (Mass.) gives a full description of the cloth he dealt in (Lupton MSS. 29 Jan. 1818).

[36] J. Bischoff, *op. cit.*, II, pp. 440–1.

[37] E. M. Sigsworth, *Black Dyke Mills, A History* (1958), pp. 17–25; J. James, *op. cit.*, pp. 354–450; R. M. Hartwell, *op. cit.*, pp. 290–3; Crump, 52; E. M. Sigsworth, 'The West Riding wool textile industry and the Great Exhibition', *Yorkshire Bulletin of Economic and Social Research*, IV (1952), 27.

[38] *ibid.*, 22; R. M. Hartwell, *op. cit.*, pp. 340–351.

[39] J. James, *The History and Topography of Bradford* (1841), p. 286.

[40] F. J. Glover, *op. cit.*, p. 93 and his 'Leeds and its industrial growth: No. 18 Blankets', *Leeds Journal*, vol. 27 (1956).

[41] W. Slade and D. I. Roebuck, *Directory of the Borough and Neighbourhood of Leeds* (1851); Kelly's *Directory of Leeds and Neighbourhood* (1881).

[42] W. Cudworth, *op. cit.*, p. 133.

[43] R. M. Hartwell, *op. cit.*, pp. 338, 350–1.

[44] *ibid.*, pp. 246, 338; *P.P.* 1833 (690) vi, 117.

[45] *P.P.* 1836 (465) viii, Part 2, 365; *P.P.* 1847 (179) xv, letter dated 7 Nov. 1846.

[46] A. Ure, *The Philosophy of Manufactures* (sixth edition, 1861), p. 704.

[47] T. W. Reid, *The Life, Letters and Friendships of Richard Monckton Milnes* (1890), I, p. 37; A. M. W. Stirling, *The Letter Bag of Lady Elizabeth Spencer Stanhope* (1913), I, pp. 120–1.

[48] E. Lipson, *op. cit.*, (1965 impression), p. 251.

[49] C. E. Camidge, *A History of Wakefield and its Industrial Fine Art Exhibition* (1866), pp. 7–8.

[50] W. G. Rimmer, 'The industrial profile of Leeds, 1740–1840', 130–157.

Other economic interests

Leeds has long been famous as a place pre-eminently superior to any other for trade and commerce, from being so advantageously placed, as it were, in the very heart of the navigation of the county, which communicates in every direction with almost every navigable river or canal in the Kingdom, affording to the Merchants and Manufacturers an expeditious and cheap intercourse with those of other places which otherwise would not be obtained.*

When the partners in a cloth firm made up their accounts at the end of the year they divided their profits in accordance with the deed of partnership. Since the size of the trading capital of the firm was usually maintained at around the same level for the duration of the partnership, surplus earnings were not consumed with the same avidity as in early factory enterprises. Each merchant had his own ideas about the way in which he spent his income. But these nevertheless conformed to a pattern. Obviously decisions were not taken every 31 December about the proportions to be allotted to consols, land purchase or loans, but when ample provision had been made for household and family expenses and after an adequate surplus had built up, resources were allocated to various ventures. One year government stock might appear the most attractive investment, three years later a few closes of land in Leeds might seem the soundest speculation. At other periods there were different calls: sons required apprenticeship fees and initial capital; daughters needed marriage portions; and cousins and acquaintances put forward good cases for loans to help them. Then when a merchant formed a new partnership it was often necessary for him to increase his capital contribution. And after many years of prosperous trading and investment he might decide to purchase a sizeable country property, which always entailed an entire reorganisation of existing commitments.

Only infrequently did savings find outlets outside these channels. This was not surprising since the range of investment in the West Riding was narrow. Industrial speculation was regarded not merely as being risky, but the majority of merchants argued that they expended enough energy and acrimony in the cloth trade without involving themselves in other ventures. In contrast, consols, land, a loan on good

* Pigot's *Directory of Yorkshire* (1830)

security returned a regular, relatively trouble-free, income. Even in enterprises like ship-owning, which were closely connected with their livelihood, interest was minimal. Of course Hull and Liverpool were a long way from the clothing areas but in the seventeenth century it was common for West Riding cloth traders to own shares in Hull ships. By 1750 the practice seems to have become restricted to only the most enterprising merchants in Leeds and Wakefield. The Elams owned several ships in the North Atlantic trade, but if the knowledge of Abraham Rhodes, who was forced into ship-owning when his firm entered the South American trade in 1808 (see p. 119), was typical, ignorance in the merchant community about the details of ownership was complete. From the day the firm bought three ships he never spent a totally restful night. Virtually every merchant in Leeds believed that shipping and insurance were matters best left to experts in Hull and Liverpool. And as we have seen the merchants steered clear of cloth-making itself, especially before the 1790's, and the working of the numerous collieries around Leeds, as in the rest of the country, was chiefly restricted to the landowners themselves. Nevertheless a small minority of merchants floated notable industrial enterprises. The Fenton family had been prominent in the Leeds cloth trade for close on a century before it turned its attention to coal-mining and farming around 1740. Soon their enterprise extended to banking, glass-making, iron- and copper-smelting and the farming of the Derwent Navigation tolls, and their industrial involvement spread south from Leeds to Sheffield and eventually beyond the county itself. When William Fenton, head of the dynasty, died in 1813, he was reputedly worth £1½ million. The partners in another Leeds cloth export firm, John Plowes (mayor in 1790) and David Dunderdale, an early merchant manufacturer and the son of a prosperous clothier, were founders of the well-known Castleford pottery.

But the more usual contribution of the merchants to industrial expansion in the county was less direct, and, given their interests, more understandable. As they were primarily traders they had a real commitment to the improvement of transport and monetary provisions. In this chapter therefore we shall examine their contribution to the transport system of the West Riding and isolate the way in which their financial activities led to the development of banking in the county.

(I)
The creation of the Aire and Calder Navigation after 1699 was the key development in the improvement of transport facilities in eighteenth

century Yorkshire. Priestley maintained in 1830 that 'the rendering of these rivers applicable to the purposes of commerce forms one of the most important features of the history of our inland navigation'.[1] By 1760 it had linked the three great woollen towns of the West Riding —Leeds, Wakefield and Halifax (by the Calder–Hebble extension of 1757)—with Hull, given that port a new lease of life and enabled the commerce of the West Riding cloth industry to become largely independent of control from London.

The detailed history of the Navigation has been told elsewhere.[2] Here it is essential only to stress four points. Firstly, the rivers were improved initially in 1699–1701 and the Navigation extended in the 1770's and 1820's largely with funds and enterprise from the merchant community in Leeds. Although ownership was technically split between two groups of proprietors, one in Leeds and the other in Wakefield, from the outset the Leeds undertakers were the much more active. In the first 20 years of the Navigation's history William Milner, who had initiated the entire scheme during his mayoralty in 1697–8, ruled its affairs. By 1720 he had raised £26,700 largely from the merchant community in Leeds. When trade improved in the late 1720's the

Map 2   Sketch-map of the Aire and Calder Navigation.
   1, Proposed Leeds–Selby canal (1769); 2, Haddlesey–Selby canal constructed 1774–6; 3, W. Jessop's proposed canal (1772); 4, J. Smeaton's proposed canal (1772); 5, Leeds–Liverpool canal.

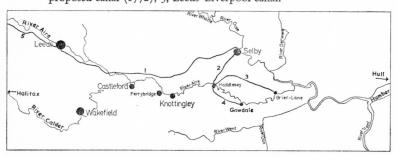

Navigation prospered for the first time. But improvements in the next 40 years, in spite of growing traffic on the rivers—Smeaton reckoned that the number of boats using the Leeds section of the Navigation had increased six or seven times between 1712 and 1771—were minimal. In 1740 relationships between the Navigation and the West Riding trading community were so bad that a network of turnpikes was initiated to provide a better, and it was believed cheaper, alternative mode of transport. And in the late 1760's plans were announced to link Leeds with Liverpool and Leeds with Hull by one vast cross-country canal. But the interest of the Navigation proprietors, now represented by Milner's grandson and Richard Wilson, recorder of Leeds and grandson of another merchant, was so strong that plans for a Leeds–Selby canal (the Selby–Hull scheme was never a serious proposition), which every trader in the county reckoned would provide a cheaper and more efficient outlet to Hull, was abandoned in spite of this endorsement and the support of the chief landowners in the area. Belatedly and as a result of this pressure the undertakers began improvements in 1774. £70,000 was expended on five cuts, a new set of locks throughout the Navigation and a five-mile canal from Haddlesey to Selby which by-passed the tortuous loops in the lower section of the Aire which had always caused problems. Again the majority of this money was raised in Leeds from the trustees, widows and daughters of merchants. When the next round of major improvements came in the 1820's, the rivers, at a cost of little short of a million pounds, were virtually canalised and the Navigation enabled ships of 100 tons to reach both Leeds and Wakefield. Once more the money came chiefly from Leeds and again one finds the same class of dependents and investors in the lists, except that the role attorneys had played in the 1770's was now taken up by bankers. Leathams, the Pontefract and Wakefield bankers, advanced £45,000; John Blayds of Leeds £17,000. The rest of the loans, like those of the 1770's, came from merchants retired from trade or their relations. Peter Rhodes of Leeds lent no less than £46,000; Arthur Heywood, a one-time Wakefield merchant, advanced £15,000. What is striking is that in the days when firms were dependent upon the support of the entire family—brothers, cousins and aunts included—this money, which a hundred years previously would have found its way into the family merchant house, was being channelled not into woollen manufacturing but into transport improvements.

Secondly, the merchant community was a great deal more evident in the history of the Navigation than the neighbouring West Riding landowners. Recently historians analysing the economic role of the gentry and nobility have argued that no one was more responsible for transport achievements than the landowner. An examination of the Aire and Calder Navigation certainly modifies this view of participation in an industrial area. Admittedly policy follows a familiar pattern and it would be difficult to argue that the vigour of Milner's direction between 1700 and 1725 was maintained. Conservatism was not a feature peculiar to the landowning class. In the 1740's and 1770's the proprietors defended their ownership, their monopoly of the water carriage of the cloth-manufacturing area, in the face of opposition from both landowners and the general trading community. Of course the proprietors claimed that the 1699 act had granted them ownership in perpetuity; and 'rights' and 'property' were not words that Parliament played lightly with in the eighteenth century. Not surprisingly, however, this entrenchment, endorsed by the House of Commons in 1772 and 1774 when it twice ejected the Leeds–Selby canal bills, meant that the direction of the Aire and Calder Navigation became increasingly reactionary. The undertakers were known locally as 'the fourth estate in the realm'. Whereas Milner and his friends in 1699 had worked hard to defeat the claims of York as the chief interior river port in the county—claims strong enough to kill all previous schemes in the preceding 70 years—once the Navigation prospered the undertakers only carried out very necessary improvements in the 1770's and 1820's when held at pistol point by the county's trading community. Their interest was chiefly in their dividends. They were not prepared to make loans for improvements. Only after 50 years of mismanagement by the lessees of the river tolls did the undertakers themselves take over the day-to-day affairs of the navigation in 1775 and appoint a professional manager. Thereafter administration was greatly improved, but the undertakers concentrated more and more upon their returns.

A cursory glance at a list of the undertakers in 1772 would have shown no evidence of their connection with trade. Not a single merchant held a share of the Wakefield stock, and only William Denison of Leeds could claim to be an active merchant. In three generations the families of the original merchant undertakers had become rentiers. The change was reflected in their obstruction of new transport plans. The real cause of the undertakers' hesitation to endorse improvements in the 1770's is delightfully shown in a pamphlet they issued in 1773:

The properties of the undertakers (were from) Time to Time conveyed and settled as Estates of Inheritance and which several widows, Femme Coverts and infants dependent upon as a great part, and in some instances, the Sole of their support, will be nearly destroyed, or very materially injured.[3]

Crucial decisions were being made by men who defended their actions in terms of their maiden aunts' and mothers-in-law's incomes. Not surprisingly such views curtailed their vision. In the 1830's the Navigation's opposition to a Leeds–Hull railway was couched in similar terms, although a defence of their position was then more difficult.

Entrepreneurial wastage was not a feature peculiar to the late nineteenth century. The Aire and Calder Navigation, on paper one of the most important and forward-looking in the eighteenth-century

Table 8 Lessees of the Aire and Calder Navigation Tolls, 1699–1774[a]

	Duration of lease	Annual amount paid for lease (£)	Names of lessees
1699	1	?	William Rooke jun.,* Joshua Ibbetson*
1704	1	800	George Dover*[b]
1705	1	1,000	George Dover,* Thomas Roebuck
1706	2	1,000	John Spencer, Thomas Roebuck
1708	7	1,000	Joseph Shaw and partners
1715	1	—	Navigation undertakers
1716	7	1,600	John Burton, George Dover,* Thomas Clarke
1723	7	2,000	Joseph Atkinson, John Burton, George Dover,* John Douglas*[c]
1730	7	2,600	Joseph Atkinson, John Burton, George Dover,* John Douglas*
1737	7	3,200	Joseph Atkinson, John Burton, George Dover,* John Douglas*
1744	7	3,600	Joseph Atkinson, George Dover,* Thomas Wilson[d]
1751	7	4,400	Joseph Atkinson, Thomas Wilson
1758	14	6,000	Sir Henry Ibbetson, Bart.,* Peter Birt
1772	21	8,500	Peter Birt.[e]

* Merchants and members of Leeds Corporation.
[a] The table is constructed from ACN.4/36.
[b] George Dover was brother-in-law of William Milner, and Mayor of Leeds.
[c] John Douglas was a cousin of Sir William Rooke, and Mayor of Leeds.
[d] Thomas Wilson was the second son of Richard Wilson, Recorder of Leeds, 1729–61. The recorder was a principal Wakefield shareholder and after Milner's death in 1740 the real manager of the Company's concerns.
[e] In May 1774 toll collection was taken into the undertakers' own hands, and Birt, by act of parliament, was given a tenth share in the estates and profits of the Aire and Calder Navigation.

economy, provides an interesting commentary on the means by which the progressive elements in our economic advance become blunted through this contact with the traditional forces of British society.

This leads us on to our third point about the Navigation. Extremely large dividends speeded up the regular process whereby the merchant was transformed into the country gentleman. Before 1720 dividends were negligible, but between 1725 and 1775 they climbed steadily from 10 to 28%. The latter year was the first in which the company managed its own affairs (previously the lessees of the tolls had been responsible for the day-to-day running of the Navigation) and subsequent dividends revealed the vast concealed profits that the toll farmers had always made.[4] By 1781 profits had risen to 100% and within 15 years they had increased by half again. They showed no decline until 1827

when heavy interest charges for improvements and the eventual competition of the railway accounted for the long slow down-turn. Since
the 1750's the undertakers' profits had been viewed with alarm and
envy. The Leeds newspapers reported in 1790 that 'a baronet in this
county now receives upwards of £5,000 per annum for what origin-
ally cost their ancestors only £5,000'. In 1817 Sir William Milner, the
baronet referred to, collected no less than £9,494, Richard Wilson,
£6,929 and Walter Spencer-Stanhope £4,550. By any standards these
were princely incomes. The smaller undertakers also did well. Miss
Kirshaw, the Vicar of Leeds' daughter, earned £900 on her £600
worth of stock: three descendants of James Armitage were paid £3,749
between them. By 1826 total dividends paid by the Navigation since
its inception had exceeded £2,250,000 and in 1824–6 the high point
of the Navigation's remarkable prosperity, 70 undertakers shared
£70,000 yearly. On these, 13 received dividends of over £1,000 each.
But behind the titles and fine addresses of the recipients hid the truth
that the majority of the undertakers were direct descendants of those
merchants who had founded the Company in 1699. Fat dividends and
large profits made before 1775 by the toll farmers had enriched many
a merchant family at a rate undreamt of in the dealings of commerce
alone.

Lastly, transport costs on the Navigation were always high. Certainly they were confined within the limits of the 1699 Act, although
this merely fixed the maximum rate of tolls to be levied for the full
distance from Leeds and Wakefield to the confluence with the Ouse at
16s. per ton from 1 October to May and 10s. for the summer months.
Within these limits the toll farmers constructed their table of rates.
Wakefield traders reckoned in 1740 'the freight from Rawcliffe (the
transit port on the Lower Aire) to Wakefield is Equal to Freight and
dues from London to Rawcliffe'. John Mills maintained

the Lock Dues upon the Rivers Aire and Calder, being very high, the Manufacturers of the Western Parts (i.e. around Halifax) as also Wool, Corn, etc.
from Lincolnshire, and other places can be conveyed by land carriage on the
said Roads, when they are passable at an easier expense than they are now carried
by Water.[5]

And there is evidence that West Riding cloth destined for London was
as likely to be sent by carrier's cart down the Great North Road as it
was to find its way there by coastal shipping. High charges were
accentuated by the shortcomings of the Navigation: the lower stretches
of the River Aire were shallow and in summer boats frequently took
several days to complete a run which should have taken 15 hours; the

toll farmers owned the majority of boats on the river and attempted 'to Monopolise the Trade'; a succession of Leeds merchants were appointed as farmers of the tolls and the practice, much criticised by the general trading community, gave an obvious trading advantage to these merchants. Not surprisingly traders attempted to work out a scheme of linked turnpikes in 1740–1 which would provide an alternative and cheaper mode of transport. In fact these roads never provided a viable alternative and trade upon the rivers grew. The number of vessels on the Leeds section of the Navigation had increased six- or sevenfold between 1711–13 and 1772: total receipts paid on the Navigation trebled between 1775 and 1800. But even with physical and managerial improvements after the 1770's there were still complaints about freight costs and dues on the river. It was inevitable in the debates about railways that someone would suggest a line from Leeds to Hull. As early as 1802 a Leeds merchant advocated a Leeds–Selby railway which he estimated would convey goods more cheaply and quickly than the Navigation and yet return a dividend of 10%.[6] Something of the old opposition to the company survived; although the undertakers had spent close on £1,000,000 in improvements in the 1820's, it came as no surprise to them that the Leeds merchant manufacturers and the Hull shippers, increasingly alarmed by the rapid growth of Goole as the Navigation's transit port after 1826, should propose a Leeds–Hull railway. The Hull–Selby part of the plan was abandoned for some reason, but a company to promote the Leeds–Selby section was formed in 1829. Resistance by the Navigation on the scale of the 1770's was out of the question. Industrialisation had made progress more difficult to impede, or at least obstruction was impossible to defend in terms of a few rentiers. The Act was passed in May 1830 and the railway opened in the following year. It is significant that three pillars of the new Leeds—Benjamin Gott, John Marshall and Edward Baines—should all be directors of the new company.

Recent economic history with its emphasis on growth and preoccupation with figures has attempted to measure the various paces of change in Britain's economic development since 1700. Although the Industrial Revolution has tended to become steam-rollered into line in this long view, it is still by common consent recognised that our economic growth began to accelerate after about 1740. The West Riding stands out as a major area of change, and was an account of the Aire and Calder Navigation, the main artery of its transport system, confined to an interpretation of its statistics—its toll receipts and dividend lists—we should take away the impression that the speed of change was rapid and that the Navigation served the Yorkshire textile area exceptionally well. A brief perusal of Priestley would confirm that improvements on the rivers were large-scale and frequent. Yet as we have seen the picture was somewhat different. The original scheme

Table 9   Aire and Calder Navigation accounts, 1775–1816

	Total receipts	Annual dividend	Reserves	Coal	Stone & lime	Corn	Miscellaneous[a]
						Lock dues paid on	
1775	40232		1725				
1776	43368		9071				
1777	52241	11250	18123	7894	2098	3777	8883
1778	41667	12000	9165	7527	1999	4579	8960
1779	40058	12000	8446	7391	2127	4339	8717
1780	41432	12000	8992	7815	1393	4168	9376
1781	40453	14250	6944	7777	1520	4362	9061
1782	40033	15000	8188	5963	1261	4046	9087
1783	45508	15000	8326	8228	1817	4985	10592
1784	45072	16000	6578	7913	1789	4006	11490
1785	53673	17000	12577	10483	2430	4546	12909
1786	52819	18000	10989	9668	2813	4596	13771
1787	57528	20000	12831	10445	3615	6283	14572
1788	55714	24000	8676	10310	4186	5819	14560
1789	59329	27000	8624	11712	4146	5718	15987
1790	64915	27000	11707	11429	4536	7038	18090
1791	67923	32000	8393	11040	4470	7857	19977
1792	69632	32000	9342	10030	4608	8075	22088
1793	64788	32000	5241	11156	5495	6533	18799
1794	68903	32000	7416	10989	6093	6196	19922
1795	69642	32000	7916	11830	4422	5560	21109
1796	75308	34000	10015	11888	5399	8078	21818
1797	91756	34000	473	14299	4125	8837	22069
1798	89062	34000	6655	14402	4773	8006	20941
1799	91124	34000	13929	14858	4184	6171	22300
1800	126292	34000	28386	18001	5663	10055	25744
1801	142638	38000	25810	17587	7569	12347	23312
1802	150268	42000	34698	19172	8346	9165	29841
1803	150325	42000	37989	19633	8103	8551	24698
1804	152090	42000	34232	21939	9116	9391	27206
1805	147135	46000	29875	19332	9785	8717	29276
1806	140766	48000	26826	20009	10268	9669	27538
1807	129666	48000	19321	20436	9645	8339	24849
1808	116773	48000	12493	21718	10059	7216	21622
1809	125993	48000	12862	21693	9812	9010	25941
1810	129758	48000	13616	21537	10693	9915	25769
1811	125716	48000	12944	22829	11939	9997	24582
1812	129173	48000	17087	22000	12346	7354	24256
1813	136161	43200[b]	21298	22745	11911	8926	27163
1814	141729	43200	31162	23012	10187	12579	28642
1815	150747	43200	35923	23201	10811	12971	29648
1816	152572	48000	41020	22526	9829	12696	29493

[a] The category 'miscellaneous' consisted largely of tolls paid transport of wool, cloth, dyestuffs and foodstuffs.

[b] A 10% property tax was deducted at source on the dividends from 1813 to 1815.

of 1699 was a brave conception fought in the teeth of York's opposition. After 1770, however, as the county's trading interests pointed out, it would have been more satisfactory and probably cheaper to construct a new canal system based upon the Leeds–Selby axis. Instead the Aire and Calder was improved at considerable cost only in the last resort. The direction of this important waterway, bold enough at the outset, had, by 1740, become as cautionary and inward-looking as that of any other river navigation in Britain. Merchant participation was not necessarily a guarantee of imaginative activity; or at least the descendants of the original proprietors soon lost their ancestors' drive. When improvements came in the 1770's and the 1820's and 1830's they were forced upon the Company by more forward-looking men who were outside the old merchant-landed group that ran the Navigation, just as changes in the Yorkshire woollen industry after 1780 did not rely upon the merchant communities who had controlled the life and trade of the Leeds and Wakefield areas for so long.

Dues on the Navigation throughout the period were undoubtedly very high, and this together with the insufficiencies of the rivers themselves was always a principal and justifiable cause of complaint by the West Riding merchants. Yet the Navigation flourished because it maintained a monopoly of the heavy goods traffic in the clothing areas. Traffic grew, however, in spite of the Navigation Company. Few railways were earlier or more widely welcomed than that between Leeds and Selby.

(II)

The history of the turnpike roads has always been neglected. As they were seldom anything more than patched up medieval routes only infrequently requiring engineering skill, and because the extent of their improvement has been disputed and their economic significance found difficult to evaluate, they have received far less attention than the canals and railways. One major misconception has arisen from discussions about the turnpikes which have been restricted to a consideration of the Acts themselves, their numbers and their chronology. A glance at the list of trustees named in each Act usually shows 100–200 men of property assigned to carry out the intended improvements. The long lists are headed by two or three peers, a sprinkling of baronets and a handful of wealthier traders and industrialists lost amongst a plethora of landowners. Historians have from this evidence assumed that those men who headed the list of trustees were the same as those who attended meetings, raised loans, let the tolls and mended the roads. In other words they have represented the creation of the eighteenth-century road system to be dependent upon those same land-owners who were active in politics and assiduous in keeping the peace. But was this pattern of participation in the improvement of roads in the agricultural areas repeated in the industrial regions? A survey of the seven trusts centred upon Leeds and created between 1741 and 1758 provides an answer for the West Riding clothing area.[7]

The general structure of the Acts for these seven roads was in no

Map 3   The roads around Leeds in 1780.

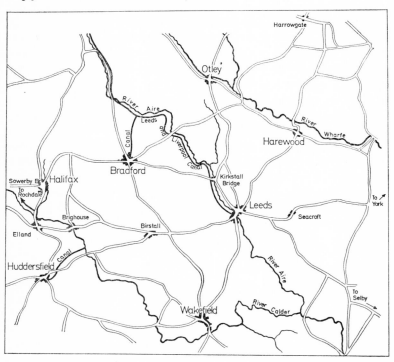

way different from that of hundreds of others. The same 150–200 names, apparently based on a minimum property qualification of £100 per annum, appear in each Act with few variations. Never more than a score of West Riding merchants can be identified, and the Halifax–Leeds–Selby Act which named the Mayor, Recorder and Corporation of Leeds *en bloc* was exceptional. Yet a study of the Leeds–Wakefield turnpike minute-book reveals that James Nelthorpe of Seacroft Hall, the cousin of a Lincolnshire baronet, was the only gentleman unconnected with trade—and even he leased a colliery from

Lord Irwin—ever present at the meetings concerned.[8] These were dominated by the Leeds merchants with a sprinkling of Aire and Calder Navigation undertakers. A meeting held in July 1758 was typical of the half dozen held every year. Besides two Navigation proprietors, the Reverend Samuel Kirshaw and the ubiquitous Richard Wilson, there were two attornies and five leading merchants, Thomas Lee, Hans Busk, Thomas and Edmund Lodge and Thomas Fenton. These men viewed the road and supervised the improvements. Since for several years the Wakefield meetings, held alternatively with those at Leeds, were unattended, the road appears to be the sole creation of a handful of merchants in Leeds. All the loans for its improvement, save £100 from a Wakefield undertaker of the Navigation, came from Leeds men in the first difficult years of development. £3,550 was raised at 5%: Samuel Davenport, Mayor of Leeds in 1764, provided £1,600; the two Richard Wilsons and Thomas Lee £500 apiece and Sir Henry Ibbetson and Thomas Fenton £100 each. Between 1761 and 1771 a further £4,400 was raised, all of which came from Leeds, except £1,000 lent by a Pontefract apothecary.

A perusal of the security ledgers of the other six turnpikes reveals a similar picture. The landowners appointed in the Acts were neither fulfilling their duties as trustees nor providing loans to repair the roads. The development of the turnpikes therefore relied upon a dozen interested merchants in Leeds. Of the original £1,250 borrowed by the Otley turnpike trustees, five Leeds men, Richard Wilson, Thomas Lee, Sir Henry Ibbetson, Benjamin Wade and Jeremiah Dixon provided £1,050. The same names are linked with other turnpike trusts: Sir Henry Ibbetson provided the first loan of £600 for the Leeds–Tadcaster turnpike in 1751; Robert Denison lent £300 to the trustees of this road in 1759 and £500 to the Leeds–Wakefield trust two years later. Only in the case of the Leeds–Selby road does the pattern vary. A similar nucleus of merchants—Ibbetson, Lee, John Noguier and Jeremiah Dixon—carried out the improvements, but this time the loans were not provided by the merchant circle in Leeds. This appears strange when the clamour with which the Leeds merchants had demanded the Act in 1741 and its extension in 1751 is considered. Or were Ibbetson and Dixon purposely obstructing attempts to improve the road? Certainly the road remained in a 'parlous' state until the 1780's, and Dixon was a Navigation undertaker and Ibbetson became a lessee of the rivers' tolls in 1758. The answer is not made easier by a consideration of the Leeds–Tadcaster turnpike, again a road constructed to provide an alternative outlet to the River Aire, for here the loans came almost entirely from merchants in Leeds.

The results of the merchants' labours to improve the roads were not very obvious before the 1780's at the earliest. The evidence is overwhelming. Arthur Young found the Leeds–Wakefield road in 1770 'stony and very ill made' and R. Brown, writing 20 years later, thought that the Wakefield–Halifax turnpike must be impassable in winter for at the end of October he found it 'in a miserable condition'. Every other topographer that jolted along the established tourist's route recorded similar strictures. Only William Marshall, the North's leading agricultural writer, could conclude 'this spirit of improvement has in no particular made greater exertions than in the forming of roads'.[9] One reason for the bad state of the roads was the relative inexperience of the merchants in the fundamentals of road construction. Although from the beginning they appear to have called in experienced road surveyors, and after 1769 the trustees of the seven roads began to meet twice yearly to co-ordinate policy and to improve the roads by the use of better materials, Brown in 1793 maintained that 'particularly near the manufacturing towns, materials are bad. To this circumstance, more than any other impropriety of management we attribute their insufficiency.' More important was the chronic state of the trusts' finances before the 1780's. Income from the tolls increased only very slowly between 1740 and 1785 when economic expansion was modest. The turnpikes were the subject of a vicious economic circle: loans were insufficient to repair the roads, further loans were impossible because the receipts were not adequate to meet additional charges. It was only with the great post-American war expansion that the roads became financially sound, and the large increase in traffic meant a rise in revenue sufficient (at least when the toll lessees chose to apply a proportion of their revenue for these purposes) to put them in good order.[10]

Certainly traffic was speeding up whatever critics in the saddle were saying. On one occasion William Milner took a week to get up to London in the winter of 1710, a journey that would normally have taken him four days. In 1785 the mail-coach promised to complete the journey in 26 hours. For the first time in the 1780's daily coaches were advertised from Leeds to London, Birmingham, Manchester, Carlisle, Sheffield, Hull and, in the season, Scarborough and Harrogate. Even the goods-waggons which plied more leisurely, but equally regularly, between the large towns became less slow, so that William Denison could enjoy supplies of strawberries sent from his estate in Nottinghamshire by carrier's cart in the 1770's.[11]

The eventual success of the turnpike was made possible by the initial enterprise of the Leeds merchants. In part conceived out of

emulation, and part by antagonism against the Aire and Calder Navigation, the roads were works that greatly facilitated the movement of
goods throughout the country between the Ouse, Wharfe and Calder,
and especially Leeds, Bradford and Halifax. In securing the Acts,
supervising their execution, and themselves usually providing the
money for early improvements, the score or so of the wealthiest
Leeds merchants were again taking the lead in important developments
in the woollen industry and county in their belief that good transport
facilities were an essential lubricant of trade. Since dividends were
limited by statute to 5%, direct pecuniary rewards were small, and
turnpike business was dull routine work. Nevertheless the merchants
wished to direct developments which were of vital significance to
themselves. That the landowners in the West Riding played so little
part is therefore not surprising. The turnpikes were major link roads
between towns and nobody had a greater interest in commercial and
urban expansion than the merchants.

(III)
The history of the bill of exchange is a long one. Far back beyond
1700 the trade bill had become the chief instrument in large commercial transactions and we have seen how important it was to merchants
in the settlement of their accounts. Here we must note something of its
wider implications in the financial system of the West Riding. Its
significance was due not simply to the fact that nowhere was its use
more widely known (except in Lancashire), nor to its great utility,
nor even that it partly remedied the chronic shortage of local cash
supplies, but that it had become a central prop in the relationship
between the clothier and the merchant. Contemporaries believed that
the paramountcy of the Yorkshire industry was dependent upon the
separation of their functions, that, unlike in the West Country where
they were fused, the apprentice and journeyman of thrift and diligence could set himself up as a clothier on a negligible capital. This
situation was only possible if the merchant was able to make frequent
cash payments for the clothiers' weekly cloth supply. Readiness to pay
cash on the clothier's delivery ensured the merchant the most competitive prices, it enabled the clothier to buy his stocks of wool from
the stapler and pay his journeymen's weekly wages. The need of the
merchant to transmute a relatively irregular supply of large bills
(payments for his cloth shipments) into regular supplies of cash and
small bills for the clothiers, cloth-dressers and dyers made his financial
arrangements important in both the industry and county.
   The merchant's key position centred upon his deep knowledge of

the London and provincial bill markets and his provision of loans and acceptance of deposits. It was these functions, long practised, that made easy the transition from trading to banking after 1770. There is evidence that merchants discounted bills for cash in two ways. Firstly, there was a purchase of bills by neighbouring estate-owners. The Temple Newsam stewards sent innumerable notes down to Leeds for 'good' bills on the strength of Lord Irwin's rents. The third Lord Irwin kept a bill account with Thomas Kitchingman, a leading merchant in the 1690's; and when the latter's wants were 'very urgent' he could ask the steward at Temple Newsam for £100 cash as 'This is ye time of ye year our clothiers buy in their wool and they are very importunate for their money.' This arrangement of mutual convenience which recognised the shortage of cash in the county is further illustrated by a letter from John Spencer of Cannon Hall to his brother-in-law Walter Stanhope:

This morning Mr. West sent to my Father for a London Bill for £140, upon which he recollected that you said (there) was a Want of Cash in the County, he hath therefore sent you the Cash and desires you will send him by the Bearer a London Bill at as short a date as you conveniently can.[12]

Secondly, a more regularised provision of cash was obtained through the Leeds merchants' participation in land-tax remittance. They played a threefold role in the collection of the tax—as commissioners for the Skyrack wapentake, as commissioners and collectors for the Borough of Leeds, and as deputies to the county receivers. The functions of the latter were the most important.

The collection of the land- and assessed-taxes was a notorious feature of eighteenth-century governmental administration. The time which elapsed between the collection and remittance provided numerous pecuniary openings for those engaged as receivers. Thomas Lee described the office of deputy-receiver as being one 'which is of some little convenience to the merchant'. But as Lee wanted his office confirming he stressed its duties rather than its benefits, and, in fact, the large amounts of cash which the deputy-receiver held for several months were invaluable in facilitating cash payments in the woollen industry, and in enabling those merchants involved to purchase consignments of cloth beyond their firm's own resources. Ample evidence of this utility comes from the account-books of Ibbetson and Koster.[13]

Sir Henry Ibbetson had handled part of the remittances of James Gee and later Marmaduke Constable, the East Riding Receivers, since at least 1738, and those of Henry Hitch, the West Riding Receiver, since

September 1751. In these two cases the receiver's office appears to have been largely titular—although it was by no means honorary—and the indirect rewards of remittance were reaped by the deputy-receivers, three Leeds merchants. As Lee wrote to Lord Rockingham concerning a dispute with William Stanhope, Hitch's successor and the younger brother of Walter Stanhope: 'The Letter (from the Treasury) to Mr. Stanhope is in reality to me and my colleagues, as his Lordship, and all this county knows that we are his sureties and have the receipt of the whole Land Tax.' Between June 1749 when Ibbetson's accounts begin and December 1761 when they close, following his death in the previous summer, he remitted to the Bank of England, where both receivers were amongst the minority who kept their accounts there, a total of £380,000 or around £31,000 on average each year. This money was remitted to the bank chiefly by bills which Ibbetson drew upon his foreign correspondents, or bills which he obtained in London and Leeds, and also, although these usually only made up the balance, bills drawn upon his London agents, Battier and Zornlin. The cash and small bills which were transferred to Leeds from the East Riding, and from closer at hand through Henry Hitch, were remitted only when the bills of Ibbetson's correspondents were notified in Leeds. His letter books show that bills, usually less than half a dozen, of varying totals between £340 and £1,730, were dispatched to Daniel Race, the chief cashier of the Bank of England, sometimes almost every other day, at other times close on monthly intervals. This method of remittance allowed considerable balances to build up in Ibbetson's favour. He held a balance of £6,600 in 1738 for James Gee, and from the evidence between 1749 and 1761, although remittances were speeded up around the mid-1750's, balances for short periods were considerable.[14]

These transactions facilitated Ibbetson's own bill dealings and enabled him to enjoy the profits of bill discount. He explained its utility to a Lisbon correspondent:

As we have an acct. of the Land Tax payment occasion to remit to the Bank of England we can have bills discounted at a much easier rate than many here . . . if therefore you do but remit us yr. bills . . . it will be a conveniency to us and enable us carry on this business of long credit with some tolerable degree of ease.

Equally important was its use to him in the woollen trade, where not only was scarce cash diffused throughout the industry—Ibbetson provided regular supplies of cash to the Oates's and Peter Birt—but he was able to buy cloth in quantities beyond the range of his capital. The

L

returns of the south European trade—a six-months market—were slow and frequently difficult. Yet between 1749 and 1760 Ibbetson's annual turnover was between two and three times his capital resources. It is interesting to note that his turnover was only slightly less than the amount he remitted each year for the land-tax receiver. When he took over part of Hitch's returns in 1751 it is significant that his share of Gee's remittances fell by almost a half. Credit from the balances he held allowed Ibbetson to purchase cloths in late autumn and early winter when they were at their cheapest. Land-tax remittance contributed in no small measure to Ibbetson's position in the woollen trade and county as a land purchaser, woollen merchant, investor in government and transport stock, lessee of the Navigation and county politician.[15]

Ibbetson was not alone in sharing the benefits of the land-tax collection. William Milner was a deputy-receiver for Francis Wyvill, Receiver for Yorkshire, Northumberland and Durham from 1698 to 1717. John Dixon and Thomas Lee handled Gee's accounts along with Ibbetson, as they also shared in returning Hitch's money from the West Riding. Lee appears to have become Receiver for the East Riding by 1760, and he certainly claimed that he could have succeeded Hitch in 1765 declining only on condition that the old deputy-receivers were reappointed. William Denison's anxiety to secure a share in the return of the land-taxes shows how valuable their remission could be to a merchant's business. In 1778 he was thanking Sir Fletcher Norton, the Speaker of the Commons, for his 'kind promise of assisting in obtaining the returning some of the publick money.' Two years later he was pestering the Duke of Newcastle to mention his willingness to remit the West Riding taxes to Lord North.[16] Denison stressed that not only could he offer security 'superior to that of any other house' but also that he believed the taxes had so increased that there was sufficient work for three or four firms in Leeds to return the taxes. The actual division of the returns between three deputy-receivers is from the evidence difficult to explain. Denison recognised that they must be of the utmost repute but supposed there was no fixed number. It is probable that the tax commissioners believed that there was a smaller degree of risk when the returns were not entrusted to one individual, and it is at least arguable that three deputies were necessary since each merchant was only interested in, or capable of, handling an amount which he could cover by his own trading transactions. Yet as the posts were subject to political manœuvres it is not necessary to account for their existence in terms that made financial sense.

Certainly whatever the reasons for the returns being divided amongst three deputy-receivers, Lee, Dixon and Ibbetson (replaced by John Blayds in 1762) had carved up the handling of the East and West Riding tax-returns very neatly. Blayds alone, however, provides an illustration of Dr. Pressnell's thesis that collectors of government revenue frequently became country bankers. Blayds was not a founding member of Beckett's Bank, but he was a partner by early 1777. In May of that year he was holding an enormous balance for William Stanhope, so large that the tax office threatened that the renewal of Stanhope's appointment would be delayed if the large amounts of money in his hands were not remitted quickly. To Stanhope's relief Blayds agreed to pay £11,500 into the former's account within seven days.[17] These large balances which Blayds leisurely remitted to the Bank of England undoubtedly aided the growth and stability of Beckett's Bank in these difficult years between 1778 and 1783.

The direct pecuniary benefits of Land Tax remittance were in fact small. Ibbetson received a 'poundage' of 4s. per cent for collecting the money from the East and West Riding centres. But the actual cash which these four leading merchants handled, the facilities it gave them in their own trading transactions and the credit the retained balances allowed them, was invaluable to them in every branch of their extensive activities.

It was not only that every merchant from Ibbetson, Dixon and Lee down made some contribution to the circulation of cash and bills throughout the West Riding in their everyday business, but also in the provision of loans and acceptance of deposits that they long-anticipated those functions more usually associated with the establishment of banking. Only the paucity of eighteenth-century merchants' accounts hides these important features of mercantile finances. Advances appear to have been of two types. Loans on bond were made by one merchant to another when the borrower was temporarily straitened or needed additional resources for some venture. Walter Stanhope borrowed £500 in 1734 from his fellow merchant George Dover. When Edward Gilyard, a brother-in-law of William Lupton and a retired dyer, died in 1755 his estate was valued at £2,520, of which £1,995 was lent on bond and note in sums ranging from £10 lent to a hatter, Thomas Barnet, to £700 borrowed by Lupton himself.[18] The incomes of the children, widows and spinster sisters of deceased merchants were frequently partly derived from interest payments made on loans of this type. By the end of the century advances were often much larger: Mathew Rhodes, who was rapidly expanding his business in the early 1790's, borrowed £7,000 from the Elams between 1790 and 1793. Secondly, loans and mortgages were arranged with the neighbouring gentry. William Milner in the 1720's was lending large sums to the Irwins who were placed in some financial difficulty by the deaths in quick succession of the third, fourth and fifth viscounts.

Over 100 years later Timothy Rhodes's investments of almost £75,000 included two mortgages for £30,000 to the Chaytor family and one for £10,000 to Sir John Lister Kaye.[19] The merchants were more prominent in negotiating mortgages than the banks, although not necessarily more than individual bank partners who in Leeds appear to have been willing to lend to landowners and merchants alike on land security. Evidence of the merchants accepting deposits is much sparser, but there is one good example in Leeds. Joseph Fountaine, Mayor in 1777 and a partner with John Wormald in a leading house, 'borrowed' on his own account £5,800 by bond and note between 1782 and 1790 in varying amounts from £50 to £1,200 from 29 different sources. These amounts were obviously deposits placed with Fountaine since he could easily have obtained far larger loans, being a merchant of great standing in the town, on much more convenient terms. When Naylors, the largest merchant house in Wakefield, broke in 1825, 'their failure brought distress and ruin to many and many a family' who had placed their savings with Jeremiah Naylor.[20]

Through their financial dealings the merchant moved imperceptibly into banking. There was nothing in the West Riding approaching the development in London where the merchant inevitably slipped from 'commercial pursuits proper to those of pure finance', for the woollen merchants were much more closely attached to an industrial region than their counterparts in London.[21] Nevertheless in Leeds banking brought no profound change in financial arrangements; it was largely a systematisation of existing monetary transactions.

Beyond a process merely imitative of national trends two features account for the growth of the West Riding country banks. The first was the need to simplify existing mercantile financial arrangements. The Leeds post-bags and the merchants' books were cluttered with letters to their correspondents and London agents concerning the complicated process of drawing, accepting, endorsing and discounting bills. The banks made at least the latter stage more convenient and cheaper. A letter from Beckett's Bank to the Aire and Calder Navigation undertakers brings out the element of simplification.

We will Furnish you with our drafts upon London for such sums as may be most convenient to yourselves and when they become due they shall be esteemed cash—any bills that you may put into our hands when they become due and are paid shall be esteemed cash also—we will furnish you with Cash here and accept of Cash from you here whenever it may Suit you to pay us any, and Cash here on Bills due in London shall be esteemed the same thing—this is reducing the whole matter to a cash account.[22]

There is evidence of the early use of banks by merchants: William Milner kept an account with Benjamin Hoare in the 1720's; Thomas Wolrich was an old customer of Smiths in Nottingham. This, together with the immediate use the merchants made of the first two Leeds banks, is further testimony to the inconvenience of earlier arrangements. The second feature was the need to provide stability of the currency within the county. The perennial shortage of cash had become chronic by the 1760's, and was further accelerated by 'clipping' and the 1767–72 boom. Attempts to enforce the acceptance of Portuguese gold were only partly successful, and the county became flooded with small bills and promissory notes, 'this hydra (which) may with propriety be compared to Pharaoh's lean kine, swallowing up in the end all real property'. The recoining of 1774—Beckett's Bank collected the deficient gold coin in Leeds—and Savile's Act in the following year to prohibit the issue of notes below £1—two years later raised to a minimum of £5—were somewhat temporary remedies. In 1787 at the height of the post-American war cycle the county was again inundated with the promissory notes payable to the bearer a number of days after sight. Meetings were held throughout the Riding to petition Parliament to prevent the abuse, and a list of north-country banks circulating such notes was drawn up, although there were many 'individual persons issuing bills or notes in the same manner'.[23] The situation was similar to that in Manchester, but Leeds was saved through the orthodoxy of its banks' policy in handling their drafts on London and note circulation. As a result local notes never fell into the disrepute that they did in south Lancashire after 1788.

The merchant partners in the various Leeds banks were cautious and skilful bankers. Beckett's Bank was perhaps the best known of all north-country banks, although the date of its foundation is uncertain. Indeed John Beckett, born in 1743 and the son of a wholesale grocer in Barnsley, was not an original partner. The bank appears to have been founded in the 1750's—the earliest notes are reputed to have had 'Established in 1758' printed upon them—by Thomas Lodge, a wealthy woollen merchant and a member of one of Leeds' oldest families, and John Arthington, a Quaker linen-draper.[24] At least Beckett was a partner by 1772 when a notice appeared that the fourth member of the bank, Thomas Broadbent, had withdrawn. Lodge, whose position in the town and trade ensured immediate success of the venture, died in 1776 and four new partners were admitted into his place to institute the legal maximum of six. Thomas Wilson was a former London and

Wakefield merchant who had succeeded to his late brother's (Richard Wilson II, the town's Recorder) extensive Leeds estates in the same year; John Blayds, merchant and twice mayor was, as we have seen, a deputy-receiver of the West Riding land-tax; John Calverley was the son of a wholesale grocer and William Walker a woollen merchant and son of a former minister of Mill Hill chapel. It was an impressive list. Wilson, a brother-in-law of Lodge and uncle of John Beckett, and Blayds were two of the wealthiest men in Leeds, and Arthington and Walker attracted the business of the Quaker and Unitarian communities. The partnership changed several times within these families but by 1800 the Beckett and Blayds families alone directed the bank's affairs. In the nineteenth century it gained an enormous reputation for stability that stretched far beyond the confines of Leeds and the Yorkshire cloth trade. When Beckett's was amalgamated in 1920 with the Westminster Bank it had 37 branches and was the largest private bank in the country.[25]

None of the other banks founded in Leeds were of comparable reputation or importance, but those founded before 1820 are interesting, like similar establishments in Wakefield and Halifax, in that their partners frequently were drawn from the merchant community. The New Bank which opened in 1777 in Boar Lane was not initially a Leeds venture, although control eventually fell to Thomas Bischoff, senior member of the well-known merchant family, who was in charge when the bank collapsed in 1827.[26] The partners of the Commercial Bank, which opened in Leeds in 1792 with a branch at Thirsk, had again close mercantile associations. William Fenton Scott, the chief partner, was the son of Henry Scott, merchant and mayor in 1748, and the son-in-law of William Fenton, merchant and colliery-owner who was mayor in 1733 and again in 1747. For a time the Commercial Bank looked like rivalling Beckett's in influence, but in January 1812 it broke through the failure of its London agent, Boldero and Lushington. Since the bank had a modest note circulation of £60,000 and could immediately realise £100,000 the *Mercury* was able to comfort its readers that there 'will be no reason for inordinate anxiety'. By August 1816 a dividend of 20s. in the £ had been paid, and two years later the grateful creditors purchased a piece of plate as a tribute to the proprietors' integrity.[27]

Another Leeds bank with a country-town branch was that of Thompson, Elam and Holtby. The date of the establishment of their partnership is uncertain, but in 1803 they were operating the Bridlington Bank. Samuel Elam and William Thompson were both Quaker merchants who had done well in the American trade. From the evidence of their monetary transactions with Mathew Rhodes, with Jowetts—Quaker wool staplers—and their association with Isaac Leatham, a Pontefract banker, in large-scale land speculation, it would appear that the Elam family by the 1790's were ranging well outside the confines of woollen merchanting and were already quasi-bankers. Samuel Elam's speculations during the uncertain years of the first decade of the nineteenth century appear to have been unsound. In October 1810 Thompson and Holtby announced that they would carry on the business without Elam, and on the same day he advertised 480 acres of land for sale at Roundhay. It must have come as no surprise that two months later all claimants of Elam were requested to submit statements in order than the estate might be 'put into a Train of Liquidation'.[28] Exactly a year after the failure of the Commercial Bank in 1812, yet another bank was opened with partners who were drawn from merchant families. Mathew Rhodes and William Williams Brown were both young men whose fathers had made fortunes in the woollen cloth trade after 1783; and the other two partners of the Union Bank, Thomas and Stephen Nicholson of Roundhay Park, were close relatives of Rhodes. After a service in Leeds second only to Beckett's this bank was amalgamated with Lloyds in 1900.[29]

Three points emerge from this brief discussion of country banking as it concerned the merchant community in Leeds. Firstly, merchants readily entered banking, although this did not always necessarily mean that they abandoned their original calling, with a result that capital gradually accrued during the eighteenth century in the cloth trade was diverted into, and occasionally fast dissipated in, banking activities. In varying degrees the resources of the Lodges, Wilsons, Rhodes, Elams, Scotts, Browns, Denisons and Blayds were utilised in the provision of banking facilities. Banking, unlike factory manufacturing, became a gentleman's profession. Lady Essex found William Beckett, the head of Beckett's Bank in the 1840's, 'a more humanised Barbarian than she had expected', and Granville Vernon recalled:

I went to my old friend Bill Beckett, expecting a good plain dinner, and a few old Yorkshire friends; instead of which I found, to my surprise, a very fine London gentleman as my host, with a number of fine London people as guests, and a dinner of the most *recherche* character with the finest of wines.

For the woollen industry the economic repercussions of this transition from merchant to banker were important. Large commercial fortunes were diverted away from the direct channels that led to large-scale manufacturing. William Denison maintained in 1778 that it was hazardous 'to commence an occupation that requires £50,000–£60,000 capital with a mere trifle', and the resources that the Leeds merchant families took into country banking, even if not in the range Denison stipulated, were very appreciable in comparison with the capital requirement of all save a handful of the very largest manufacturers before the 1830's.[30] Secondly, bankers' drafts on London became the chief form of currency used in the Yorkshire trade, for with their numerous endorsements they were good securities. Not only did these drafts alleviate the serious shortage of cash, but they facilitated merchant accounting. John Micklethwaite in the 1790's held a typical merchant's account with Beckett's. He received a few large and comparatively infrequent payments from America—sometimes less than one a month —and yet he had to make many small but regular payments to the clothiers with whom he dealt, and the cloth-dressers he employed. As a result Micklethwaite had resort to Beckett's almost daily for drafts upon them at short notice. In 1796 he had 444 separate transactions with his bank for drafts and cash totalling £10,647. Moreover the banks provided greatly improved facilities for foreign exchange.[31] Lastly, the banks were important in the provision of short-term loans in the form of temporary overdrafts. Obviously the size of the overdraft was gauged on the respectability of the merchant house, and it was the wealthier houses, in the last resort least needing them, which obtained the largest amounts. In January 1825 J. H. Oates was informed by Beckett's that they had reduced their charges to 4% and that the firm could have 'what we like there at that rate', although it later transpired that the amount was to be the underside of £10,000. Arrangements like these meant that the merchant could keep the minimum amount of cash in his current account, knowing that in the case of extra heavy buying in the cloth markets, or delay in correspondents' remittances, his obligations would be temporarily met by his bank. Abraham Rhodes' ultimate success in building up a firm that 'became almost one of the first in this town' was largely due to his bank's forbearance in guaranteeing an overdraft in the region of £30,000 for at least two years in the critical period at the conclusion of the Napoleonic Wars.[32]

The close-knit nature of the merchant community in Leeds and the banks' dealings in government securities, the chief area of mercantile investment besides land until the 1820's, meant that the bankers had a shrewd knowledge of the merchants' reliability. The system was a convenient arrangement necessitated by the seasonal nature of cloth-merchanting, and it saved many enterprising firms like the Rhodes' that would otherwise have been drawn down into the periodic whirlpools in trade after 1790. In the provision of these facilities and in their thorough knowledge of the requirements of the woollen industry the bank directors made a contribution to industrial development that was not unworthy of their merchant forbears.

Notes to Chapter 7

[1] J. Priestley, *op. cit.*, (1831), p. 7.

[2] This section is based upon R. G. Wilson's '*Leeds Woollen Merchants: 1700–1830*', University of Leeds Ph.D. thesis (1964), pp. 185–239. Part of this material of the Aire and Calder Navigation has been published in *The Bradford Antiquary*, New Series, Part XLIV (1969) as 'The Aire and Calder Navigation Part III. The Navigation in the second half of the eighteenth century'. See also his 'Transport dues' (1966), and R. W. Unwin's two articles in *The Bradford Antiquary*, Parts XLII, XLIII, (1964, 1967).

[3] The pamphlet is amongst the Aire and Calder Navigation papers in the British Transport Commission Historical Records (York), ACN 4/117.

[4] Three toll farmers at least made substantial fortunes from the toll farm of the Navigation: Thomas Wilson between 1744–58; Sir Henry Ibbetson (and his executors), 1758–72; Peter Birt, 1758–74. The entire Wilson family did well from the Navigation. Wilson's father and brother ruled its affairs from the 1730's to the early 1770's. Thomas Wilson was a partner in Beckett's Leeds Bank and his family, after the Denison's, was the wealthiest in late eighteenth-century Leeds (see p. 201). Ibbetson's family made more money from the toll farm than they did in the cloth export trade and when Ibbetson's heir came of age in 1772 he was able to commission John Carr to build a fine new house at Denton on the family's Wharfdale estate (see p. 244). When Peter Birt was removed in 1774 as toll farmer he retired to Wenvoe Castle in Glamorganshire. Thereafter the company, not unwisely, collected its own dues.

[5] *C.J.*, XXIII, 570, 614; *L.M.*, 6 July 1741.

[6] *L.M.*, 16, 23 Jan. 1802.

[7] In 1741: Leeds–Elland (Halifax); Leeds–Bradford–Halifax; Leeds–Selby; 1751: Leeds–Tadcaster; 1753: Leeds–Harrogate; 1758: Leeds–Wakefield and Leeds–Otley.

[8] This and the following paragraph are based upon Leeds–Wakefield Turnpike Minute Book (1758–79); Leeds–Wakefield Turnpike Mortgage Ledger (1760–1854); Leeds–Selby Turnpike Securities Ledger (1751–1872); Leeds–Tadcaster Ledger (1751–1841); Leeds–Otley Turnpike Securities Ledger (1780–1841); Leeds–Elland Turnpike Securities Ledger. All are deposited in the County Record Office, Wakefield.

[9] A. Young, *A Six Months Tour Through the North of England* (1770), I, p. 136; R. Brown, *op. cit.*, p. 213; J. Aikin, *op. cit.*, p. 567; W. Marshall, *The Rural Economy of Yorkshire* (1788), p. 180.

[10] *L.M.*, 7 March 1769; R. Brown, *loc. cit.*; R. G. Wilson, 'Transport dues', 110–23.

[11] *Diary*, II, 12; *L.M.*, 2 Aug. 1785; Denison MSS. De H/45, W. Denison to J. Hayes, 28 June, 9 July 1777.

[12] Temple Newsham MSS.; Spencer–Stanhope MSS. (Sheffield) 60560/19. See also *Thors. Soc.*, XXI (1912), 7, 67–8.

[13] W. R. Ward, *The English Land Tax in the Eighteenth Century* (1953), pp. 167–168; L. S. Pressnell, *Country Banking in the Industrial Revolution* (1956), pp. 56–60; W. G. Hoskins, *Industry, Trade and People in Exeter*, pp. 45–6; Wentworth Woodhouse MSS., Thomas Lee to the Marquess of Rockingham, 22 July 1765.

[14] W. R. Ward, *op. cit.*, pp. 48, 103–5; W. M. Acres, *The Bank of England from Within 1694–1900* (1931), pp. 231, 254–5, 374; Sir J. Clapham, *The Bank of England: a History* (1944), I, p. 199; Wentworth Woodhouse MSS., Thomas Lee to Lord Rockingham, 3 May 1766.

¹⁵ Compare King's Lynn where the merchants complained to the town's M.P.s about a Mr. Taylor, receiver for part of Norfolk and all Cambridgeshire, who 'was a great dealer' in Lynn and 'it is no small advantage to him to have the power of so much money for sometimes six, seven or eight months', *A Supplement to Blomfield's Norfolk* (1929), p. 178.

¹⁶ *Diary*, II, 439; W. R. Ward, *op. cit.*, p. 104; Denison MSS. De H/46, 15 Dec. 1778, 27 Feb. 1781.

¹⁷ L. S. Pressnell, *Country Banking*, pp. 56–71; *L.M.*, 18 March 1777; Spencer–Stanhope MSS. 2186, William Stanhope to Walter Spencer-Stanhope, M.P., 27 May 1777.

¹⁸ Spencer-Stanhope MSS. 114; Lupton MSS.

¹⁹ Temple Newsham MSS., William Milner to Hon. Chas. Ingram, 19 Oct. 1720; and the same to Isabella, Lady Irwin, 31 May, 21 Aug., 14 Oct. 1721, 14 April, 9 June, 29 Oct., 1722; DB/39 Armitage Rhodes Papers.

²⁰ Gott MSS. small notebook lettered 'Acct. of Money borrowed by J.F.'; H. Clarkson, *op. cit.*, p. 52.

²¹ L. S. Sutherland, *A London Merchant, 1695–1774*, p. 15. See also L. B. Namier, 'Brice Fisher M.P. A mid-eighteenth century merchant and his connexions', *Ec.H.R.*, XLII (1927), 514–22.

²² ACN 1/36, 4 July 1774.

²³ *L.M.*, 11 May 1773, 30 Jan., 6 Feb., 6 March, 10 April, 13 May, 10, 17 June 1787. See also T. S. Ashton, 'The Bill of exchange and private banks in Lancashire, 1790–1830' in T. S. Ashton and R. S. Sayers (eds.), *Papers in English Monetary History* (1953), pp. 37–49.

²⁴ H. Pemberton, 'Two hundred years of banking in Leeds', *Thors. Soc. Miscellany*, vol. 13, part I (1958). T. E. Gregory in *The Westminster Bank Through a Century* (1936), II, p. 136, states, on the evidence of William Beckett in 1832, that the bank was founded in 1774. He thinks the Beckett brothers came to Leeds in the early eighteenth century and made an ample fortune in the Portuguese trade. But Beckett was not born until 1743. Certainly he was quickly accepted in Leeds: he was mayor within two years of election to the corporation, and he married the third daughter of Christopher Wilson, later Bishop of Bristol, and grand-daughter of Richard Wilson I.

²⁵ *L.I.*, 6 Oct. 1772; *L.M.*, 8 March 1777, 26 March 1800; T. E. Gregory, II, 137–140.

²⁶ *L.I.*, 11 March 1777; H. Pemberton, *op. cit.*, pp. 62–3; Oates MSS.

²⁷ L. S. Pressnell, *Country Banking*, p. 463; *L.M.*, 31 March 1792, 11, 18 Jan. 1812, 10 Aug. 1816; *L.I.*, 11 Jan. 1812, 16 Nov. 1818.

²⁸ *L.M.*, 18 June 1803; *L.I.*, 24 Dec. 1810; John and Joseph Jowett's Ledger No. 2 in the Brotherton Library, Leeds; M. Phillipps, *A History of Banks, Bankers and Banking in Northumberland, Durham and North Yorkshire* (1894), p. 284.

²⁹ *L.I.*, 23 Nov. 1812; R. V. Taylor, *op. cit.*, pp. 461–2; H. Pemberton, *op. cit.*, pp. 64–6.

³⁰ A. M. W. Stirling, *op. cit.*, pp. 206–7. Denison MSS. De H/46, W. Denison to Mrs. Cooke, 7 Dec. 1778.

³¹ *L.I.*, 4 Jan. 1827; Micklethwaite MSS. 4932A; L. S. Pressnell, *Country Banking*, p. 365.

³² Oates MSS., J. H. Oates to E. Oates, 17, 22 Jan. 1825; R. G. Wilson, 'Fortunes of a Leeds merchant house'.

8   *Politics and religion*

> I believe the only information that will be conveyed by the com-
> missioner who came into the town of Leeds . . . will be that he
> found the Corporation of Leeds as pure as holy water.★

We should have a strange view of merchant society if we were left
with the impression that the merchant never looked beyond his
counting-house window or walked further than the cloth halls. When
he retired, after a good dinner, over a pipe and bottle of wine with his
partners and friends, talk shifted—when it was serious—from trade to
affairs of state and church. National events that shook London were
discussed a few days later in terms of their impact on Leeds and its
industry. They gained a certain perspective: arguments about Dr.
Sacheverall's trial shifted to talk about the High Church party in the
town; the American war was seen not so much as a crucial event in
the development of the Empire as in its relation to the Yorkshire
woollen industry. In this metamorphosis, politics and religion became
as much a mainspring of a merchant's life as his trading interests.
Together they provided a framework of thought into which his social
and economic actions fitted.

The merchants' political participation was on two levels. It is convenient therefore to separate their activities in governing Leeds, from
their share in formulating policy in the county. Several themes can be
explored. In the town the corporation was attacked by the new manufacturing class—men largely of Whig and Dissenting sympathies—
thrown up in the rapid changes which overtook Leeds after 1783. The
old merchant community was charged with inefficiency and corruption in grappling with the problems of a quickly growing town. In
the county the importance of the merchant was much less evident in
an area always dominated by the landed aristocracy and gentry. Yet
the woollen industry, and the merchants especially, provided far the
most important economic interest in the county besides the landed
preponderance. After 1780 this interest was the most potent force to

★ Sir John Beckett, 1834.

be reckoned with in Yorkshire politics, and by the 1820's it was claimed that the county's elections were being settled in Leeds without reference to the county at large.

(I)

The pre-eminence of Leeds amongst the clothing towns was emphasised in that it alone was incorporated by Royal Charter. The original Charter of 1626 had been granted at the request of the merchant community, 'the ablest men of Leedes for their owne ends' as their opponents identified them, to secure its economic and political control of the town. The revision and renewal of charters in 1643, 1661, 1684 and 1689 well illustrates the interaction of English national and urban history during the seventeenth century. At the last date the charter of 1661 was renewed. Its statutes made provision for a body of 24 assistants or common-councilmen, 12 aldermen and a mayor to enact by-laws for the regulation of the woollen industry within the town and the government of the borough which was co-extensive with the 32 square miles of the parish.[1]

Although there were attempts to form a class of freemen and revive guild organisations after 1662 in the anxious desire to return to normality, these endeavours to force an expanding trade into the strait jacket of medieval regulation had been abandoned by 1720. Hence there were no restrictions to debar any male residing within the borough from becoming a member of the corporation. As elections to vacancies, however, were made by the corporation itself, on its own nominations, recruitment was almost entirely from the merchant and professional classes.

The seventeenth-century corporation had always been merchant-dominated, but the full measure of their control can only be calculated after 1710 when the occupations of the assistants are for the first time always given. 63% of the assistants elected between 1706 and 1795 were woollen merchants. An even greater predominance of merchants occupied the aldermanic benches: of the 107 aldermen elevated between 1710 and 1835, 77 were engaged in the woollen trade. And in the same period woollen merchants occupied the town's chief honour as mayor on no fewer than 92 occasions.[2] Save for a sprinkling of surgeons, apothecaries and, after 1770, bankers, the corporation was drawn wholly from the merchant community. To peruse the list of elections given in Wardell leaves the impression that the corporation was a very large family company. The names of the town's chief merchant dynasties appear generation after generation—Denisons, Blayds, Cooksons and Dixons present themselves with great regularity.

The only other recurring additions outside the long-established oligarchy were those young well-to-do merchants who had just completed their apprenticeships in the town's leading firms. Without the slightest exaggeration, the Municipal Corporation Commissioners could report in 1835:

The close constitution of the Corporation is obvious, all vacancies in each branch of it being filled by the Select Body, gives to that body absolute and uncontrolled self-election . . . Family influence is predominant. Fathers and sons and sons-in-law, brothers and brothers-in-law succeed to the offices of the Corporation, like matters of family settlement.[3]

An examination of the corporation court-books suggests that the town governed itself. Election entries and fines, by-laws to encourage recalcitrant members and a few petitions cover their pages. The desire to control the woollen industry within at least the borough, the principal reason for incorporation in 1626, had largely disappeared by 1720. *Laissez-faire* in Leeds appears to have preceded Adam Smith's great treatise by 50 years. One wonders why anyone ever bothered to pay the large fines for refusal to serve office as the duties of common-councilman at least appeared so light and only very rarely did the corporation meet more than three or four times a year. Most meetings concluded in one of the town's better managed taverns since 'treats' were customary on the election of every councillor, alderman and mayor. Yet there was room for action. In 1723 even the Moot Hall itself, where the corporation met, was in 'great decay' through butchers whetting their 'knives . . . upon both the Moothall stairs and likewise upon the Pillars and Walls of ye said Hall'. The town's roads and bridges were often in disrepair. Bad surfaces were made worse by the careless disposal of refuse. The Rev. Dr. Scott's coach was smashed to pieces and he himself badly bruised when it was overturned by a large heap of rubbish which had lain in the middle of St. James's Street for many weeks in 1802. One offender placed with premeditated exactitude 'ten cart loads of manure, ten cart loads of dung, ten cart loads of ashes, ten cart loads of dirt and ten cart loads of filth' in the road at Mill Hill five years later.[4]

It would be wrong, however, to represent the corporation as a convivial dining club which met whilst the town became putrefactious. The corporation minutes taken alone are somewhat misleading. A different view of the activities of the aldermen at least is gained from the Quarter Sessions records. From the Moot Hall a rota of aldermen, who were the borough's justices of the peace, dispensed an informal daily justice, and every three months they, the mayor and recorder sat at general Quarter Sessions. From this position they supervised the entire administration of the town: they managed the collection of the poor- and highway-rates, appointed the overseers of the poor, the constables, road surveyors, cloth- and leather-searchers. Their attention to problems was somewhat spasmodic. Action appears to have depended upon the drive of the mayor. During the years of office of energetic merchants like William Cookson in 1712, 1725 and 1739, and Joseph Fountaine in 1777 a good deal was achieved: Cookson had plans in 1725 for building both a new workhouse and prison; and Fountaine carried out a thorough investigation of the working of the assize of bread and weights and measures within the borough. At other times business was largely routine, offices were filled, disputes about poor-rate assessments settled, the occasional felon was ordered to be stripped naked to the waist and whipped smartly up and down Briggate, and attempts were made to undermine what the magistrates regarded as the four pillars of sin in Georgian Leeds, public houses, prostitutes, gaming dogs and billiard tables. Certain economic regulations appear to have been vigorously enforced. The apprenticeship laws, especially in respect of the town's pauper apprentices, were observed down to about 1770 when the magistrates either lost control through the sheer problem of numbers, or they turned a blind eye to the stipulations of a law that was becoming generally disregarded. The assize of bread was always thoroughly administered, although the appointment of cloth-searchers within the borough, even before supervision passed to the county magistrates by the act of 1725, was fitful.[5] Moreover the evidence of prosecutions concerning the fraudulent manufacture of cloth is ambiguous. Contemporary statements about the poor quality of Yorkshire cloth were numerous. Prosecutions, however, were rare which suggests that the laws were neglected rather than that large fines were a deterrent. The merchants' own thorough inspection of the cloth, the price negotiated by both parties and the requirements of the customer made the laws unnecessary except in a mere handful of cases. Since regulations were customary, both merchants and clothiers clung to them as an ultimate and remote safeguard.

Of the corporation's financial administration we know little; as it owned no property its income was derived almost entirely from fines paid on admission to and resignation from office.[6] But evidence from the administration of the parish rates suggests that this paucity of resources in fact allowed the corporation to preserve a better reputation. For the poor-rate assessment, the town's basic tax, on which the highway and constable's rates were also reckoned, was again estimated and supervised by a group of aldermen; and here there was ample room for chicanery. The town's justices compiled the valuations, and heard appeals against rating of both property, and before it fell into disuse, personal stock.[7] Their obvious discrimination against foreigners and newcomers and their tendency to allow appeals from their families and friends indicate that sharp practices were not unknown.

The Webbs maintained that the 'Lighting and Paving Act' of 1755 which set up a body of improvement commissioners, instigated a committee outside and opposed to the corporation.[8] Nevertheless the commissioners named in this act, and a subsequent one of 1790, came almost entirely from the merchant community, and it was not until 1810 that any concerted effort to exclude the old oligarchy was made. These remarks are even more applicable to the composition of what might be described from their membership as sub-committees of the corporation which were responsible for the running of various institutions within the town. The Committee of Pious Uses which managed the town charities, the Charity School, Workhouse Committee, even the Lordship of the Manor, where merchant families held the majority of the nine shares, were all dominated by the same caucus of merchants that monopolised the membership of the corporation.[9] Until 1810 the government of the town rested entirely within the merchant fraternity. No one opposed this state of affairs, because no one was so fitted to regulate the welfare of the community. By contemporary standards their magistracy was vigilant. After 1780 expansion in the town was entirely unprecedented; the corporation attempted to retain control, but, given its outlook, the task proved too much. On the surface it appeared moribund, and many common-councilmen probably did little more than attend two or three council meetings a year, but the aldermen's duties as magistrates and membership of the town's numerous administrative and charitable committees were exacting. This most probably explains why William Denison refused the mayoralty four times in the 1750's, and why those members newly elected to the corporation were often prepared to pay fines of as much as £500 by the 1780's to avoid office. The borough justices were far busier in the execution of their commissions than their country counterparts whose activities have received far greater attention by historians.

(II)

Leeds returned no members of parliament and consequently the corporation's political action at the national level was somewhat sterile. One beneficial result was that Leeds suffered little interference from the county's political magnates. Defoe thought that Leeds, Sheffield and

Wakefield held an advantage over towns like Norwich and Exeter in that '. . . the frequent elections having no influence here to divide the people they live here in much more peace with one another than in other parts'.[10] In general Defoe's observations held, and only at major crises as in 1715, 1745 and throughout the 1770's was the storm of national events sufficient to stir the still waters of the town's political life. Then feeling in the town ran high, especially in 1710–15 when religious and political issues became inextricably entwined, and the merchant community became sadly divided.[11] But the immediate influence of the merchant community on the course of county politics before 1780 was small. William Milner saw his son elected M.P. for York in 1722, and Henry Ibbetson on the strength of a long purse and exemplary conduct in the Forty-five canvassed York in 1747 only to withdraw at the last minute.[12] Otherwise the Leeds merchants played no obvious role on the hustings at York Castle. Certain county M.P.s like Sir John Kaye and his son Arthur, however, relied strongly for support on Leeds and the clothing towns. The good opinion of the merchant community in Leeds, particularly as its voice was authoritative throughout the woollen-manufacturing area, was well worth securing by any interest. The borough was always canvassed before an impending election which was more than could be said for the majority of towns within the county. The leading merchants dined and lodged the candidates for the night, and with their fellow citizens rode to York for every election. There, amongst the great preponderance of landed gentry, they appeared lost.

Only in events concerning the woollen industry was the merchants' influence decisive. Their role in guiding its affairs was similar to their part in developing the roads and waterways around Leeds. Again their control of affairs rested on their acquaintance with both the political world and all branches of the cloth trade. As semi-official spokesmen for the fastest growing sector of the country's most important industry they emerged as an important economic interest in county and, at times, national politics.

Timely petition to Parliament was the chief weapon employed by the merchants as watchdogs of the woollen trade, although personal solicitations of the Secretaries of State by prominent merchants on behalf of the community was not unknown.[13] When an important merchant like William Denison pursued an individual line he was not without political connections: Denison was able to pester the Duke of Newcastle, Lord Chesterfield and the Speaker of the Commons, Sir Fletcher Norton, besides putting his case to 'his particular friends' in Parliament, Edwin Lascelles, 'Governor' Thomas Pownall and George

Prescott.[14] William Cookson's obituary in the *Gentlemen's Magazine* emphasised the reliance politicians placed upon his judgement of events in the West Riding, 'His commercial knowledge and opinions were held in high estimation and respect by Mr. Wilberforce and Mr. Pitt; to whose presence he was frequently admitted as a delegate from the town of Leeds.'[15] By a similar network the merchant community as a whole was able to represent its views on every piece of legislation and in every Commons committee that touched upon the Yorkshire woollen industry between the Act of 1708 and the abolition of the 6*d*. duty on imported wool in 1825.[16] They were liberal with their purses, tireless in their journeys up to London. There they lobbyed the M.P.s of Yorkshire and its boroughs and put their case to the country gentlemen and merchants of their acquaintance.

The merchants were influential in the making of policy for the Yorkshire woollen industry for three reasons. Firstly, they were the most important, if least numerous group, within the industry itself; secondly, the government relied on local initiative in the formulation of economic policy and here the merchants took the lead; lastly, M.P.s for the Yorkshire constituencies, who filled the Commons' committees and had influence with the government knew their repute and recognised their standing as men of wealth in the county and key figures in the country's premier export trade. In this fashion the merchants' grasp on economic legislation was a good deal more significant than most political historians, even those of the Namier school, have conceded. This fusion of political action and economic interest in the West Riding was observable in every major industry and port in England.

(III)

It was the revolt of the American colonies which led to a full-scale discussion of issues and events in county politics for the first time within living memory. Never again were they merely the province of party leaders. In Yorkshire criticism of Lord North's handling of the war (William Denison maintained he knew 'no more of the Trades and Manufactures of this country than a child') and contemporary constitutional arrangements resulted in the formation of the well-known Yorkshire Association. Falling rents and dwindling trading profits sharpened the demand for 'economical reform' and 'a hundred knights' to represent the counties and counteract the great majority of members returned by 'decayed and indigent boroughs'.[17]

All merchants were prepared to apportion a good deal of blame for the crisis in 1780 to Lord North, but the particular branch of reform that the wealthier merchants demanded was limited. Denison wished

M

'all the petty Boroughs were suppressed and the qualifications of a Voter £40 per annum at least and the number of Peers limited'. Moreover since the Association comprehended every Dissenting merchant in the town the Anglican community had some misgivings. Again Denison supported the Association 'so far as they recommend economy . . . but the chief promoters of it in this County are the Oates [the leading Unitarian merchants in Leeds] who were Promoters and Supporters of the American rebellion and consequently the cause of our present distresses'.[18] But in spite of qualifications about its supporters and some of its aims the Association was liberally supported by the foremost Leeds and Wakefield merchants, several of whom were members of its executive committee. There was general approval when the Association was able to return its candidates in the 1784 election in both the county and York itself, and the merchant community felt especially fortunate in having its views represented by Richard Milnes the Wakefield merchant, who became one of the York M.P.s. Aristocratic interest in the county suffered a crushing defeat. A percipient correspondent of the *Mercury* isolated a new authority which claimed attention: 'By the late glorious election, the independence of Yorkshire is established, and the power and patriotism of the trading interest exemplified and confirmed.'[19]

Peace subsisted in the county throughout the rest of the 1780's, but the outbreak of the French wars revealed a potentially dangerous situation in the West Riding which upset the existing political balance. The Leeds corporation's and the Anglican merchants' wholehearted support of the government in their suppression of 'Republican and Levelling Principles' marked their growing Tory predilections. On the other hand the clothiers and cloth-workers were restive at the introduction of weaving-frames into the scribbling- and spinning-mills and the growing use of the gig-mill and shearing-frames in finishing, the threat of merchants becoming manufacturers and the rapid rise in prices. They found allies amongst the numerous Dissenters of all occupations. Christopher Wyvill, the leader of the sadly depleted 'Association,' attempted to exploit this division in the autumn of 1795 when the treason and seditious assembly bills came before Parliament. He called on the 'honest and industrious clothiers' to come forward and assert their independence of the merchants. But Wyvill's political star was on the wane, and there was massive support for the government's legislation. The meeting at York to petition Parliament to implement the restrictive acts was 'the largest assemblage of gentlemen and freeholders which ever met in Yorkshire'. Wyvill's meeting was virtually ignored.[20]

If the moment was not ripe to make full political gain of the division between the merchants and clothiers in 1795, the time came in 1806. In the election of this and the following year, the power of the trading interest emerged as the decisive factor. The relationship between the merchants and large manufacturers on the one hand and the clothiers and cloth-workers on the other had deteriorated rapidly after 1802 in the squabble over the retention of the woollen laws. Underneath lay the clothiers' fear of the new factories and the big manufacturers' desire to be rid of all restrictions. The crisis came to a head with the suspension of the woollen laws for a probationary period. When Henry Lascelles (the second son of the Earl of Harewood), who was elected M.P. for Yorkshire in 1796, and the darling of Leeds corporation, failed to oppose the suspension bill in 1804 his effigy was burnt in half a dozen clothing villages and shot by clothiers in the Volunteer Corps.[21] The clothiers found the conclusion of the committee of enquiry into the woollen manufacture little to their liking with its recommendation that all restrictive statutes should be repealed, and their resentment of Lascelles' offensive treatment of their witnesses in London was at its height when parliament was suddenly dissolved in October 1806.

Where Wyvill had failed in 1795, Lord Fitzwilliam and the West Riding Whigs now succeeded. William Fawkes, an 'independent Whig', whose tag 'Jacobin' disclosed his leanings, was selected as their candidate. He had the support of the remnant of the old Rockingham interest, the Dissenters, and the vast majority of clothiers and cloth-dressers. William Cookson informed his friend Wilberforce of the state of the clothing districts:

a very unfair advantage has been taken, at the expense of Mr. Lascelles and yourself, of the exasperated state of the clothiers in every direction of our Riding, as well as of the general class of workmen, who all make common cause with them, against any opposition to their combination system . . . the clothiers who were before the committee are violent beyond all conception and the whole body in the two [Cloth] Halls would not . . . produce 10 votes for Mr. Lascelles.

Fawkes was rapturously received in Leeds. Again Cookson reported events, this time to Lascelles himself:

Those gentry that were sent to the Committee in London are particularly virulent, my names-sake [Robert Cookson a Holbeck clothier and trustee of the White Cloth Hall] most Bitter. Mr. Lascelles had 'used him like a dog', he is a firm Presbyterian and acted under the Double Virus—For nearly all of the Merchants who attended Fawkes are of that Ingenious sett—a Wharfdale squire or two, Amitage, Ridsdale, C. Smith were with him.

Fawkes' carriage was drawn by the croppers from hall to hall. In Halifax and Wakefield he met with the same reception. Lascelles dared not show his face through the cloth hall doors.[22]

Wilberforce, the other county M.P., was certain of his return although his parliamentary conduct during recent years did not go uncensored by the clothiers and Dissenters. He was at least secure of their second vote where plumpers were not promised for Fawkes. Certainly he could not afford to make common cause with Lascelles as he had done in 1802.[23] Fawkes with his massive support among the innumerable clothiers and small tradesmen seemed unassailable.

Lascelles relied almost solely for his support on the woollen merchants and larger manufacturers of the three clothing towns and the Sheffield and Rotherham cutlers and ironmasters. It appeared a strange alliance, the son of a Tory peer depending on the county's chief commercial interests. In Leeds a committee of merchants met daily under the chairmanship of the mayor to return both Lascelles and Wilberforce. The town clerk, Lucas Nicholson, was deputed Lascelles' chief election agent, and the Leeds merchants organised his canvass of the West Riding. However those Leeds men who travelled to York for Wilberforce's committee meeting soon realised that Lascelles had no hope of success. Lascelles who appears to have remained curiously inactive throughout the preliminary skirmishes had no alternative but to retire from the contest.[24]

Within six months parliament was dissolved again. Fawkes stood down for Lord Milton, the 21-year-old heir of Earl Fitzwilliam, and as Lascelles was determined to seek re-election for the county a contested election—the first since 1741—appeared inevitable from the beginning. Lord Harewood, to vindicate the family honour was 'ready to spend in it his whole Barbadoes property'. Again Wilberforce's election was in no doubt. The real struggle was between Lascelles and Milton. Torrents of abuse prohibited any clear statement of the facts. Lascelles was castigated by the clothiers with all the venom they had heaped upon him in 1806. But in a speech reported in the *York Herald* he revealed that the true cause of his unpopularity amongst the clothiers and small traders was more substantial than the reason always tendered (his personal manner), 'the domestic system of the chief manufacture of Yorkshire', he asserted, 'was expiring; he might almost say extinct; and therefore he supported a Manufacture upon large capitals, where less profit could be expected, and consequently the articles would be sold at a cheaper rate and would conduce more to the National Interest'. A pamphlet supporting Milton saw the contest between him and Lascelles as a conflict between clothiers and merchants, and both candidates realised that their fate would be resolved in the cloth-making area.[25]

The merchants in Leeds, as if to atone for Lascelles' defeat in the previous year, espoused his cause with even greater assiduity. A Leeds manufacturer wrote:

On this occasion observe with what avidity a great body of merchants have come forward to force upon us that Member, whom six months ago, we so decidedly rejected. They have tried and found him well suited to their purposes ... You will probably hear a good deal about aristocracy, though that will come with a bad Grace from the Aristocratic Confederacy of Leeds. For the true Definition of an aristocracy is, the Tyranny of the few over the many.

Again the corporation openly canvassed Lascelles return; indeed it was the rock on which his support was built. Walter Fawkes, at a dinner in London given in Milton's honour, said that the latter 'had not only the Pope to contend against', in a reference to the Catholic question, 'but a still more formidable phalanx, the Corporation of Leeds'.[26] It was to their vexation that, after perhaps the most celebrated and expensive contest in British electoral history, the corporation learned that Lascelles had again been defeated.

Both Fawkes and Milton's victory over Lascelles was the triumph of a coalition between aristocratic influence, the clothiers and clothworkers and the Dissenting industrial middle class over the merchants and the country gentry of the three Ridings.[27] In other words political decision had switched from the landed to the commercial and industrial communities, since voting patterns in the West Riding determined the fate of both elections. The North and East Ridings stood on the touchlines whilst the real issues were fought out in the West Riding towns. It is significant that Lascelles' nomination in York was not proposed by the two greatest Tory magnates in the county, but by J. B. S. Morritt, whose son William was a merchant in Leeds, and John Hardy the Recorder of Leeds. Now the voice of leading merchants like William Cookson carried as much authority in political manœuvres as that of any baronet. Moreover the elections witnessed not only a transfer of political power but also one of opinion. The merchants opposed all idea of reform which the Whig peers and new manufacturers advocated. That seemingly strange alliance of Anglican gentry and Tory merchants that produced the Ten Hours Bill and yet opposed all notion of Parliamentary reform was already in embryo.

(IV)

If the full implications of the divisions between the clothiers and merchants was at times lost in the county, the split between the Tory merchant community and Whig and Dissenting Reformers was more obvious in the town. It was further sharpened by the town's two newspapers. Baines, the editor of the *Mercury*, always regarded the *Intelligencer* as being in the pay of the leading Tory merchants. Its proprietors were given a seat on the corporation, and after 1790 it came more and more to be regarded as the voice of the Anglican merchant community. The *Leeds Mercury*, which had appeared to be on its last legs in 1800, had become by 1810 the most influential Whig newspaper in the county. Baines, its editor, one of those displaced persons of the Industrial Revolution, had arrived in the 1790's almost penniless in Leeds from Preston, where his father had clashed with the reactionary corporation. As a young man of drive and intelligence Baines brought himself to the notice of those 'temperate but steady Reformers' the Unitarians. In 1801 with the help of a £1,000 loan from the leading worshippers at Mill Hill, he was enabled to purchase the *Leeds Mercury* for £1,552 from the widow of the late proprietor who had allowed the paper to fall into bad shape. 'It was suggested that a new journal might be established', wrote Baines' son and biographer, 'which would do justice to their opinions.' The Vicar of Leeds saw the acquisition of the newspaper centring on Walter Fawkes, the Whig candidate in the 1806 election:

a number of his Presbyterian friends and late officers of his corps have entered into a subscription to purchase and publish Mrs. Binn's newspaper which now endeavours to Enlighten the Public Mind and which has been since its change of Hands pretty severe upon the Clergy and Church Establishment.[28]

Naturally its support came from the Dissenting community, but equally significant was its popularity among the new manufacturing class. These hardworking men ranging from prosperous factory-owners to small traders and shopkeepers had done well in the two decades following the American war. Often professing Nonconformist beliefs and desirous of reform, they had little time for the old merchant community which defended every existing institution and admitted no degree of change. When Edward Baines switched his attack to exposing the corporation's inefficiency in running the town, they gave him their wholehearted support.

The corporation's general unpopularity amongst this new middle class stemmed from its 'restricted system and want of a more popular method of election' and its political and religious affiliations.[29] Until its dissolution the old corporation continued to be dominated by a caucus of Tory, Anglican merchants, who only admitted new common-councilmen of their own breed and on their own terms. Above all the politics of the merchant oligarchy became increasingly unpopular in the town and throughout the woollen manufacturing district. Their support of Henry Lascelles was only the beginning of the antagonism.

The Tory merchants opposed every petition for peace before 1815, and every motion for reform after the war. Their great dinners on the Prince Regent's birthday, and the meetings of the Pitt and True Blue Clubs, were concluded with vast speeches and innumerable toasts that called for support of the Constitution, the Established Church and the preservation of social order. Dissent they regarded as a peculiar form of Anglicised Jacobinism. Baines, writing after the True [Blue Club's dinner in honour of Henry Lascelles in 1812, commented on the toast:

'The Land we live in, and they who don't like it leave it'—it will always be a favorite with a party who would, if they had the power as they have the inclination, crush or expatriate everyman and everybody of men, that dare to differ in opinion with them on any subject of Trade, Politics and Religion.[30]

Address after address was dispatched to the Regent, on the conduct of his wife and his numerous bereavements, motions so cringing in their tone as to infuriate the majority of the town's inhabitants. None excelled that presented to the King on the Duke of York's death in 1827:

We regret that the expression of our lamentations must renew your majesty's sorrows for the loss of so dear a relative whose heart had been knit with your majesties from earliest life in the closest bond of affection, but permit us, Sire, to mingle our Tears with those of our friends whom His Royal Highness's kindness had cheered and of the widow and orphan whom his compassionate bounty had sustained; to express our high sense of His Royal Highness's unparalleled administration as commander-in-chief of the British Army, who while he raised it to its highly efficient state by a system of rigid discipline and judicious regulations, won the hearts of the whole army by the impartial dispensation of its honours, by acts of personal kindness to its individual members and by a general attention to its comforts.

The corporation was in no doubt that there was a place assured for the Duke of York in the bosom of God and Mary Ann Clarke. Baines summarised the opinion of his readers on this and similar addresses, when he wrote 'it would not be easy to find, in so small a compass, so much of falsehood, absurdity and inanity'.[31] Opposition to the corporation's actions grew as the movement for reform gathered momentum.

In fact no one questioned the corporation's diligence and few its integrity as it strove manfully to deal with the problems of the growing town. To cope with the mass of judicial administration, the mayor and two aldermen held Petty Sessions twice a week, and one alderman sat 'daily to transact business as a borough justice attended by the town clerk'. John Hardy, the Recorder of Leeds, commenting that William Hey, the distinguished Leeds surgeon, twice held the mayoral office, wrote 'None but those who have filled that office can form any just estimate of the labour, the patience and the personal sacrifices which the discharge of its ordinary duties requires.'[32] In 1823 Edward Brooke, Benjamin Gott and John Blayds found the office of mayor so burdensome that they each submitted to fines of £200 to escape serving. When Hardy himself retired from office in 1833 he wrote, in a moving letter of resignation:

in these days of jealous but laudable scrutiny into the concerns of public bodies that of the Corporate Magistrates of Leeds will come out of the ordeal leaving no other impression on the minds of the Inquirers than that of astonishment at their great and gratuitous sacrifice of private comfort and convenience to the laborious and too often thankless performance of public duty.

Hardy's prediction was correct. The municipal corporation commissioners admitted 'the great respectability of the present members of the Corporation and their impartial conduct as justices were universally acknowledged'.[33] Baines and his followers objected to the means rather than the end: they felt it deplorable that the affairs of the town should be directed by a handful of self-elected Tory merchants, and their criticism was basically one of genuine disagreement about the nature of authority in the town. The crying need for parliamentary reform was brought home daily to the Whig manufacturers. The town provided a perfect microcosm of the national political scene.

There was, however, a loophole in the corporation's omnipotence. The vestry and the improvement commissioners' meetings were outside its immediate control. The merchant community had always dominated vestry meetings and since 1755, when an Act for cleansing, lighting and paving the streets of Leeds instituted the improvement commissioners, they had been principal members of this body.[34] Indeed the high property qualification of £1,000 personalty or £40 per annum in land that was required for qualification as an improvement commissioner excluded all save the town's middle class from membership. Few cared about the vestry and its meetings were ill-attended throughout the eighteenth century.[35] With the emergence of the manufacturing class after 1780, however, there was an alternative body of respectable, well-informed citizens outside the merchant community equally capable of managing the town's affairs. Since the corporation was closed to them the Unitarian merchants and later Baines in the *Mercury* urged them to attend all the vestry and improvement commissioners' meetings. Gradually after 1790 they filled some of the places vacated by the merchant community. It was noticeable that the latter were losing interest in poor-law administration and street cleansing. Not until 1809, however, was the authority of the improvement commissioners *vis-à-vis* the corporation of any great significance. In this year a new Act enlarging previous legislation, not only enabled the commissioners to erect a court house and prison, increase the number of overseers of the poor and amend the water-works, but also to levy a rate to make these improvements possible. This was an important departure, since the power to levy rates had never been exercised by the corporation although they were empowered to do so had they wished. The corporation could not easily block the very necessary improvements which the Act made possible, but its support of the legislation was decidedly half-hearted. They agreed on the improvements so long as the rate did not exceed 3*d*. in the £ and gave £200 towards defraying the expenses of obtaining the Act only on condition that it was 'repaid with the interest out of the first monies that shall be raised under the powers of the said intended act'. When the committee, which the corporation had appointed to confer with that elected by the vestry, reported, the corporation adjourned, 'a sufficient number not attending'. The lead in securing the Act was clearly taken by the vestry and Baines applauded that 'spirit of improvement in many of the principal towns . . . particularly in the West Riding'.[36] Even now the 'reform' party had not sufficient control of the vestry or the improvement committee to launch an all-out attack on the merchant oligarchy. Not until after 1815 did the final bid for power in the two bodies begin.

Control of the vestry was essential. The parishioners at the annual Easter vestry meeting elected the overseers of the poor, the eight churchwardens and half the street commissioners. Baines and the Dissenters centred their attack on the maladministration of the workhouse —the treasurer admitted deficiencies of £1,800 in 1818—and the failure of the churchwardens and Poor Rate overseers to publish their accounts. The campaign came to a climax on Easter Sunday 1819. Three thousand men crowded the parish church as Baines stood up to denounce those churchwardens who opposed the publication of the public monies. Benjamin Gott replied on behalf of the corporation, until John Hardy, the Borough Recorder, summoned from his dinner, arrived half-way through the meeting to expound the Tory merchants' views. On a show of hands Baines won his point.[37] The subsequent election of churchwardens and workhouse trustees showed the ascendency of the Reformers in the town. Michael Sadler, the merchants' chief spokesman issued the warning that he 'had seen the inconveniences arising from this spirit in the large and populous town of Birmingham where almost every man of respectability has been driven from parochial offices'.[38] In Leeds the situation Sadler predicted did not exactly take place. The merchants smarted as Radicals and Nonconformists filled the offices of churchwarden, workhouse trustee and overseer of the poor, positions they and their forbears had monopolised for generations. But the new men, as the *Mercury* was at pains to point out, were not from a noticeably different social group since the Tory claim to monopolise 'all the respectability of the place' was bogus.

The Reformers had triumphed, and yet the result of this religious and political struggle fought for control of the town's administration could end, as the Webbs discovered, only in deadlock:

> by 1833, in fact, the government of Leeds, split up between Tory corporation and Whig commissioners, Dissenting churchwardens and church overseers—in the background a turbulent vestry confronting an obstinate bench of magistrates —had, in spite of the good intentions and honesty of all the parties concerned, ceased to provide a possible administrative machine.

This situation was by no means unique to Leeds. The result was the reform of the municipal corporations in 1835, a measure long envisaged by the Whig leaders. In Leeds, as the commissioners had forecast, popular election produced a body of very different political complexion. The Whig reformers had a majority of almost four to one on the new council. The proud old Tory corporation was extinguished overnight, and its members lamented that power was likely to be vested 'in a class of persons who although numerically the greater are from their education, habits and station in life not likely to be the most intelligent or independent'.[39] In fact as Dr. Hennock has discovered the social grouping of the new corporation was not unlike that of the old: there was still a large number of merchants—although they represented an appreciably smaller percentage of the whole council—who gained seats after 1835.[40] He maintains the change 'that had taken place in the composition of the Council apart from its party complexion, was not social, it was religious'. Certainly the rival team of Whig Dissenters swept the honours in 1835, but the principal change was more fundamental than Dr. Hennock in his comparison of occupational groups would admit. The unified voice of the corporation was hushed and its exclusiveness, guaranteed by self-election, smashed. Moreover the great Tory Anglican dynasties largely disappeared. The Whigs and Dissenters might have the same calling, but they were frequently 'new' men who had achieved prosperity after the 1780's, men of very different aims, background and traditions from those of the old merchant oligarchy.

(V)

In the county the alliance between the Tory landowners and the West Riding merchants became a force to be reckoned with in Yorkshire, and even national, politics. Their thinking on key issues of the day—peace, the Corn Laws, social disorder, catholic emancipation and re-form—was influential. Yet what is not always realised is that the core of this union in the 25 years before the first Reform Act was to be found in the corporation of Leeds. In the election of 1812 Benjamin Gott maintained that 'the Commercial Interest had only abstained from coming forward sooner, lest they should be thought as arrogating too much'. Lascelles was returned in place of Wilberforce, who was re-tiring from the county seat, without a contest. The *Intelligencer* in jubilant mood attacked the *Mercury* and the Reformers whose 'poisoned darts' had been manufactured, 'with a view of creating jealousies, schisms and disunion between the landed and commercial interests—between *the merchants and manufacturers*—and between the commercial interests at Leeds, and those at Sheffield, Halifax, and the trading dis-tricts'. The *Mercury* could arrive only at a very different conclusion. Commenting on the fact that out of 96 gentlemen dining with Lascelles at York to celebrate his victory, 49 came from Leeds, Baines wrote:

It is not, we believe, generally known, that in the earlier periods of British History, the Borough of Leeds returned two members of Parliament (1653–60) and we should congratulate our fellow Burgesses on the partial recovery of our ancient privileges by the return of Mr. Lascelles to Parliament, did it not happen that in so doing, the Freeholders of the County of York have been deprived, for the present, of one half of their elective franchise.[41]

This assessment was a fair representation of the facts. At the next election in 1818, Sir Francis Wood, in proposing Lord Milton as Whig M.P. for the county, denounced the West Riding merchants. He did not deny that their interest should have its proper weight, but he believed that it was a new interest, and that they 'should assemble on and determine who shall be the representatives of this county was an unheard of thing'. The baronet was a little confused. The West Riding merchants had long been a pressure group of sig-nificance in the county. It was the alliance of the Tory landowner and merchant which was the new force. The predominance of the latter in the union led Wood and the Whig landowners to represent it as the 'electoral college of West Riding merchants'. In reply to Wood's attack the *Intelligencer*, although it admitted their commercial interests had on the whole been well represented by the landed interest, left no doubt where political power was now centred.[42] Speaking of the strength of the 'Mercantile Interest' it continued:

> If united it would be found perhaps, irresistible. Even in this county, with their votes, their money, and their influence, it is doubtful whether they could not succeed in sending up two merchants as members of the House of Commons for Yorkshire.

The merchants' views on the Corn Laws and social disorder were perhaps most indicative of their political position. Their attitude to the former placed them in a difficult situation. Not only were they socially and politically allied with the Tory squires but also they were rentiers themselves and frequently had pretensions to becoming land-owners. Nevertheless instinctively they realised that they should oppose the 'obnoxious measure' of 1815. Observing that agricultural rents had at least doubled in the previous 20 years, and believing themselves to have been much harder hit by the war, they argued that a 40–50% reduction in rents should be effected before protection policies were adopted. High food prices could only have the most adverse effects on industry. The legislation led to murmurings even amongst the corporation of Leeds that the balance of the landed representation should be redressed in the interest of the manufacturing population. These expressions, however, were never formulated be-yond the sly warnings given of the strength of the merchants' interests. Their affiliations with the Tory landowners led the Leeds merchants to believe that a simple modification of the laws was necessary. Only in the repeal of the 6*d.* duty on imported wool—a measure to bolster up the falling prices of the home clip—was the commercial interest deter-mined and united enough to overthrow the landowners' policies. As James Bischoff recorded, the Leeds merchants played a conspicuous part in obtaining the rescission of the wool and rape-seed duties in the half-dozen years following their institution in 1819. If the landowners in Parliament agreed to the repeal of these duties—partly through their failure to produce the desired stimulation in English wool prices—it made them even more tenacious in their determination to retain the Corn Laws. As the meeting to petition for the revision of the Corn Laws in 1826 showed, the merchants, whatever their innermost doubts about them, would not openly speak one word against them. Meekly they followed their allies, the Tory landowners, into acquiescence.[43]

It was their attitude to social unrest, however, which identified the

merchants most closely with the Tories. The real danger of the unemployment and unrest in the five years after 1815, unlike the earlier
Luddite disturbances, was its link with the demand for extensive parliamentary reform. This connection led the Leeds Tory merchants to
associate reform with disturbance and disaffection.

Yet it is not always realised that the threat of social revolution so
often in men's minds after 1815 loomed nowhere larger than with the
old merchant oligarchies, threatened as they were by a new class of
manufacturers and reformers who held different political and religious
opinions. In fact there was little cause for apprehension in Leeds.
Baines and his followers were never the 'set of Hired, Disaffected
Ragamuffins' and 'illiterate Jacobins' the *Intelligencer* represented them
to be, for as they were always at pains to point out they strictly
adhered to all middle-class virtues. But the Tory merchants continued
in their belief that they were about to be engulfed by a union of
insurgent reformers ranging from Nonconformist merchants to
Radical hand-loom weavers and croppers. The petition of the corporation against the Reform Bill is illustrative of this fear; it found the
bill too sweeping:

. . . granting the Population a preponderant influence over Property . . .
your petitioners dread consequences of entrusting the interests of the few to the
protection of the many which would . . . too likely to be swayed in the choice
of their Representatives by matters of partial and temporary interest at the
dictation of ambitions or the inter-meddling of Political associations formed for
the purpose of controlling Elections.

It was this threat of insidious social pressure which inseparably joined
the causes of the merchants with those of the Tory landowners.

Catholic emancipation brought the struggle between the two parties
in Leeds to a climax. The Dissenters' long espousal of the Rockingham
and Whig interest had always depended on the latter's promise to
secure religious freedom. In the mid-1820's party feeling never ran
higher in Leeds. During the 1826 general election, which was fought
on the platform of emancipation, Joshua Oates, a leading Unitarian,
wrote to his brother in London: 'The election sends us all to logger-
heads and there is scarcely a *blue* Mercht. in town who wd. at present
admit me within his doors—and perhaps the gr. bulk of our *Merchts.*
are blue.' The county election in fact was uncontested and it reached a
perfect compromise. The Whigs returned two M.P.s for Yorkshire
for the first time, in Lord Milton and John Marshall, the Leeds Unitarian flax-spinner, but, since through the disenfranchisement of Grampound, four M.P.s were elected by the county, the Tories secured the

return of William Duncombe and Richard Fountayne Wilson, the
head of the well-known Leeds family.[44] Indeed the town could
congratulate itself on its representation.

Finally the story of the reform agitation in Leeds has been told at
length elsewhere.[45] What is of interest here is the seemingly anomalous
position of the merchant community. That they should consistently
reject all notion of parliamentary reform from the moment Lord John
Russell proposed transferring the Grampound seats to Leeds in 1820
is not surprising. Reform was as great a threat to their ascendency in
the town as to the squirearchy in the shires. In contrast their support
of the legislative reform of factory conditions is more paradoxical.
They welcomed Oastler's bitter attacks on the Whig manufacturers,
and supported M. T. Sadler—the chief exponent of the political views
of the corporation, and M.P. for Newark and later Aldborough—
who, after Hobhouse's defection, became parliamentary leader of the
movement. When Sadler, elected an assistant of the corporation in
1820, was canvassed as the prospective Tory candidate for the first
Leeds election in 1832, the Ten Hours Bill overshadowed parliamentary reform as the chief political issue. Baines denounced the
strange alliance of Tory merchants and Radical factory operatives as
'contemptible trickery' on the part of the former. He wondered that
proud Tories like Robert Hall and William Beckett allowed themselves to sit on the same platform as some of the working-class leaders
of the movement.[46] Its support by the Tory merchants has a long
history which can be traced through their support of abolition of
slavery and the Evangelical movement. Charity had always been the
foremost of their virtues. There was no inconsistency when they
applauded Robert Oastler's attacks on the Dissenting manufacturers,
and welcomed the medical and statistical evidence produced by Sadler
and Thackrah to prove the debilitating effects that factory conditions
produced on the artisans' health. In many ways the support of the Tory
landowners and merchants for factory reform was a response to the
threat to their position as the traditional leaders of society. They therefore met this attack with an alliance of factory-workers in an attempt to
destroy the pernicious union of reforming Whig landowners and the
new Dissenting mill-owners and masters. Yet in spite of the Tory
merchants' massive support for Sadler and the popularity of the factory
movement amongst the working classes, their worst fears were realised
when the newly enfranchised lower middle class, headed by the Dissenting merchants and factory-owners, returned the Whig candidates
John Marshall, jun., and T. B. Macaulay, the historian, by a substantial
majority.

(VI)

When William Cookson died in 1811 an obituary notice pointed out that the props of his life had been his zealous support of his 'King, Church and Constitution'.[47] A similar attachment sustained the entire corporation and the majority of merchants in Leeds; it gave them an entirely united voice in politics, religion and economic policy. And since their strains were welcome to the majority of the landed gentry in Yorkshire they assumed great authority as the mouthpiece of the commercial interest which everyone recognised to be of growing importance in the affairs of the county. In two respects their policies were apparently contradictory. Since they were vitally interested in the mechanisation of at least the finishing processes in the woollen industry, and were especially perturbed by the cloth-workers' attempts to invoke the Tudor laws against gig-mills and shearing-frames and their actual refusal to work them, they were thrown together with the large manufacturers who demanded the entire abolition of the woollen laws. Hence arose the bitter division between the clothiers and merchants that was crucial in the elections of 1806 and 1807. Later they supported attacks on the Whig and Dissenting factory owners in the Ten Hours movement, which allied them with those radical elements which traced their ancestry to the clothiers and cloth-workers opposition to the factory system during the French wars. Their views are not difficult to reconcile. Economic interest accounts for their action in the abolition of the woollen laws; and a thorough distrust of those Whigs and Dissenters who were clamouring for a reform of the corporation led them into the factory movement under Oastler's banner of altar, throne and cottage. The radicals as early as 1819 had dismissed Baines and his middle-class reformers as wolves in sheep's clothing, and the corporation's ready relief of unemployment and a desire to avoid any repeat of Peterloo in Leeds during the summer of 1819 had somewhat confused the radicals' identification of distress with the corruption of the representative system in Leeds. Yet the swing of national opinion manifested in catholic emancipation, the Reform Act and the Municipal Corporations Act, smashed the Tory merchants' oracle—the unreformed corporation itself—and the united voice of its old authority in the town, the trade and the county was stilled.

The 1832 election was a crushing defeat for the Tory oligarchy. As a political force they appeared spent. It required only the Municipal Corporations Act to remove them from political authority. When the Whig reformers secured a four to one majority in the new council, the long period of the Tory merchants' complete ascendency in the affairs of the town was at an end, although the fortunes of the Tory party in Leeds did revive again in the late 1830's. Their deposition by a profusion of Whig Dissenting merchant-manufacturers, engineers and retailers—a class largely created after the 1780's—was a major factor in the Tory merchants' disappearance from the town. The way was left wide open for the great Liberal captains of industry who dominated Victorian Leeds. The names of the prominent eighteenth-century merchants were soon forgotten in Leeds by all save a few of their remoter female descendants who could not afford the comforts of Cheltenham or the south coast.

(VII)

The merchants' role in the religious history of the town is in large measure a reflection of their dominant place in its political life. The same group of merchants who held the whip-hand in the corporation wielded authority in the vestry and workhouse committee meetings. In their appointment of the vicar and the perpetual curates of Holy Trinity and St. John's Churches, this group controlled an important field of ecclesiastical patronage. The administrative structure of the two chief Dissenting places of worship was little different, for both Mill Hill and Call Lane Chapels relied on a caucus of merchants for their management and financial support.

By the early years of the eighteenth century the majority of merchants were of the Anglican persuasion. There were fewer than a dozen Dissenters amongst the merchant community who clung tenaciously to their fathers' beliefs throughout the eighteenth century. A large number brought up as Dissenters like Sir Henry Ibbetson and William Milner were gradually admitted into the Anglican communion. First attending both the parish church and meeting houses they soon found that they were not allowed to serve two Lords. To what extent the civil disabilities to which the Dissenters were subjected guided their steps into the Anglican fold it would be difficult to estimate. Dissent—and perhaps the majority of seventeenth-century merchants were Dissenters—was on the wane. Lord Oxford wrote on his visit to the town in 1725:

what is much to be wondered at, in a place inhabited by such a numerous low multitude, there are but two meeting houses in it for Dissenters, which must doubtless be owing to the blessing of God upon the pious Labours and prudence of those worthy clergymen, who have so successfully laid out their plans in cultivating this vineyard.[48]

There is little reason to believe, however, that the paucity of Dissenters owed anything to the endeavours of the Anglican parish priests.

If the vestry meetings provide any indication of the vigour of church life, then that in Leeds was indeed in poor spirit. Meetings were infrequent—between 1716 and 1740 there was seldom more than one a year—and they were always ill-attended. On the other hand the numerous charitable benefactions made by the merchants might suggest that the spiritual life of the more affluent parishioners was still healthy. In the building of Holy Trinity in the 1720's, an undertaking completed solely on the merchants' initiative under the leadership of William Cookson, there was, as the subscribers showed in their petition to Parliament, a concern for the inadequacies of the two existing churches to cope with the growing population. Yet one can be forgiven the suspicion that the new church was raised more to the glory of Leeds and its merchants, than to that of God. The merchants, who already owned adequate accommodation in the parish church and St. John's, purchased the majority of the pews. The poor, had they wished to attend, were virtually excluded. The workhouse, again revived by William Cookson during his second mayoralty in 1726, was closed within three years since he could find little support amongst his fellow merchants.[49] Like the great marble memorials that the merchant families erected in the parish church, charity at its worst was merely a form of self-advertisement. It depended so much on the motives of the individual that it is quite unsafe to judge the community by its standard.

In the appointment of the parish clergy the Anglican merchants exercised what they regarded to be their most important Christian duty. The advowson of the parish church was purchased by the parishioners in 1583, but a tumultuous popular election in 1614 had led to a decree of Sir Francis Bacon's restricting the patronage to 25 trustees. The right of presentation to St. John's church, completed in 1634 at the sole expense of a merchant, John Harrison, was vested in the mayor, vicar and three senior aldermen; that of Holy Trinity lay with the mayor, vicar and recorder. As the 25 trustees were self-elected they were drawn almost entirely from the merchant community, which led to the appointment of a number of clergymen closely related to the town's leading families. By the early eighteenth century, presentation to the town's three churches was looked upon as a suitable reward for those merchants whose sons and sons-in-law had taken Holy orders. Vacancies were infrequent and there was usually a superfluity of candidates. Therefore elections to the vicarage were always bitterly contested amongst the 25 trustees. One election in 1745 took six years to sort out.[50]

This zealous execution of their patronage was always easily defended by the merchants. The biographer of Dr. Kirshaw (vicar from 1745 to 1788) made a significant catalogue of his virtues: he was lauded as a

N

conciliator, a shrewd patron of the parish perpetual curacies, and as a man of the world. Not one word of his piety or godliness was mentioned. The author explained the springs of his actions:

But so long as men are actuated by the principles of human nature, they must be biased by interest. They must be allowed a partiality for their connections. They must respect the attachments of friendship and of blood; and their attempts to draw close these natural or artificial ties must be deemed, not only innocent, but even laudable. The claims of merit can therefore have no place, where they would interfere with duties of prior obligation.[51]

This homily on 'interest' might equally well have served as an apologia for the conduct of the merchants in all their public actions.

The torpor of the Anglican church in Leeds was shaken by the Methodist and Evangelical revivals.[52] Methodism was ill-fitted to the merchant rationale, and its only converts from the merchant community came from a small fringe group headed by James Armitage, a prosperous clothier and eventual merchant, and Arthur Ikin, a blanket merchant whose father, the town's leading upholsterer, had helped to refurnish Temple Newsam in the alterations of the 1730's. The merchant oligarchy could comprehend no one with Methodist leanings, and the pull of tradition forced Ikin and Armitage away from the paths of Methodism. Ikin's son was mayor in 1803 and colonel of the Leeds volunteers; Armitage's son Edward became a staunch Anglican landowner.

Evangelicanism was far more important in reawakening the merchants to the actualities of practical religion. Yet the early movement was not very different from nascent Methodism, save in the social standing of its converts. The affinities of the two movements are brought out well in the unpublished diary of the Rev. Henry Crooke, a record of considerable interest in that diaries of early Evangelical ministries in large industrial parishes are rare.[53] The Wesleys' concerns were with the working and lower middle classes, Crooke's chief problem on the other hand was to shake the wealthy merchant families and the clergy from their spiritual lethargy and worldliness. There was room for action. If the condition of the church in Leeds was entirely dependent upon its clergy it was in a parlous state. When the vicar and the curates of the parish met monthly at their 'club' at the Angel Inn, they were as Crooke noted 'all clergymen and yet not one word of spiritual things among us'.

Later, through Miles Atkinson (lecturer at the parish church 1770–1811) and Isaac and Joseph Milner, two well-known divines born in the town, Leeds became a centre of the evangelical movement.[54] Sunday-schools flourished, and the merchants contributed very liberally with their time and money in founding a number of religious societies. Charitable effort reached a high point. Over £26,000 was collected between 1794 and 1822, principally for additional relief of the poor in Leeds, but also for 'sufferers' in Russia, Portugal, Germany and Ireland. Moreover the merchants also covenanted a number of annual subscriptions to the Infirmary, the House of Recovery, the Bible societies and the Lancastrian and National Schools. Including the contribution he made to his church the charitable effort of a substantial merchant around 1800 could amount to over £100 a year. Not only, however, did the merchants subscribe to a variety of good causes, but they participated in the distribution of money, soup and blankets. Through this organisation they became acquainted with the problems of poverty—through visits to the destitute both as distributors of charitable relief and in their official capacity as overseers of the poor —to an extent that we more often associate with late Victorian benefactors and social workers. The response to their despair at the social upheavals after 1800 in Leeds was primarily a utilitarian one: they supported and organised relief works, the new schools and later the Mechanics' Institutes and the Savings Banks that mushroomed after 1815. Their other solution, the building of more churches—three were built by parliamentary grant in the 1820's—was more hypothetical.[55]

The impact of the evangelical movement on the merchant community was important, not only in reawakening its members to a re-invigorated religious life, but also in contributing to their political thinking. Atkinson and his converts insisted that virtue must be enforced by crown and government. The Church alone could not achieve a moral rejuvenation. As magistrates the merchants were instrumental in setting the example of and enforcing the new morality. This belief in the utility and infallibility of the Constitution led them to give it unqualified support. Their apparent utter conservatism was relieved, however, through their participation in the Anti-Slave Trade movement and their work amongst the poor. Out of this forcing house sprang their support of factory reform. And undoubtedly evangelicalism was responsible for raising the spiritual life of the merchant community to a higher level than it had been for at least four generations. A caucus of merchants endeavoured to enlighten their actions as magistrates by its principles for many years. They were tolerably successful if we can judge from the impression that John Russell formed from his visits to the town to paint the wealthier merchant families. In 1799 he wrote:

I do not hear the evil language in the streets of Leeds as in London. I have not heard an oath, nor have I been witness to an immoral action. This place is very remarkable in respect to religion, and what is more so, that amongst the rich and great a very considerable body are devout, approve and receive the gospel.[56]

It is very difficult to isolate factors of economic significance from a study of the Anglican church in Georgian Leeds. The meaning of worship illuminated men's private lives and found an expression in the building and adornment of a number of churches and many charitable works. But because religious belief and political affiliation went so closely hand in hand the emergence of an influential Anglican Tory party was a more important consequence in Leeds. Religious affairs could take on all the animosity of politics; together they defined a framework of friendship within which a number of merchant partnerships were formed and a system of mutual business assistance was built up. The opportunities given by communal worship meant that in an economic sense, although business morality might be loosely related to an interpretation of religious doctrines, the ethical aspects of religion were more significant than the dogmatic implications of its theology.

Dissent made a notable contribution to life in eighteenth-century Leeds. Yet in spite of its strong activist tradition an apparent stagnation existed as far reaching as that in the Anglican Church.[57] Doctrinal controversies and the spread of Methodism helped to whittle away the congregation. The increasing wealth of well-to-do members of the congregation and the lure of the Established Church was a recurrent problem. It is the organisation of the meeting-houses, however, that concerns us here, together with an examination of the generally accepted view that they acted as an agency for the entrepreneurs of the early industrial revolution in which freedom from the distinctions and traditions of the Anglican church enabled the Dissenters to form extensive partnerships and aid each other in common economic activity.[58]

Having no formal creed, the Unitarians emphasised works rather than faith. Religion was a search for Truth, a truth expressed daily in honesty, hard work and philanthropy. That this rational progressive faith held attractions for mercantile society there is no doubt. Yet was the daily organisation of this down-to-earth, unemotional brand of religion very different from that of the Anglican church? Did the merchants dominate the two chief centres of Dissent in Leeds, Call Lane and Mill Hill Chapels, to the extent that they ran the town churches? Were the shopkeepers and journeymen of any more consequence here than in Holy Trinity or St. Paul's?

Call Lane Chapel, the meeting house of the Independents, had been built largely through the activity of Samuel Ibbetson, a leading merchant in the 1690's.[59] Few of the merchant community, however, appear to have worshipped at the chapel. Of the founders the Ibbetsons slowly but surely transferred their affections to the parish church, and the wealthy Spencer brothers were the last of their family engaged in woollen-merchanting. In the various elections to the office of Chapel Trustee merchants seldom appeared; clothiers and cloth-workers were more prominent. The appointment of Jacob Busk and Bernard Bischoff as trustees in 1740, however, secured the adhesion of two prominent naturalised merchants who gave vigour to at least the finances of the chapel.

After 1780, when the great expansion of the woollen industry brought into prominence a new group of men, the chapel took on a new lease of life. The trustees list of 1797 shows that they had been comprehended within the life of the chapel very well. At the top of the list were two Bischoffs; further down came four newcomers to merchanting, William Glover, Arthur Lupton, Thomas Kighley and David Dunderdale; Benjamin Lister and James Motley were wool-staplers and Samuel Glover and Thomas Cadman wealthy wholesale tobacconists. All save the Bischoffs were 'new' men, interlopers amongst the chapel elders and intruders in the merchant community. This group is small, but a close examination shows a number of interesting alignments. The Busks' and Bischoffs' social and economic relationships were far more extensive than those of the rest of the congregation. But a very close relationship existed between the Darntons, Luptons, Riders and Cadmans. These families had for generations been regular attenders at Call Lane, but none of them were considered to be 'substantial, sufficient and honest' enough to be elected trustees before the 1790's. The four families were all related by marriage, which provided a complicated pattern of partnerships and financial arrangements. In the depression after 1815 William Lupton's firm was kept going by large loans from his father-in-law John Darnton and the latter's partner Thomas Cadman. Yet connections forged in the congregation alone failed to provide a pattern of advancement. Certainly the small group of trustees which ran the chapel was much quicker to recognise up-and-coming families than the Anglican merchant oligarchy which dominated the running of the churches. Nevertheless the fortunes of the Darntons and Luptons, initially launched in Sir Henry Ibbetson's dressing shops, were consolidated like those of the Dunderdales and Glovers in the expansion of trade after 1783. Position in the chapel was a recognition of worth and wealth, not their cause.

One of the most important features in the religious history of Leeds is the widespread influence of the Unitarians. Mill Hill was, as Thoresby noted, the first and grandest Presbyterian meeting-house in the north. Doctrinal difficulties existed but they were more easily contained than at Call Lane through the guidance of a succession of distinguished ministers that included Joseph Priestley and Charles Wicksteed, the political economist.[60] And if the Anglicans, and particularly the Evangelical clergy, regarded Unitarianism as little better than atheism, several factors combined to give the Unitarians a unique position in Leeds that was at variance with the general disapproval of them. The congregation was well established. Many members had been worshipping there since its inception in 1672 and some like the Oates and Lees were amongst the oldest and wealthiest merchant families in the town. Unlike Call Lane, the Mill Hill district increased in fashion with the development of the Wilson's Park estate, and the chapel was well situated on the edge of this sought-after area.[61]

Little is known of the administration of Mill Hill before 1770, but it was always far more merchant dominated than the Independents' meeting-house, and, save for the Bischoffs and the Busks, the chapel elders were more prominent in the town and woollen trade. The chapel was in the care of 25 trustees, who when their number fell to less than 9, filled the vacancies with 16 more 'honest and substantial inhabitants of the Parish of Leeds'. The election of 1774 observed this provision: no fewer than 10 of the 16 new trustees were merchants. The trustees dominated all the chapel meetings and acted as chapel wardens. The minister was excluded from their meetings and they wielded extensive powers: five or more trustees had power 'to move or rescind such orders and resolutions respecting the affairs of the chapel consistent with the trusts thereof'. It was difficult for a minister to assert independence when his stipend depended entirely on the congregation's subscriptions. The Rev. William Wood, a well known natural historian in his day and minister between 1773 and 1808, derived much of his influence through his marriage with the daughter of George Oates, a connection which related him to the leading families in his congregation. As his biographer shrewdly commented, it was 'a matter of no little importance to his comfort'.

Yet there was another side to the Mill Hill coin beside the impression of the merchants' authority. A large measure of the success of the Unitarian church in Leeds was due to its recognition and comprehension within its system of church government of the small tradesmen and manufacturers. The Unitarians' approach to the problems of the new industrial society, of wealth and poverty, were refreshing. They were forward in good works, especially in door-to-door relief of the poor. Frequent charity sermons were rewarded by large collections. The chapel in 1801 contained 17 pews for the poor and a few years later the chapel wardens were encouraged to draw up a list of the poor, 'who by their regular attendance . . . are entitled to relief from the subscriptions made in the chapel for the Poor and to claim the Privilege of being buried in the chapel burial ground'. It was the continuing attraction of the chapel to all sections of the community and its easy assimilation of the new manufacturing classes who were to play so large a role in Victorian Leeds—the Kitsons, Fairbairns, Greenwoods and Talbots—that gave Unitarianism its importance in the city down to the present century.

As at Call Lane the Sunday services were not the end of co-operation. Excluded from civic office and sharing common Whig political opinions the Unitarians were thrown very closely together. Civic restrictions fused their economic interests. Possessing the same views, receiving the same education, it was not surprising that partnerships were formed between members of the congregation. Thomas Wolrich had formed a dyeing and merchanting enterprise with George Oates in the late 1740's. This partnership was dissolved when David Stansfeld, a member of a well-known Halifax Unitarian family, married Wolrich's only daughter, and the young man and his father-in-law formed a new house. When the Rev. William Wood married the daughter of Wolrich's old partner George Oates, the family eventually took their son into the family concern. Rayner and Dawson was a partnership between two old Unitarian families, but the most interesting firm was that of Thursby, Hainsworth and Dunn, a merchant house that brought together no fewer than three trustees at Mill Hill. This search for partners amongst fellow members of the congregation was a continuing feature in the floating of firms right through the nineteenth century when cloth-merchanting had long been in decline.

These formal partnerships were only one of the aspects of chapel life that bound the interests of the congregation closer together. In difficult times financial help was canvassed amongst the wealthier members of the chapel. John Marshall was able to raise £700 at a crucial stage of his fortunes in 1793 from his friends at Mill Hill. A more notable and extensive enterprise was the floating of the new *Leeds Mercury* under the editorship of Edward Baines. Marriage provided further connections.[62] There were many unions of mutual interest which were calculated to advance the few families who headed the Mill Hill congregation.

As at Call Lane, membership brought benefits only to those already established on the path to success. Yet the introspection of the congregation, and their homogeneity of interests provided a web of connection and consanguinity that was more evident than in the Anglican church. It was this, rather than any singularity in the tenets of their faith that levered them into positions of economic dominance. Moreover the reformist political opinions of the Unitarian merchants— induced by their own civic disabilities more than any convinced democratic belief—dovetailed with those of the new manufacturers and engineers. Together they formed a powerful political group in the county. Thus when the ranks of the old merchant families diminished after 1800, the nineteenth-century giants, the Marshalls and Kitsons, took their place. It was this easy absorption of new talent that secured such a lengthy and notable role for Mill Hill chapel in the history of Leeds.

Notes to Chapter 8

[1] For a good account of the Charters see Heaton, pp. 220–42; W. G. Rimmer, 'The evolution of Leeds to 1700', pp. 117–25. They are printed in J. Wardell, *op. cit.*, Appendices VII and XIII.

[2] L.C./M 1–3 Leeds Corporation Court Books (1660–1835). The practice of giving occupations in the court books is discontinued around 1795, and the town directories must be consulted after this date. Bankers held the office of mayor nine times, apothecaries and surgeons thirteen, 'Esquires' and 'Gentlemen' nine and linen merchants twice.

[3] *P.P.* 1835 (116) XXV Municipal Corporations, I, 620.

[4] This and the following paragraph are based on the Order and Indictment Books of the Leeds General Quarter Sessions (1698–1809), L.C./QS 1–12.

[5] Compare Heaton, *op. cit.*, p. 236.

[6] Fines fixed by the corporation were amongst the highest in the country. They rose steadily throughout the eighteenth century. When Edward Armitage refused to serve as common-councilman in 1792 he was fined £400; Harry Wormald declined advancement to the bench of alderman and paid £500 into court in 1803. As the corporation relied so heavily for its income on these fines its selection of members was not always guided by the purest of motives.

[7] See above, p. 21.

[8] S. and B. Webb, *op. cit.*, pp. 414–15. The records of the improvement commission have not been traced since 1945 although the Webbs consulted them.

[9] L.L./M 1–6 Minute and Order Book of the Vestry Workhouse Committee of Leeds township, 1726–1824.

[10] J. Wardell, *op. cit.*, p. 71; *H.M.C. Portland MSS.*, IV, 142.

[11] R. G. Wilson, *Leeds Woollen Merchants: 1700–1830*, pp. 345–53 gives details of these disputes.

[12] *Diary*, II, 333; Add. MSS. 32, 712, f. 7, Henry Ibbetson to the Duke of Newcastle, 1 July 1747.

[13] e.g. Add. MSS. 32, 863ff. 259–60, Sir Henry Ibbetson and Thomas Lee to the Duke of Newcastle, 12 March 1756.

[14] Denison MSS. De/H 46. See also Sir L. Namier and J. Brooke, *The History of Parliament, The House of Commons 1754–1790* (1964), iii, pp. 22–3, 316–18, 324–5.

[15] *The Gentlemen's Magazine*, LXXXI (1811), 94.

[16] For an example of the way in which the West Riding merchants and landowners compromised on a piece of legislation (the important Stamping Acts of 1765–6) see R. G. Wilson, 'Three brothers', 109–118.

[17] Ramsden MSS., W. Weddell, M.P., to his wife, 9 April 1784; I. R. Christie,

Wilkes, Wyvill and Reform (1962), pp. 68–120, and his 'The Yorkshire Association, 1780–4; a study in political organisation', *Historical Journal*, iii (1960), 144–61.

[18] Denison MSS. De/H 46, William Denison to George Prescott, 17 Jan., 5 Feb., 24 Dec., 1780; *L.M.* 6 April 1784.

[19] See several letters of William Weddell and Lord Fitzwilliam in Ramsden MSS; also R.I. and S. Wilberforce, *The Life of William Wilberforce* (1838), I, pp. 52–67; N. C. Phillips, *Yorkshire and English National Politics, 1783–1784* (1961), *passim*; *L.M.* 20 April 1784; 'Return of Canvass, Yorkshire Election of H. Duncombe and W. Wilberforce Esqs. 1784' in Leeds Central Library.

[20] R. I. and S. Wilberforce, *op. cit.*, II, pp. 120–8; *L.I.* 14 Dec. 1795.

[21] *L.M.* 4 Aug. 1804.

[22] See R. V. Taylor, *op. cit.*, pp. 296–8, for a brief sketch of Fawkes' career; also R. I. and S. Wilberforce, *op. cit.*, III, pp. 278–9, and Harewood MSS. William Cookson to H. Lascelles, n.d.

[23] *L.M.* 1 Nov. 1806; R. I. and S. Wilberforce, *op. cit.*, III, p. 279.

[24] Harewood MSS., Robert Markham to H. Lascelles, 27 Oct. 1806; W. Cookson to same, n.d.

[25] *Y.A.S.* Records Series, vol. 96, part 2, 153; [E. Baines] *Yorkshire Contested Election* (1807); E. A. Smith, 'The Yorkshire elections of 1806 and 1807: a study in electoral management', *Northern History*, II (1967), 62–90; *York Herald*, 16 May 1807; Fitzwilliam MSS. F426, 'Letter to the Manufacturers of the West Riding of Yorkshire' (1807).

[26] *L.M.* 9 May; *L.I.* 22 June 1807.

[27] E. A. Smith, *op. cit.*, 84–5.

[28] Sir E. Baines, *Life of Edward Baines, Late M.P. for the Borough of Leeds* (1851), pp. 14–15, 45–7; Spencer-Stanhope MSS. 2169, Rev. P. Haddon to W. Spencer-Stanhope, M.P., 19 April 1801.

[29] *P.P.* (1835) (116) XXV Municipal Corporations, 1620.

[30] *L.M.* 31 Oct. 1812.

[31] L.C./M3, f. 329; *L.M.* 1 Feb. 1817.

[32] *P.P.* Municipal Corporations, 1622; J. Pearson, *The Life of William Hey, F.R.S.* (1822), II, pp. 107–8.

[33] L.C./M3 entry for 22 March 1833; *P.P.* Municipal Corporations, 1620. See also the *Leeds Times*, 4 April 1833, which, Radical as the newspaper was, printed a tribute to the administration of the corporation.

[34] 28 Geo II C.41.

[35] The Vestry Minutes (1716ff.) are at Leeds parish church.

[36] This Act (49 Geo III C.122) superseded those of 1755 and 1790. For Baines' views see *L.M.* 25 Feb. 1809, also L.C./M3 entries for 1 and 15 March 1809.

[37] S. and B. Webb, *The Parish and the County* (1906), p. 94; *L.M.* 25 Nov. 1815, 17 April 1819; *L.I.* 16 March 1818, 12, 19 April 1819.

[38] *L.M.* 1 May 1819; *L.I.* 3 May 1819.

[39] S. and B. Webb, *The Manor and the Borough*, p. 423; D. Read, *Press and People* (1961), p. 126; L.C./M3 entry for 28 July 1835.

[40] E. P. Hennock, 'The social compositions of borough councils in two large cities, 1835–1914', in H. J. Dyos (ed.), *The Study of Urban History* (1968).

[41] *L.I.* 12 Oct., 26 Oct. 1812; *L.M.* 31 Oct. 1812.

[42] *L.I.* 29 June, 6 July 1818.

[43] J. Bischoff, *op. cit.*, II, pp. 1–67; *L.I.* 16 Nov. 1826; *L.M.* 2, 9, 16, 23 Nov. 1826.

[44] Oates MSS., J. H. Oates to E. Oates, 10 June 1826; J. Mayhall, *The Annals and History of Leeds*, p. 327; *Y.A.S.*, Record Series, vol. 96; part II, 115–18, 155; *Speeches and Addresses of the Candidates for the Representation of the County of York in the Year 1826* (1826).

[45] A. S. Turbeville and F. Beckwith, 'Leeds and Parliamentary reform, 1820–1832', *Thors. Soc.*, XLI, part I (1943), 1–88. See also A. Briggs, 'The background

of the Parliamentary reform movement in three English cities (1830–2)', *The Cambridge Historical Journal*, X (1952).

⁴⁶ *L.M.* 'Extraordinary', 11 Dec. 1832. For an account of the early Factory Act agitation in Leeds see J. T. Ward, *The Factory Movement 1830–1855* (1962), pp. 32–106, and his 'Leeds and the factory reform movement', *Thors. Soc.*, XLVI, part 2.

⁴⁷ *The Gentlemen's Magazine*, LXXXI (1811), 194.

⁴⁸ *H.M.C.* Portland MSS., VI, 141.

⁴⁹ Vestry Minute Book, 1716–81 (Leeds parish church); L.L./M1–6 Minute and Order Books of the Vestry Workhouse Committee of Leeds Township. A list of the first pew holders at Holy Trinity is given in Thomas Wilson's collection, DN/204.

⁵⁰ R. J. Wood, 'Leeds church patronage in the eighteenth century', *Thors. Soc.*, XLI, part 2 (1945), 103–113; C. M. Elliott, *The Economic and Social History of the Principal Protestant Denominations in Leeds*, unpublished Oxford University D.Phil. thesis (1962), pp. 385–8; William Cookson's Commonplace Book (Thoresby Society). Memorandum Book of John Lucas, f. 47, gives another account of the 1715 election.

⁵¹ *A Sketch of the Life and Character of the Late Dr. Samuel Kirshaw, Vicar of Leeds* (1788), p. 23.

⁵² A good account of early Methodism in Leeds is to be found in the Rev. J. Wray's 11 vols. MSS., 'A Compilation of Facts Illustrative of Methodism in Leeds' (*c.* 1835). His version was largely based on the evidence of John Hebblethwaite, a nonagenarian retired merchant and the son of a clothier who had been an early adherent to the new teaching.

⁵³ Clark MSS. (Leeds). The diaries cover the years 1757–69. For the merchants' connections with Cooke, see R. G. Wilson, 'Leeds woollen merchants', 399–403.

⁵⁴ For biographical notes on Atkinson and the Milners see the *D.N.B.* and R. V. Taylor, *op. cit.*

⁵⁵ The information on public subscriptions in Leeds is taken from the newspapers between 1794 and 1822. It should also be remembered that no less than £15,748 was subscribed to the Volunteers Corps in 1803, and the Quakers then made large donations to the hospital.

⁵⁶ G. S. Williamson, *John Russell, R.A.* (1894), p. 66.

⁵⁷ There were numerous pamphlets on the subject, Gough's *Enquiry into the Causes of the Decay of the Dissenting Interest* (1730) and Doddridge's *Free Thoughts on the Most Probable Means of Reviving the Dissenting Interest* (1731). For the state of Dissent in Leeds see 'Diary of a Leeds layman', *Transactions of the Unitarian History Society*, IV (1927–30), 248–67. Its author Joseph Ryder (1695–1768) belonged to a family of Mabgate clothiers.

⁵⁸ A section on the Quakers has been omitted since I was unable to see the minutes of the Leeds and Brighouse Meeting. Therefore although several merchants, especially after 1750, were Quakers I have been unable to establish how important individually they were in the running of their religion. Certainly a study of the Elam family (see p. 32). who in the course of two generations emerged from cloth-making through shopkeeping and the importing of tobacco to cloth-merchanting, landowning and banking, would be useful. Allott's 'Leeds Quaker Meeting', *Thors. Soc.* L (1966), 1–77, suggests that the Meeting exhibited several features that were present elsewhere in Dissent and which set it apart from the Anglican Church in terms of its organisation as much as its beliefs. Members knew each other well through pastoral visiting, regular discussions about financial arrangements of the Meeting and the oversight that was exercised over the business affairs of all friends. Moreover at quarterly county Meetings for Yorkshire and at the annual Meeting in London leading Leeds Quakers came to know their fellow-believers throughout England. In comparison with the Church of England and in respect of mutual economic assistance in business organisation all these

features were important. The more well-to-do Quakers, as Dissenters in general, had few occupational opportunities outside business, but they were part and parcel of a nation-wide body whose being was committed to promoting the interests of its members in industry and trade.

[59] Diary, I, pp. 206–7. This section is derived from material relating to Call Lane Chapel in the Lupton MSS.

[60] Arianism and Trinitarianism were problems which each pastor at Mill Hill faced. Priestley summed up his doctrinal position at Leeds in a number of pamphlets. See E. M. Wilbur, *A History of Unitarianism in Transylvania, England and America* (1952), p. 297.

[61] The remaining paragraphs of this chapter are largely based upon the Mill Hill Minute Books 1771–1858. See also C. Wellbeloved, *Memoirs of the Rev. William Wood* (1809) and W. D. Schroeder, *Mill Hill Chapel, Leeds: 1674–1924* (1924).

[62] W. G. Rimmer, *Marshalls of Leeds*, 40; *supra*, p. 320.

9 *The merchants in Leeds*

Leeds is a busy town, wine and company, noyse and mony, are the great things your Corporation deales in.*

(1)
It was probably with some surprise that Defoe's public learnt that Leeds was not merely the chief centre of the Yorkshire woollen industry, but also boasted the greatest cloth market in England.[1] Readers remembered that Lord Danby had been created Duke of Leeds in 1694, but otherwise the town possessed few other claims on their memories. To those visitors who looked for themselves the town was puzzling. It was not so much the statistics—the parish, co-extensive with the borough, covered 21,000 acres and contained 13 villages and a conflicting number of hamlets besides Leeds township itself—which were difficult to digest, but they were astonished by the scenic diversities. They found the country around Headingley, Chapeltown and Potter-Newton well-wooded and undulating, the air salubrious, and although the villages were within two miles of the centre of Leeds, they were quite unspoilt by any industrial concerns since the woollen manufacture inexplicably stopped within a mile of Leeds on this north side. Holbeck and Hunslet to the south, on the other hand, were low-lying and crowded with the houses, sheds and tenter grounds of scores of clothiers. Leeds township presented a similar contrast within an area of no more than half a square mile.

The most usual introduction to Leeds was for travellers to ride across Leeds Bridge from the south and view the town from its medieval artery, Briggate. As likely as not they came to see the cloth market that filled the broad street on Tuesday and Saturday mornings until 1757. Once the stalls had been cleared and the throng resorted to nearby ale-houses they could gain a clearer impression of the town's main street. It was a jumble of architectural styles. A report in 1628 described it thus:

a large and broad streete . . . the houses on both sides thereof are verie thicke and close compacted together, being ancient, meane, and low built, and

---

* The Rev. George Plaxton to Ralph Thoresby, 8 July 1707.

generallie all of Tymber; though they have stone quarries frequent in the Town, and about it; only some fewe of the richer sort of the Inhabitants have their houses more large and capacious, yett all lowe and straitened on their backsides.[2]

By 1700 there had been more rebuilding in stone, but many houses, including the large merchant residences built around 1600, were being redeveloped as shops and inns and their long gardens and warehouses behind were subdivided into tenements, the origins of the notorious 'yards' of a century later. Those who walked along the industrial nucleus of the town, along Swinegate and the Calls, commented on the number and smell of the finishing shops in this area, and noted the town's warehouses and granaries when they wandered down to the north bank of the River Aire. Usually they continued across the parish church yard to Timble Bridge. Here, from Marsh Lane along Sheepscar Beck to Mabgate, they found jumbled together the houses of the clothiers and their journeymen, and the innumerable mills along the beck which drove fulling-stocks and the gear to grind dye-stuffs and rape-seed. It was for this part of the town visitors reserved their severest strictures about dirt, stench and poor building.

Between Briggate and the cloth-making area on the eastern edge of the town, especially in Kirkgate, to the west in Boar Lane and in the New Town, or Town End as it was often known, around St. John's church on the northern extremity of the town, lived the merchants. It was their establishments which gave the town its variety, and provided some visitors with the view that Leeds was full of good houses and large gardens. Certainly a glance at John Cossin's plan of Leeds executed in 1725 gives this impression. The 15 houses which embellish the margins of the map—14 were occupied by merchants—and several more shown on the map are pleasant indeed, good solid early eighteenth-century houses, domestic rather than stately, but nevertheless commodious houses in which one could entertain one's business connections and country relatives for long periods very comfortably. Many of the houses appear more stylish than those illustrated in Cossin's contemporary map of York. There was a certain rivalry amongst the merchants which encouraged improvement. Thoresby noted in 1715: 'From the church to the Bridge, is a Foot Path way thro' the Fields by certain gardens, particularly Alderman Cookson's who has lately erected here a very pleasant seat, with Terras Walks etc.', and 'in the adjoining orchard . . . John Atkinson Esq., J.P. for the West Riding and Mayor of Leeds in 1711 is now building a delicate House, that for the exquisite Workmanship of the stone work, especially the Dome, and for a painted stair case excellently performed by Monsieur

Parmentier etc. exceeds all in Town.'[3] As the merchant enjoyed a good garden and needed at least two small closes of grass nearby for his carriage horses, his hack, a couple of cows and sufficient hay for them in winter, the town retained a rural look. These requirements together with the fact that Briggate was changing accounted for the merchant's removal to the New Town, Boar Lane, and Meadow and Hunslet Lanes, south of the river, after 1660. Yet since warehouses and packing shops were becoming increasingly difficult to find in overcrowded Briggate and Kirkgate, and personal supervision was an all-important requisite in the highly-skilled job of finishing cloth, the merchant usually found that he had to build warehouses and packing shops at the end of his yard. Business came first. It was a slight inconvenience, but one understood by one's neighbours, that the impression made by the summer-house and long flower borders was a little spoilt by a vista of packing shops and pressing rooms. The resulting confusion of gentleman's residence and business premises is illustrated by the property in Woodhouse Lane that Samuel Elam's executors were letting in 1777. Besides the house, packing and dressing shops there was 'also at the Back a close of Land, containing about two acres, and a neat garden planted with diverse sorts of choice Fruit Trees with a Hot-House and Fish Pond therein'. William Denison's premises opposite the Assembly House in busy Kirkgate managed to crowd a large residence, counting-house, packing shops, stable and coach-house, an enormous dung hill, a garden and close within an area not more than 30 yards wide by 120 yards deep.[4]

Around the middle of the eighteenth century as the merchant began to finish his own cloth and employ cloth-dressers as paid journeymen, the pressing shops and warehouses grew until they rendered many of the properties in Kirkgate, Boar, Hunslet and Meadow Lanes undesirable. Coal consumption was large in the finishing shops and the smell noisome. Cottages were built for the cloth-workers, public houses erected and some of the merchants' mansions subdivided. Hunslet, the busiest cloth-making centre in the county, crept towards Leeds. In 1779 Richard Cotton, William Milner's grandson, was letting his subdivided house in Hunslet Lane. A handsome summer-house and greenhouse was sole evidence of its former glories. Four years earlier a property in the same street, 'fit for a Merchant, Gentleman, etc. . . . with Packing shops, workshop, stable, chaise, six acres of garden and close, a Public House and five tenements' was advertised for sale. Boar Lane was deteriorating in the same fashion. John Lee was selling an entire yard there in 1773, and although three new sashed houses fronted the street, a dozen cottages were huddled in the yard behind. Over 20 years later Lee's nephew Richard was selling his 'Mansion' and warehouse in the same street, with over two acres of land, very suitable for building.[5] By 1800 the area was frequented by few merchants. Like many other towns faced with a fast expanding population Leeds built in on itself. As the old spacious gardens were built over one by one the town temporarily solved its building problem in this jumbled, unhealthy way. And since the township itself was largely owned by the leading merchant families there were no Common rights nor the obstruction of a single landowner to block developments. One by one, and for various reasons, those merchants who owned land in the centre of the town realised these assets after 1750.

The most remarkable feature of Leeds before 1770 is that a not insignificant increase in population was contained within roughly the early seventeenth-century confines of the town. Growth between 1625 and 1700 was, for a number of reasons modest, and the town of some 5,000–6,000 people when incorporated in 1626 had no more than 7,000 inhabitants in 1700. After 1700 acceleration was more rapid, especially after 1740, and by 1771 the town's population was estimated at 16,380. It was a growth accounted for as much by the immigration of apprentices and journeymen labourers and their families, as by the small surplus of births over deaths. Yet Professor Rimmer has reckoned that the 3,327 houses the township contained in 1772 were gathered in an area little larger than the 1,200 houses in 1700. His estimate for 1700 is too low unless there was a marked fall from around 5·83 to 4·90 occupants per household, which seems unlikely.[6] Certainly population density doubled. If we take the built-up area of the township from Cossin's plan as being around 350 acres it has risen from 20 to 46 people per acre. This figure is high, for although the area was small there was a marked variation in the density of housing over the township. If the shading of Thomas Jeffrey's plan of Leeds (1770) has any meaning, Briggate had become a solid agglomeration of houses and tenements. The urban sprawl intensified in the old working-class areas of the town, Marsh Lane, Quarry Hill, the Leylands and Mabgate where the cottages, dyehouses, weaving sheds and press shops were jumbled together in a confusion which shocked visitors to the town. One in 1768 noted that although the town was large and populous it was also 'exceedingly dirty, ill-built and badly paved'. The gardens of Thoresby's cousins and friends in the Calls area were disappearing beneath warehouses and a blanket of refuse and grime. Aikin observed in 1795 that amongst 'the lowest rank of people there is often more than one family to a house'.[7] The pressure of rapid population growth and increasing industrialisation at the centre of the town drove the merchants away to villages north of Leeds and to create a new area, the Parks, which was developed on the western edge of the town.

(II)

Richard Wilson, Recorder of Leeds, inherited the Parks from his ancestors the Sykes. It was an area of some 140 acres, a pleasant expanse of green fields—completely rural save for a solitary dyehouse at Drony Laith—between the river and the old Bradford turnpike, that provided peace on earth for the Unitarian meeting-house in Mill Hill and an open outlook for the Wilson mansion. Following the example of his son Christopher, a canon of St. Pauls who had greatly increased his prebendal income at Finsbury by the sale of building leases, Wilson sanctioned the area for development with the sale of land for the site of the new Coloured Cloth Hall in 1755. His son, another Richard and also recorder, released a plot for the Infirmary in 1768. Private residential building commenced at this latter date but building was slow at first. By 1780 only a dozen houses had appeared in two new streets, Park Row and South Parade. With a return to normal conditions in 1783 construction was accelerated. East Parade, begun in 1785, completed a large square bounded by Park Row and South Parade with the Coloured Cloth Hall and Infirmary on the south side. A second square, Park Square, was begun in 1788 with another terrace, Park Place, to the south. By 1793, 64 houses had been constructed on the Wilson 60-year leases.[8] These terraces were part of a general urban expansion in the 1780's. In Birmingham, the Crescent was a grandiose scheme interrupted by the war in 1793. Nearer Leeds, Paradise Square at Sheffield and the St. John's development at Wakefield were areas designed to provide spacious and fashionable houses, away from the town centre, for the wealthiest sections of the community.

The houses remaining in Park Place and on the north and east sides of Park Square are unexceptional late Georgian brick town houses. Their interiors have been gutted to provide office accommodation, but their dignified facades still indicate their one-time respectability. All the houses were spacious. In 1776 Richard Markham, a partner in Tottie and Markham, sold his newly built house in Park Row. Besides the drawing- and dining-rooms fitted with carved marble chimney-pieces and the extensive servants' quarters, there were six bedrooms with 'genteel chimney pieces and very fashionable papers'. William Cookson's house in South Parade was rather larger: the dining- and drawing-rooms were each 28 feet by 18 feet; there was besides a breakfast room and library, a housekeeper's room, a butler's pantry, servants' hall, kitchen, etc., 11 main bedrooms, a double coach-house and stabling for

8 horses.[9] William Wilberforce and other visiting notabilities were lodged very comfortably here.

The cost of the houses is more difficult to determine than their size. When a working-man's cottage in Leeds could be built for around £40 before the French wars, and double that amount by 1820, the prices paid for housing in the Parks were prohibitive to all save the most well-to-do. Miss Eastland thought herself very fortunate to secure a small house in East Parade for £500 in the 1780's. A few years later Miss Catley found she had to pay £800 for a similar residence. These were amongst the smallest houses in the new area. Mrs. Arthington, the widow of a founding partner of Beckett's Bank, sold a pair of houses in Park Place for £3,000 in 1796.[10] William Cookson's house must have cost at least £2,000 when it was built in 1780.

The former exclusiveness of the area is now only revealed in the Wilsons' 'Ledger of Ground Rents'. A short study shows the large majority of occupants to have been merchants, their widows, daughters and dependants with a sprinkling of clergy, attornies and surgeons. Nothing epitomised the tone of the new area so readily as the list of the five inhabitants of South Parade in 1792: three mayors and leading merchants in the town, Edward Markland, William Cookson and Thomas Lloyd lived next door to each other; the fourth was occupied by Charles Barnard, a wealthy attorney; Mrs. Busk, a merchant's widow whose two daughters had married into the Milnes family of Wakefield, resided in the fifth. In 1797 no fewer than 7 of the town's 12 aldermen lived in the Park area.[11] A glance at any charity subscription list—and those printed, area by area, were very numerous throughout the French wars—confirms that this was by far the wealthiest area in the town.

Nevertheless this attempt to create an exclusive west end with a working-class area concentrated entirely to the east of Briggate failed. The war after 1793 brought private building to a standstill compared with pre- and post-war proportions and this badly delayed the completion of Park Square. But much more important for the fate of the whole area was the Wilsons' lack of interest in the entire project. It is most unlikely, simply because Leeds was a centre of industry, that the Wilsons could have created a provincial parallel to the development of the Grosvenor, Bedford and Chelsea estates in London. Yet after 1793 there was no attempt to maintain the planning and character of the earlier Park terraces. This situation arose through the rapid change in ownership of the estate. Richard Wilson died in 1774 and his extensive properties were not long in the control of his elderly brothers—Thomas, a bachelor, one-time London merchant and partner in

o

Beckett's Bank, and Christopher, Bishop of Bristol. When the latter died in 1792 the major part of his estates passed to his grandson, a minor, although he allowed his second son, Christopher, then unmarried, to retain a life interest in the Leeds properties. Christopher Wilson had not the slightest concern with the growth of Leeds or its trade. Eagerly giving up all pretence to a legal career on his father's death, he devoted the rest of his long life and large income to establishing himself as a leading racehorse-owner. To maintain a massive expenditure in London and Yorkshire he was prepared to convert every square yard of his valuable Leeds estate into building plots with no consideration of the properties to be erected beyond that the sites realised him the highest price.[12]

In fact as Wilson argued, when he obtained Acts in 1803 and 1816 to reverse his father's will to sell the Leeds property and invest the proceeds in the broader acres of rural Yorkshire, the Parks area was under pressure from all sides. His father had sold Gott and Wormald a plot of land at Bean Ing to the west of the two squares in 1791; and the largest factory in the woollen industry began to belch its smoke, conveniently carried by the prevailing wind, into the drawing-rooms of Mrs. Busk and her neighbours. Moreover the south side of the estate was threatened: Wilson in 1803 maintained he had never lived at the family home in Mill Hill since 'from the great number of fire engines and other Erections for carrying on the Manufactures the . . . Mansion House would be a very unhealthful place of Residence'. Eight years later the tenants of the house brought a smoke pollution case against George Nussey. The evidence revealed that three other dye-houses, almost as close as Nussey's large works, lined the north bank of the river, and the factories in Swinegate and to the south of the river were equally troublesome. It is an interesting commentary on the use of printed travels as a historical source that Bigland in the same year described the Wilson house as 'commanding beautiful prospects'.[13]

Even if Wilson argued that the early character of the Parks could not survive the inroads of industrialism, as ground landlord he made no attempt to enforce development restrictions written into the leases. The open space before South Parade 'was partly laid out in gardens, but the largest proportion . . . used as a tenter ground'. Park Lane was allowed to become crowded with dressing shops, warehouses and even scribbling- and fulling-mills, so that when Robert Coulman had difficulty in selling his house in South Parade in 1817 he advertised:

From the peculiar Eligibility of their situation, these premises are particularly suitable for any respectable Stuff or Cloth Merchant, as a Part of them might be converted at a moderate Expense into an Extensive or middle sized Warehouse, thereby considerably reducing the Window and House Duty and still leaving a House sufficiently large for the Reception of a genteel family.[14]

In the same year, 1817, the fate of the whole area was irrevocably sealed when Wilson obtained sanction to sell all the remaining land south and west of Park Square, and the lots were bought to provide cheap housing for the workers of Gott's factory and the other new mills which were now built even closer to Park Square (see Map 4).

Map 4   Building in the west end of Leeds in 1821.

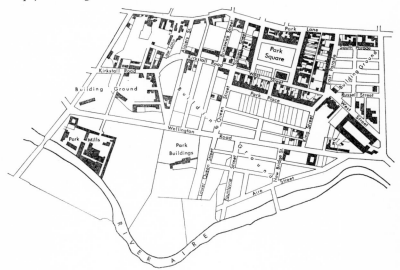

Edward Parsons in the early 1830's was able to assess the effects of these developments:

Large dyehouses and immense manufactories line the Northern side of the river, streets of cottages open from the great Western Road; a vast population pours forth at specific periods of the day to their avocations of industry and toil, and although the avenue to the town by the Wellington Road is commodious, open and airy, the other which conducts the traveller to St. Paul's Church and Park Square is now one of the meanest, the most irregular, and the most unpleasant in the whole circumference of Leeds.[15]

Although topographers were still ready to make the sharp contrast between the eastern and western halves of the town, neatly bisected by Briggate, their device was becoming less meaningful as the Parks became surrounded on three sides by mills, workshops and back-to-back housing, and was effectively cut off from open country to the west.

This encompassment induced the wealthier merchant families to move away into the outer Leeds townships or away from the borough altogether. Any attempts to secure smoke abatement was useless: court cases revealed the agony of housemaids and the despair of gardeners, but Benjamin Winter obtained 1s. damages from Nussey in 1811, and the inhabitants of Park Square were unsuccessful in their prosecution of Gott for smoke nuisance in 1824. The impression of outsiders made depressing reading. Had not Sir George Head thought Leeds the grimiest manufacturing town in England? Was it not Edward Parsons who could think of no more dismal scene on earth than Hunslet on a rainy day?[16] Moreover the rate of population increase was at its height between 1810 and 1830.

Table 10   The population of Leeds, 1771–1871

	Leeds township	Out-townships within the borough	Rates of increase (on previous census returns %)
1771[a]	16,380		
1775	17,121	13,288	
1801	30,669	22,493	
1811	35,951	26,583	17·6
1821	48,603	35,193	34·0
1831	71,602	51,791	47·2
1841		152,054	23·2
1851		172,023	11·7
1861		206,881	16·8
1871		258,817	20·0

[a] F. Beckwith, 'The population of Leeds during the Industrial Revolution', *Thors. Soc.*, 41, part 2 (1945), 127–9, 177–8.

The most disturbing aspect of the population explosion was the increasingly lurid light thrown upon the healthiness of the town by a number of its more prominent medical practitioners. As early as 1801–2 there had been a particularly violent outbreak of typhus which had raged in some of the yards off Briggate for as long as four months. When in February 1802 the *Intelligencer* reported that it was 'not now as at first confined to the lower orders' there was great alarm. The merchant community hurriedly subscribed £2,300 to open an isolation hospital, but when its first real test in containing a widespread typhoid epidemic came in 1817 it was found wanting.[17] Furthermore there had been complaints about the inadequacies of the town's water since 1810. The supply was itself totally insufficient to meet new demands and an inhabitant in 1826 found it 'so impregnated with almost every noxious Matter that the Mind of Man can conceive'. It therefore took little ingenuity in 1832 to make the connection between the cholera epidemic which carried off 702 people in the town and the deplorable state of its sewers and watercourses.[18] In fact a survey of the incidence of the typhoid outbreak in 1817, by a young and clever doctor, Charles Thackrah, the basis of an important volume on the relationship of health and occupations, had already secured a good deal of publicity. His findings, long made known in Leeds and eventually published in 1831, were received with immediate acclamation by Sadler and Oastler, the champions of factory reform. The merchants with their superior houses and food, shorter hours of work and ample opportunities for exercise came off best in the study. But neither this knowledge nor the fact that Mill Hill was shown to be appreciably the healthiest ward in the township could reassure the merchant community when it thumbed through the rest of the book. And Michael Sadler's figures for Leeds, however severely handled by Ure and Macauley, could not be banished from the mind. When he compared very unfavourably the death and longevity rates of Leeds, Ripon and Pickering, the wealthiest inhabitants were able to draw their own conclusions.[19] That the position in Leeds was no worse than in Sheffield or Liverpool was immaterial. There was ample proof of air-pollution, contagious disease and a high mortality rate. An obvious solution was to quit the Parks terraces. The Rhodes who had lived in Park Square bought a house in Headingley where the doctor assured them, 'the air came there direct from Ilkley'. Their departure was part of a general exodus which had begun as early as 1800.

(III)

One of the first things that John Kighley and John Dunderdale did when they came back from the United States in 1805 was to walk to Harewood Bridge, something they had 'often spoken of in America'. Writing in his diary Kighley thought that nothing 'can exceed the richness of the country on all sides' around Gledhow, Moortown and Chapeltown, 'cultivation appears to have reached its zenith'. The out-townships to the north of the parish had since the seventeenth century attracted a handful of merchants who were in search of a purer air and a more rural way of life. It was their properties, their gardens and model farms, which gave the landscape its air of cultivated richness. When Jeremiah Dixon, merchant and High Sheriff of the County in 1758, bought the Gledhow estate in 1764 he engaged John Carr to build a grand new house '. . . and during the remainder of his life continued to adorn it with beautiful plantations'. The Rev. Joseph Ismay riding through Chapeltown saw the house on its completion and those of the two 'Mr. Oates, particularly that on ye North side, which is an elegant Box with neat Gardens and Pleasant Walks enclosed with Palisades to a small farm house, where ye Poultry etc. are Kept. We saw White Turkeys at this place which it seems are much in Fashion at present.' Indeed Chapeltown 200 years ago put Ismay in mind of Montpelier. There was a very good inn at the Bowling Green, a cricket club, card assemblies, horse-racing and 'the Gentlemen and Ladies from Leeds frequently make an Excursion either on Horseback or in their chaises to Chapeltown, in order to enjoy fresh air upon this Moor in ye Mornings, that they may eat their Dinner with a keener appetite and a better Relish at ye return'. In 1798 Chapeltown, within two miles of Leeds, was described as 'a very genteel neighbourhood and in the centre of fine sporting country'.[20]

This building of solid Georgian houses in the north Leeds villages, like those of the Oates which caught the Reverend Ismay's eye, provides a parallel, on a small scale, with developments in the Home Counties, where the London merchants were buying small estates and erecting stylish houses for their relaxation and retirement throughout the eighteenth century. Houseman in 1800 observed that, 'merchants frequently accumulate very large fortunes, if we may judge from their many and elegant seats, with which the neighbourhood of Leeds is studded'. Writing in 1849 George Dodd still found the out-townships and neighbouring parishes 'interspersed . . . with mansions, parks and farms'.[21]

The wholesale opening up of the northern side of Leeds parish came with the break-up of two large estates around 1800. For over two centuries Headingley had been largely owned by the Wades of New Grange, a small landed family connected with several merchant families in Leeds. By the close of the French wars the directories reveal a number of merchants living in this pleasant wooded village: familiar names are cited—Nicholas Bischoff, Thomas Ikin, the Rhodes and John Marshall, the great flax-spinner, who occupied the Wades' old mansion. Besides the salubrity of the air one of the village's attractions was that 'Parochial Taxes were very, very trifling.' Roundhay, the second estate, was just beyond the original confines of the borough, and it provides the best documented example of the migration of the merchant classes to the villages surrounding the towns. It was in 1797 that Lord Stourton decided to sell his Roundhay property of some 1,300 acres. The purchasers were Thomas Nicholson, a London banker, and Samuel Elam, a young Leeds banker and merchant. They paid £60,000 for the estate and split it into two halves. Elam never appears to have lived at Roundhay, and from the outset began to sell parcels of land to his first cousin Robert Elam. When Samuel Elam was in dire financial straits in 1810 the 450 acres which remained were purchased by Nicholson, Robert Elam and another merchant, John Goodman. After this second sale was completed development was more rapid. The village took on a dual character, it retained 'an air of the seat of ancient nobility' but was 'chiefly in the possession of oppulence connected with the town of Leeds'.[22]

Entirely given over to farming before 1800, the village had now become the residence of the Nicholsons (connected by marriage with the Armitages and Rhodes, both leading merchant dynasties after 1800), and five other wealthy merchant families. Thomas Nicholson had built 'the greatest of the late Georgian mansions in Leeds' and created the Waterloo lake which is now the centre of Roundhay's celebrated public park. A church was erected in 1825, and an Act of Parliament obtained to maintain the road from Leeds. Not only were the surroundings attractive and within easy reach of Leeds, but the rates were low. Robert Elam was assessed at £20 for his house, coach-house, stable, vinery, plantations and gardens with two cottages and a greenhouse; Mrs. Nicholson was rated at £92 for the mansion house, out-buildings and park of 132 acres. The rate furthermore was 1s. in the £, which was trivial when compared with the amounts now paid in the Park Square area where rates had greatly increased since the Court House Acts enabled the corporation to make levies for public improvements. Assessments were high and increasing especially in the 1820's when there was a spate of clearance and public building in the centre of the town. Developments at Roundhay were typical of what was happening in every village from Kirkstall to Gipton on the north side of the parish, and representative of progress in many urban communities where the movement of the wealthier members to areas outside the town was accelerated after 1790 by changing industrial profiles and profits obtained in trade. Suburbia was one of the innumerable, unplanned offspring of the Industrial Revolution.

If the majority of merchants were only too pleased to escape from central Leeds to a pleasant Regency villa in Headingley or Roundhay, others like Benjamin Gott, Thomas Ikin, John Blayds and James Armitage—all men of very ample means—followed in Jeremiah Dixon's footsteps at Gledhow to build up large model estates around Leeds. The great success of Wormald and Gott's manufacturing concerns in the 1790's enabled Gott to purchase Armley House and the manor of Armley from the executors of another merchant, Thomas

Wolrich in 1803. For a few years he and his family drove there to spend their leisure time, before he invited Sir Robert Smirke, the architect of the British Museum, to design a new house in the fashionable neo-Grecian style and Humphrey Repton to landscape the grounds. John Blayds engaged the same pair at Oulton Hall, and a few years later in 1827 he built in the park 'one of the most chaste and elegant churches of pointed architecture to be met with in the Kingdom'. He expended £16,000 on its construction and purchased £4,000 worth of 3% consols for its upkeep.[23]

Properties like Armley and Oulton were the envy of those left behind in Leeds. The ideal of 'a country life in business' was a cherished one, especially when the reality of an industrial town became unbearable. The reward of great success in merchanting had always been a country estate with political and social activities maintained at county level. Yet this was the prize of the retired or one's children. What were the prospects of those men who wanted a country life but at the same time had to keep on the family business? Cloth-buying, dressing and packing had always required close supervision; and merchanting, with the great increase in variety of cloths and the unsettled market conditions after 1800, was a more arduous task in an increasingly competitive world than it had been 50 years earlier. The new merchant manufacturers, men of non-merchant origins, were prepared to work hard to secure a good livelihood. Those who attempt to live in both worlds, like the Milnes and Jeremiah Naylor in Wakefield, crashed or were brought low in the many crises after 1800. The question of residence was only one factor in the decision to continue merchanting. Yet it was an important one. Gott found Armley House; Thomas Ikin bought Leventhorpe Hall, a delightful house built by John Carr in 1773 with 450 acres, 'happily situated in one of the richest vales of a fruitful country, too distant to be annoyed by the Nuisances and yet near enough to share the important advantages of a Manufacturing District'.[24] Others less determined to stay in the woollen industry made the question of residence one on which their decision turned. Many merchants were prepared to make the ultimate break and sever connections with the town and its trade. They chose to buy a small country estate and turn their resources accumulated in the woollen trade into government and other securities to provide themselves with a regular fixed income, rather than continue in an increasingly depressing and unhealthy town and in an industry where conditions were fast changing and the prospects of profits uncertain.[25]

(IV)
Throughout the eighteenth century the merchants' ascendancy in
Leeds was never questioned. William Milner and Henry Ibbetson did
not waste a moment's thought on their right and adequacy to direct
its welfare. Not only did they and their fellow merchants dominate the
corporation, but also every administrative body in the town. Church
life, poor relief, charity, the improvement commission, the Infirmary
and grammar school, even the lordship of the manor all came under
their survey and supervision. Yet in the 50 years after 1780 when the
population increased four times not only did physical control of this
development become increasingly difficult, but the town was swamped
by a crowd of manufacturers, machine-makers, general dealers, shopkeepers, soap boilers and leather manufacturers. It has been estimated
that there was a net increase of almost 3,500 new firms in the town
between 1800 and 1840.[26] These changes posed unprecedented problems
for the merchants' direction of affairs, and their control, as we have
seen, was questioned after 1800 by the new manufacturing classes for
the first time. The wealth of many of these newcomers provided no
ticket of admittance either to the dwindling merchant community's
ranks or the administration of the town.

Yet was it not the merchants' own wealth that gave them their
status? The answer is a complex one. Certainly it would be too simple
an assumption to maintain that wealth alone was the basis of their
position in the town. It must be remembered that the machinery of the
oligarchy had by 1800 been running smoothly for close on 200 years.
Since the incorporation of the borough there had been a small number
—never more than a dozen at any time—great merchant dynasties that
had run the Leeds woollen trade and the town's administration. There
had always been a larger number of merchants admitted to both these
mysteries on terms determined by this caucus. Apprenticeship had
regulated the admittance of newcomers to the profession of merchant,
and the fact that both premiums with the best houses and initial capital
requirements were high had ensured that recruits were of good standing, but actual inclusion to their society and the running of the town
was managed by a less formal mechanism. Common business interests
did not in themselves provide a ticket of entry to the inner group; the
latter's interpretation of respectability in the matters of education,
calling, marriage and connections, and style of living were essential
tests which had to be passed by newcomers and the satellites of lawyers,
surgeons and clergy who owed their livelihood chiefly to the merchants' patronage. The system was concealed but its force nonetheless
powerful. The *Mercury* mentioned Assemblies, 'confined exclusively

. . . to the "quality" of the town, to which the tradespeople are, in some way or other prevented from subscribing'. The situation was identical to that in Coventry (portrayed by George Eliot in *Middlemarch*) where the old master ribbon manufacturers were being swamped by smaller masters of a new kind after 1810. Socially the former were still able to hold their own:

there were nice distinctions of rank in Middlemarch; and though old manufacturers could not any more than dukes be connected with none but equals; they were conscious of an inherent social superiority which was defined with great nicety in practice, though hardly expressible theoretically.[27]

If we consider the requirements of acceptance in education, marriage and establishments we shall see the buttresses of the old merchant social order, and the difficulties that the self-made merchant, and after 1790 the manufacturer, had in breaking these conditions down. The replacement of the old guide lines of eighteenth-century urban society, borrowed from the landed gentry, by the new rules of the manufacturing classes is an important stage both in the development of the pattern of industrial society and urban history.

(V)

On the surface there appears little in the merchants' formal education to set them apart from the rest of their townsmen. The majority of merchants—wealthy and less well-to-do alike—sent their sons to the Free Grammar School in Leeds during the eighteenth century. Relying on the benefactions of two seventeenth-century merchants John Harrison and Godfrey Lawson, the school, however, was by no means restricted to the children of the merchants, attorneys and clergy. William Lupton the cloth-dresser was able to send his three sons there, and the Rev. Isaac Milner, Dean of Carlisle, Professor of Mathematics and Master of Queen's College Cambridge 'made his way from the humblest ranks of life to the first honours of one of the first universities in the world', by way of Leeds Grammar School. He and his brother Joseph, another pupil and celebrated evangelical divine, were the sons of a Mabgate weaver.[28]

The heavy emphasis on the classics at the grammar school was not the ideal preparation for the practicalities of cloth-merchanting. A number of private 'writing' schools attempted to cater for these deficiencies by the teaching of book-keeping, mathematics and languages. Many of these establishments from their prospectuses published in the newspapers were very dubious places of learning. Edward Moor, teaching in the King's Arms Yard, ended his advertisement with the note: 'I engrave Plate, Shields and Stamps for Merchants, Prints for Haberdashers, Tobacconists, Peruke-Makers etc. I likewise engrave, lacker and silver clock faces at the lowest prices.'[29] Seldom were these institutions patronised by the merchants' sons for anything more than an occasional special course in accounts or a language.

By far the most important part of a merchant's education, however, was his apprenticeship. It commenced when he was about 15 years old and extended from 4 to 7 years. He lived with his master's family, went daily into the counting-house and finishing shops and regularly visited the cloth markets of Leeds, Wakefield and Halifax. If the apprentice was being trained with one of the large export firms in the town he spent a year abroad visiting its foreign correspondents and learning languages. Occasionally a merchant sent his son abroad to complete his education in a more formal and extended manner. In the seventeenth century this appears to have been customary. James Ibbetson and William Milner both spent several years in Holland during the early 1690's. By 1750 a period of education abroad was becoming rare, especially as Holland's hold on the north European cloth trade was greatly diminished, although some merchant trainees were still being sent abroad to learn languages for a short time. Arthur Lupton was receiving instruction in 'High Dutch', French and accounts in Frankfurt-upon-Main in 1764, and Henry Hall, Dutch and French at Delph about 1790.[30] For the apprentice completing his training with a home merchant a tour collecting debts and obtaining orders from customers served the same purpose as the period spent abroad by those intending to take up the export trade. It was the long period of expensive training and their ability to buy a partnership which gave the young merchants their status, rather than their initial schooling which was within the range of other sections of the community.

Not all the merchants were satisfied with this pattern of education for their sons. William Milner with his vast pride and income broke out of the grammar school and apprenticeship circle when he sent his son to Eton and Jesus College, Cambridge. At the same time, around 1710, James Ibbetson, not to be outdone, sent his elder son Samuel to the Inns of Court. Both Milner and Ibbetson had ambitions for their sons beyond the woollen cloth trade, but a number of merchants who wished to settle their sons in the church or the law were sending their sons to universities—almost always to Cambridge—or the Inns of Court, although this did not necessarily entail any basic education beyond that provided by the town's grammar school.[31] Only when a merchant intended his son for some other profession was he sent to university: for the one chosen to carry on the business the money was set aside for a good apprenticeship.

The number of pupils at the grammar school fell from 120 in 1760 to 40 in 1808. From 1777 to 1815 the school was discredited by a bitter Chancery suit when the 15 trustees, the majority of whom were aldermen and merchants, attested that its classical education was too narrow and attempted to introduce French, German and Mathematics; 'those parts of learning which might render it a sort of commercial academy for the children of mercantile and manufacturing inhabitants in this town'. The Lord Chancellor, Lord Eldon, ruled in 1805 that this proposal was incompatible with the founders' will, although a mathematics master was afterwards employed. If the trustees' attempt was to stop the drift of merchants' sons being educated elsewhere it was belated. As early as the 1740's the stock of the grammar school had fallen to the extent that a number of prominent merchants like Walter Stanhope and William Cookson were sending their sons to the neighbouring grammar schools at Bradford and Wakefield. Joseph Randall's celebrated academy at Heath was popular, as was that at Dronfield in Derbyshire.[32]

After the 1780's the tendency for merchants to have their sons educated further afield and more frequently at universities increased. Not only did the Dissenting academies, but also a large number of Anglican private schools less well known to history, provide a wider education than the grammar school whose reputation at this period was fast declining. Moreover there was a deliberate attempt by the merchants to avoid it as increasing numbers of shopkeepers and manufacturers began sending their children there. The schooling of Benjamin Gott's sons was typical of the education that the wealthy Anglican merchants provided for their sons after 1780. Benjamin and John Gott were first sent to the academy at Heath, before going for two years to Richmond in Yorkshire, where Canon Tate kept an excellent school, which boasted that one in six of the Fellows of Trinity College, Cambridge had been educated there in the early nineteenth century. They were then transferred to a school at Dumfries before going on to Edinburgh University to attend lectures there for two sessions in 1809–1811. Later Benjamin made an extensive tour of Europe, and he died in Athens in 1817.

An education on this scale was beyond the range of all save the wealthiest of the long-established merchants. Nevertheless more and more emphasis was placed on actual education as opposed to vocational training, especially now that many merchants' sons were beginning to look to the professions for their livelihood. In the early eighteenth century it had been the merchants' expensive apprenticeship that had set them apart from the rest of the community, but by 1800 it was their superior education that gave them an enhanced status *vis-à-vis* the manufacturing classes.

(VI)

A merchant's marriage was as important as his education in fixing his rank in society. The more pedestrian considerations of marriage—frequently uppermost in the contract—were concerned with questions of money and settlements. The announcements in the newspapers, at least before 1780, usually gave the brides reputed dowries. Three typical examples were those of Henry Smithson, D'arcy Molyneux and William Wilson. Henry Smithson married 'a young lady possessed of every amiable and endearing accomplishment and a fortune of £12,000'; D'arcy Molyneux's wife had a dowry of £6,000; William Wilson, mayor in 1762, married Ann Pawson a Leeds heiress with £20,000.[33] A good marriage was the cause for great celebration. When James Blayds married Peter Birt's daughter in 1770 there were tumultuous rejoicings in Leeds. Open house was kept for three days for the Blayds' cloth-dressers, 'firing of Cannon, ringing of Bells and other demonstrations of joy were likewise shown on the occasion'. Annuities were guaranteed in the case of widowhood, but the merchant was able, when necessary, to plough his wife's resources into the business, and marriage portions were an important source of business finance. From the evidence, by 1750 an aspiring merchant sought a wife who could provide a dowry of at least £1,000.

Yet the merchant community was not entirely concerned with these financial aspects, for the arbiters of its social conventions insisted on certain other requirements. The newspapers dwelt on the accomplishments and connections of the merchants' brides in a style that any contemporary novelist might have envied, for it was recognised that the tone of a merchant's social life was largely determined by the background and dowry of his wife.

The easiest passport for any newcomer to Leeds into the ranks of the inner merchant circle was by marriage. It could give an immediate entry to the town's social round and administration. Although Sir Henry Ibbetson had been dead ten years and the doors of his counting-house closed almost as long, when his two daughters married, their husbands—both outsiders—were immediately elected to the corporation.[34] That John Beckett, newly arrived from Barnsley, became mayor in 1775, two years within election to the corporation—a record achievement for a newcomer—was largely due to his excellent marriage into the Wilson family, and his success as a banker was in no small measure attributable to the same fact. For the merchant oligarchy was perpetuated by a complex pattern of intermarriage between the families that composed it. A sample of 132 merchant marriages taken from the Leeds newspapers between 1740 and 1830 shows that 69 married within the town, and of these 43 married the daughters of other merchants. Considering that the merchant was perhaps the most mobile member of the community, the percentage of marriage within the town was high. The result was that a merchant like Ralph Thoresby on his own account and his wife's—she was a Sykes—could claim cousinship with almost every merchant in the town. The extensive marriage alliances of several merchant dynasties like the Cooksons, Lodges, Wilsons, Ibbetsons, Lees and Oates made them key families in the structure of the merchant community for three generations.

There is ample evidence of the merchants' wider connections with the neighbouring gentry from the pedigrees that Whitaker brought up to date for the second edition of Thoresby's *Ducatus* in 1815.[35] Occasionally love, or ambition, took the merchant beyond the small gentry's marriage market. Thomas Medhurst's wife was the daughter of the Rev. Granville and Lady Catherine Wheler, a niece of the Earl of Huntingdon and Lady Betty Hastings; and although Lady Huntingdon's Methodist leanings brought the family into some disrepute, it was obviously a brilliant match since Wheler was reputably the wealthiest man in Holy orders in England. Richard York, the son of Whitell Sheepshanks (afterwards York) wedded the daughter of the first Earl of Harewood and the Milnes of Wakefield married several times into Lord Galway's family.[36] These women with their fine manners were the leaders of taste and fashion in the town.

Marriage then could enhance the merchant's status not only in that his wife's dowry often gave him new resources, but also in that she set the standard of his entire establishment. In this way the merchant's already high standing in the community was sealed by a good marriage with the daughter of a well-established merchant or neighbouring landowner. This range of marriage, built on the firm cornerstone of the exchange of ample settlements, was quite beyond the ambitions of the rest of the town. It was not therefore surprising that the hard-working manufacturer and his homely wife found it impossible, as had the self-made merchant before them, to break into the social round of the closely related oligarchy of the wealthier merchants with their fine houses and entertainments, their excursions to Bath and Scarborough and their long sojourns with their relations in the country.

(VII)

There was a uniformity of upper-class taste and design in Georgian England which saved the rich from the censures of vulgarity that were later levelled against the leaders of the new industrial society. There was no division between north and south, no clash between the gentility of the aristocracy and the barbarity of urban society, no contrast between the life devoted to good works and the life wasted in money-making that industrialism created in the nineteenth century. Before 1780 there was one ideal pattern of living, that manifested by the aristocracy. As it percolated through the provinces to the landed gentry and merchants many of its excesses disappeared. Simply because a merchant possessed a similar income to the lesser gentry, simply because there was a homogeneity of style in housing, furniture and fashion they enjoyed the same simplified version of the ideal. Someone commented in Leeds in 1793 that the merchants' wealth enabled 'them to vie with the nobility in their magnificence'.[37] It was this style of living that set them socially apart in the town.

Close attention was paid to the dictates of fashion. The merchants and their wives read the newspapers, perused the latest novels and like all good upper-class Englishmen had their children, horses and dogs painted by a stream of minor painters who had fallen out of favour in London, or who were about to make their name there. Parmentier (1658–1730) came from Lord Carlisle's new palace at Castle Howard to paint a mural on the staircase of John Atkinson's house and the portraits of several merchant families. When William Cookson died in 1743 he left his son 'five pictures in the Great dining Room of his Grandfather, Grandmother, Father, Mother and Uncle done by Mr. Parmentier'. Benjamin Wilson, R.A. (1721–88), a cousin of Richard Wilson the recorder, boasted a large clientele of Yorkshire gentlemen and Leeds merchants. England's leading pastelist John Russell (1745–1806) did some of his best work when he was in Leeds during the 1790's painting the town's worthies.[38] The wealthiest merchants patronised architects and artists of national fame. John Carr submitted plans for a number of houses for merchant clients in Leeds, Wakefield and Halifax. Benjamin Gott employed Sir Robert Smirke and Humphrey Repton at Armley, and then he and Mrs. Gott went up to London to have their portraits painted by Sir Thomas Lawrence. The Milnes and Denisons could afford Gainsborough, Reynolds, Romney and George Stubbs to commit them to posterity. But nothing exceeded Robert Denison's grandiose scheme when his brother William died in 1783.[39] He invited Carr to build a new church and mausoleum at Ossington, and his own will demanded that his executors should finish a Monumental Statue at full length to the memory of my late Brother agreeable to his Directions and also shall set up ... a Tomb or Monumental Statue to my memory and I will that not less than the sum of one thousand pounds shall be laid out and expended ... to finish the same in the most compleat manner.

Robert probably had in mind something like the statue of the Marquess of Rockingham that, in 1774, Joseph Nollekens had executed for Wentworth Woodhouse. Nollekens and William Tyler, R.A., were invited to submit schemes, but Robert cared nothing for Tyler's plan of attiring William in Roman tunic and Nollekens was commissioned to supply both statues for which he was paid £921.[40] The result would have gladdened the brothers' hearts. The base of William's statute bears a fine relief with a ship, wool bales and sheep—a fitting allegory of the Denisons' lives and riches. Such catholic patronage of the arts suggests a taste which no contemporary could have faulted. The only point that separates the Denisons and the average north-country squire is that whereas the latter was unlikely to afford even a half-length Gainsborough portrait, much less a Nollekens memorial, William and Robert Denison could proudly sit for two of the leading painters of their day and plan their park with the north's most fashionable architect.

Beyond this automatic patronage that was the preserve of the wealthy, some merchants, in the unpretentious ways of the north, showed themselves to be men of genuine culture and wide interests. William Denison enjoyed travelling abroad, and he made a fair collection of Italian pictures for his house in Kirkgate. When J. P. Neale visited Denton in 1822 he noted that the best pictures, including a good Rubens, had been collected by Sir Henry Ibbetson over 60 years previously.[41]

If the merchants kept half an eye cocked at posterity they were not blind to the satisfaction of their more immediate comforts. The stray inventories that have survived, and the sale notices which appear in the newspapers after the 1790's disclose the ample contents of their houses. They kept an excellent table. William Milner was able to entertain liberally the Archbishop of York, the county M.P.s and a host of country acquaintances from Lord Irwin to the humblest neighbouring curate. The leading merchants kept up this hospitality throughout the century. Even when there were no visitors business was over by three o'clock, and the merchant was able to take a leisurely dinner. Through this constant round of polite morning calls, dinners and assemblies, the news of the woollen trade and the gossip of Leeds circulated. Country visitors like the Rev. George Paxton were amazed at the pace of social life. Only in the hot summer of 1723, when everyone seemed to be out of town, could William Cookson report that Leeds was utterly quiet except for the monthly ravings of poor Sir William Rooke.[42]

The self-made merchant and the manufacturer found it difficult to fit into this way of life. It was not simply that the grandest merchants kept a good carriage and employed a butler and footmen besides more menial hands but that their families had done so for as long as three generations.[43] The barrier was not one of wealth, but of social form. The old merchant families knew each other intimately, they shared the same background, education and connections, they enjoyed the same tastes and they had together ruled the town's administration and social life for 200 years. Newcomers were not welcomed unless they could conform to their views of society.

(VIII)

When the woollen industry expanded more rapidly after 1783 a new impetus was given to a whole range of other industries, and the instigators of these changes emerged as a new class of self-made, newly-rich men largely outside the old merchant group that had managed the town and its trade since the sixteenth century. These men did not immediately diminish the merchants' control of every feature of town life. The Corporation retained its exclusiveness until 1835 and the trustees of the advowson of the parish church, the Infirmary and other public works were still drawn from the same sector of the community that they always had been. Nevertheless, as we have seen, Baines, after 1802, canalised the new dissenting manufacturers' dissatisfaction with affairs in a precise political direction by his attack on the old Tory Anglican merchant oligarchy. Political expressions were the outward and visible signs of deeper economic and social tensions. The merchants' social paramountcy survived so long as they could maintain effective economic leadership in the industry. When after the 1780's they allowed this leadership to drain away—as much through their own inaction as by the threats of the new merchant-manufacturers—their social exclusiveness was menaced. The march of industry and the merchants' own capitulation gave their relaxation of control a tone of inevitability. Firstly, many of the oldest and largest merchant houses had by 1815 already closed their doors on Leeds and the cloth trade. The big six firms of the eighteenth century—Dixon's, Lee's, Ibbetson's, Milner's, Denison's and Cookson's—had all gone by 1811; the heads of the families all lived the lives of solid, prosperous landowners with the exception of Francis Cookson whose family connections allowed him to obtain the perpetual curacy of St. John's, Briggate. Secondly, since these, and similar, firms were disappearing the stream of their trainees,

P

who had always been welcome to the town and trade as young men of means and good connections, dried up. Lastly, the merchant community's ranks split when the old Dissenting merchant families accepted the new manufacturers, often men of their own religious and political persuasions, quite readily. Those merchants left of the old Tory Anglican beliefs answered the onslaught on their position largely in terms of their social superiority.

At the lowest level this statement was nothing more than an attempt by many merchants to trace their pedigrees back into the seventeenth century. Registers were avidly perused, coats of arms quartered. In 1815 Edward Oates spent £73 10s. at the College of Arms verifying the Oates' lineage, and with typical merchant attention to detail the cost was split between five members of the family. By diligent research impressive pedigrees and coats of arms were constructed.[44] The result was a splendid re-edition of Thoresby's *Ducatus Leodiensis* with the family trees brought up to date. The work was definitive and excluded all but the oldest Leeds families. None of the new manufacturing class received a footnote.

Something of the old social exclusiveness survived in another form. Mrs. Benjamin Gott's diaries, which recorded little besides the innumerable times she and her husband dined with, or entertained the Leeds aristocracy—the Becketts, Bischoffs, Blayds and Dixons—are a remarkable testimony to the cohesion of the leading merchant families.[45] As one of the leaders of Leeds society she found no need to comment on the rise of the new manufacturing class. Others were not so reticent. Mrs. Wainhouse and Mrs. Buckle, two octogenarians and both members of old merchant families who had felt the new social pressures after 1815, told their reminiscences to Charles Oates in the 1880's. As Oates commented, they had had the opportunity of observing in their long lives a number of extensive social changes. They lamented the removal of the old merchant families into the country and their replacement by a set of upstart manufacturers and engineers. Who was Sir Peter Fairbairn? Had not Sir James Kitson's maternal grandfather been a letter-carrier? Then there was Mr. Waite, a wholesale plumber and glazier, who bought Burley Lodge and caused 'considerable amusement to his acquaintances that he had two very large mirrors in the drawing-room, the full height of the room'. If Mrs. Buckle and Mrs. Wainhouse denounced the new class, they recalled with joy every detail of the merchant families who had left Leeds. One might dismiss these recollections as the highly coloured wanderings of two old ladies unless one discovered a very similar set of reminiscences that Henry Clarkson published about Wakefield. He again looked over a great chasm of social change to recall the gold age of the 'merchant princes' who ruled Wakefield in the eighteenth century.[46]

This very stress on social pre-eminence was a symptom of a deep-rooted malaise. Political and social divisions in Leeds after 1800 underlined two fundamentally different approaches to the leadership of the industry and the town. The new class—the manufacturers, engineers and their allies the Whig dissenting merchants—pinned their faith in moderate political reform and uninhibited economic expansion, while the remnants of the merchant hierarchy defended its political position in terms of inherited right and lamented the economic changes that had undermined the pillars of the old industry, the cloth halls, the small clothiers and the non-manufacturing merchants. Since political and economic forces after 1800 were working on the side of the new class eventual victory lay with them. The reverberations of their triumph resulted in the final departure of the old merchant families from Leeds. As their economic existence in the industry and their social and political position in the town were harassed they began an unprecedented exodus. Only the wealthier, better-known merchants were saved from the oblivion that swallowed up the rest.[47]

Notes to Chapter 9

[1] D. Defoe, *op. cit.*, II, pp. 204–7.

[2] Nicholas Raynton, 'Survey of Leeds in 1628', Corporation of London MSS., R.C.E., No. 60. See also W. G. Rimmer, 'The evolution of Leeds to 1700' *op. cit.*, 91–129.

[3] *Ducatus*, 76.

[4] *L.I.*, 29 July 1777; Denison MSS. De/H 21.

[5] *L.M.*, 6 April 1773; 14 March 1775; 4 May 1779; *L.I.*, 8 June 1795.

[6] W. G. Rimmer in *Leeds Journal*, vol. 27 (1956), 15. See also his 'Working men's cottages in Leeds, 1770–1840', *Thors. Soc.*, Miscellany, vol. 13, part 2 (1961), 171; F. Beckwith, 'The population of Leeds during the Industrial Revolution', *Thors. Soc.*, vol. XLI, part 2 (1945), 125–31, 177–8.

[7] *H.M.C.* Verulam MSS., 239; J. Aikin, *op. cit.*, p. 571.

[8] Wilson estate papers, DB 32/1, 19, 26. See also M. W. Beresford and G. R. J. Jones (eds), *Leeds and its Region* (1967), pp. 186–97; C. Gill, *A History of Birmingham* (1951), p. 122.

[9] DB 32/20; *L.M.*, 1 July 1776; 18 May 1811.

[10] W. G. Rimmer, 'Working men's cottages', 189; DB 32/7; *L.M.*, 9 April 1796.

[11] The ground rent ledger covering the years 1792–1829 is in DB 32/7. See also DB 32/19–22 and the *Leeds Directory* (1797).

[12] The family pedigree is in *Ducatus*, 2–3. The substance of this paragraph is derived from the wills of the three Wilson brothers, a few stray letters and an account-book of Christopher Wilson (DB 32/12) in the Wilson papers, DB 32.

[13] 'An Act to carry into execution certain articles . . . between Christopher late Lord Bishop of Bristol and Messrs. Benjamin Gott and Harry Wormald . . . 1794', and 'An Act for Vesting Parts of the Estates divised by the Will of Christopher late Lord Bishop of Bristol . . . 1803'; DB 32/5–7 and *L.M.*, 27 April 1811; J. Bigland, *op. cit.*, p. 776.

[14] G. A. Cooke, *A Topographical and Statistical Description of the County of York* (*c.* 1810), p. 181; *L.M.*, 27 Sept. 1817; 21 Feb. 1818.

[15] Compare the estate plans of 1793, 1806 and 1817. See also 'Report of the Trial . . . against Benjamin Gott and Son for an alleged public nuisance in neglecting to ensure the smoke of their Steam Engine Furnaces at Leeds', (1824), and E. Parsons, *op. cit.*, I, p. 171.

[16] *ibid.*, pp. 175, 179; Sir George Head, *A Home Tour through the Manufacturing Districts of England* (1836), p. 169.

[17] *L.I.*, 7 Dec. 1801; 13 Dec. 1802; *L.M.*, 13 Nov. 1802; 5 Jan. 1805; 13 Dec. 1806; 17 Sept. 1817.

[18] *L.I.*, 20 Feb. 1809; 8 Aug. 1814; 19 Jan. 1826; *L.M.*, 6, 27 Aug. 1814; E. Parsons, *op. cit.*, I, p. 157.

[19] See bibliography under C. T. Thackrah; M. T. Sadler, *The Law of Population* (1830), 2 vols.; A. Ure, *op. cit.*, p. 396; *Journal of the Statistical Society of London*, II (1839-40), 397-424; F. Beckwith, *op. cit.*, pp. 147-8.

[20] Kighley's Diary, 21 Aug. 1805; R. V. Taylor, *op. cit.*, pp. 181-2; H. M. Colvin, *A Biographical Dictionary of English Architects* (1954), p. 123; 'Journal of the Rev. Joseph Ismay', *Thors. Soc.*, vol. XXXVII (1937).

[21] J. Houseman, *A Topographical Description of . . . Part of the West Riding of Yorkshire* (1800), p. 186; *The Land We Live In* (1849), III, p. 96.

[22] Oates MSS., the section on Roundhay is based upon the Armitage MSS. MD 279/A 5, 6. See also J. W. Morkill, *The Manor and Park of Roundhay* (1893), pp. 32-6.

[23] D. Stroud, *Humphrey Repton* (1962), pp. 148, 165, 171; N. Pevsner, *The Buildings of England, Yorkshire: The West Riding* (1959), pp. 57, 336, 387; E. Parsons, *op. cit.*, II, p. 458.

[24] *L.I.*, 15 July 1815; N. Pevsner, *op. cit.*, p. 351.

[25] *Infra*, p. 220, note 47 and pp. 229-30.

[26] W. G. Rimmer, 'Working men's cottages', 189, and his 'The industrial profile of Leeds', 147.

[27] *L.M.*, 10 Nov. 1821; Quoted in J. Prest, *The Industrial Revolution in Coventry* (1960), p. 51.

[28] The school registers begin in 1820. A short list of distinguished eighteenth-century pupils appears in the *Register of Leeds Grammar School: 1820-1896*, (1897), pp. 2-7. See also R. V. Taylor, *op. cit.*, pp. 205, 277; A. C. Price, *A History of the Leeds Grammar School*, (1919), pp. 117-21.

[29] *L.M.*, 16 June 1741; 27 Dec. 1743.

[30] *Diary*, I, 310-11; J. Mawman, *op. cit.*, p. 33; Lupton MSS., William Lupton to Arthur Lupton, 2 June 1764; *Thors. Soc.*, Miscellany, vol. 12, part 4 (1953), 329.

[31] *Complete Baronetage*, V (1906), p. 39; *Diary*, II, p. 232; A. C. Price, *op. cit.*, p. 121.

[32] Price., 133-48; *L.M.*, 6 Aug. 1808; Spencer-Stanhope MSS. 2169; M. H. Peacock, *The History of Wakefield Grammar School* (1892); J. Randall, *An Account of an Academy at Heath Near Wakefield* (1750).

[33] *L.M.*, 16 Jan. 1750; *L.I.*, 11 April 1758; 27 Feb. 1759.

[34] Ingram Rider, 'gentleman', was elected to the corporation in 1769; Major Thomas Rea Cole in 1775.

[35] e.g. Sir Henry Ibbetson, Thomas Lloyd and Walter Stanhope, *infra*, pp. 244-245, 247.

[36] Burke's, *Landed Gentry* (1952), 'Wheler of Otterdon Place', 'York of Hutton Wardesley'; Burke's *Peerage* (1959), 'Galway, Viscount'.

[37] *L.I.*, 21 Oct. 1793.

[38] *D.N.B.*, XV, 322; Cookson's will proved at York, 1743; Herbert Randolph, *The Life of Sir Robert Wilson* (1862); G. S. Williamson, *op. cit.* John Miers, a leading silhouettist, made his name in Leeds drawing the town's gentry.

[39] H. M. Colvin, *op. cit.*, pp. 122–5; J. Pope-Hennessey, *Monckton Milnes, The Years of Promise, 1809–1851* (1949), p. 7.

[40] Denison MSS. De/H 47.

[41] J. P. Neale, *Views of Gentlemen's Seats* (1822). See also Sir Henry's will proved at York, August 1761.

[42] The inventory of the contents of Walter Stanhope's house (Spencer-Stanhope MSS. 1214), and the sale of Wade Brown's furniture (*L.M.*, 28 Nov. 1807), provide good examples of these sources. Plaxton's letters are published in *Letters of Eminent Men Addressed to Ralph Thoresby* (1832), 2 vols.; 'Letters addressed to Ralph Thoresby F.R.S.', *Thors. Soc.* (1912), xxi; 'Letters of the Rev. George Plaxton', *Thors. Soc.*, vol. xxxvii, Part I, (1936) 30–104.

[43] Sir James Graham believed there were about a hundred carriages kept in Leeds in 1806 (1806 Report, 444); Thomas and James Fenton each kept four male servants in the 1780's and John Milnes, six. J. Batley, *A History of Rothwell* (1877), p. 191; J. W. Walker, *Wakefield, Its History and People* (1934), p. 398.

[44] Oates MSS., Edward Oates to Rev. T. D. Whitaker, 21 Nov. 1814; 16 March 1815.

[45] Gott MSS. The diaries for 1810–11 are incomplete. After a long break a complete set for the years 1830–50 exists. A similar view of society in Halifax emerges from 'Miss Lister's Diary Extracts and Comments', *Trans. Halifax Ant. Soc.* (1950), 69–83, and 'Mrs. William Rawson and her diary', *Trans. Halifax Ant. Soc.* (1958), 29–50.

[46] Oates MSS. and H. Clarkson, *op. cit.*

[47] Taylor in his *Biographia Leodiensis* mentions 15 families which were prominent around 1800, who later gave up merchanting and left Leeds. The Oates papers record a further nine which followed in their footsteps. Mrs. Wainhouse stressed the desire to break connections with Leeds completely: Richard and William Lee wanted to lead the lives of country gentlemen; 'Thomas and William Gatliffe both had families but they disappeared from Leeds a long time ago'; Richard Wilson 'bought an estate in the North and was no more heard of in Leeds'.

10   *The merchants in the county*

> Trade is so far here from being inconsistent with the character of
> a gentleman that trade in England makes gentlemen, and has
> peopled this nation with nobles and Gentlemen too: for, after a
> generation or two, the children of traders or at least their grand-
> children come to be as good gentlemen, statesmen, parliament
> men, privy counsellors, judges, bishops and noblemen as those of
> the highest births and most ancient families.*

The purchase of a country estate from the profits of trade is as old a
phenomenon as urban development itself. It is the highest common
factor in a discussion of the relationship between town and country
society in all countries and at all periods. If the gentry provided occasional recruits to merchanting, the merchants in return provided the
greatest channel of recruitment to the landed classes. As Postlethwayt
pointed out time after time, trade admitted men to 'honour and pre-
ferment' and 'estates of consideration' more easily and frequently than
by any other profession. Burke's *Peerage* and *Landed Gentry* are full of
the names of families which purchased their estates from the profits of
trade, and the landed family which had no alliance with the commercial
world was almost unknown. Fortunes made in the Leeds woollen
trade secured the place of at least two dozen families in Burke's compilations, and over 40 names connected with commerce in Leeds,
Wakefield and Halifax found their way into Langdale's *Topographical
Dictionary of Yorkshire* (1809) which listed the seats of the county's
gentry. The same process, whereby merchants became landowners
through the profits of trade, was taking place not only in Leeds,
Bristol and Newcastle, but in every town that could boast a merchant,
banker and attorney. In the eighteenth century it was a movement
which broke down almost all social barriers between the gentry and
merchant classes.

Not that the merchant was ashamed of his activities or felt compelled
to hide his profits beneath the garb of broad acres, but, as Colonel
Henry Liddell explained, he desired to live 'a country-life in business'.[1]
The peak of any merchant's ultimate ambition was not to build up the
largest firm in his trade, but ultimately to found a prominent and stable

* M. Postlethwayt, *Dictionary of Trade and Commerce* (third edition, 1765), I,
see under 'commerce'.

landed dynasty. Families that became by-words in Leeds lore were those like the Milners, Ibbetsons and Denisons who had made a fortune in the town and then transferred their riches and talents to the country. This predilection for a landowner's life had most important social and economic consequences.

The old explanation of the accumulation of capital necessary for industrialisation in Britain after 1750 was that a high proportion of new industrial enterprises were floated from profits accumulated by merchants in the home and export trades. Recently historians have questioned this assumption. Professor Flinn warns us that this percolation of commercial profits into the key growth industries must not be exaggerated: 'The first goal of many a merchant was the acquisition of a landed estate with a stately home, and an unknown proportion of all mercantile profits in the eighteenth century was poured into this form of conspicuous consumption.'[2] What happened in Leeds? What answers do the activities of William Milner and William Denison, in this as in every other merchanting activity leading examples, provide to questions of the merchants' motivation in land purchase, integration with traditional country society and the effects of their migration on Leeds and the woollen industry?

(I)

William Milner was very fond of relating his success in life for there are at least two extant accounts of his good fortune. It was not for nothing that he was variously known to the coterie of antiquarians that met at his cousin Thoresby's as 'Alderman Million' 'Earl Percy' and the 'Bashaw of Pannopolis'. Riding from Newcastle back to Leeds in 1707 with Milner, Thoresby

> was mightily pleased with some remarkable providences that have attended this worthy magistrate who is of good family . . . yet began the world with little, being the youngest son . . . [he], with a thankful heart to God recounted to me the various steps of his growth, the first year he had commissions for £5,000; the second for £10,000; the third for £15,000; the fourth for 20 or 25,000£; and has now dealt for £80,000 per annum.[3]

In his direction of the Aire and Calder Navigation, in merchanting and town administration Milner was obviously a man of great drive. The concerns of the Navigation together with his work as a West Riding J.P. and as a receiver of the land-tax extended his interests beyond Leeds and cloth merchanting. Brought by these means into close contact with the West Riding landowners, it was not surprising that Milner decided to purchase Nun Appleton, an estate only 17 miles from Leeds, on the break-up of the great Fairfax properties at the beginning of the eighteenth century.

Although the high land-tax which Godolphin had imposed for the upkeep of Marlborough's army had lowered land prices Milner was doubly resolved to drive a hard bargain.[4] When serious negotiations began in 1708 he demanded the rents from Lady Day 1707 onwards, and hoped that he would be reimbursed 'for my loss of time and charges of my two fruitless Journeys to London, wch. were £100 to my prejudice'. He offered £17,000 for the 2,385 acres (by 1873 the Milners had acquired 5,558 acres[5]) of the Bolton Percy and Nun Appleton estates, including 'The manor house which cost building £30,000 and the orchards, Gardens and Walks where the house stands.' It is not quite clear whether Milner paid a large proportion of the price with £13,000 that he temporarily had in his hands from the land-tax collection, for Thoresby's account of his visit with Milner to the Bank of England and the Exchequer a few days before he finally signed the deeds in February 1709 is very brief. Certainly £3,500 was withheld from payment for legal reasons until June 1718.

The estate was run down, but the rents were low and the property was capable of great improvement. Milner had secured a good bargain. With his usual vigour he demolished the old house at Nun Appleton, where Lord Fairfax and General Monk had planned Charles II's return in 1660, and within three years had built a smaller, more convenient house with some of the materials. It provided a fine inheritance for Milner's only son, who in 1716 married Elizabeth Dawes, the daughter of the Archbishop of York, and with obvious satisfaction Milner wrote across the fat settlement 'My son's marriage writings.' In 1717 the son was created a baronet, and in 1722, elected M.P. for York.

Although Milner himself still continued to work hard for the rest of his long life in Leeds, he had the satisfaction of knowing that through his ample provision his son moved with any gentleman in the county on equal terms. And since he provided dowries of £5,000 each for his daughters they easily found husbands. One married the son of a Staffordshire landowner, the other an ambitious lawyer, Richard Witton, who immediately built a good country house near Wakefield with the proceeds of his wife's settlement. In the peace of old age Milner could recount in 1737: 'My son and two of my daughters are very happily married to persons of good familys, good Estate and good humours, and they all live very plentifully and comfortably.'

On Milner's death in 1740 the firm was carried on in a half-hearted fashion for a few years by a nephew, but the major portion of the large resources that the Milner family had accumulated in the woollen trade

passed to Nun Appleton. There a fixed rent-roll—the bogey of so many
eighteenth-century landowners—was augmented by the Leeds inheritance and an increasing income from William Milner's investment in
the Aire and Calder Navigation. A total income of over £12,000 a year
by 1800—over half was the return on Navigation stock—placed the
Milners on parity with the average income of the peerage and allowed
them to maintain an establishment that was the envy of the old landed
gentry in Yorkshire. They directed the affairs of the Navigation, represented York in Parliament on several occasions, but otherwise—except
that they were brought back to be buried in state at Leeds parish church
—their connection with Leeds and its trade was by and large severed
in 1740. But William Milner troubled by the demise of the Fairfaxes
and many other West Riding landed families, both large and small, at
the turn of the seventeenth century, could have rested assured that his
descendants did not have the same financial worries. Savings made from
his trade with Hamburg, the sale of the valuable Leeds properties and
transport dividends allowed them over the next two centuries to build
up as well-run a medium-sized estate and found as stable a landed
dynasty as any in Yorkshire.

(II)

Answers to the questions of the merchants' motivation in land purchase
have almost always been stated in terms of social and political advancement. The mere enumeration of the seven estates[6] scattered across four
counties which William Denison left to his brother in 1782 suggests
a piecemeal acquisition which does not square with this traditional
reason. His letter-books suggest that an economic incentive provides
a sounder explanation. One large central estate would have served his
purpose better were his ambitions purely to emulate the great landowners. On the other hand this haphazard accumulation reflects two
considerations. William remained a bachelor, and although by the
1750's he was probably the wealthiest man in Leeds, his success—and
this was unusual—did not lessen his diligence in the cloth export firm,
but it meant that there was not the direct stimulus to create a first-class
consolidated estate. Secondly, the estates were in some degree purchased
out of current earnings by the merchant house, and this probably
limited the size of property purchased at any given period. As a large
surplus built up—and unlike later manufacturing concerns the capital
required by the larger export houses in Leeds probably never exceeded
£20,000 before 1783—Denison looked round for the best possible
investment.

If the size and scattered nature of William Denison's properties reflect his personal and financial arrangements we must look elsewhere for the motives which led him into land purchase. Perhaps like William Milner he wished to fix the ultimate seal of success on his career, but comparisons are not explanations, especially in this case for Denison was a man of independent views. Certainly there was no question of him neglecting business in Leeds to spend time in country pursuits. In 1779, when he tried to evade serving as High Sheriff of Nottingham he wrote to the Speaker: 'Nor do I call myself an inhabitant of that country for tho' I have a large house upon my estate and keep an old woman there to light fires for its preservation, I have never been in Nottinghamshire 14 days per ann. since I purchased it, and then only upon business.'[7] Yet he claimed Ossington was his favourite estate. What leisure time William had was spent taking the waters each spring at Bath.

Although William purchased his first estate in Lincolnshire in 1759 the factors which influenced this departure and subsequent ventures emerged from a perusal of his only surviving letter-books which cover the years 1777–81. By the 1770's the firm's involvement appears to have been entirely in the Italian market, and as we have seen (p. 49) after 1778 his firm was badly hit by the closure of the Mediterranean trade. Denison felt he was better doing nothing at a time when insurance costs were high, exchange rates unfavourable and remittances behind hand. He summarised his position when he wrote to his nephew: 'My capital during the year 1778 had better have been at 2 per cent. Interest than in trade . . . and 1779 promises no better success, tho' goods are cheap.'[8]

As debts came slowly in, William curtailed his orders with the clothiers and his purchases in the cloth halls and began to investigate the best available investment opportunities. He considered three alternatives: annuities, government stock and land. In 1779 he explored opportunities for the negotiation of suitable annuities. For a number of years William had occasionally speculated in this field, and in 1779 he agreed to let Lord Chesterfield have £4,800 on an undisclosed annual repayment. In the following year, however, he was writing, 'Little money to be made in the annuity business—only with trustworthy private gentlemen. Foley's family have robbed the publick near £300,000 that way.' His doubts came too late. When the executors settled his brother's estate in 1789 they commented that both had been lax in keeping their annuity accounts—many of the annual payments were unpaid—and it was reckoned that Lord Chesterfield, Lord Seaforth and Lord Foley together owed them £9,881.[9] The second and third investment categories were more important. In these difficult years William constantly weighed the monetary returns of consols against land. Rents fell sharply after 1778 and large arrears were forcing the necessitous to sell. In the winter of 1777-8 Denison was offered several West Country estates at Bath, and in the following autumn he was considering properties in Lincolnshire and the East and West Ridings, but as he told a York land agent: 'If I can't make four per cent or upwards in elegible purchases my spare money will go into the funds.' As the war dragged on and the depression deepened, rents fell further—William reduced his by one-fifth in the spring of 1780—and the value of land in some places fell by as much as one-third. As the land market became increasingly uncertain, the problem of management, outlay and rent arrears weighed heavily with him: 'I will not purchase unless I can do it upon as good terms as I enjoy in the funds which is 5 per cent clear of all charges and expences whatsoever, where I have no delays, no disappointments, no bad Tennants, nor no Stewardships.' The yield of government stocks rose sharply between 1777 and 1780, from an average of 3·7 to 5%. By early 1780 William realised that his trading surplus was nowhere so well invested as in stocks producing 5%. The difficulty was to obtain them. He was prepared to advance £10,000–£12,000 in early 1780, but only £6,000 was accepted. In February 1781 he wrote demanding £20,000 worth of that year's issue. Yet in spite of persistent letters to John Robinson at the Treasury reminding him that his distant relative Joseph Denison, the banker, had been allowed his full quota of £100,000 he was only allowed £5,000 of his £20,000 application. He was forced to conclude: 'those that get such large sums have a private ear to either my Lord North's or Robinson's ears especially when the loan is advantageous'.[10]

The evidence on Denison's monetary transactions in these years confirms the view that his estates were purchased as the best outlet for his surplus cash. Only a narrow range of investments were considered: in 1759, when he bought his Lincolnshire properties, and 1768, when he expended £89,000 on two estates in Nottinghamshire and the East Riding, he believed land to be the better speculation; in 1780 and 1781 the return on government stocks was more attractive. Denison's attitude was significant in two respects. Firstly, land was viewed entirely in the utilitarian terms of improvement and return. Distance, tradition, beauty mattered little; improvement potential was of far greater interest. Moreover he was prepared to resell his property. In January 1779 he was offering Ossington for sale at £60,000 (a £26,000 advance on the purchase price in 11 years). 'It always seemed to me to be a favourite Estate of my Broths.', wrote Robert Denison, 'and never imagined he wo'd part with it at any rate . . . I know my bror. will abate nothing of the last price sett, nor will he take it, if the value of money sho'd alter.' Property was never once considered for its built-in social guarantees or political advantages: William well knew he could have afforded any pocket borough he chose; his wealth and position in Leeds gave him a sufficient status. Secondly, he eschewed any form of industrial investments in the West Riding woollen and coal industries, or even in transport improvements beyond a minimum share in the Aire and Calder Navigation. The executors accounts of Robert's will showed that not a penny found its way outside land, annuities, government stock, and of course the firm itself. Certainly, for an old gout-racked man, William expended an incredible amount of energy and thousands of pounds in agricultural improvements on his estates. At Ossington alone Robert wrote: 'he has laid out an Immensity of money in building planting and improving the Estate and has cut down very little timber only some offall decayers that the woods are better by some thousands than they were when he had it'.[11] Here on the threshold of Britain's industrialisation, the eve of Rostow's 'take-off', was a merchant, who according to the traditional interpretations should have been channelling surplus earnings into industrial enterprises of one form or another, completely ignoring this outlet. And William Denison was extremely rich by any contemporary standards—the Leeds papers estimated his fortune between £500,000 and £700,000 when he died in 1782.[12] Few early industrialists' wealth could compare with this. Yet his actions are entirely explicable: his was the classic but common merchants' attitude that one pursued one's trade vigorously but did not become involved in industry. It was far easier when depression frequently came to curtail activities as a merchant than it was to keep going as a manufacturer. The minimum capital was employed, surplus earnings were canalised into the safest and most easily realisable outlets—land and government stocks.

(III)

In these examples of land purchase by two of the wealthiest men in the West Riding different motives were uppermost in their minds. Milner simply wanted to found a landed dynasty. His only son, educated at Eton and Cambridge, was never intended for trade. When he married Archbishop Dawes's daughter it was inevitable that his father should give him Nun Appleton. Denison bought far more property—possibly as much as 10,000 acres—scattered from Durham through Yorkshire into Nottinghamshire and Lincolnshire because land was about the best investment open to him. Of course Milner realised that Nun Appleton was an excellent outlet for his savings, and Denison knew that his purchases would provide his nephew with a princely inheritance, but their reasons were basically different. Where did the rest of the merchants in the town stand on this question?

It should be remembered that the majority of merchants never purchased a landed estate, although bankruptcy sales reveal that partners in the smallest firms owned parcels of land, houses and industrial premises—the latter often taken in the settlement of debts—scattered across Leeds and the clothing districts. This fact did not reflect that such disbursements were unwise, but that their purses were confined. The wealthiest merchants, however, those who headed the export trade and became aldermen, those who had interests in the county and moved on the fringe of landed society were attracted to the life of the country gentleman. Since the frontier between town and country was difficult to determine, and the merchant who knew nothing of the ways of the land was unknown, the transition for the man of wealth to the ideal way of life in eighteenth-century society was not difficult. Without exception he had country cousins—usually well-to-do ones—and he was able to talk problems over with lawyers, men like Richard Wilson in Leeds and Robert Benson in Wakefield, who managed estates for the landed gentry and who knew when a good unencumbered property would become available. But every merchant in Leeds was aware that the proper management of an estate required more resources than a rent-roll in itself could provide. Buying an estate was not a venture lightly undertaken for it meant a complete rediversification of interests. When Robert Denison—a cousin of the brothers William and Robert—decided to give up merchanting in Leeds in 1783 and become, through his purchase of Sir William Anderson's Kilnwick Percy estate, an East Riding squire, his finances were straitened for some years. The acquisition and improvement of the estate necessitated the sale of his property in London and the foreclosing of a number of mortgages. In the early 1790's Meanwood Hall (his Leeds home), the Woodhouse property, land formed around the nucleus of his clothier ancestors' establishment and part of the Beeston estates were sold. When in 1792 he purchased an adjoining manor to Kilnwick for £17,000 he was obliged to raise £10,000 on mortgage from two partners in Beckett's Bank. By 1794 he had borrowed £8,000 from one of them, his old merchant associate John Blayds, and there were many other sums borrowed of £1,000 and less from friends in Leeds. His steady income of around £2,000 from dividends paid by the Aire and Calder Navigation, the West Riding turnpikes, Barnsley canal and his Beeston rent-roll enabled him to raise the money and pay the interest regularly.[13] Investments of profits by earlier Denisons in transport securities and Leeds property were being converted into the broad acres of the Yorkshire wolds.

Few merchants were as well-to-do as Robert Denison, and therefore their different circumstances and aims led to a variety of approaches to landownership. These might be conveniently classified under four heads. Firstly, a number of the wealthiest merchants followed William Milner's example in buying an estate primarily to found a landed dynasty. At least a dozen partners in the largest firms in Leeds bought large properties well away from the town. Besides the two branches of the Denison family, the Ibbetsons (Denton Park, Otley), Lloyds (Cowsby Hall, Northallerton, and Stockton Hall, York), Fentons (Underbank, Sheffield), Prestons (Flasby Hall, Skipton, and Moreby Hall, York), Scotts (Woodhall, Wetherby), Dixons (Gledhow Hall and Weeting Hall, Norfolk), Browns (Rossington Hall, Doncaster, and Copgrove Hall, Boroughbridge), Yorks (Wighill Park, Tadcaster), Sheepshanks (Arthington Hall, Otley), Medhursts (Kippax Hall and Ledstone Hall, Ferrybridge), Wormalds (Sawley Hall, Ripon) and the Oates (Besthorpe and Gestingthorpe Hall, Essex), transferred their resources to the land and filled Burke's pages with pedigrees that were undistinguishable from the rest of his compilations. Sons became soldiers and justices of the peace, daughters were sacrificed to canons and colonels. Secondly, since merchant trainees were often recruited from landed families and made fine marriages, they and their children frequently succeeded to good estates that allowed them to discontinue trade in Leeds. The Kitchingmans and Micklethwaites returned to the estates their families had originated from; John Markland inherited his mother's ancestral home at Foxholes in Lancashire; William Lee, the fourth generation of a leading merchant family, through his wife obtained Grove Hall near Pontefract; Walter Stanhope succeeded to two large estates from his uncles, lawyer John Stanhope of Horsforth and John Spencer of Cannon Hall, Barnsley. They hyphenated or changed their names, quartered their arms and settled down to the lives of country squires. Thirdly, a small number of merchants bought estates for speculative purposes. The Elams ventures have a modern ring. In 1795 Samuel and Emmanuel Elam, reputed to have made £300,000 between them in the American market, together with a fellow Quaker, Isaac Leatham, a Pontefract banker and model farmer in the North Riding, bought an estate of 5,463 acres near Malton for £155,000 (James Armitage, another Leeds merchant, was the under-bidder) and split it into several lots for sale. Samuel Elam, jun., a banker in Leeds, was involved in a number of similar, but smaller deals, in land around Leeds and York.[14] Transactions of this type by other merchants in Leeds property were frequent by 1800 when land values began to rise sharply. The prospects of a quick and easy profit were good, and land was a useful security to raise loans upon or sell when a firm's obligations were acute. Lastly Leeds was ringed by the small, well-kept estates of the merchants. We have already seen the examples of Benjamin Gott, John Blayds and Thomas Ikin,[15] and at least two dozen more names could be added of merchants who purchased similar properties of between 100 and 300 acres. Here their owners kept an eye on their interests in Leeds, farmed and gardened in exemplary fashion, hunted with the Leeds harriers, shot game over their land, and liberally entertained their neighbours and families. Theirs was a country life in miniature. When Leeds grew rapidly after 1800 some moved further afield and bought or leased larger, more rural estates. When William Smithson became Colonel of the Volunteers Corps he seems to have entertained very grand notions and leased two of the finest houses in the county, Ledstone and Heath Hall. William Prest, mayor in 1817, moved to Toulston Lodge, Tadcaster, and severed most of his connections with Leeds. Another alderman, Robert Coulman, bought Wadworth Hall near Doncaster for £11,600 in 1825.[16] The Oates papers record a number of families who followed in their footsteps.

If land purchases can be classified in this fashion, it is more hazardous to draw conclusions from their chronology. Inheritance observed only the dictates of chance, and compact properties within easy reach of Leeds had always been a favourite retreat for the town's merchants, although some landed families who owned several of them and had little or no connection with the woollen trade, were increasingly replaced after 1750 by men who had made a fortune in Leeds. Investment in land became more frequent after 1800 when conditions in the town and trade began to change rapidly and more men could afford the outlay from the large profits made after 1783. Nevertheless the most notable estates, those bought by William Milner, James Ibbetson and William and Robert Denison, were purchased before 1785. In the West Riding the evidence does not entirely support Professor Habakkuk's thesis that the trade in land was cut down after 1700 and that which did come up for sale was acquired by the larger existing estate-owners to consolidate their properties. Like the area around London land changed hands more rapidly because the main stimulus to the market was fortunes made in commerce which tended to rise and fall more dramatically than those of the old landed gentry in the shires. Purchases were related to the price of land comparative with other securities and the resources of individual merchants. Because the way

of life of the landowner was the ideal of commercial society, because
land conferred political and social privileges and because it was often
the best means of holding wealth, landownership was always the goal
of the wealthiest merchants. For this same reason, and, from the sample
of the merchants who became landed proprietors from the Yorkshire
woollen trade, it is difficult to accept Professor Mingay's assertion that
eighteenth-century merchants were less likely to become landowners,
in comparison with previous centuries, because 'investment in the
funds made stocks an acceptable alternative to land, both as a pure
investment and as a means of settling an income on a wife and children'.
Moreover he argues marriage was the easiest means by which merchants could improve their social status and political influence by
connection with the landed classes.[17] Certainly marriage alliances of
this type paved the way for the merchant who moved into landed
society, but the wife accepted the status of her husband rather than vice
versa. And landownership was not a pursuit to be renounced for a fat
holding of government stock. It was an acclaimed existence in itself.
This constant aim of the merchants to become landed proprietors
blurred the emergence of any chronological pattern of purchase
between 1700 and 1830: as much as this reflected anything it was the
long-term state and prospects of industry in the West Riding. Of more
interest here are the social and economic consequences of the merchants'
ventures into landownership.

(IV)
The extent to which the landowning merchant integrated with landed
society has always been debatable. Eighteenth-century comedy represented him as a fish out of water, proud of his wealth yet careful with
his money, devoid of taste, accomplishments and polish. In fact his
passage into the world of Squire Western, itself not one of exquisite
refinement, was not difficult. Accounts have tended to obscure two
pieces of evidence. Historians have accepted the landowner's views on
the merchant community as being identical with their unfavourable
reaction to the new manufacturers after the 1770's. There was in fact
a marked discontinuity. Many of these manufacturers, like Arkwright,
Strutt and Peel were entirely self-made men who had no recognised
place in the hierarchy of eighteenth-century social order.[18] Moreover
in contrast with the new industrialists it must be remembered that those
merchants who embarked upon large-scale landownership already had
considerable status in the urban community. In Leeds their standing
was defined by a delicately balanced series of factors that included
social connections and position in the town and trade. Moreover these

men through their economic relationships and social recreations with the gentry had served an apprenticeship which stood them in good stead when they came to set themselves up in the country.

The income of the wealthier merchants in the woollen industry placed them on economic parity with the middling and smaller gentry. The late Professor Hughes showed how modest the incomes and establishments of very respectable Cumberland squires were in the mid-eighteenth century.[19] Partners in leading firms in Leeds and Wakefield were already long used at least to an equal affluence, and their way of life was quite as comfortable as that of modest West Riding squires. The link between the two groups, however, was not one of income parity but an economic relationship which pulled them together at four points. Since at least the seventeenth century the merchants had provided loans and mortgages for the neighbouring landed gentry. Secondly, they shared common business interests in transport and mining ventures. Some landowners placed their sons as apprentices with firms in Leeds. Thirdly, the leading merchants shared the burden of county administration with the landed gentry since they were the only two groups who could meet the requisite property qualifications. Three merchants, Henry Ibbetson, Jeremiah Dixon and William Denison were elected to the office of high sheriff whilst they were still active in trade, and many more became deputy-lieutenants and county justices, especially after the Militia Act of 1757. Lastly—and the relationship was still basically an economic one—the majority of merchants had some connection with the landed gentry through marriage.[20]

Out of this joint economic and political participation grew an exchange of visits and dinners. Leeds in reality, if not in name, was the county town of the West Riding, the centre of the woollen trade and the legal and financial metropolis of the county. Sheffield was not so central nor Wakefield so large and neither enjoyed the corporate status that gave Leeds a further cohesion and its society a focus. As a social capital York stood pre-eminent in the county, but Hull in the East Riding and Leeds in the West provided the same social round as any other English county town. The merchants were wealthy, therefore their entertainments were large and frequent. William Cookson found that Zurich, Berne and Lausanne in 1712 were much less lively than Leeds, and the Rev. George Plaxton, inviting the antiquary Thoresby to spend a few days with him in the country, wrote: 'Leeds is a busy town, wine and company, noyse and money are the great thing your Corporation deals in, now these are enemys to old MSS. and records, and will not allow a man time to pore over them.'[21] To the Yorkshire gentry this bustle of constant entertainments was a welcome diversion, and Leeds, itself not an unpleasant town before 1800, was the centre of some fine country. Therefore they flocked to Leeds to stay with their relatives, to enjoy the cock-fights, races, assemblies, plays, and a constant round of dinners when the corporation entertained visiting notabilities and the common-councilmen, aldermen and mayors celebrated their election to office.

In all these activities the merchants joined with gusto. The early newspapers are full of advertisements of race-meetings on Chapeltown Moor and cock-fighting matches between the Leeds gentlemen and those of the neighbouring West Riding and Lancashire towns. Hunting and shooting were common pursuits that again brought the merchants and gentry together. The earliest reference to the Leeds hunt is in 1740. Fifty years later it was meeting no fewer than three times a week. Some merchants hunted with neighbouring packs in the county, whilst Thomas Medhurst, William Fenton and Edward Armitage all kept harriers which they followed regularly with their friends. Owners of property at Chapel Allerton—within two miles of the centre of the town—were so incensed by the damage done to crops and fences by the too frequent hunting of different packs of hounds that they inserted a long notice of complaint in the newspapers in 1794.[22] And for those who wanted a break from, or wished to avoid these more raffish pursuits, the theatre, where after it was built in 1771 the stars of the Georgian stage, Mrs. Siddons, Mrs. Jordan and Charles Kemble made occasional appearances, the Assembly Rooms, part of the new White Cloth Hall built in 1774 and 'allowed on all hands to be as complete and highly finished as any set of rooms of that kind in the whole of the Kingdom', and the Music Hall provided further diversions. Commenting on their recreations a correspondent in the *Mercury* was surprised 'that many of the merchants divide the week between their Pleasures and their Business and what they gather with one Hand scatter with the other'. He had mistakenly assured himself that 'the merchant himself was but a mere ant ever solicitous for what he had never time to enjoy'.[23]

(V)

These social occasions had more important economic consequences than their transience would at first sight suggest. Not only did the close association between gentry and merchants welded in this fashion create a society that was far more open than on the Continent, but also there was a perfect mutual understanding of each other's world. In an economic sense this was vital. It was not simply that the landowner recognised the contribution of trade to his own and his country's welfare or that every merchant was conversant with benefits of agricultural improvement, but that their social attitudes and economic responses were linked in a way that played a decisive role in the pattern of British industrialisation. Through their association together in selected business enterprises, local government administration and social pursuits the landowners condoned the changes that took place in the eighteenth-century economy. It was this fusion of interest between land and commerce, the fact that the landowners encouraged what happened in industry that created the ideal environment for the first crucial stages of rapid industrialisation. After 1815 controversies surrounding the Corn Laws and factory system threw the two groups apart and created a division that was of little advantage to either party.

In another sense the close understanding between merchants and landowners in the eighteenth century had its price. With the tradition that they were quasi-country gentlemen in their ideals and pursuits it is not surprising that after 1800 the majority of merchants—especially the more well-to-do and old-established ones—would not take the decision to begin manufacturing cloth, lock their resources up in factories and give the attention to business that this resolution would have necessitated. They were not prepared to waste their lives shut up in a mill for 14 hours a day, or endlessly crossing the Atlantic to collect bad debts in the backwoods of America. John Dixon and John Denison provide excellent examples.

Dixon's father Jeremiah had been a partner with Thomas Lee in one of the half-dozen leading houses in the town between 1750 and 1780. Success came easily to him: in business, a deputy-receiver of the West Riding land-tax and an Aire and Calder proprietor; in public life, a prominent Rockinghamite and High Sheriff of Yorkshire in 1758; in retirement, squire of Gledhow Hall and a Fellow of the Royal Society. Whether his eldest son John had ever been trained for business or whether he merely showed no interest it is now impossible to determine. He resigned from the corporation within a year of election and only came into his own as Colonel in the West Riding Volunteer Corps during the Napoleonic Wars. No sooner was the war over than he sold Gledhow to Sir John Beckett and moved to a country estate in deepest Norfolk. The firm, carried on by brother Jeremiah for a time, had been out of business for 20 years.

John Wilkinson, the son of a London merchant, was 27 when he succeeded to a large portion of his uncle Robert Denison's ample estate in 1785. Robert was adamant that his nephew having trained as a merchant with the family house in Leeds, should remain to direct its affairs:

It being my express intent and meaning that such of them the said John Wilkinson the Younger Edward Wilkinson and Robert Wilkinson as shall retire from the said Business or shall behave and conduct himself unsteadily therein in the Opinion of my said Trustees shall not in any manner be benefitted by or interested in any of the said Estates funds and Effects.

John Denison (he had changed his name from Wilkinson in 1785), however, had little intention of being tied down to the West Riding woollen trade. Why should he spend his time in Leeds when his uncle had left him estates flung across four counties and an income that was far superior to the majority of country gentlemen? In the event he was indecisive. He built quite the grandest of the merchant houses in Leeds in 1786. The *Mercury*, with barely concealed wonder, informed its readers that the house had taken only 101 days to build; 'it is 104 feet long, the wings two stories high, the middle of the building three stories, and it contains 13,680 feet of stone-work executed in masterly manner'. But within five years he had somehow evaded the injunctions of his uncle's will (as did his brother Edward—Robert died in 1789) and retired completely to his country estate at Ossington. He married the daughter of the M.P. for Westbury and after 1796 he himself spent his time as Member for a succession of constituencies and rearing a very large family. Many Nottinghamshire squires must have envied Ossington. The old woman who lit fires for its preservation in William's time was replaced by a staff which included six male servants and a French butler. Half a dozen architects from Sir John Soane down were consulted over the next 30 years about a large number of improvements ranging from a complete remodelling of the house to a 'very coarse rustic' sheep cot. His eldest son married the Duke of Portland's daughter and became Speaker of the House of Commons. The Denisons had established themselves as a leading Nottinghamshire family.[24]

The significance of Dixon's and Denison's example—and many other commercial fortunes in both Leeds and Wakefield went the same way —was that here were the two largest firms in the industry virtually withdrawing their capital from trade at the critical stage of the first period of rapid industrialisation. And in comparison with the early industrialists they had unlimited financial resources. William Denison had ploughed far more money into land than Benjamin Gott and the Wormalds had expended in establishing the first major factory in the wollen industry. The emulation of his example on a lesser scale amongst the West Riding cloth merchants suggests that Mantoux's assertion that there was 'a gradual transformation of commercial to industrial capital' and Charles Wilson's similar conclusion that 'capital came to industrialists in need from merchants of an older generation . . . everywhere there is unbroken continuity' are at least an oversimplification of the position.[25] There is no doubt that this diversion of capital, accrued in generations of trade, away from new developments in the industry into land had serious effects. It is possible to argue that the woollen industry grew relatively slowly in comparison with worsteds and cottons after 1783 simply because its largest source of savings was not ploughed back into investment in machinery and savings. As we have seen Wakefield's economic stagnation during the nineteenth century was partly due to its merchants' refusal 'to permit mills or manufactures to be established here'.[26] In Leeds, where the business community was larger and there was not the same reliance on a single industry, the merchants were unable to curtail developments to this extent. Nevertheless the town had been declining in importance as a centre of cloth production as early as the 1770's. Even as a marketing and finishing centre its position was being undermined by the 1820's. The factory manufacturers marketed their own output, merchant communities and finishing establishments appeared in Bradford, Huddersfield and even the lesser centres after 1815. This relative decline in Leeds' key position in the Yorkshire woollen and worsted industries should partly be explained by the long-established merchant houses' refusal to embrace wholeheartedly the factory system.

But the effects of the merchants' defection was lessened by their entrepreneurial shortcomings. From the evidence of their increasingly conservative outlook about the prospects of the industry, expressed by merchants like William Cookson and Jeremiah Naylor before the major enquiries of 1806 and 1821, and given the outlook of a whole generation of young men like John Dixon and John Denison between 1785 and 1815, they were ill-equipped to lead the industry through its transition from a domestic- to a factory-based system of production. Their abdication gave the new manufacturers, men like Benjamin Gott and Abraham Rhodes in Leeds,[27] and a whole range of clothiers and dealers (in every woollen centre across to the Lancashire border) who by hard work and vision reaped the early entrepreneurial profits of power-driven machinery, the leadership of the woollen industry.

One should not completely dismiss the merchants in this fashion. Those who went into landownership brought a fresh approach to its problems. Adam Smith reckoned the merchants who became land-owning proprietors 'were the best of all improvers'. In William Denison's example, vast financial resources and a keen eye on the accounts were linked with a considerable knowledge of the latest agricultural developments to effect major improvements on his country estates. Few landowners could afford to renovate their farmsteads, lime, hedge and ditch on his scale. Thus where the merchants were engaged in active improvement, as possibly the majority were, the transference of capital was not unproductive. The only large-scale alternative considered by the merchants before the 1820's in their investment schemes was government securities. And it is feasible to argue that the expansion of productive capacity was more rapidly achieved by expenditure in land than in 3% consols. Moreover the merchants' transference to the ranks of the landowners had wider social implications. The significance of change went deeper than the fact that they became country gentlemen and gave their children such fine educations that they became more genteel than the gentry themselves. John Denison sent his nine sons to Eton, and besides the eldest, Lord Ossington who was Speaker of the House of Commons from 1857 to 1872, they included a Governor-General of Australia, a Bishop of Salisbury, a judge, a colonel and an archdeacon. Thomas Lee's son John became Attorney-General in Lord Rockingham's second administration; Robert Milnes of Wakefield refused the Chancellorship of the Exchequer in 1809 at the age of 25.[28] Here in microcosm was a process essential for continuity and stability in English society. On the one hand the traditional landed society easily assimilated these wealthy merchant families, while on the other the contribution of the new element was critical in the revitalisation of England's upper classes during the readjustments of the eighteenth and nineteenth centuries.

Notes to Chapter 10

[1] E. Hughes, *op. cit.*, I, p. 71.

[2] M. W. Flinn, *The Origins of the Industrial Revolution* (1966), pp. 44–5.

[3] *Diary*, I, pp. 429–30. See also J. Mawman, *op. cit.*, p. 33, and 'Letters addressed to Ralph Thoresby, F.R.S.', *Thors. Soc.*, XXI (1912), *passim*.

[4] The four following paragraphs are largely based on unsorted deeds and letters amongst the Milner papers, DB/65 and *Diary*, II, 12–42.

[5] *Return of Owners of Land*, 1875 (C-1097).

[6] Leeds and Potterton Hall (West Riding); Beswick (East Riding); Rimswell and Coatham (North Riding); Grindon and Chilton (Co. Durham); Ossington and Sutton-on-Trent (Notts.); Kelstern and Calsthorpe (Lincs.). It is impossible to date the exact chronology of Denison's purchases from his surviving papers. Kelstern was bought in 1758–9, Ossington and Sutton in 1768 for £34,000, Beswick for £55,000 in the same year (Glentworth in Lincolnshire was considered at £58,000 but turned down). In 1879 W. Denison owned 6,309 acres in Nottinghamshire and Lincolnshire only (J. Bateman, *The Great Landowners of Great Britain and Ireland* [1879 edition]).

[7] De/H45, W. Denison to Sir Fletcher Norton, 6 Feb. 1779.

[8] *ibid.*, same to J. Wilkinson, 13 Feb. 1779.

[9] *ibid.*, same to R. Bignell, 20 May 1780 and De/H47 'Report and Statements of the Transactions of ye executors of ye will of ye Deceased Robert Denison Esquire' (1789).

[10] De/H45 letters to J. Butler, 20 Nov. 1778; S. Field, 5 June 1780; G. Prescott, M.P., 17 Jan., 13 March 1780, 18 Jan. 1781; J. Robinson, M.P., 24 Feb. 1781. See also T. S. Ashton, *Economic Fluctuations*, p. 187.

[11] De/H45, R. Denison to W. Cartwright, 12 Jan. 1779.

[12] *L.I.* 16 April 1782; *L.M.* 30 April 1782.

[13] The papers relating to Robert Denison's Leeds affairs are in DB/129/4.

[14] *L.I.* 19 Oct. 1795; *L.M.* 5 March 1796, 4 March 1797.

[15] *supra*, p. 207.

[16] T. Langdale, *A Topographical Dictionary of Yorkshire* (1809 edition); *Contemporary Biographies: West Riding of Yorkshire* (1902), p. 31.

[17] H. J. Habakkuk, 'The land market in the eighteenth century' in J. S. Bromley and E. H. Kossmann (eds.), *Britain and the Netherlands* (1960), pp. 154–173; also his 'English landownership: 1680–1740', *Ec.H.R.* (1940), 1–17; G. E. Mingay, *English Landed Society in the Eighteenth Century* (1963), pp. 47, 73.

[18] W. Bowden, *Industrial Society in England Towards the End of the Eighteenth Century* (1925), Chapter 3.

[19] E. Hughes, *op. cit.*, II, pp. 67–8, 117.

[20] *Supra*, pp. 212–14; 'West Riding Justices of the Peace Qualification Book' (1745–1819) at the County Record Office Wakefield.

[21] William Cookson's 'Commonplace Book'; *Thors. Soc.*, XXI, *op. cit.*, p. 153.

[22] See *L.M.* 15 April 1740; 5 Dec. 1780; *L.I.* 27 Sept. 1763; 18 Oct. 1790; 22 Dec. 1794; 2 Nov. 1807. The Spencer-Stanhope MSS. contains a fine set of cock-fighting records, and lists of those paying the annual Game Duty Certificates appeared in the newspapers (e.g. *L.I.* 20 Oct. 1794).

[23] *L.I.* 17 June 1777; *L.M.* 15 April 1740. See also E. Parsons, *op. cit.*, II, p. 135 and *The Leeds Guide* (1806), pp. 59–60.

[24] The paragraph of John Dixon is constructed from stray newspaper references and the Leeds directories, that on John Denison from the Denison MSS. and private family papers belonging to Lt.-Col. W. M. E. Denison.

[25] P. Mantoux, *op. cit.*, p. 62; C. Wilson, 'The entrepreneur in the Industrial Revolution in Britain', *Explorations in Entrepreneurial History*, vii (1955), 130.

[26] C. E. Camidge, *op. cit.*, p. 8; J. Wilkinson, *op. cit.*, p. 163.

[27] R. G. Wilson, 'A Leeds merchant house'.

[28] *Complete Peerage*, X, 188–9; *D.N.B.*, V (1908), 802–7; F. Boase, *Modern English Biography* (1965 impression), I, p. 858; V, pp. 72–3. See also for the Milnes, T. W. Reid, *op. cit.*, I, pp. 1–37, and J. Pope-Hennessey, *op. cit.*, pp. 1–10.

Appendix A

*The trade of Leeds (home and foreign) in manufs., January 1782**

	Foreign	Home
Rawstornes		5000
Mirfield & Son	500	500
Dixon & Lees	40000	
S. Oates, Sons & Co.	35000	
Asquiths		5000
Wolrich & Stanfield	35000	
Horner & Co.	18000	
Lister	5000	
W. & S. Smith		5000
Thompson	1000	17000
Thin & Co.		12000
Lloyds & Co.	35000	
Markland & Sons	20000	
Elam & Buck	4000	
Plowes		10000
Wormald & Co.	10000	30000
Strother & Story	20000	
Blayds	40000	
Sheepshanks & Co.		18000
Clayton & Strother	30000	
Rhodes's & Hebbte	15000	
Bischoff & Sons	45000	
Molyneux	8000	
A. Hall	500	4500
John Wood		4000
Jo. Wrigglesworth	3000	9000
Thos. Wigglesworth		1000
Greens & Ridsdale	20000	
Denison	50000	
Clapham & Hall	3000	12000
Micklethwait	3000	
Lee & Leathley	4000	6000
Cotton	2000	
Routh & Co.	10000	
Goodmans & Co.	3000	15000
C. & J. Brown	1000	5000
Eyre & Co.	6000	6000
Thursby & Co.	10000	
J. & E. Brooke	5000	
Peacopp	3000	
Sutton, Powell & Co.		6000
Jones & Bustard		20000
Green	5000	
Tolson & Son	8000	

---

* 'Extracts from an old Leeds Merchant's Memorandum Book: 1770–1786',
Thors. Soc., XXIV, Miscellanea (1919), p. 37.

	Foreign	Home
Wareing	2000	10000
Smithson	12000	
Jno. Greaves	3000	
J. T. Wade	8000	
T. Wilks & Co.		8000
Sam. Dixon		8000
Jas. Armitage & Co.	35000	
Johnsons	18000	
Cookson & Son	20000	
Bacon & Allen		8000
Bensons	1000	9000
G. Oates & Sons	20000	5000
R. & R. Bramley	20000	
Alexr Turner & Co.	18000	
Jno. Cookson		4000
Browne & Wilsons	1000	3000
Fisher	12000	
Hill	30000	
Wm. Blackburne	(?)	(?)
Smithies & Co.		2000
Jno. Clapham		4000
Geo. Hutton		3000
Pratt & Co.	5000	
Lupton	5000	
E. Elam	10000	
Eli Musgrave		4000
Rayner, Dawson & Co.	15000	10000
John Wright		4000
Harrison & Holly	5000	
Expd	738000	273000
		738000

Total £1,011,000

Appendix B

Biographical notes on principal merchants

Armitage, James (d. 1803). Youngest son of Joseph Armitage (d. 1750) a prosperous Hunslet clothier. Formed partnership with two elder brothers, and the firm prospered after 1760 in the Portuguese, and later, American markets. Succeeded to his brothers' property and bought the Farnley Hall estate in 1800 for £49,500 for his only son, Edward, and sufficient Aire and Calder Navigation shares in the 1790's to return an income of over £3,000 per annum from this source alone. Neither his son nor his grandsons were concerned in trade.

Berkenhout, John. A native of Holland who came to Leeds as a woollen merchant *c.* 1715. Naturalised by Act of Parliament 1722. Married daughter of James Kitchingman, mayor 1702. Elected to corporation 1741, but election annulled. His son John (1731–91) was a celebrated naturalist.

Bischoff, Bernard (1696–1764). Born at Basle, settled in Leeds *c.* 1715. Married Martha Unwin of Castle Headingham, Essex. Four sons all merchants in Leeds: of these the eldest, John James (1729–1806), who married the daughter of a London silk-mercer, had three sons, again merchants; the second, George (d. 1812) married twice into the Whitaker family (two members ministers at Call Lane Chapel). George's eldest son, Thomas, was a banker in Leeds, and his second son, James, who died in 1845, was the author of *The Comprehensive History of the Woollen and Worsted Manufactures.*

Blayds, James (d. 1715). Elected to Corporation 1710. His elder surviving son John (d. 1731) was Mayor in 1729. Younger son Francis (1699–1764) was elected to the Corporation in 1725, but resigned two years later. Francis had two sons: (1) *John Blayds* (1730–1807). Merchant and partner in Beckett's Bank. Mayor 1761, 1774 and 1794. Married daughter of John Brooke, merchant, mayor 1736, 1754. Moved to Oulton Hall in the 1780's and left his large estate when he died to John Calverley, a partner in Beckett's Bank, who assumed the name of Blayds the same year. Calverley was mayor, in 1785 and 1798, as had been his father, a Leeds grocer, in 1772. (2) *James Blayds* (1735–72). Elected to Corporation 1761. Married in 1770 the daughter of Peter Birt of Airmin, later Wenvoe Castle, Glamorgan, a wealthy colliery-owner and farmer of the Aire and Calder Navigation Tolls.

Breary, Thomas. Fourth son of Archdeacon William Breary, a member of one of York's chief seventeenth-century aldermanic families. Married daughter of Solomon Pollard, mayor in 1715. Elected to corporation 1717, mayor 1720. Left Leeds 1730 and died without issue. In partnership with Scudamore Lazenby, mayor in 1719, the son of Thomas Lazenby, mayor in 1700.

Brown, James (1758–1813). Made a fortune in the post-American War boom. Two sons: (1) *James Brown* (1786–1845) of Harehills Grove, D.L., J.P., merchant-manufacturer; married daughter of Matthew Rhodes (*q.v.*). Son, James (1814–77) succeeded to his large fortune and bought estate near Doncaster and Boroughbridge. Gave up manufacturing on becoming M.P. for Malton, 1857. High sheriff of Yorkshire, magistrate and D.L. (2) *William Williams Brown,* J.P. (1788–1855). Elected to Corporation 1835. Banker of repute in Leeds and London. His only son left Leeds on marrying daughter of Sir Joseph Radcliffe Bt. of Rudding Park; elder daughter married Thomas Benyon, D.L., J.P., of Gledhow Hall, Leeds, a prosperous linen-yarn manufacturer.

Browne, Wade, D.L., J.P. Grandson of John Wade a prominent merchant. Elec ted to corporation 1788, mayor 1791 and 1804. Left Leeds for Shropshire 1807. His only son Wade (1796–1851) married daughter of Edward Pennefather,

Lord Chief Justice of the Queen's Bench in Ireland, and purchased an estate in Wiltshire.

Busk, Jacob H. (1688–1755). Native of Gottenburg, Sweden. Settled in Leeds *c.* 1715 as a woollen merchant. Naturalised by Act of Parliament 1721. Married Rachel co-heiress of John Wadsworth of Horbury, merchant. Youngest son, Sir Wadsworth Busk, Kt., Attorney-General of the Isle of Man.

Busk, Hans (1718–92). Eldest son of the above. Married Martha, heiress of Richard Rodes Esq. of Long Houghton Hall and Bull House, Peniston. Two daughters each with reputed dowries of £100,000 married James and Richard Milnes, eminent Wakefield merchants. The former was M.P. for Bletchingley and the latter, who bought Fryston Hall, was M.P. for York. Busk left upwards of £150,000 when he died in 1792.

Cookson, William (1669–1743). Father settled in Leeds around 1650. Married daughter of Michael Idle, mayor 1690. Brother Joseph (1678–1745) vicar of Leeds, 1716. Imprisoned in Newgate in 1715 for a short period for supposed Jacobite sympathies. Three times mayor, 1712, 1725, 1738. Great benefactor to the church and poor. In partnership with younger brother, Samuel.

Cookson, Thomas (1707–73). Son of above. Elected corporation 1742, resigned 1744. Married daughter of William Dawson Esq., of Longcliffe Hall, Settle.

Cookson, William (1749–1811). Son of above Thomas. Mayor 1783, 1801. Married Mary, daughter of Henry Scott (mayor 1748). Friend of Wilberforce and prominent 'Church and King' advocate in the West Riding, and exemplary magistrate in both the county and Leeds. Death 'caused . . . by the sudden intelligence of the rascality of his partner or agent in America'. Son, Francis Thomas (1786–1859), incumbent of St. John's at age of 24.

Denison, Robert (d. 1766). Son of Thomas Denison, merchant. Elected to corporation 1717; mayor 1721, 1737. Two sons: (1) *William Denison* (1714–82).★ Leading partner in the largest export house in Leeds, 1740–82. Elected to corporation 1749, refused to serve the office of mayor no fewer than four times in the 1750's. In 1773 a partner in the London merchant house of Denison, Smith and Colebroke. Four years earlier had purchased estates at Ossington, Notts. and Kilnick in East Yorkshire. High sheriff of Nottinghamshire 1779. Died leaving estate of over £500,000 to his brother Robert. (2) *Robert Denison* (1720–85). Brother, partner and heir of above William. Elected to Corporation 1772. Denison's estates passed to John and Edward Wilkinson of Potterton Lodge, Wetherby, nephews and partners in the Leeds house. John assumed the name of Denison.

Dixon, Jeremiah (1670–1721). Son of Joshua Dixon of Heaton Royds, Bradford who settled in Leeds *c.* 1650. Married daughter of Alderman John Dodgson. Elected corporation 1696, resigned 1712.

Dixon, John (1695–1749). Third son of above. Married daughter of Thomas Gower Esq. of Hutton. Resigned corporation year after election in 1731.

Dixon, Joshua (1708–75). Cousin of the above John, and son of Joshua Dixon, merchant. Mayor 1765. Only son Jeremiah, D.L., J.P., vicar of Woolley, married Ann, sister of Benjamin Gott (*q.v.*).

Dixon, Jeremiah, F.R.S. (1726–82). Son of above John. Married daughter of Rev. Henry Wickham of Guiseley. Like father, resigned from corporation within a year. High sheriff of Yorkshire, 1758. Purchased estate at Gledhow 1764 and engaged John Carr to build a new house there. Prominent Rockinghamite, undertaker of Aire and Calder Navigation and deputy-receiver of the West Riding land-tax. In partnership with Thomas Lee (*q.v.*). Eldest son John (1753–1824),

---

★ R. V. Taylor, *Biographia Leodiensis*, (1865), pp. 180-1, states the above William Denison to be the son of a William Denison, merchant; but I have been unable to trace this connection.

Colonel of West Riding Militia, left Leeds; second son Jeremiah, mayor in 1785, married daughter of John Smeaton, F.R.S., the famous Leeds engineer who rebuilt the Eddystone Lighthouse. He was the last of the family engaged in merchanting.

Elam, Gervaise (1679–1771). A prominent Quaker clothier. Four sons, all of them eventually merchants in Leeds: (1) *John Elam* (d. 1789). Described as a tobacconist 1744. Through importing tobacco from America began to export cloth across the Atlantic. An early pioneer of the American cloth trade, where the Elam family made their fortune after 1760. Retired from business some years before his death. (2) *Emmanuel Elam* (d. 1796). Like his brother concerned in the American trade. Retired from trade with upwards of £100,000. In 1795 purchased a 5,500 acre estate near Malton with his brother Samuel, and Isaac Leatham, a fellow Quaker and model farmer. His will was fiercely contested for over 20 years after his death. (3) *Samuel Elam* (d. 1797). Described as 'grocer' in 1750, but became a merchant by 1770. In 1772 married daughter of William Greenwood of Hatfield. She had a reputed fortune of £5,000. Succeeded by his son Samuel (d. 1811) who joined his fellow Quaker merchant, William Thompson, to form a bank in Leeds around 1800. Purchased half the Roundhay estate in 1800, but continued to live in Leeds. In dire financial difficulties in 1810, died the following year. (4) *Joseph Elam.* Merchant, declared bankrupt 1769. This family, concerned in exporting cloth, ship-owning, land speculation and banking between 1780–1810, quickly fell from prominence after Samuel Elam's virtual bankruptcy in 1810.

Fenton. This was a large and important family in Leeds. *William Fenton* of Woodhouse Hill, Hunslet was a merchant and chief alderman in 1658. His grandson *William* (1685–1743) married daughter of Capt. Richard West of Underbank. This branch of the family established a line of country gentlemen, lawyers and clergymen. One descendant Lewis Fenton was M.P. for Huddersfield in the first Reformed Parliament. Another grandson *Thomas* (1647–1705) married the daughter of Sir Charles Houghton, Bt., and one of their sons *Samuel* (1723–94) was a merchant in Leeds. His son *Samuel* (1761–1804) followed in the same footsteps and his daughter Anne married M. T. Sadler, a merchant in Leeds, M.P. for Newark and an early leader of the factory reform movement. Another grandson of the original William, also *William*, was a merchant and mayor in 1733, and 1747. His daughter married Henry Scott, also a merchant and mayor in 1734 and 1748. Their son William Fenton Scott inherited the large estates of this branch of the family in 1790 and two years later he founded the Commercial Bank in Leeds. Yet another grandson of the first William, *James*, established a dynasty of merchants (later colliery-owners, glass-manufacturers and farmers of the Derwent Navigation Tolls) at Rothwell Haigh between Leeds and Wakefield. James had two sons, *Thomas* (b. 1731) and *William* (d. 1774). Thomas' elder unmarried son William (1764–1813) died reputedly worth £1,500,000; William's son *James* (1753–1823) married a daughter of Sir Henry Ibbetson. And of his daughters, one married Sir Richard Kaye, Bt., one Richard Lee (*q.v.*) and another John Cleaver, vicar of New Malton.

Fountaine, Joseph. Member of a wealthy Linton-in-Craven landed family. Served apprenticeship in Leeds and elected to corporation 1766; mayor 1777. Married twice, secondly to the eldest daughter of Alderman Henry Atkinson, whose wife was a Stanhope of Horsforth Hall. Partner with John Wormald in one of the largest houses in Leeds. They took Benjamin Gott as an apprentice in 1780. Fountaine died 1791, leaving one daughter.

Gott, Benjamin (1762–1840). Famous early factory owner. Son of John Gott, surveyor of the West Riding bridges and deputy-engineer on the Aire and Calder Navigation works. Educated Bingley Grammar School. Served five-year apprenticeship with Wormald and Fountaine, 1780–5. In the latter year he became a junior partner. Fountaine had no sons, and Wormald's were not of age. His acceptance into the firm was the turning point of his career. By 1792 his two senior partners were dead, and he began building the famous Bean Ing factory, the first full-scale factory in the Leeds woollen industry. Within ten years he had commenced operations in two other mills at Armley and Burley. He still, however, retained the merchanting side of the business, and continued to purchase cloth from the clothiers.

Elected to corporation 1791; mayor 1799. Refused to serve office a second time 1823. Purchased Armley House 1803 and engaged Sir Robert Smirke to build a new house there in 1820. Collector of pictures and books, close friend of Rennie and Watt. Founder member of Leeds Philosophical and Literary Society, and first president of the Leeds Mechanics Institute. Married Elizabeth, daughter of William Rhodes of Badsworth in 1790. His two surviving sons John and William continued the business without the drive of their father for 27 years after his death.

Hebblethwaite, John (1744–1840). Son of Robert Hebblethwaite, a Holbeck clothier. Married (1) Ann Keighley; (2) Sarah Rhodes, the sister of Hebblethwaite's partners. Made a fortune between 1783–1800; gave evidence before the committee of enquiry into the state of the woollen industry. Retired after 1815 to Hilary Place.

Hall, Henry, I (1683–1758). Son of Henry Hall (d. 1691) of Stumperlowe Hall, Sheffield. Settled in Leeds 1716 after selling the family home. Described as a 'cloth worker' when he entered the corporation in 1727. Mayor 1751.

Hall, Henry, II (1743–1805). Son of above: 'a severe, stern and self-willed man'. Married Elizabeth Broadbent, daughter of the manager of Austhorpe Colliery and a relation of John Smeaton, the engineer. Elected to corporation in 1790; mayor 1796. A stuff merchant in partnership with Charles and William Clapham.

Hall, Henry, III (1773–1859). Son of Henry Hall II. Educated Hipperholme School, Halifax, and in Holland. Election to corporation 1805; mayor, 1812, 1825. Retired early from merchanting to devote himself to local politics and charitable works. A strenuous Evangelical Tory. When he died he was described as 'the representative of the oldest Leeds family then resident in the town'. His son Robert (1801–57) was educated at Leeds Grammar School and Christ Church, Oxford. Married daughter of Thomas Tennant, merchant and three times mayor of Leeds. Barrister and recorder of Doncaster after 1845. Energetic supporter of factory reform. M.P. for Leeds for two months before his death.

Ibbetson, James (1674–1739). Son of Samuel Ibbetson (1650–97), merchant. Dissenter, although elected to corporation 1715. He played no active part in its affairs, however. Married daughter of John Nicholson, a York surgeon. Bought Denton Hall, Otley, a seat of the Fairfaxes, in 1717 which was settled on his eldest son Samuel, who had a legal training and took no part in the woollen trade.

Ibbetson, Sir Henry (d. 1761). Younger son of above. Like his father one of the most prominent merchants in the town. Married (1) daughter of F. Foljambe, Esq. of Aldwarke; (2) Isabella, daughter of Ralph Carr Esq. of Cocken, Co. Durham. Offered to raise 100 men for the defence of York, 1745, and on strength of his patriotism was canvassed as M.P. for York in 1747 but he stood down at the last minute. Created baronet 1748. Elected to corporation 1753, and mayor in same year—a record promotion. Played prominent part in West Riding economic affairs. In 1758 obtained a half share of the lease of the Aire and Calder Navigation, with Peter Birt with whom he was concerned in coal-mining ventures. His son James, although elected to the corporation in 1770, spent all his time at Denton, which he inherited from his uncle.

Kirshaw, Samuel (d. 1727). Son of the rector of Ripley. Elected to corporation 1711. Like his brother Richard, also rector of Ripley, he married a daughter of Samuel Sykes, mayor 1684. Thoresby noted in 1700 he had the first negro servant in the district. His children died young. His nephew and namesake was vicar of Leeds (and rector of Ripley) 1751–86.

Kitchingman, Thomas (d. 1713). Probably a second generation settler in Leeds. Mayor 1688 and 1705. By his death one of the largest merchants in town, as well as being a colliery proprietor and owner of the manor of Beeston. Economic activities so wide that he does not fit easily into the usual woollen merchants' category. Married daughter of Thomas Driffield, a York merchant. His son Thomas elected to corporation 1713 and immediately advanced to alderman—an indication of the family's power in the town at this period. He died shortly afterwards, or left Leeds.

Kitchingman, James. Brother of above. Mayor 1702. Married daughter of John Fenton of Woodhouse Hill. Son, *James*, mayor 1722, but nothing more is known of him after this date. Some of the family moved back to Carlton Husthwaite in north Yorkshire, their ancestral home; but this merchant dynasty, perhaps the most important in the town in the first decade of the eighteenth century disappeared from the town virtually without trace, in the male line, by 1730.

Lawson, Godfrey (1629–1709). Second son of Edward Lawson Esq. of Brunton, Northumberland, a family of 'ancient descent'. Mayor of Leeds, 1669. Married Elizabeth, daughter and co-heiress of Joseph Watkinson Esq. of Ilkley. Son and daughter married into the Trotter family of Skelton Castle, Cleveland.

Lee, Thomas (1692–1736). A newcomer to Leeds, the son of a Sheffield barber who married the daughter of a Woodehouse clothier, yet died very rich.

Lee, Thomas (1718–73). Son of the above and like his father a Unitarian. Married the daughter of a merchant, Anthony Markham. Eminent merchant in partnership with Jeremiah Dixon (*q.v.*). Deputy and eventual receiver of the East Riding land-taxes, and a staunch political supporter of Lord Rockingham. His brother *John* (1733–93) was a barrister-at-law and M.P. for Higham Ferrars, Attorney-General, 1783, in Lord Rockingham's second ministry. Thomas had two sons: (1) *Thomas Lee* (b. 1744). Married Ann Foster of Greenwich who had a fortune of £10,000. His father settled on him an estate at Barnsley, but he was virtually disinherited in his will. (2) *Richard Lee* (b. 1750). Married younger daughter of William Fenton Esq. of the Glasshouse, Rothwell. Carried on business in Leeds in partnership with the Dixons, but his two sons gave it up around 1800. The elder, *William*, married daughter of Sir Thomas Wentworth Blackett and lived at Grove Hall, Pontefract.

Lloyd, Gamaliel (d. 1817). Son of George Lloyd, F.R.S., a Manchester merchant, later of Barrowby Hall, Leeds. Married daughter of James Attwood Esq. of Bristol. Entered Leeds woollen trade *c.* 1765. Elected to corporation 1771, mayor 1778. Left Leeds 1789, died in London. Minor politician of some interest.

Lloyd, Thomas (1751–1828). Brother and partner of the above. Married daughter of Walter Wade Esq. of New Grange, Leeds. Elected to corporation 1778, resigned 1786. Gave up merchanting to become Colonel of the Leeds Volunteer Infantry in 1794. Rented Horsforth Hall and later moved to York. His son George bought Cowesby Hall, Northallerton.

Lodge, Thomas (d. 1710). Third-generation merchant. His father built Red Hall, Leeds. Elected to corporation 1696, resigned 1706.

Lodge, Richard (d. 1749). Had two sons: (1) *Thomas Lodge* (1718–76). Elected corporation 1746, resigned 1749. Married Elizabeth, daughter of Richard Wilson, recorder of Leeds. Founder partner of Beckett's Bank. Daughter, Mary, married (1778) Sir Richard Sullivan, a director of the East India Company. (2) *Edmund Lodge* (1721–99). Mayor 1759, 1771. Married (1) Ann, daughter of Richard Micklethwaite, merchant; (2) Grace, daughter of Thomas Sawer, merchant and mayor, 1726, 1740. Ceased to reside in Leeds 1776 and moved to Willow Hall, Halifax, where he combined the business of a merchant and cotton manufacturer.

Lupton, William (1700–71), chief cloth-dresser to Sir Henry Ibbetson and executor of John Koster's partnership with Ibbetson in 1760. Three sons educated at grammar school: *Francis* (1731–70), merchant in Portugal; *William* (1732–82), perpetual curate of Headingley and vicar of Blagdon; Arthur (1748–1807), merchant in Leeds, married daughter of a Mabgate clothier. His eldest son William (1777–1828) married Anne Darnton, daughter of a wealthy Leeds wholesale tobacconist. Of his 11 children, eldest son, *Darnton* (1806–73), continued firm in

Leeds and was mayor and prominent citizen for many years. Two other sons J.P.s in Leeds.

Markland, John (b. 1740). Son of John Markland of Manchester. Mayor 1786, succeeded to his grandmother's estate in Lancashire in following year.

Markland, Edward (1750–1832). Brother and partner of above. Mayor 1789 and 1807. Shortly afterwards left Leeds to become a resident magistrate in Westminster. Two sons: (1) *Ralph* (1789–1860). Merchant, mayor 1828. Married daughter of Thomas Wright, proprietor of the *Leeds Intelligencer*. (2) *John* (1780–1848), Rear-Admiral.

Medhurst, William (1688–1745). Son of John Medhurst who died at Bremem, and grandson of a physician. Settled in Leeds around 1710. Described as 'cloth worker' in 1719, 'merchant' in 1721. Elected to corporation 1719, but election rescinded, and not elected again until 1731. Married daughter of Thomas Armistead, a Leeds apothecary. Bought estate at Kippax and left Leeds to reside there in 1740. His was one of three names put forward for the office of high sheriff in 1743. Two surviving sons: (1) *Thomas Medhurst*, D.L., J.P. Elected to the corporation 1753. Mayor 1760, 1773. Married in 1757 Elizabeth, daughter of Rev. Granville and Lady Catherine Wheler of Otterden Place, Kent. Improved Kippax estate, but bankrupt in 1780. Son, William, murdered his wife in 1800. Their issue succeeded to the Kippax, Otterden and Ledstone Hall estates. (2) *John Medhurst*. Junior partner who carried on the business in Leeds. Elected to corporation 1764.

Milner, William (1662–1740). Son of William Milner (1630–91) merchant, and grandson of Richard Milner, mayor 1652. Married daughter of Joshua Ibbetson, merchant and mayor 1685, whose wife was daughter of Christopher Breary, lord mayor of York 1666. Mayor 1697, and by this time largest merchant in Leeds and principal promoter of the Aire and Calder Navigation scheme. Purchased Lord Fairfax's historic seat Nun Appleton in 1708. West Riding D.L. and J.P. His only son created a baronet in 1717, soon after his marriage with Elizabeth, daughter of Sir William Dawes, Archbishop of York. Milner carried on his business until his death with the aid of William Read, his clerk and—after his master's death—a merchant on his own account. The Milner firm was carried on for a short time by Francis Milner, a son of one of Milner's two elder brothers, who had been merchants in Holland.

Oates, Joseph (1675–1729). Second son of Josias Oates Gent. of Chickenley, near Dewsbury. Four sons all prominent merchants and Unitarians in Leeds: (1) *Thomas Oates* (1710–50) died without issue. (2) *George Oates* (1717–79) acquired Low Hall and Carr House, Leeds. He had three sons, again all merchants: (a) *Joseph* (1743–1819), married Elizabeth, daughter of Joshua Rayner (*q.v.*). He bought Weetwood Hall and his issue continued merchanting in Leeds. (b) *George* (1748–97) married Mary, daughter of Robert Hibbert, a Manchester merchant. Her brother was an M.P. and chairman of the West India Dock Company. Thus George Oates' three sons all concerned in West Indies trade. (c) *Frederick* (1750–1803) married third daughter of William Read, merchant. Son Frederick William continued merchanting. (3) *Josiah Oates* of Chapel Allerton (1722–82) died without issue. (4) *Samuel Oates* (d. 1789) married Mary, daughter of Samuel Hamer, of Hamer Hall, Rochdale, by daughter of James Ibbetson (*q.v.*). Four sons: *Samuel Hamer* (1752–1811) D.L., J.P., who married Sarah, daughter of William Coape Esq. of Arnold, Notts., and sister to General Sir John Coape-Sherbroke; and three others. Various members of Oates family prominent in Leeds until mid-nineteenth century when they bought estates in Essex and Suffolk.

Preston, William (d. 1772). Son of John Preston, merchant and mayor 1691, and Martha, daughter of Sir Benjamin Ayloff. Elected corporation 1719, resigned 1730. Married twice: issue by first wife settled at Flasby Hall, York; by second wife at Moreby Hall, York. Youngest son, vicar of Scalby, married daughter of Dr. Prescot, Master of St. Catherine's College, Cambridge.

Preston, Croft. Brother of above William. Elected to corporation 1714, mayor 1714. Married Frances, daughter of Benjamin Wade Esq. of New Grange, Leeds. His son Wade Preston a merchant died unmarried.

Rayner, Joshua (1703–57). Son of Thomas Rayner, Gent., of Ledsham. Unitarian. Claimed to be largest stuff-merchant in England when he died in 1757. In partnership with Obadiah Dawson. Son, *Milnes Rayner* (1753–92) a merchant in Leeds died unmarried. Estate passed to his two sisters, Elizabeth who had married Joseph Oates of Weetwood Hall, and Sarah who married William Smithson (*q.v.*).

Rhodes, William (d. 1772). A large dyer in Leeds. Four surviving sons all merchants: (1) *Timothy Rhodes* (d. 1790). Together with his brother, Mathew, gave up the family dyeing business in 1780 to form a cloth-exporting firm with John Hebblethwaite. His will—he made bequests of £10,060—disclosed the business had prospered. (2) *Mathew Rhodes* (d. 1796). Formed a new partnership with Martin Hind in 1793. Left £40,000. His son John William (d. 1861) was later of Hennerton House, Berkshire. He died very wealthy, leaving property in Yorkshire, Berkshire and Ireland to his family. (3) *Abraham Rhodes*. First mentioned in Italy in 1788 travelling for his brothers' firm. Later in partnership with Hebblethwaite, and by 1810 had formed a new partnership with his nephew Henry Glover and his brother William Rhodes. Engaged in the European and American trade, and after 1810 commenced manufacturing on a large scale at Woodhouse Carr. By 1815 he considered his firm was one of the largest in the town. In the 1820's living at Roundhay and Wold Newton Hall, Yorkshire. (4) *William Rhodes* (d. 1811). Died in America, where he was representing the firm in New York.

Rooke, Sir William (d. 1743). Son of William Rooke, merchant and mayor 1683, and, through his mother, grandson of William Busfeild, one of the most prominent seventeenth-century Leeds merchants. Mayor 1713, although refused the office in 1705 and was fined £100. One of the principal promoters of the Aire and Calder Navigation. Knighted 1727, but shortly afterwards insane. His estate passed to Wingate Pulleine Esq. of Carlton, his relative and guardian and one-time governor of Bermuda. Pulleine's grand-daughter and heiress married Walter Spencer-Stanhope (*q.v.*).

Scott, Henry. Descendant of John Harrison and Rev. Henry Robinson, two famous Leeds benefactors, and son of John Scott, Gent., of Wakefield. Elected to corporation 1731; mayor 1734, 1748. His elder brother was perpetual curate of Holy Trinity Church, Leeds, vicar of Bardsey and domestic chaplain to George III's father. By second wife, Alice Fenton, had numerous children: his daughter Mary married William Cookson (*q.v.*), and his eldest son *William Fenton Scott* was senior partner in the Leeds Commercial Bank that failed in 1812. He married in 1779 the sister of Sir John Lister Kaye, Bt., and lived at Woodhall, Wetherby.

Sheepshanks, Richard (1711–79), a well-to-do yeoman of Linton-in-Craven, had seven sons, three clergymen and four merchants: (1) *Whittel Sheepshanks*, assumed name of *York* (1743–1817). Served apprenticeship in Leeds and became a prosperous merchant. Elected to corporation 1788, mayor 1795, 1815. Married widow of William Peart of Grassington. Only son Richard (D.L., Colonel of the West Riding Yeomanry and high sheriff, 1832) married Lady Mary Lascelles, youngest daughter of the first Earl of Harewood. (2) *Richard Sheepshanks* (1747–97). Merchant in Leeds and Philadelphia, where he died. Son, William (b. 1774), merchant and manufacturer, like father trading both at home and in America. (3) *Joseph Sheepshanks* (b. 1755). Merchant, married Anne, daughter of Richard Wilson of Kendal. Commenced manufacturing, and his four sons all derived large incomes from the family mill. *John Sheepshanks* (1787–1863), at one time engaged in the cloth business became a great art and book collector; his brother, *Richard Sheepshanks*, F.R.S. (1794–1855), was a Fellow of Trinity College, Cambridge. (4) *James Sheepshanks* died in 1789 unmarried. Of the three brothers in the Church: William, the eldest, was a Prebendary of Carlisle, rector of Ovington in Norfolk

R

and perpetual curate of St. John's, Leeds. John, the youngest, was vicar of Wymes-wolde, Leicestershire, and perpetual curate of Holy Trinity, Leeds.

Smithson, William (1750–1830). Son of Robert Smithson (1701–63) a Leeds merchant. Married daughter of Joshua Rayner (*q.v.*) and partner with her brother Milnes Rayner. Leading merchant and mayor 1781. Succeeded Thomas Lloyd (*q.v.*) as Colonel of Leeds Volunteers. Gave up merchanting and resided at Heath Hall, Wakefield. Only child married Thomas Burough, barrister-at-law of Chetwynd Park, Salop.

Stanhope, Walter (*c.* 1704–58). Second son of John Stanhope Esq. of Horsforth Hall and Mary, daughter of Sir William Lowther Bt. Apprenticed with William and Croft Preston (*q.v.*) 1721. Elected to corporation 1730, resigned 1737. Married (1) Mary, daughter of Patience Warde Esq. of Hooton Pagnell Hall, Doncaster; (2) Ann, daughter of John Spencer Esq. of Cannon Hall, Barnsley. Only surviving child *Walter* succeeded to the Cannon Hall and Horsforth estates and assumed the additional name of Spencer. M.P. for Hull and later Carlisle Income of £10,000 per annum in 1800.

Wilson, William (1718–64). Son of Richard Wilson, recorder of Leeds 1729–61. Apprenticed in London, where his elder brother Thomas was a merchant. Married Ann, daughter of Henry Pawson of Leeds. Mayor 1762. Bought Gled-how Hall, Leeds. Only child married Col. Norcliffe Dalton of Langton Hall, Malton.

Wolrich, Thomas. Descendant of an old landed family. Apprenticed with Richard Wilson, the recorder of Leeds, about 1735. Gave up the law to form a partnership with a fellow Unitarian, George Oates, in the 1740's. Their merchant-ing and dyeing business prospered, and Wolrich's brother, Hatton, joined the firm. Bought Armley House in 1772. His only child, Sarah, married *David Stansfeld* (d. 1822), a member of a well-known Halifax family. Of their numerous issue *Thomas Wolrich Stansfeld*, the eldest son, succeeded his father and grand-father in the family firm. It was declared bankrupt in the 1825–6 depression.

Wormald, John (d. 1786). Apprenticed in Leeds. Elected to corporation 1761, mayor 1776. Married (1) Rebecca, daughter of R. Thompson Esq. of Staincliffe Hall, Batley; she had a reputed fortune of £4,000. The couple moved into Walter Stanhope's old house; (2) Sarah, daughter of late Alderman Atkinson in 1766, the sister-in-law of his partner Joseph Fountaine (*q.v.*). They had three sons: (1) *Harry Wormald* (d. 1816). Lived at Denison Hall, Leeds. Elected to corporation 1793. Refused to serve the office of alderman in 1803, fined £500. Provided much of the capital for Bean Ing factory, and in fact remained in partnership with Gott until 1816, when on Harry's death, the Wormald family withdrew their capital from the firm. (2) *John Wormald* (d. 1809). Partner in Wormald and Gotts. Elected to corporation 1803. (3) *Richard Wormald* (d. 1823). Joined the firm 1795. He con-ducted the cloth-buying activities of the firm. Moved to Cookridge Hall. Married in 1823 Elizabeth, daughter of Benjamin Gott. He died the same year and there was much gossip in the town. She lived another 40 years and the Wormalds had to pay her annuity of £2,000. Cookridge passed to a son of Harry Wormald.

Bibliography

(I) *Manuscript sources:*

Brotherton Library, Leeds

Gott MSS.
Jowitt Business Records.
Lupton MSS.
White Cloth Hall Papers.

Leeds Central Library, Archives Department

Apprentice Register of the Leeds Workhouse Committee, 1726–1809.
Business Records of Grace and Jepson, 1815–61.
Clark MSS. (Rev. Henry Crooke's diary).
Dartmouth Estate Records.
Ledston Documents (Medhurst).
Leeds Corporation Court Books, 1662–1835.
Leeds Quarter Sessions, Order and Indictment Book, 1698–1809.
Minute and Order Book of the Vestry Workhouse Committee of Leeds
    Township, 1726–1824.
Newby Hall MSS.
Oates MSS.
Poor Rate Assessment Books for the Township of Leeds, 1713–1805.
Ramsden MSS.
Temple Newsam MSS.

The following collections have been temporarily deposited by a firm of Leeds
solicitors in the archives department. I was allowed to consult other papers in
their own keeping.

Coloured Cloth Hall Papers, DB/24
Bland Estate Papers, DB/29
Denison Papers, DB/36, 129
Armitage-Rhodes MSS, DB/39
Hebblethwaite Deeds, DB/43
Milner MSS, DB/65
Fearne Bolland Papers, DB/68–9
William Hey's Accounts and Papers, DB/75
Calverley of Oulton Hall, Estate Deeds, DB/179
Minute Books of the Pious Uses Committee 1664–1844, DB/196–7
Thomas Wilson's Commonplace Book, DB/204
Trinity Church Repair Charity, DB/211

Leeds Reference Library

A compilation of facts illustrative of Methodism in Leeds, 1735–1835, by John
    Wray.
Dugdale, Sir William, Visitation of Yorkshire, 1664, with continuations and
    additions by William Radclyffe up to 1827.
Return of Canvass, Yorkshire Election of H. Duncombe and W. Wilberforce,
    Esqs., 1784.
Rusby, J. (compiler), Pedigrees and Arms of Leeds Families, 1892.

Thoresby Society, Leeds

Commonplace Book of William Cookson, *c.* 1700–43.

Yorkshire Archaeological Society, Leeds
Correspondence of Ralph Thoresby, F.R.S.
Papers of the Armitage Family of Hunslet and Farnley Hall.

Mill Hill Chapel, Leeds
Minute Book, 1771–1858.

Leeds Parish Church
Vestry Minute Books, 1716–1844.

The Cartwright Memorial Hall, Bradford
Cunliffe-Lister MSS.
Spencer-Stanhope (Horsforth Hall) MSS.

Sheffield Public Libraries, Archives Department
Bacon Frank Papers.
Crewe MSS.
Spencer-Stanhope (Cannon Hall) MSS.
Wentworth Woodhouse MSS.

Harewood House, Leeds
Political Papers of the Second Earl of Harewood.

The County Record Office, Wakefield
Land Tax Returns: Skyrac Division, 1753–1830.
Return of Cotton and Other Mills, 1803–4.
Return of Justices and Deputy-Lieutenants in the West Riding, 1757–1820.
Turnpike Records:
  Leeds–Otley Turnpike Securities Ledger, 1780–1853.
  Leeds–Selby Turnpike Securities Ledger, 1751–1872.
  Leeds–Tadcaster Turnpike Securities Ledger, 1751–1841.
  Leeds–Wakefield Turnpike: Minute Book, 1758–79; Mortgage Ledger, 1760–1854; Securities ledger, 1780–1853.

West Riding of Yorkshire Deeds Registry, Wakefield
Abstract of Deeds, 1705–50.
Land Indenture Memorials, 1704–65.

British Transport Commission Archives, York
Aire and Calder Navigation Papers, 1699–1830.
Barnsley Canal Papers, 1792–1830.
Calder-Hebble Navigation Papers, 1757–1830.

Borthwick Institute, York
Leeds wills, 1700–1830.

Department of Manuscripts, University of Nottingham
Denison MSS.

John Ryland's Library, Manchester
Papers relating to the Micklethwaite family of Leeds and Ardsley Hall, Barnsley.

British Museum, London
Additional Manuscripts.

Public Record Office, London
Apprenticeship Registers, 1711–65.

Official Publications
Historical Manuscripts Commission: *Dartmouth MSS.*; *Portland MSS.*; *Verulam MSS.*; *Sackville MSS.*
House of Commons Journals.
House of Lords Journals.

(II) *British parliamentary papers:*
1752. Report from the Committee upon the Petitions relating to the false winding of wool, and the marking of sheep with Pitch and Tar.
1788. Report from the Committee on the Laws relating to the Exportation of Live Sheep and Lambs, Wool, Wool Fells etc.
1802–3 V. Report from the Committee on the Woollen Clothiers Petitions.
1802–3, V and 1803–4, V. Reports from the Select Committee on the Petitions of Manufacturers of Woollen Cloth in the County of York.
1802–3, VII. Minutes taken before the Committee . . . [on] the Laws Relating to the Woollen Trade.
1806, III. Reports from the Select Committee . . . [on] the State of the Woollen Manufacture in England.
1808, X. Minutes of Evidence . . . respecting the Orders in Council.
1816, VI. First and Second Reports from the Select Committee on Seeds and Wool.
1820, XII. Accounts and Papers.
1821, XVII. Accounts and Papers.
1821, VI. Reports from the Select Committee on the Laws Relating to the Stamping of Woollen Cloth.
1828, VIII. Report of the House of Lords Committee on the British Wool Trade, 1828.
1833, VI. Report from the Select Committee on Manufactures, Commerce and Shipping.
1833, XX. Factories Inquiry Commission, First Report.
1834, XIX, XX. Factories Inquiry Commission, Supplementary Report, Parts 2 and 3.
1835, XXV. Reports from the Commissioners. Municipal Corporations (England and Wales) appendix, part III.
1836, XLV. A Return of the number of Persons Employed in . . . Factories in the United Kingdom.
1845, XVIII. Second Report of Commissioners of Inquiry into the State of Large Towns and Populous Districts.

(III) *Newspapers and periodicals:*
The Leeds Intelligencer
The Leeds Mercury

(IV) *Directories and maps:*
1781. Bailey, W. *Northern Directory* (Warrington).
1784. Bailey, W. *The British Directory for 1784.*
1790. *Universal British Directory* (second edition).
1797. Ryley, J. *The Leeds Directory.*
1800. Binns and Brown, *A Directory for the Town of Leeds.*
1807. Wilson, G. *A New and Complete Directory for . . . Leeds.*
1809, 1814, 1817. Baines, E *Directory of . . . Leeds.*

1822. Baines, E. *Directory for the County of York.*
1826. Parson, W. *General and Commercial Directory . . . of Leeds.*
1830. Parson, W. and White, W. *Directory of . . . Leeds and the Clothing District.*
1830. Pigot and Co. *Directory of Yorkshire.*
1837. White, W. *History, Gazetteer and Directory of the West Riding.*
1851. Slade, W. and Roebuck, D. I. *Directory of the Borough and Neighbourhood of Leeds.*
1881. Kelly's Directories, Ltd. *Directory of Leeds.*
1725. Cossins, J. *A New and Exact Plan of Leeds.*
1770. Jefferys, T. *A Plan of Leeds.*
1797, 1810, 1817. [Wright, T.] *A Map of Near 10 miles Round Leeds.*
1806. Heaton, J. *Plan of the Town of Leeds with its Modern Improvements.*
1815. Giles, N. and F. *Plan of the Town of Leeds and its Environs.*
1821. Fowler, C. *Plan of the Town of Leeds with its Recent Improvements.*
1831. Fowler, C. *Plan of the Town of Leeds and its Environs.*

(V) *Unpublished theses:*

Edwards, J. K. 'The Economic Development of Norwich 1750–1850 with Special Reference to the Worsted Industry', Ph.D. thesis, Leeds (1963).
Elliott, C. M. 'The Economic and Social History of the Principal Protestant Denominations in Leeds', D.Phil. thesis, Oxford (1962).
Gary, A. T. 'The Political and Economic Relations of English and American Quakers (1750–1785)', D.Phil. thesis, Oxford (1935).
Glover, F. J. 'Dewsbury Mills: A History of Messrs. Wormalds and Walker Ltd., Blanket Manufacturers of Dewsbury', Ph.D. thesis, Leeds (1959).
Hartwell, R. M. 'The Yorkshire Woollen and Worsted Industries, *1800–1850*', D.Phil. thesis, Oxford (1956).
Jackson, G. 'The Economic Development of Hull in the Eighteenth Century', Ph.D. thesis, Hull (1960).

(VI) *Books, pamphlets and articles published before 1900:*
(Unless otherwise stated, London is the place of publication.)
Aikin, J. *A Description of the Country From 30–40 Miles Around Manchester* (1795)— *England Delineated, or a Geographical Description of Every County in England and Wales* (1788)—*England Described, Being a Consise Delineation of Every County in England and Wales* (1818).
Allen, T. *A New and Complete History of the County of York* (1828), three volumes.
An Account of the Proceedings of the Merchants, Manufacturers and Others Concerned in the Wool and Woollen Trade . . . in their Application to Parliament (1800).
An Alphabetical List of The Proprietors of the Leeds and Liverpool Canal (Bradford, 1789).
Anon. *Old Leeds, its Bygones and Celebrities* (Leeds, 1868).
Atkinson, D. H. *Ralph Thoresby the Topographer: His Town and Times* (Leeds, 1885), two volumes.
Atkinson, Rev. M. *The Duty of a Minister* (Leeds, 1784)—*Practical Sermons* (1812), two volumes.
Babbage, C. *On the Economy of Machinery and Manufactures* (1832).
Bailey, W. *Lists of Bankrupts, Dividends and Certificates from the Years 1771–1793* (1794).
Baines, E. *Yorkshire Contested Election* (Leeds, 1807).
Baines, E., jun. 'On the woollen manufacture of England; with special reference to the Leeds clothing district', *Journal of the Statistical Society of London,* xxiv (1859)—*The Life of Edward Baines* (1859)—*The Social, Educational and Religious State of the Manufacturing Districts; in Two Letters to Sir Robert Peel* (1843).

Baines, T. *Yorkshire, Past and Present* (1875), four volumes.

Baker, R. 'On the industrial and sanitary economy of the borough of Leeds in 1858', *Journal of the Royal Statistical Society*, xxi (1858).

Banks, W. S. *Wakefield and its Neighbourhood* (1871).

Batty, J. *The History of Rothwell* (Leeds, 1877).

Bigland, J. *A Topographical and Historical Description of the County of York* (1812).

Billam, F. J. *A Walk Through Leeds, or a Stranger's Guide* (Leeds, 1806).

Bischoff, J. *A Comprehensive History of the Woollen and Worsted Manufactures* (1842), two volumes.

Bourne, H. R. F. *English Merchants* (1886), two volumes.

Bray, W. *Sketch of a Tour into Derbyshire and Yorkshire* (1783).

Brown, R. *A General View of the Agriculture of the West Riding of Yorkshire* (Edinburgh, 1799).

Burnley, J. *The History of Wool and Woolcombing* (1889).

Camidge, C. E. *A History of Wakefield* (1866).

Clarkson, H. *Memories of Merrie Wakefield* (Wakefield, 1889).

Cooke, G. A. *Topographical and Statistical Description of the County of York* (c. 1810).

Crabtree, J. *A Concise History of the Parish and Vicarage of Halifax* (Halifax, 1836).

Cudworth, W. *Round About Bradford* (Bradford, 1876).

Dayes, E. *An Excursion Through the Principal Parts of Derbyshire and Yorkshire* (1805).

Defoe, D. *A Tour Thro' the Whole Island of Great Britain*, ed. G. D. H. Cole (1927).

Dikes, Rev. T. *A Sermon Preached on the Occasion of the Death of Rev. Miles Atkinson, A.B.* (Hull, 1811).

Dodd, G. *The Textile Manufacturers of Great Britain* (1851).

Eden, F. M. *The State of the Poor* (1797), three volumes.

Fawcett, J. *The Rise and Progress of the Town and Borough of Bradford* (Bradford, 1859).

Fortunes Made in Business: A Series of Original Sketches (1884–7), three volumes.

Gaskell, P. *The Manufacturing Population of England* (1833).

Haynes, J. *A View of the Present State of the Clothing Trade in England* (1706).

Head, G. *A Home Tour Through the Manufacturing Districts of England, in the Summer of 1835* (1836).

Hirst, W. *History of the Woollen Trade for the Last Sixty Years* (Leeds, 1844).

Hobkirk, C. E. P. *Huddersfield: Its History and Natural History* (1859).

Housman, J. *A Topographical Description of . . . Part of the West Riding of Yorkshire* (Carlisle, 1800).

Hunter, J. 'Familae Minorum Gentium', *Publication of the Harleian Society*, xxxvii–xl (1894–6).

James, J. *The History and Topography of Bradford* (1841)—*A History of the Worsted Manufacture* (1857)—*The History of Bradford and its Parish* (1866).

Langdale, T. *A Topographical Dictionary of Yorkshire* (Northallerton, 1822).

Leeds Corporation (Statistical Committee). 'Report upon the condition of the town of Leeds and its inhabitants', *Journal of the Royal Statistical Society*, ii (1839).

Luccock, J. *The Nature and Property of Wool Illustrated, With a Description of the British Fleece* (Leeds, 1805).

Lupton, J. H. *Wakefield Worthies* (Wakefield, 1864).

Macpherson, D. *Annals of Commerce* (1805), four volumes.

Marshall, W. *The Rural Economy of Yorkshire* (1788).

Mawman, J. *An Excursion to the Highlands of Scotland and the English Lakes* (1805).

Mayhall, J. *The Annals and History of Leeds* (1860–6).

Memoirs of the Life and Writings of Michael Thomas Sadler (1848).

Mortimer, T. *A General Commercial Dictionary* (1823), third edition.

Neale, J. P. *Views of Gentlemen's Seats* (1822).

Parsons, E. *The Civil, Ecclesiastical, Literary, Commercial and Mercantile History of Leeds . . . and the Manufacturing Districts of Yorkshire* (Leeds, 1834), two volumes.

Parsons, E. *The Tourist's Companion; or the History of the Scenes and Places on the Route by the Railroad and Steam Packet from Leeds and Selby to Hull* (1835).

Pearson, J. *The Life of William Hey* (1822), two volumes.

Philipps, M. *A History of Banks, Bankers and Banking in Northumberland, Durham and North Yorkshire* (1894).

Priestley, J. *Historical Account of the Navigable Rivers, Canals and Railways Throughout Great Britain* (1831).

Randall, J. *An Account of an Academy at Heath, Near Wakefield* (1750).

Rees, A. *The Cylopedia* (1819–20), six volumes.

Register of the Leeds Grammar School: 1820–1896 (Leeds, 1897).

Samuel Bros. *Wool and Woollen Manufactures of Great Britain; a Historical Account* (1859).

Scatcherd, N. *The History of Morley* (Leeds, 1830).

A Short View of the Rise, Progress and Establishment of the Woollen Manufacture (1755).

A Sketch of the Life and Character of the Late Doctor Samuel Kershaw, Vicar of Leeds (Leeds, 1788).

Smeaton, J. *Reports of the Late John Smeaton, F.R.S.* (1812), three volumes.

Smith, J. *Chronicon Rusticum Commerciale, or Memoirs of Wool* (1747), two volumes —*A Review of the Manufacturer's Complaints Against the Wool Grower* (1753). *A Summary View of the Proposed Canal from Leeds to Liverpool* (Bradford, 1770).

Taylor, Rev. R. V. *The Biographia Leodiensis* (1865).

Taylor, W. Cooke *The Handbook of Silk, Cotton and Woollen Manufactures* (1843).

Thackrah, C. T. *The Effect of the Principal Arts, Trades and Professions, and of Civic States and Habits of Living, on Health and Longevity: With a Particular Reference to the Trades and Manufactures of Leeds* (1831).

Thoresby, R. *The Diary of Ralph Thoresby, F.R.S.*, ed. Rev. J. Hunter (1830), two volumes—*Ducatus Leodiensis*, ed. Rev. T. D. Whitaker (Leeds, 1816), second edition—'Letters addressed to Ralph Thoresby F.R.S.', ed. W. T. Lancaster, *Thors. Soc.*, xxi (1912)—*Letters of Eminent Men, Addressed to Ralph Thoresby* (1832), two volumes—*Vicaria Leodiensis* (1724).

Turner, J. H. *Biographia Halifaxiensis* (Bingley, 1883).

Ure, A. *The Philosophy of Manufactures* (1835).

Walker, J. *Report to the Committee of the Proposed Railway from Leeds to Selby* (1829).

Wardell, J. *The Antiquities of the Borough of Leeds* (1853)—*The Municipal History of the Borough of Leeds* (1846).

Wellbeloved, C. *Memoirs of the Life and Writings of the Late Rev. W. Wood, F.L.S.* (Leeds, 1809).

Whitaker, Rev. T. D. *Loidis et Elmete* (Leeds, 1816).

Wilberforce, R. I. and S. *The Life of William Wilberforce* (1838), five volumes.

Wilkinson, J. *Worthies, Families and Celebrities of Barnsley and the District* (1883).

Williamson, G. S. *John Russell, R.A.* (1894).

Woodcroft, B. *Brief Biographies of Inventors of Machines for the Manufacture of Textile Factories* (1863).

Young, A. *A Six Months Tour Through the North of England* (1771), four volumes.

(VII)) *Recent books, pamphlets and articles.*

Ashton, T. S. *Economic Fluctuations in England, 1700–1800* (Oxford, 1959)—*An Economic History of England: The Eighteenth Century* (1955)—'The bill of exchange and private banks in Lancashire 1790–1830', in *English Monetary History*, eds. T. S. Ashton and R. S. Sayers (Oxford, 1953).

Aspinall, A. *The Early English Trade Unions* (1949).

Astrom, S-E. *From Cloth to Iron* (Helsingfors, 1963).

Atkinson, F. *Some Aspects of the Eighteenth Century Woollen and Worsted Trade in Halifax* (Halifax, 1956).

Bailyn, B. *The New England Merchant in the Seventeenth Century* (Harvard, 1956).

Beckwith, F. 'The population of Leeds during the Industrial Revolution', *Thors. Soc.*, xli, part 2 (1948).

Beresford, M. W. *The Leeds Chambers of Commerce* (Leeds, 1951).

Bowden, P. J. *The Wool Trade in Tudor and Stuart England* (1962)—'Wool supply and the woollen industry', *Ec.H.R.*, ix (1956).

Bowden, W. *Industrial Society in England Towards the End of the Eighteenth Century* (New York, 1925).

Bradfer-Lawrence, H. F. 'The Merchants of Lynn', in *A Supplement to Blomefield's History of Norfolk*, ed. C. Ingleby (1929).

Briggs, A. 'The background of the parliamentary reform movement in three English cities (1830–2)', *The Cambridge Historical Journal X* (1952).

Brooke, S. 'Notes on the Hall family of Stumperlow and Leeds', *Thors. Soc.*, part 4 (1953).

Buck, N. S. *The Development of the Organization of Anglo-American Trade, 1800–1850* (Yale, 1925).

Burke's Genealogical and Heraldic History of the Landed Gentry (1914 and 1952 editions). *Burke's Peerage* (1956).

Burley, K. H. 'An Essex clothier of the eighteenth century', *Ec.H.R.*, xi (1958).

Butler, A. E. (ed.) *The Diary of Thomas Butler of Kirkstall Forge* (1906).

Carroll, R. 'Yorkshire parliamentary boroughs in the seventeenth century', *Northern History*, iii (1968).

Carus-Wilson, E. M. *Medieval Merchant Ventures* (1954)—and Coleman, O. *England's Export Trade 1275–1547* (Oxford, 1963).

Christie, I. R. *Wilkes, Wyvill and Reform: The Parliamentary Reform Movement in British Politics, 1760–1785* (1962)—'The Yorkshire Association, 1780–4: a study in political organisation', *Historical Journal*, iii (1960).

Clapham, J. H. 'Industrial organisation in the woollen and worsted industries of Yorkshire', *Economic Journal*, xvi (1906)—'The transference of the worsted industry from Norfolk to the West Riding', *Economic Journal*, xx (1910)—*The Woollen and Worsted Industries* (1907).

Cokayne, G. E. *Complete Baronetage* (Exeter, 1900–6), five volumes.

Cole, A. H. 'A new set of stages', *Explorations in Entrepreneurial History*, vii (1955).

Collyer, C. 'The Rockingham connection and country opinion in the early years of George III', *Leeds Phil. & Lit. Soc.*, vii, part 4 (1955)—'The Rockinghams and Yorkshire politics, 1742–1761', *Thors. Soc.*, xli, part 4 (1954)—'The Yorkshire election of 1734', *Leeds Phil. & Lit. Soc.*, vii (1952–5)—'The Yorkshire election of 1741', *Leeds Phil. & Lit. Soc.*, vii (1952–5)—'Yorkshire and the "Forty-five" ', *Y.A.J.* (1952).

Colvin, H. M. *A Biographical Dictionary of English Architects, 1660–1840* (1954).

Crump, W. B. (ed.) 'The Leeds woollen industry 1780–1820', *Thors. Soc.*, xxxii (1931).

Crump, W. B. and Ghorbal, G. *History of the Huddersfield Woollen Industry* (Huddersfield, 1935).

Davis, R. *Aleppo and Devonshire Square* (1967)—*The Commercial Revolution*, Historical Association Pamphlet No. 64 (1967)—'English foreign trade 1660–1700', *Ec.H.R.*, vii (1954)—'English foreign trade 1700–1774', *Ec.H.R.*, xv (1962)—*The Rise of the English Shipping Industry in the Seventeenth and Eighteenth Centuries* (1962).

Deane, P. 'The output of the British woollen industry in the eighteenth century', *J. Econ. Hist.*, xvii (1957)—and Cole, W. A. *British Economic Growth, 1688–1959: Trends and Structure* (Cambridge, 1962).

'Diary of a Leeds layman, 1733–1768', *Unitarian Historical Society Transactions*, iv (1927–30).

Dictionary of National Biography (1908–9).

Driver, C. *Tory Radical: The Life of Richard Oastler* (Oxford, 1946).

Dyos, H. J. (ed.) *The Study of Urban History* (1968).
East, W. G. 'The port of Kingston-upon-Hull during the Industrial Revolution', *Economica*, xi (1931).
Edwards, M. M. *The Growth of the British Cotton Trade 1780–1815* (Manchester, 1967).
Fitton, R. S. and Wadsworth, A. P. *The Strutts and Arkwrights, 1758–1801: A Study of the Early Factory System* (Manchester, 1958).
François, M. E. 'The social and economic development of Halifax, 1558–1640', *Leeds Phil. & Lit. Soc.*, xi, part 8 (1966).
Gayer, A. D., Rostow, W. W. and Schwartz, A. J. *The Growth and Fluctuation of the British Economy* (Oxford, 1953).
Gregory, T. E. *The Westminster Bank Through a Century* (1936), two volumes.
Gill, C. *Merchants and Mariners in the Eighteenth Century* (1961)—and Briggs, A. *History of Birmingham* (1951), two volumes.
Glover, F. J. 'Government contracting, competition and growth in the heavy woollen industry', *Ec.H.R.*, xvi (1964)—'Philadelphia merchants and the York-shire blanket trade, 1820–1860', *Pennsylvania History*, xxviii (1961)—'The rise of the heavy woollen trade of the West Riding of Yorkshire in the nineteenth century', *Business History*, iv (1961)—'Thomas Cook and the American blanket trade in the nineteenth century', *Business History Review*, xxv (1961).
Hamilton, E. J. 'Prices as a factor in business growth', *J. Econ. Hist.*, xii (1952).
Heaton, H. 'The American trade', in *The Trade Winds*, ed. C. N. Parkinson (1948)—'Benjamin Gott and the Anglo-American cloth trade', *Journal of Business and Economic History*, ii (1929)—'Benjamin Gott and the Industrial Revolution', *Ec.H.R.*, iii (1931).—'Financing the Industrial Revolution', *Bulletin of the Business Historical Society*, xi (1937)—(ed.) *The Letter Books of Joseph Holroyd and Sam Hill* (Halifax, 1914)—'A merchant adventurer in Brazil, 1808–1818', *J. Econ. Hist.*, vi (1946)—'Yorkshire cloth traders in the United States 1770–1840', *Thors. Soc.*, xxxvii (1941)—*The Yorkshire Woollen and Worsted Industries* (Oxford, 1920).
Henderson, W. D. 'The Anglo-French commercial treaty of 1786', *Ec.H.R.*, x (1957).
Hinton, R. W. K. *The Eastland Trade and the Common Weal in the Seventeenth Century* (Cambridge, 1959).
Hoffman, W. G. *British Industry, 1700–1950* (Oxford, 1955).
Homans, G. C. *The Human Group* (1951).
Hoskins, W. G. *Industry, Trade and People in Exeter, 1688–1800* (Manchester, 1935).
Hughes, E. *North Country Life in the Eighteenth Century* (Oxford, 1952–65), two volumes.
Jackman, W. T. *A History of Transportation in Modern England* (Cambridge, 1916).
John, A. H. 'Aspects of English economic growth in the first half of the eighteenth century', *Economica*, xxviii (1961)—'War and the economy in the eighteenth century', *Ec.H.R.*, vii (1955).
Killick, H. F. 'Notes on the early history of the Leeds and Liverpool canal', *Journal of the Bradford Historical and Antiquarian Society*, i (1900).
Lipson, E. *The History of the Woollen and Worsted Industries* (1921)—*A History of Wool and Wool Manufacture* (1953).
Lloyd-Pritchard, M. F. 'The decline of Norwich', *Ec.H.R.*, iii (1951).
McGrath, P. (ed.) 'Merchants and merchandise in seventeenth century Bristol', *British Record Society's Publications*, xix (1955).
Mann, J. de L. (ed.) 'Documents illustrating the Wiltshire textile trades in the eighteenth century', *Wiltshire Archaeological and Natural History Society*, xix (1964).
Mann, J. de L. 'Textile machinery, 1760–1850', in *A History of Technology*, eds. C. Singer, E. J. Holmyard and A. R. Hall, iv (Oxford, 1958)—'Wiltshire textile industries since 1550', in *V.C.H., Wiltshire*, iv (1959).
Mantoux, P. *The Industrial Revolution in the Eighteenth Century* (1928).

Mathews, R. D. *The History of Freemasonry in Leeds, 1754–1954* (Leeds, 1954).
Mathias, P. 'The social structure in the eighteenth century: a calculation by Joseph Massie', *Ec.H.R.*, x (1957).
Minchinton, W. E. 'Bristol—metropolis of the west in the eighteenth century', *Transactions of the Royal Historical Society*, iv (1954)—'The merchants in England in the eighteenth century', in *The Entrepreneur*, papers presented at the annual conference of the Economic History Society, April 1957 (Harvard, 1957)—(ed.) 'Politics and the port of Bristol in the eighteenth century', *Bristol Record Society's Publications*, xxii (1961).—'The trade of Bristol in the eighteenth century', *British Record Society's Publications*, xx (1957).
Morse, H. B. *The Chronicles of the East India Company Trading to China 1635–1834* (Oxford, 1926–9), five volumes.
Namier, L. 'Brice Fisher M.P. A mid-eighteenth century merchant and his connections', *Ec.H.R.*, xlii (1927).
Pankhurst, L. M. 'Investment in the West Riding wool textile industry in the nineteenth century', *Y.B.*, vii (1955).
Parkinson, C. N. *The Rise of the Port of Liverpool* (Liverpool, 1952).
Pares, R. 'Merchants and planters', *Ec.H.R. Supplements*, No. 4 (1960).
Pares, R. *A West-India Fortune* (1950).
Pevsner, N. *The Buildings of England; Yorkshire: The West Riding* (1959).
Phillips, N. C. *Yorkshire and English National Politics: 1783–1784* (Christchurch, N.Z., 1961).
Pollard, S. 'Fixed capital in the Industrial Revolution in Britain', *J. Econ. Hist.*, xxiv (1964)—*The Genesis of Modern Management* (1965)—'Investment consumption and the Industrial Revolution', *Ec.H.R.*, xi (1958).
Ponting, K. *A History of the West of England Cloth Industry* (1957).
Pressnell, L. S. *Country Banking in the Industrial Revolution* (Oxford, 1956)—(ed.) *Studies in the Industrial Revolution* (1960).
Price, A. C. *A History of the Leeds Grammar School* (Leeds, 1919)—*Leeds and its Neighbourhood* (Oxford, 1909).
Raistrick, A. *Quakers in Science and Industry* (1950).
Ramsey, G. D. *The Wiltshire Woollen Industry in the Sixteenth and Seventeenth Centuries* (1943).
Read, D. *Press and People, 1790–1850: Opinion in Three English Cities* (1961).
Redford, A. *Manchester Merchants and Foreign Trade, 1794–1939* (Manchester, 1934–1956), two volumes.
Rimmer, W. G. 'The evolution of Leeds to 1700' and 'The industrial profile of Leeds, 1740–1840', *Thors. Soc.*, i, part 2 (1967)—*Marshalls of Leeds Flax-spinners 1788–1886* (Cambridge, 1960)—'Middleton colliery, near Leeds (1770–1830)', *Y.B.*, vii (1955)—'William Hey of Leeds, surgeon (1736–1819): a reappraisal', *Leeds Phil. & Lit. Soc.*, ix (1961)—'Working men's cottages in Leeds 1770–1840', *Thors. Soc.*, xlvi (1961).
Robson, R. *The Attorney in Eighteenth Century England* (Cambridge, 1959).
Schroeder, L. W. *Mill Hill Chapel, Leeds 1674–1924* (Leeds, 1924).
Scott, E. K. (ed.) *Matthew Murray* (Leeds, 1928).
Schumpeter, E. B. *English Overseas Trade Statistics 1697–1808* (Oxford, 1960).
Sigsworth, E. M. *Black Dyke Mills* (Liverpool, 1958).
Silberling, N. J. 'British prices and business cycles, 1779–1850', *Review of Economic Statistics*, v, supplement (1923).
Smelser, N. J. *Social Change in the Industrial Revolution* (1959).
Stirling, A. M. W. *Annals of a Yorkshire House* (1911), two volumes—*The Letter-bag of Lady Elizabeth Spencer-Stanhope* (1913), two volumes.
Sutherland, L. S. 'The accounts of an eighteenth century merchant', *Ec.H.R.*, iii (1932)—*A London Merchant, 1695–1774* (Oxford, 1962).
Thomas, J. 'A history of the Leeds clothing industry', *Y.B.*, Occasional Paper No. 1 (1955).

Thompson, E. P. *The Making of the English Working Class* (1968).

Tomlinson, W. W. *The North-eastern Railway, its Rise and Development* (Newcastle upon Tyne, 1914).

Turberville, A. S. and Beckwith, F. 'Leeds and parliamentary reform, 1820–1832', *Thors. Soc.*, xli (1946).

Unwin, R. W. 'The Aire and Calder Navigation', *The Bradford Antiquary*, new series, parts xlii–iii (1964, 1967).

Victoria County History of Yorkshire (1912).

Victoria County History, the City of York (1961).

Wadsworth, A. P., and Mann, J. de L. *The Cotton Trade and Industrial Lancashire* (Manchester, 1931).

Ward, J. T. *The Factory Movement, 1830–1855* (1962)—'Leeds and the factory reform movement', *Thors. Soc.*, xlvi (1961)—'West Riding landowners and the railways', *Journal of Transport History*, iv (1960).

Ward, W. R. *The English Land Tax in the Eighteenth Century* (Oxford, 1953).

Waters, S. H. *Wakefield in the Seventeenth Century* (1933).

Webb, S. and B. *English Local Government from the Revolution to the Municipal Corporation Act: The Manor and the Borough* (1910)—*The Parish and the County* (1906).

Welbourne, E. 'Bankruptcy before the era of Victorian reform', *The Cambridge Historical Journal*, iv (1932).

Wesley, J. *The Journal of John Wesley*, ed. N. Curnock (1938), eight volumes.

Westerfield, R. B. *The Middleman in English Business Particularly Between 1660–1760* (Yale, 1916).

Willan, T. S. *The English Coasting Trade, 1600–1750* (Manchester, 1938)—*River Navigation in England, 1600–1750* (1936).

Wilson, C. *Anglo-Dutch Commerce and Finance in the Eighteenth Century* (Cambridge, 1941)—'Cloth production and international competition in the seventeenth century', *Ec.H.R.*, xiii (1960)—'The entrepreneur in the Industrial Revolution in Britain', *Explorations in Entrepreneurial History*, vii (1955).

Wilson, R. G. 'The fortunes of a Leeds merchant house', *Business History*, x (1967) —'Transport dues as indices of economic growth, 1775–1820', *Ec.H.R.*, xix (1966).

Wood, A. C. *A History of the Levant Company* (1935).

Wood, J. R. 'Leeds church patronage in the eighteenth century', *Thors. Soc.*, xli (1948).

Y.A.S. Record Series, volumes 71–2, 77–9, 'Archbishop Herring's visitation returns' (Wakefield, 1928–31)—volume 96, 'The parliamentary representation of the county of York' (Wakefield, 1938).

Index of subjects and places

pressions in, 44–9; exports of, 10, 44–5; fluctuations in output of, 4–5, 7, 37, 41–9, 111–15; periods in growth of, 51, 90; progress of, 6, 11, 16, 47; proportion of output consumed at home and exported, 42–3; reasons for growth, 52; recessions in, 134; share of national output, 37–44; slow change in, 90; stagnation of, 45–6; well-sited for European trade, 12–13
woollen laws, repeal of, 101–06
Woollen Manufacturers Bill (1809), 104
wool staplers, 48, 53, 94
Worcester, 4
worsted industry, 7, 47, 90, 96, 128–9;

changes in the late eighteenth century, 33; concentration of, 129; exports of British, 117; growth of, 116–18; output in 1771–2, 42–3
worsted manufacturers, 59, 128
worsted weavers, 30, 48

York, 11, 17, 140, 145, 166, 195, 231; Corporation of, 16; decline of cloth trade, 9–12; merchants, 13; rivalry with Leeds, 10–14, 16
Yorkshire Association, 167–8
Yorkshire elections (1784), 168; (1806), 169; (1807), 170–1; (1812), 177; (1818), 177; (1826), 179–80; (1832), 180–1

Index of names and firms

(Those names shown in italics were cloth merchants in Leeds, Wakefield and Halifax)